HERBERT HOOVER

HERBERT HOOVER

· A LIFE ·

Glen Jeansonne

with David Luhrssen

NEW AMERICAN LIBRARY
New York

NEW AMERICAN LIBRARY
Published by Berkley
An imprint of Penguin Random House LLC
375 Hudson Street, New York, New York 10014

Copyright © 2016 by Glen Jeannsonne
Penguin Random House supports copyright. Copyright fuels creativity, encourages diverse voices, promotes free speech, and creates a vibrant culture. Thank you for buying an authorized edition of this book and for complying with copyright laws by not reproducing, scanning, or distributing any part of it in any form without permission. You are supporting writers and allowing Penguin Random House to continue to publish books for every reader.

New American Library and the NAL colophon are registered trademarks of Penguin Random House LLC.

Library of Congress Cataloging-in-Publication Data
Names: Jeansonne, Glen, 1946–, author.
Title: Herbert Hoover/Glen Jeansonne.
Description: New York, New York: New American Library, 2016.
Identifiers: LCCN 2016005097 (print) | LCCN 2016006468 (ebook) |
ISBN 9781101991008 | ISBN 9781101991022 (ebook)
Subjects: LCSH: Hoover, Herbert, 1874–1964. | Presidents—United
States—Biography. | United States—Politics and government—1929–1933. |
United States—Politics and government—1929–1933.
Classification: LCC E802.J429 2016 (print) | LCC E802(ebook) |
DDC 973.91/6092—dc23
LC record available at http://lccn.loc.gov/2016005097

First Edition: October 2016

Printed in the United States of America
1 3 5 7 9 10 8 6 4 2

Jacket photograph © Bettman/Corbis
Jacket design by Emily Osborne
Book design by Tiffany Estreicher

To David Luhrssen,
the best writer I know, and to whom
I owe more than I can ever repay.

CONTENTS

viii   *Contents*

PROLOGUE

—————

erbert Hoover's birthday, August 10, is not observed as a federal holiday, an occasion for patriotic parades or shopping mall clearance sales. Banks do not close, and the mail is delivered on time. Ordinary Americans attribute no unusual significance to the date. Yet in the minuscule village of West Branch, Iowa, descendants of Hoover, townspeople, and, occasionally, state dignitaries gather annually to pay homage to a man they consider the patron saint of their town, but whom much of America remembers as an economic Satan. When not demonized, he is relegated to a historical footnote, remembered bitterly as the incumbent president during the first four years of America's Great Depression, a calamity laid at his door. Few presidents have been so routinely vilified. In polls ranking chief executives, he sinks to almost the bottom. High school textbooks often dismiss him in a few paragraphs; college texts allot only a little more.

Nonetheless, Herbert Hoover was one of the most extraordinary Americans of modern times. The kaleidoscopic range of his life's work, constituting an almost unbroken record of success and offering writers and readers little fodder for criticism, would justify an inclusive biography even if he had never become president. The most versatile American since Benjamin Franklin, Hoover led a life that was a prototypical Horatio Alger story, except that Horatio Alger stories stop at the pinnacle of success. As one of Hoover's early biographers wrote, "Truth does what fiction dares not try to do."[1]

Orphaned before the age of ten, by twenty-one Hoover had earned his way through Stanford University, where he won a reputation as a diligent student, a superb administrator, and an astute campus politician who demonstrated brilliance in his chosen field of geological engineering. He met his future wife, who soon joined his adventures as he roamed the world, finding fame and fortune. By twenty-four, Hoover was superintendent of an enormously rich gold mine in the arid wasteland of Western Australia. At twenty-seven, he managed a coal-mining operation in China and narrowly escaped death during the Boxer Rebellion. By forty, he was legendary in the mining community and a multimillionaire, having accumulated a fortune that supported his family for the remainder of his life.[2]

From the cornfields of Iowa to the apple orchards of Oregon, the goldfields of Australia, and the coalfields of northern China, Hoover's early life was spent at or bordering frontiers. Herbert Hoover was an eminently practical idealist, lacking a scintilla of cynicism, with a profound moral compass firmly steeped in the American dream. Although Hoover's own dream was tarnished by heartrending interludes and leavened by national tragedy, he refused to relinquish it. America, he believed, was the world's most open society, imperfect yet pregnant with hope, flexible, resilient, and inspiring, a land that nourished and appreciated personalities as varied as Henry Ford, Ralph Waldo Emerson, and Jonas Salk.

Hoover personified the American dream he extolled. The first president born west of the Mississippi, he was the first to use radio during a campaign, the first to have a telephone on his desk in the Oval Office, and the first commerce secretary to reach the White House. He was summoned to service by more presidents than any other American chief executive, including Woodrow Wilson, Calvin Coolidge, Harry Truman, and Dwight Eisenhower. At his death, he had been awarded more honorary degrees than any other American. Most important, it is estimated that his relief efforts saved more human lives than those of any other individual in human history.[3]

Although he never carried a firearm or endured the shelling, gas, barbed wire, and machine guns of the First World War, Hoover emerged as the greatest humanitarian of the bloodbath that claimed well over 10 million lives. Amid the carnage, he saved the lives of millions of starving Belgians trapped in the vortex of war. After the fighting had consumed the lives of soldiers and destroyed the reputations of statesmen, Hoover rose above the embittered, self-serving peacemakers who gathered at Versailles and, as his friend John Maynard Keynes observed, became "the only man who emerged from that ordeal with his reputation enhanced."[4]

Although the war ended in 1918, Hoover's relief work was only beginning. His postwar American Relief Administration (ARA) fed nations from the North Sea to the Urals. The ARA's European Children's Fund, the forerunner to CARE, fed millions of children. During 1921–23, when drought, famine, and disease threatened 15 million people in the newborn Soviet Union, Secretary of Commerce Hoover set aside his antipathy toward Communism and persuaded President Warren G. Harding and Congress to allocate $20 million to distribute food and medicine to the Soviet peasants. Ironically, although most Americans remember Hoover for the anguish of the Great Depression, abroad he earned a reputation among common people as a selfless patron who staved off starvation, typhoid, and cholera during their periods of distress. In 1927, Hoover brought his reputation as a "Master of Emergencies" home when he rescued and rehabilitated the Mississippi Valley during the Great Flood that inundated hundreds of thousands of acres, sweeping away towns, cattle, and people.[5]

The catastrophic flood was a prelude to Hoover's presidency, when he found himself deluged by human misery. His stained reputation as

president is at least partly undeserved. A Progressive in the lineage of Theodore Roosevelt and Woodrow Wilson, Hoover was neither a do-nothing
nor a laissez-faire president. On the contrary, he became the first chief
executive to pit the government against the economic cycle. Erecting
more public works in four years than were constructed during the previous twenty, he pushed through a divided Congress a greater array of
constructive legislation than had any previous chief executive who
served during hard times, and incubated ideas integral to the New Deal.
American politics could hardly have leaped from Coolidge to Franklin
Delano Roosevelt without Hoover in between. Still, Hoover was not simply FDR writ small. Hoover considered deficit spending during a recession a necessity, yet he did not believe that infinitely greater spending
would yield infinitely greater prosperity. He advised that the government
could only redistribute wealth, not create new wealth. He distributed
public works according to counties of highest unemployment, irrespective of political influence, refusing to barter patronage for votes. Hoover
did not end the Depression in his single term, yet no other democratic
government worldwide ended it that quickly either.[6]

Although the Great Depression was Hoover's major concern, it was
not his only one. He pioneered summit diplomacy, initiated the Good
Neighbor Policy with Latin America (fleshed out by FDR), and tried to
cobble together international peace in a world bursting apart at the
seams. Hoover reformed prisons, revised the legal code, ameliorated
conditions for workers with the Norris–La Guardia Act, and improved
the health and welfare of children. The president respected the separation of powers. No law he signed was declared unconstitutional. No federal appointee was dismissed for corruption. He created a lean bureaucracy
and preserved labor peace. His administration cracked down on bootlegging—not surprisingly, unsuccessfully, although Al Capone was ap-
prehended and sentenced to federal prison.[7]

As the Depression deepened, the president's popularity plummeted.
Despite his increasingly aggressive legislative assault on the Depression,

the nation remained mired in steep unemployment and business stagnation. He found himself poised above an earthquake fault sufficient to swallow any president. Any incumbent elected in 1928 would likely have been defeated in 1932. After winning his first term in a landslide, Hoover lost out on a second in a landslide. Voters could not have been correct both times. Although historians often charge that Hoover's exertions were too little, too late, his Democratic opponent in 1932, Franklin Roosevelt, during his campaign denounced the incumbent for doing too much, too soon, for piling up a mountain of debt, bloating the bureaucracy, and wasting taxpayer dollars. Roosevelt promised to slash spending by 25 percent and balance the budget if elected.

As an ex-president, Hoover sought historical vindication. Never again considered infallible or invincible, in time he recovered and served his country ably in his reincarnation as an elder statesman. Hoover's public service—political, humanitarian, philanthropic, and literary—following his White House years embellished his stature, though it never fully restored his place in presidential history. Yet he was constitutionally incapable of remaining merely a spectator to public life. Because Hoover was an author and a highly sought speaker, his energy, productivity, and resolve were extraordinary. He did not turn from one task to another during this industrious period; he performed them simultaneously. He was constantly on the move, mentally and physically, striving to remain near the action.

Hoover gravitated incrementally to the right after his presidency in response to the swelling of the federal bureaucracy, the growth of executive power, and the increasing national debt. He became the conscience of the GOP philosophy during his exclusion from the inner circles of official Washington, a consistent champion of the conservative Republican principles—leading some to conclude retroactively that his presidency had been more conservative than it actually was. Following the Second World War he led another mission of mercy to alleviate the scourge of famine. The former president chaired commissions to reorganize the executive branch under Presidents Truman and Eisenhower, and he participated in two foreign policy debates that gripped the nation: entry into World War II prior to Pearl Harbor, and the use of nuclear power versus land armies from the 1950s onward. The frontier orphan, country bred but city polished, also aided slum boys through the Boys Clubs of America, a deterrent to juvenile delinquency.

From his suite in the Waldorf Towers, high above Manhattan, an endless stream of books flowed out, increasingly polished in style, provocative in discernment, and versatile in content. Having been denied political vindication, he sought historical acceptance and left a record of the history he had witnessed and helped shape. Throughout these years, he was the single most important bearer of the torch of American conservatism between his own administration and that of Ronald Reagan, who tapped a reservoir of political philosophy that might have vanished except for Herbert Hoover's principles, conscience, tenacity, and ideals.[8]

ONE

A Quaker Orphan
on the Frontier

erbert Hoover nearly died young. At two, he became infected with croup and lay on his tiny bed, coughing himself to exhaustion, unable to breathe, while his parents and relatives struggled to revive him. His father, Jesse, in futility, finally pronounced the stony, cold, purple little body dead. At that moment, the boy's uncle, Henry John Minthorn, a physician, arrived and began to work desperately on the still child. Nothing worked. At last, he applied his mouth to the child's and breathed air into his lungs. The infant choked, heaved, and slowly began to revive. It was the first, but not the last, close brush with death for Herbert Hoover.[1]

He had been born about midnight on August 10–11, 1874, in West Branch, Iowa. A midnight birth meant he could have selected either August 10 or 11 as his birthday. He chose the eleventh, yet his biographers selected the tenth. Nicknamed Bertie, he had an older brother, Tad, about four years his senior, and a sister, May, approximately two years younger. By the time he turned three, he and Tad were inseparable, a bond severed only by death, though he and May never became close.

The Hoover children were descended from six generations of Quakers, about one-third Swiss and three-quarters British. Their ancestors had migrated in the mid-1700s for a variety of religious and political motives, but chiefly seeking free or cheap land. Bertie's paternal ancestors had lived initially in Pennsylvania, then moved south to Maryland and North Carolina, thence to Ohio, and finally to the village of West Branch in 1854, always relocating in groups connected by kinship and religion. His maternal heritage also originated in Pennsylvania; from there his mother's family migrated to Canada, lived briefly in Ohio, and finally landed near West Branch in 1859. Two paternal ancestors were colonial governors; none on either side fought in the American Revolution. Both sides of the family converted to Quakerism, the paternal from Lutheranism, the maternal from Congregationalism. The Quaker lineage was intense as well as lengthy. It included evangelists, physicians, missionaries, and agents who ministered to the needs of Native Americans. The early generations were predominantly farmers.[2]

Hoover's father, Jesse, was gaunt and muscular, with brown hair and eyes and a Quaker beard, and was infused with kinetic energy, a trait Bertie also inherited from his mother, Huldah. As the village blacksmith, Jesse was mechanically gifted, like both his sons, and his quick wit and storehouse of tall, spellbinding tales made him popular in the community. He won election to the town council and became village assessor.[3]

Jesse's devout Quaker wife likely did not appreciate his humor. The two were such opposites in personality that some initially considered their marriage a mismatch. At twelve, the serious, slender, green-eyed, brown-haired girl stopped fights among boys on the playground. At her father's funeral the following year, she consecrated her life to God. Huldah Minthorn was well educated for a woman of her time, graduating from a Quaker academy and attending two semesters at the embryonic state university at Iowa City. Then she taught at nearby Muscatine, where she was known as a biblical scholar and hard-nosed disciplinarian who converted all eighteen of her students to the Quaker creed during a single year. Intense and solemn, Huldah taught her children to be direct, to set priorities, to avoid gossip, "to live in peace, and to work for the common good among all men of all races." Though firm, she was tolerant and embraced the couple when one of her relatives married outside the faith. When Tad asked his mother if her doctrines represented the only way, she invariably answered, "Yes." Yet she explained that her version of heaven included multitudes who had entered in some other way.[4]

Once a stop on the Underground Railroad, the secret network that smuggled fugitive slaves to freedom in Canada, West Branch was a bustling farm village of about four hundred, located at a crossroads on the Iowa prairie. Notably lacking a tavern, West Branch had twelve stores and a few paved sidewalks, but no paved streets, public lighting, or municipal water except for a town pump. Frugality and thrift were ingrained by religion and necessity. Farmers raised corn, wheat, hogs, dairy cows, and chickens, mostly for domestic consumption. Winters were frigid, with winds that whipped across the virtually treeless prairie. Summers were torrid, offering little shade, punctuated by thunderstorms and occasional tornadoes. Typhoid, malaria, diphtheria, tonsillitis, and tooth loss were endemic. Malnutrition resulted from an abundant but unbalanced diet. In a setting where only the hardy survived, Bertie overcame mumps, measles, diphtheria, and chicken pox. "It was a Montessori school in stark reality," he later wrote.[5]

The Hoover family lived in a tiny cottage measuring only twelve by twenty feet, wedged together in a combined sitting room and kitchen, an adjoining bedroom where the children slept, and another bedroom for the parents. Outside there was a back porch, and an outhouse near the well. The building rested upon the banks of the west branch of the Wapsinonoc, usually a mild creek. After thunderstorms it sometimes swelled, surged up to the front door, and swept away fences, bridges, horses, cattle, and people. A footbridge connected the modest home with Jesse's blacksmith shop on the adjoining bank. The setting was humble yet not bleak. A white picket fence surrounded the front yard, where Huldah planted marigolds, snapdragons, and tiger lilies. "My life started amid golden love and glorious sunshine," Tad remembered.[6]

Bertie's life began auspiciously. His parents were kind, upright, popular in the community, upwardly mobile, and caring. He was surrounded by a nurturing environment of fellow Quakers, including aunts, uncles, and cousins. Their stable community included no rich and no poor. The family was attuned to the changing of seasons, the sowing and reaping of crops, and the rhythms of nature.[7]

No twentieth-century president, with the exception of Theodore Roosevelt, derived such spiritual replenishment from nature. Hoover would later look back on his time in West Branch with nostalgia for small-town life and scenic beauty. It marked his lifelong addiction to the outdoors, a taste for pastoral settings, and empathy for rural America. "I prefer to think of Iowa as I saw it through the eyes of a ten-year-old boy," he later wrote, "and the eyes of all ten-year-old Iowa boys are or should be filled with the wonders of Iowa's streams and woods, of the mystery of growing crops."[8] He recalled Cook's Hill, "that great long hill where, on winter nights, we slid down at terrific speeds with our tummies tight in home-made sleds." Local creeks and rivers were swarming with sunfish and catfish, which he and his brother caught, cooked, and ate. Their primitive tackle was a willow pole with a butcher line for a string and cheap hooks. For good luck they spit on their bait—a worm.[9] As a world-known figure, Hoover was asked which subject he liked best in school as a young man. "None," he answered. "They were something to race through so I could get out of doors."[10]

Hoover remembered his childhood in Iowa as a time of daily adventures and exploration, "the wonder of growing crops, the excitements of the harvest, the journeys to the woods for nuts and hunting, the joys of snowy winters, the comfort of the family fireside, of good food and tender care."[11] Not only did he learn character-molding lessons that tested his mettle and stretched his imagination; life on the frontier also gave him a tough, resilient body, and neither farm nor village chores daunted him. He dutifully planted corn, hoed gardens, milked cows, and sawed and carried wood. As he worked, Hoover tapped his fertile young mind and planted seeds that blossomed as he matured and made him an

unusually creative person with enormous drive. He learned to be resourceful, to rely on his intuition and instincts and, because he was sometimes
alone, to trust his own judgment. He learned to soften loneliness.

Bertie demonstrated unusual industry in a hobby that foreshadowed his
profession. Frequently trekking to the Burlington railroad tracks, where
the construction engineers had hauled glacial gravel and dumped it as bal-
last along the road, he foraged for specimens, finding agate, coral, crystals,
and fossils of ancient creatures embedded in stone, which provoked his
curiosity. He searched along the edges of ponds, creeks, and rivers, carried
the rocks home, and labeled them. The collection became his most prized
possession. Bertie was fortunate to find a local dentist, Dr. William Walker,
who shared his hobby of collecting stones and was an amateur geologist
who owned agate from Colorado and marble from Vermont.[12]

Much of the boy's time, when he was not at home, at school, or outdoors, was spent in Quaker worship. The creed dominated the small
communities of his youth. Officially known as the Society of Friends,
the Quaker denomination was created in England by George Fox in 1652
to restore Christianity to its humble origins, to strip away the ceremony
and worldly ostentation that had crept into Anglicanism, Catholicism,
and Presbyterianism. Quakers rejected adornments such as steeples,
stained glass windows, and organs. Dress was plain, emphasizing subdued colors of gray and black, and language was candid. The Friends, as
they were known, did not recognize any person as their superior and
employed no form of salutation that might be interpreted as a sign of
servility. They considered all men brothers, none exalted over another.
All agreements between Quakers were oral; their word was sufficient.
They evinced resolute individualism, tolerance, thrift, directness, and
transparent honesty. Any type of honest labor, mental or manual, received
due respect, and education was venerated. Modesty, humility, an aversion
to idle gossip, and protection of privacy, all Quaker traits, would later
prove handicaps to Hoover as president.[13]

Although Quakers were stubbornly individualistic, they also believed
in bonds of unity and in cooperation, especially within their immediate

communities. They cared for one another, and Quakers were rarely in dire need. Yet they did not want to encourage sloth and helped only those in want through no fault of their own. Despite their equability, there was a hard edge to Quaker charity. The able-bodied were expected to support themselves. An ill person, for example, would be helped only for the duration of his or her hardship. Hoover's sect was highly disciplined, rarely wasted time, and believed in social order. Thus, freedom was never absolute. The ideas of liberty and responsibility were merged, and Hoover described his own ideal as "ordered liberty." From his religion Hoover also derived his philosophy combining idealism and practicality. His sect did not oppose wholesome recreation, yet life was a serious business, and individuals should be purpose driven. They received fulfillment through assisting, serving others, and close friendships, with an unusual affinity for lifelong bonds. Men were entitled to the rewards of honest labor, and the Friends strove for social justice yet discouraged the flaunting of wealth.[14]

Quakerism took root in West Branch from its founding, and it remains influential to this day. After outgrowing services in private homes, the early settlers erected a one-room meetinghouse that seated about a hundred. With no predetermined programs, congregants relied on spirit to inspire them to pray, to speak, or, rarely, to sing. Singing or excessive speaking by an individual was attributed to vanity or to inspiration from a dark source. Sunday entertainment of any kind was discouraged. Services lasted about two hours, much of the time devoted to silent meditation.

While he occasionally chafed at discipline, Hoover never rebelled against the essential doctrines of his childhood faith, although he developed minor vices such as smoking cigars and drinking in moderation, and his Sabbath attendance was irregular. Hoover was whimsical about some Quaker customs, which he remembered nostalgically. "Quaker children were submitted to a certain mild discipline," he wrote. They were, for example, required to read a chapter of the New Testament every morning. "Out of which I became for life a walking Concordance," he explained. "But in a large way there were no inhibitions on the non-destructive energies of children." Though Huldah rejected novels as untruth and limited the family library to the Bible, an encyclopedia, and tracts denouncing alcohol, her mischievous sons sneaked peeks at adventure novels such as *Robinson Crusoe* and *The Deerslayer* when they visited the homes of more lenient relatives. Hoover remembered that his parents and extended family stimulated the imaginations of their children by encouraging fantasies, including beliefs in Mother Goose and Santa Claus. "But any taint of militarism, including wooden swords and toy soldiers, were rigidly excluded." Christmas was a time for homespun enjoyment. He remembered, "Cutting down a Christmas tree was a ceremony. It was decorated with strings of popcorn for snow. Roasting the popcorn, collecting nuts from the woods and making the candy from maple and sorghum molasses were children's privileges." On Christmas morning, the children awakened to stockings stuffed by Santa Claus, and that day's service at the meetinghouse featured the reading aloud of the second chapter of Luke and the Sermon on the Mount. At noon, "there was a superlative Christmas dinner," he recalled, "with all the fixings known even to New York City, except caviar and alcohol."[15]

Hoover was proud of the self-sufficiency of his pioneer Quaker ancestors. "They operated their own creameries, meat packing, and fruit preserving," he wrote. "They ground their own cornmeal, made their own maple and sorghum syrup, made their own soap and repaired their own machinery." The children worked after school and enjoyed it, and everyone practiced thrift.[16]

Hoover carried most Quaker traits all his life. His reticence, for example, and self-effacing style, his preference for privacy, and his devotion to his immediate and extended family, as well as his commitment to those legitimately in need, were common among Quakers. Still, the adult Herbert Hoover did not emerge from a mold. In some respects he was atypical, or possessed certain traits to an unusual degree. It would be an oversimplification to consider Hoover's environment deterministic. After all, West Branch produced many Quakers yet only one Herbert Hoover.

Bertie entered the first grade at five, the youngest student, somewhat ill prepared. He missed the first week and was often absent. Temporarily held back from promotion to the next grade, he compensated for the lost time and rejoined his classmates. He soon proved an average student who excelled at math. Popular with teachers and schoolmates, he was at times a target for school-ground bullies because he had been taught not to fight back. His first-grade teacher, Mrs. Stephen Sunier, reflected, "He was studious. A real cherub. Just a sweet little boy. Bertie was a smiling boy and good-natured but he had a reserve about him that was puzzling. Yes, he had wonderful dignity for a little fellow. You didn't have to tell him to study." Mollie Brown, who taught Bertie in the third and fourth grades, was especially fond of him. Brown instructed him in arithmetic, geography, language, and physiology, for which no textbooks were used. She spent her own spare time helping him keep abreast when he missed class. By fourth grade he had become more serious and somewhat withdrawn, though still likable. "His mother was rather strict with him," Brown said, "but when she gave him permission to go to the swimming hole he would fairly fly to see who got there first, and he would be half undressed before he got there. He was a playful boy, yet he remembered his lessons and was quiet."[17]

When he was a small boy, Bertie's attention was not always directed on his studies. The Hoover brothers played pickup games of baseball and football at recess, after school, and between chores. Bertie was a better-than-average baseball player. A bit chubby, he possessed average speed yet was agile and determined. Huldah enrolled Bertie in the Band of Hope, a youth organization that promoted Prohibition. Though uninterested in politics as a boy, he later remembered when his mother remained at the polls all day to help persuade men to vote Iowa a dry state, which they did. Bertie claimed that even the town drunk voted for abstention.[18]

The Hoovers lived in their small cottage only a few years before Jesse sold the house and blacksmith shop, began selling and repairing farm implements and home accessories, and purchased a second, larger home. Here, sister May was born. Bertie enjoyed watching his father coat barbed wire with smoldering tar in order to preserve the barbs. Once, while alone in the shop, wondering whether tar might burn, the boy tossed a hot ember into the boiling vat, which burst into flames, nearly destroying Jesse's business and engulfing an adjacent store. Quickly, townsmen assembled a bucket brigade to douse the inferno. Two years later, his business prospering, Jesse bought a more spacious home. A mansion by the standards of Bertie's tiny birthplace, the house sat on about an acre of land. Five red maples grew on the front lawn, with a crab apple tree and a vegetable and flower garden in the backyard. The Hoover boys later recalled family picnics, Fourth of July celebrations, county fairs, and visits to relatives. Nonetheless, the happy memories were overshadowed by the tragic events of those years.[19]

Until the winter of his sixth year, Bertie's world seemed nearly idyllic. His parents nurtured their children and enjoyed life. A strong, robust man in his prime, Jesse exuded vibrant health. Energetic and fun loving, he had a new home, a large circle of friends, and a thriving business. Then Jesse contracted what initially appeared to be merely a cold, but actually constituted the early symptoms of typhoid. An epidemic had spread throughout the village, disseminated by contaminated water. The children were sent to visit their uncle Benjah, who owned a farm near West Branch, while Jesse recovered, but he grew worse. On December 15, Benjah loaded Jesse's children into his one-horse sleigh and sped them home, where they found their aunts and uncles praying over the corpse of their father, dead at thirty-four. Tad took the loss hardest, writing that his father's unexpected death had created "a void unfillable and unfilled forever. Here, then, passed out of my life my hero, the one in whom were found all those qualities and noble attributes which, in the budding ambition of later years, I desired for my own."[20]

Huldah now became the dominant figure in the children's lives and virtually their sole support. Though she inherited his small estate, Jesse left a modest life insurance policy, and his farm-implement business was sold. To supplement her family's income, Huldah harvested vegetables from the garden, took in sewing, and rented rooms to boarders. With her husband gone, profound religious emotions began to surface in the sensitive young widow. She spoke out more frequently at meetings, earned a reputation for inspired soliloquies, and soon became an itinerant preacher, traveling to nearby meetinghouses. As her reputation grew, she sometimes stayed away several weeks, boarding her children with relatives. Huldah was conflicted by the varied responsibilities of raising her family, earning a meager subsistence, and serving God. She wrote her sister Agnes, "I just keep myself ready first for service to my master—then to work at whatever I can to earn a little to add to our living and then the care of my little ones." Her life a constant tug-of-war between her preaching and her children, she was plagued by a guilty conscience because she loved both. "Every day is full," she explained, "and sometimes the nights. I will try to do what I can and not neglect the children."[21]

While Huldah was traveling, Bertie, Tad, and May often stayed with their uncle Benjah and aunt Ellen. Benjah had married a Methodist and converted to his wife's faith, but that did not disrupt the family relationship; they had habitually dined with Bertie's parents and their children each Sabbath. Bertie and Tad became close friends with their cousin George and enjoyed high jinks on the farm, where discipline was somewhat milder. On one occasion the boys kidnapped an owlet from its mother's nest and tried vainly to train it as a pet. The nocturnal bird provided little amusement; it was awake only when the boys slept, and eventually it escaped.[22]

Bertie and Tad spent one magic summer in the company of six young Osage Indian braves who attended the Indian Industrial School at West Branch and remained during the vacation period. The young Native Americans and the Hoover boys built a hideaway secluded within a twenty-acre grove of trees, away from the prying eyes of adults. The boys learned Native American lore, such as making and shooting bows and arrows and building fires by rubbing sticks or rocks together to strike a spark. Tad and Bertie also made slingshots for shooting birds, which could be concealed from their mother more easily than a quiver. Usually they shot at robins, doves, or prairie chickens, but on one occasion they ambushed and roasted a flock of domestic chickens that had strayed from a farm. Bertie was too young to hunt seriously, but he tagged along, and the expeditions whetted his appetite to spend more time in the wilderness.[23]

A few years later, Hoover spent an entire summer on the Osage Reservation in Indian Territory (Oklahoma), where his uncle, Laban Miles, was the Indian agent. Bert and the Miles family were the only white people on the reservation, and Bert played daily with a tribe of young Osage Indians who taught him their wilderness lore, lessons that were implanted for life. Bert attended the Indian school and immersed himself in their lifestyle. For the moment, he experienced a summer of glorious freedom without Quaker restraint, onerous chores, or loneliness.[24]

If the death of Jesse had been a trauma to the children, the next loss was devastating. In the bitter winter cold of 1884, Huldah left home for Muscatine to preach. With no transportation available, she walked about four miles after she had given her bed to an older person the previous night and slept on a chilly floor. She contracted a severe cold, which worsened, despite treatment, and evolved into pneumonia. Huldah died on February 24 at the age of thirty-six and was buried next to Jesse in the family plot. Tad was inconsolable. He complained of "a poignant grief for the early ending of a life of one who was always loving and kind and tender." He expressed his anguish with heartrending words: "The lady of the golden sunshine of the little brown house had gone away and there were left only three small children, adrift on the wreck of their little world."[25]

Bertie, age nine, was publicly stoic, yet the pain carved a gorge of despair that the years could not bridge. The final prop of stability had been knocked from beneath the heartbroken orphans. The trauma compelled Hoover to become independent and self-reliant while yet a boy. It deprived him of love and physical affection, which as an adult he found difficult to express demonstrably. Some fifty years later, he wrote of the time spent in West Branch: "As gentle as are the memories of that time I am not recommending a return to the good old days. Sickness was greater and death came sooner."[26] Still, he repeatedly advised children to take their time growing up, enjoy their early years, and avoid trepidation about the future. He was speaking from experience.

Huldah had entrusted a local Quaker attorney, Lawrie Tatum, respected for his scrupulous probity, to become legal guardian of the children should she die, and the probate court approved her choice. The family property was auctioned, and Tatum invested the revenue at 8 percent interest, to be preserved, if possible, for the children's college education. Bertie's share of the estate was $718.32, his sole financial resource between the ages of ten and twenty-one. All the relatives were young and none could afford to take in all three orphans, so the despondent children were apportioned among relatives in the West Branch area. May, age eight, was raised by Grandmother Minthorn. Tad, about fourteen, lived for a time with his uncle Merlin, then was taken in by his uncle Davis, who dwelled in a sod house and groomed the boy to become a yeoman farmer like himself. Bertie's fourth-grade teacher, Mollie Brown, offered to adopt her favorite pupil, but the family council rejected Brown on the grounds that she was unmarried and worked full-time.[27]

Bertie was thus assigned to his uncle Allan, who owned a farm about two miles outside of West Branch, and had a son, Wally, near Bertie's age, who became his cousin's best friend. Allan was a subsistence farmer whose life was a constant struggle to meet payments on his mortgaged farm, with little remaining disposable cash. Bert adapted well, though he had to work harder than he had for his own parents. Together the family boiled soap, weaved carpets, refined sorghum into sugar, churned butter and cheese, canned fruits and vegetables, and made jam. The children helped to plant and harvest crops, feed the livestock, milk cows, and curry horses. Bert and Wally walked ten miles to the nearest forest to cut trees for firewood, diced them into smaller pieces, and carried them home in repeated trips. Allan paid the boys 1 cent per hundred for capturing potato bugs, 2 cents for cleaning out the barn, and 5 cents for each hundred thistles cut. Bertie never shirked the tedious work and enjoyed being outside. He liked his hardworking, good-humored uncle and would have been content to grow to maturity in this familiar and cheerful environment. Yet his odyssey was unfinished. His life had come to resemble *The Pilgrim's Progress*, with similar challenges and segues. But like all challenges, it meant opportunity for growth.[28]

In the fall of 1885, Uncle Allan received a letter from Huldah's brother, Dr. Henry John Minthorn, an erudite, versatile, devout man who was superintendent of Friends Pacific Academy in Newberg, Oregon. Minthorn's son had died recently and he wished to adopt Bert, whom he could provide with a better education and superior vocational opportunities than were available at West Branch. The Hoover-Minthorn clan ruminated about uprooting the boy again, yet the educational argument clinched their decision. Eleven-year-old Bertie, who rarely cried, burst into tears. He was leaving everyone and everything he loved. He soon boarded an emigrant train, a barely spruced-up cattle car in which travelers had to supply their own food and bedding, for the seven-day, two-thousand-mile journey. With Aunt Millie's repast of fried chicken, ham, bread, and meat pies, the apprehensive youngster was dispatched under the watchful eyes of Oliver Hammel and his emigrant family of West Branch Quakers. Hoover later reflected that the Minthorns were correct in believing that he could obtain a better education in the Far West, and without being transplanted, he would not have become the same man.[29]

Dr. Minthorn met Bertie at the train depot in Portland and they boarded a stern-wheeled steamer down the Willamette River to Newberg, a rustic Quaker trading post barely larger than West Branch. The orphan's new home was a wonderland of virgin fir trees, which, clustered closely, shaded out the underbrush and created the canopy of an arched cathedral. The Willamette Valley was a place like none Bertie had seen, an enchanting frontier of beauty and mystery, permeated with a mild, inviting climate. The rivers were majestic, leaping with schools of silvery fish. If West Branch had been Utopia, this was Eden.[30]

John Minthorn had trekked west with his Quaker family to build a New Jerusalem in the green forests of Oregon. He settled on land near Newberg, where in 1885 he helped construct the Friends Pacific Academy he hoped would grow into a college—today called George Fox University. Minthorn was humorless and less indulgent than Uncle Allan, and he loathed wasted time. There was no devil in Minthorn's workshop because there was no idleness. If Cedar County had stamped a work ethic onto Bertie, life in Oregon hammered it in on an anvil. Minthorn, the same man who had breathed life into Hoover when the boy lay dying of croup, was a dominant figure in the Quaker community. He managed a land company, was the town's sole physician, and acted as superintendent at the academy where both he and his wife also taught. A devout Quaker, he possessed unusual drive and a vivid imagination, as did his protégé.

Bertie, now called Bert, worked arduously. Before school and on weekends, he watered and curried Minthorn's ponies, fed the livestock, milked the cows, and split firewood. Once, after the boy forgot to water the animals, Minthorn wakened him after midnight and sent him scurrying to the pump. During the summer recess Bert helped Minthorn saw down trees, some of them four feet in diameter, then burn the stumps, wasting priceless timber in a headlong rush to till the virgin soil. Hoover swept and mopped the academy and, because Minthorn's three daughters were too young to help, did household chores such as washing dishes and laundering clothes. Bert's childhood had evaporated. Gone was much of the leisure of youth, the latitude to grow up slowly. Minthorn was hard yet not heartless, tolerant and fair, yet all business, habitually clad in drab Quaker colors. He further instilled a work ethic in Hoover, yet he admitted, "I do not think he was very happy."[31] He added, "Our home was not like the one he left with his own parents and almost no work."[32] Bert did not grumble, but neither did he beam.

If the weekdays were demanding, the Sabbath seemed downright grueling. Chores began at dawn, followed by the interminable observance in the meetinghouse, frequently in stoic silence. Then the family walked home in silent contemplation. Following a period of enforced meditation, there was a meeting of the Band of Hope in which the instructor depicted the damnation of an alcoholic by exhibiting graphic photographs of emaciated, broken-down hard drinkers. At home, Bert was expected to read a redeeming book before falling asleep exhausted. One Sunday he persuaded some of his cousins to skip Sunday school to go fishing. They accidentally tipped over the boat and returned covered with mud. The next day, the local Quakers prayed for twelve hours for the sinners. Yet Bert did not believe God frowned at him. "My God is a good, kind God," he said privately.[33]

Minthorn was no ogre—quite the contrary. Beneath the stern exterior lay a gentle heart. He was unselfish and forgiving, possessing a superb mind, which he did not flaunt; he and Bert were, in fact, much alike. John possessed imagination, communication skills, and human empathy for his patients. Hoover concluded that Minthorn was "a severe man on the surface but like all Quakers kindly at the bottom."[34] Before he left Oregon, they had forged bonds that went beyond mere acceptance. Not the least of the lessons Bert partook of were self-discipline and sympathy for the world's downtrodden. Though demanding, Minthorn was not cruel, and he could be generous. He treated the poor free of charge. As a young man Minthorn had driven a wagon on the Underground Railroad. He was a Quaker pacifist, yet with a caveat: he served in the Union Army as a surgeon and participated in the Battle of Shiloh. "Turn your other cheek once," he told Bert, "but if he smites it, then punch him."[35]

The physician invited his adopted son to ride his buggy with him when making house calls, and on these long rides he unwound and regaled the boy with exciting stories about his adventurous life, exhibiting the same low-voltage magnetism that would later be attributed to Hoover himself. Having served as a missionary and Indian agent among

Native Americans in Oklahoma and Oregon, John had a strong sense of social justice. At Friends Pacific Academy, he taught not only physiology, drawn from his medical expertise, but history and literature, in which he was well-read. Intellectually, he was a cut above Hoover's West Branch relatives and Bert's own parents. Unlike Bert's parents, Uncle John believed in reading a variety of genres and could discuss national politics. He encouraged the young Hoover to delve into fiction, poetry, and classical literature, and he stocked Friends Pacific Academy and his home with an eclectic selection of books. The physician gave Bert his own room in their spacious home and respected his privacy. He had no objection to having fun, so long as chores were done first. Minthorn was a man of character, impeccably honest, who taught the youth valuable lessons from books and from life. He was resolute and organized and set priorities, all qualities Hoover took to heart.[36]

When land prices soared in 1888, Minthorn seized the opportunity to reap a quick profit by moving his land company to the town of Salem, the rapidly growing territorial capital. Hoover, now fourteen, moved with the family and became the office boy for the land company rather than completing high school. Bert quickly adapted to the world of business. "My boyhood ambition," the orphan later explicated, "was to be able to earn my own living without the help of anybody, anywhere."[37] Life had forged a strong, determined, independent young man.

The new office boy quickly mastered the rudiments of typing, bookkeeping, and filing while striving to improve his writing skills, penmanship, and organizational abilities. The company grew, as did Hoover's responsibilities. The boy bought and sold land, planted and cultivated orchards, constructed houses, and placed new settlers. The company built a church, school, and hotel; operated a sawmill, flour mill, and railroad; laid out streets; and installed sewers. Hoover was involved in all facets of this expansion. Hundreds of letters a week poured in, and he could locate any specific letter in less than a minute. He was placed in charge of advertising and drafted ads that appeared in a thousand Eastern newspapers, bringing hundreds of emigrants weekly to Salem.

Bert met them at the train depot, found temporary quarters and food, showed them homes and lots, and demonstrated the potential for fruit orchards.[38]

Bert even participated in stockholders' meetings. The young Hoover possessed vision; he knew the country was migrating west, that Oregon was a magnet and real estate seemed likely to soar. Salem had opened new horizons for Bert, and he thrived. The young entrepreneur enrolled in night school at a new business college in Salem. His instructor, finding him gifted at math, tutored him in algebra, geometry, and advanced arithmetic, and also in Latin, at which he was less adept. Sometimes Bert slept in the back room of the land office after returning late from night school. Briefly, Tad and May moved to Salem and the family was temporarily reunited.[39]

Bert acquired a second teacher-mentor, Miss Jennie Gray, daughter of a Salem banker, and his learning curve arced upward. Gray took him to the public library, signed him up for borrowing privileges, and channeled his imagination into new dimensions. He eagerly digested classics by Sir Walter Scott, Charles Dickens, and Voltaire. He sped through *David Copperfield* and his favorite, *Ivanhoe*, and dived into Thackeray, Shakespeare, and American history. His appetite for books unveiled another side to his practical, mechanically oriented mind, and for the first time people came to see flashes of brilliance and to note his unusually supple intelligence, his curiosity to explore the universe of knowledge. Miss Gray, who also became Bert's Sunday school teacher, invited him to socials and picnics, where he met young people, including at least one brief paramour, Daisy Trueblood. Bert participated in a Quaker debate club in which he successfully vanquished his opponent with his argument that war had destroyed more men than alcohol had.[40]

Hoover made time for fun in his crowded life, cultivating friendships, playing baseball, swimming, and configuring jigsaw puzzles. As always, the outdoors beckoned. He grew to love Oregon's vast expanses of forests, mountains, and streams. He found a greater variety of fish than in Iowa, and he learned the art of fly-fishing. While using worms to fish with young companions, Bert was approached by a kindly stranger who gave each boy three flies. Suddenly, Bert caught more and bigger fish. From that point onward, he fished exclusively with flies and dismissed as amateurs anyone who used live bait. He fished the Willamette and its tributaries, as well as other rivers, streams, and, occasionally, millponds for panfish. His favorite adversary was the cutthroat trout, hungry as it battled upstream to spawn. As an adult, he returned frequently to Oregon, enjoying not only the fishing, but frying and eating his finny prey, the camaraderie of the campfire, and camping in the wilderness. Solaced beneath the sunset or the stars, his mind rested.[41]

The description Hoover paints in his *Memoirs* verges on poetry. "Oregon lives in my mind for its gleaming wheat fields, its abundant fruit, its luxuriant forest vegetation, and the fish in the mountain streams," he writes. "To step into its forests with their tangles of berry bushes, their ferns, their masses of wild flowers, stirs up odors peculiar to Oregon. . . . Within these woods are never-ending journeys of discovery." He remembered waters crowded with hungry trout, where fishermen were sparse and nature bounteous, where one could catch a day's limit within hours, where descending a thousand-foot canyon to a stream and climbing back up loaded with fish was an afternoon's diversion. Years later, the joy reverberated.[42]

In hindsight, the time spent at Newberg and Salem assumed a positive perspective. Uncle John was less a demon than a reasonably perceptive foster parent, the tension between the boy and the man basically a struggle between two strong-willed individualists, each well-meaning. When Bert left Oregon, he learned that Minthorn had not deducted a penny for board or expenses during the six years he lived there, and Bert's remainder of his parents' estate, wisely invested, had actually increased.[43]

Salem broadened Hoover's vistas. Every day a host of individuals tromped through the waiting room of the land company, where Bert tuned in to their conversations and serendipitous facts stuck to his magnetic brain. Hoover soaked up information from farmers, ranchers, soldiers, explorers, lawyers, businessmen, speculators, and migrants. The boy heard familiar names such as Jefferson and Lincoln, and new ones such as Chester Arthur, Grover Cleveland, and Benjamin Harrison. At times the conversations drifted to the dawn of the Republic and the Civil War, and the men hashed out the relative merits of Robert E. Lee and U. S. Grant, as well as the merits of free trade versus protectionism. Hoover's curiosity was titillated by one argument between Quaker Republicans who embraced transferring the county seat and Democrats who opted for the status quo. Democrats were reactionaries who never wanted to change anything, Bert complained. Already as a teenager, he was a Progressive Republican.[44]

While political discussions whetted the young man's appetite, they were less important to his immediate future than his meeting with a mining engineer named Robert Brown. Unlike conversation with most visitors, theirs was neither trivial nor accidental. Brown was an old friend of Bert's father who had come to Salem to meet Jesse's son. Their conversations extended over several days, focusing on the geological engineer's profession. He explained to Bert that mining engineers spent most of their time roaming the outdoors, exploring the boundaries of their minds. Brown emphasized the importance of precision and management, which Hoover possessed. Skill at mathematics, Hoover's forte, was essential. Mathematics was to an engineer what a scalpel was to a surgeon. The chat with Brown was a spark that struck kindling waiting to burst into flame. It infused the youth with a sense of purpose for the first time—of fitting his gifted mind to an undertaking molded for it. Further, geologists were rare in the West, where opportunities were greatest. A college degree, however, was essential. The encounter proved providential, yet Hoover never met Brown again.[45]

The teenager ruminated over his future. He talked to other engineers, visited local foundries, and inspected sawmills, repair shops, and mines before settling on the specialty of mining engineering. Then he began scrutinizing college catalogs. Substantial obstacles existed. He lacked sufficient money and had not earned a high school diploma. His relatives approved of his ambition to attend college and encouraged it, raising no objections to his becoming an engineer. However, the close-knit family insisted that Bert enroll at a Quaker university. Dr. Minthorn even obtained a scholarship for his foster son at Earlham College, a Quaker institution in Indiana. Yet Earlham did not offer a diploma in mining engineering and Hoover could find no Quaker college that did. A war of wills seemed to leave Bert at a dead end. It would not profit Hoover, his God-fearing relatives inveighed, to sharpen his mind and yet mortgage his soul.[46]

Bert read in a Portland daily newspaper a prominent story pertaining to the founding of a new public university to open October 1, 1891, for admission of its first, or pioneer, class. California's millionaire U.S. senator Leland Stanford, a railroad magnate who had lost his only son, intended to devote much of his fortune to the creation of a university at his ranch near present-day Palo Alto that would become the West Coast equivalent of the Ivy Leagues. The faculty would be recruited nationally and already promised star quality. Dr. David Starr Jordan, a prominent scientist, left Indiana University to become Stanford's first president. He raided the Indiana faculty for luminaries that included Dr. Joseph Swain to head the Mathematics Department and Dr. John Casper Branner to chair the Department of Geology and Mining. Bert read further that Swain would arrive in Portland that spring to administer entrance examinations. Hoover craved the opportunity, yet his family resisted stubbornly. Then Minthorn, who was well connected, asked if the Dr. Swain giving the exam was Joseph Swain, a devout Quaker, which indeed he was. That carried the argument. No institution that employed Swain could be either second-rate or worldly, the physician declared.[47]

Now all Bert had to do was pass the exam. He had a meager formal education, but a sharp mind and a ton of determination. Swain talked with the youth beforehand and watched him industriously plow through the lengthy test. Hoover did extraordinarily well on some sections, yet fell woefully short on others. He could not be admitted on the basis of the exam. His Achilles' heel was English, which would continue to challenge him throughout his collegiate career. Hoover had sound, imaginative ideas and could express himself clearly, yet his spelling, punctuation, and grammar, largely self-taught, were lacking, and he could not conjugate irregular verbs. Nonetheless, Swain was impressed by Hoover's tenacity and his intention to make something of himself. He was exactly the type of student Stanford wanted, given encouragement and embellishment, perhaps the proverbial diamond in the rough. Swain encouraged Bert to come to Stanford during the summer, receive tutoring in his weak areas, and retake the exam in time for the fall opening on October 1. As for money, he could work his way through. It was a gamble, but Swain recognized the young man's character and spirit.[48]

Hoover boarded the train for Palo Alto that summer with all his belongings, including a bicycle, and his modest savings, plus a surprise $50 given to him by Uncle John at the station. Having arrived at Newberg a small boy of eleven, he left not quite seventeen, a tall, gangly, yet muscular young man. He was opening a new chapter of his education. Grandmother Minthorn, now living in Oregon, tearfully kissed him good-bye and said, "I think thy mother would like to see thee now."[49] It might seem that the distance from Oregon to Stanford was much shorter than Hoover's journey from Iowa to Newberg, Oregon. Actually, it was much greater.

TWO

Cardinal Red

Hoover stepped off the train at Menlo Park and pedaled his bicycle, packed with his clothes and meager possessions, the three miles to Palo Alto, in its own way as much a frontier outpost as West Branch, Iowa, or Newberg, Oregon. With the university's buildings still incomplete, he took lodging at Adelante Villa, an old home converted to a boardinghouse for early arrivals. Construction workers raced to hammer and plaster together the campus's buildings in time for an avalanche of students—no one knew exactly how many—in the midst of a vast pasture that would ultimately make Stanford the largest university, in geographical terms, in the nation. Hoover had not waited until his arrival in California to study for his second attempt to pass the entrance examination; he had crammed in the Minthorn barn every night since his failure. Now President David Starr Jordan and Dr. Joseph Swain, who also resided at Adelante Villa, helped to tutor Bert in their spare time. His chief tutors, however, were the two women who owned the boardinghouse.

The diligent, impoverished young Quaker paid for his room and board by performing odd jobs. He groomed horses and drove by buggy to Menlo Park to purchase groceries and pick up the mail for President Jordan, whom he also transported to his office on campus. Hoover's work ethic was already ingrained, his goals were high, and from the beginning he understood his objective. Though he would enjoy college immensely, plunge into extracurricular activities with gusto, make life-long friends, and meet the love of his life, he was driven by his goal to become an engineer, and a good one. No one anticipated how good, but they were about to find out.[1]

After a summer of intense study, he faced his second, and doubtless last, attempt to pass the entrance exam. The tutoring and hard work paid dividends. Bert fared well in geometry, algebra, and American history. He scored lower on literature, yet passed easily. Needing one more subject, an elective, he picked physiology, which deals with the structure and functions of the organs of the human body. Most of his data was gleaned from long carriage rides with Dr. Minthorn, who had discoursed upon his medical practice. Hoover also bought two used textbooks, read them from cover to cover during a full day and a sleepless night, and passed physiology the next morning. Yet his nemesis, English composition, continued to haunt him. He could express himself clearly and accurately, yet he did not give the meticulous attention to spelling, grammar, and punctuation that he applied to subjects he enjoyed. He failed English 1B and was admitted on the condition that he remove the deficiency before graduation, a stipulation that would hover for almost the entire next four years. In microcosm, 1B epitomized his academic career. Bert had come to Stanford to learn, not to make superlative grades, and his interests were selective. He excelled at subjects he found fascinating and went far beyond the required reading, while skimming others.[2]

Now a member of Stanford University's pioneer class, Hoover became the first, and youngest, resident of Encina Hall, the incomplete men's dormitory, which during the early weeks lacked electricity and hot water. Encina was a portion of a quadrangle that constituted the centerpiece of the new Stanford campus, enclosing a grassy commons. Carved from Senator Stanford's enormous ranch, the campus was surrounded by fields and meadows that evolved into rolling hills and then rose to mountains in the distance. Beyond that lay the Pacific. The budding geologist felt like Alice in Wonderland, all the delights of his mind's eye within his reach. Inwardly, Stanford represented an equally auspicious universe to explore. Students who enrolled at the school during its early years did so because it was different from other colleges; thus, it was likely that their characters were different from those of other students. They arrived at a university evolving on the spot, one that offered a different kind of college atmosphere. Isolated from urban life, the Stanford faculty and its students relied upon one another for companionship, entertainment, and the ambience of home. Each department formed a smaller family within this larger family. The Geology Department was tightly knit, with the students and faculty developing a special kinship. Faculty invited students into their homes for casual discussions on Friday evenings, and new ideas gestated informally.[3]

For Hoover, Stanford marked his first independence outside a predominantly Quaker environment. The work was rigorous, the pace breathtaking, offering Bert the opportunity and challenge to grow and succeed, liberated by more freedom than he had ever known. He would grow up with Stanford, and they would forever remain connected. The university would provide something Hoover had lacked since he was orphaned: a truly nurturing environment. Stanford provided some of the best years in his life.[4]

Under the hot California sun, an intellectual garden blossomed. Hoover was eager to sink his roots into the heart of his curriculum, geology and engineering. However, the renowned professor John Casper Branner, chair of the Department of Geology and Mining, notified Stanford officials that he had been unable to disengage from his obligations as state geologist for Arkansas until January and could not join the faculty until the spring semester. Hoover was disappointed, but he found other academic manna to feed his voracious mental appetite until Branner arrived.

For the first semester of his freshman year, Bert declared a major in mechanical engineering. Through the fall term he took solid geometry, algebra, trigonometry, linear drawing, freehand drawing, and mechanical engineering.

To support himself, Hoover obtained a job in the registrar's office. He also instigated a part-time paper route, picking up the San Francisco daily, delivering it on campus, and collecting the payment, keeping part of it as his profit. This required rising before dawn and working for several hours before his first class. It was a schedule he would keep throughout his life, habitually sleeping only five or six hours, relying on his robust stamina.[5]

When Branner arrived to begin the spring semester, Hoover's morale soared. He promptly changed his major to geological engineering and signed up for as many Branner-taught courses as he could. Branner had a well-founded reputation as a superb teacher who took a special interest in helping his students. At the onset, only eleven pupils enrolled in the Geology Department, allowing the master mentor to devote a great deal of individual attention to each. Hoover, the brightest and most industrious, quickly became his favorite, and Branner strove to draw him out of his shell of shyness. "He rarely spoke unless spoken to," a classmate said. "It wasn't until later I realized how much it was possible to like him."[6]

Hoover sparkled with the arc of a shooting star, much of it purely by instinct. He was brilliant and patient, and his passion for geology rivaled Branner's. On the basis of Bert's experience as an office boy in Oregon, Branner hired him to assist in routine office chores, such as filing and sweeping, but soon promoted him to laboratory assistant at a higher salary. Branner was delighted because he could delegate a task to Hoover and the aspiring geologist accomplished it without further ado. Unlike Branner's previous lab assistants, he did not pester his instructor with details. "Most men fumble jobs, have to be supervised and directed," Branner said. "But I can tell Hoover to do a thing and never think of it again." The eminent professor considered Bert the best-organized student he had ever met.[7]

Branner did not believe in cramming the heads of students with miscellaneous facts. Instead, he opened their minds and inspired them to think independently, to imagine and innovate. He encouraged rather than repressed originality because he knew engineers in the field must improvise. Branner gave his students a solid background in all the basic sciences. He emphasized a theoretical rather than an applied education for the engineers he taught, and he expected them to learn their practical tasks on the job. Branner significantly influenced Hoover's personal method of dealing with subordinates in many aspects of his career, from mining to the presidency. Hoover wanted assistants who demonstrated the initiative he had demonstrated as a laboratory assistant. His later administrative style, which reflected, on a larger scale, Branner's method, was to decentralize authority. That meant selecting able subordinates, giving them general instructions, and then permitting them the latitude to accomplish their tasks in their own way. He took responsibility for mistakes and allowed second chances. This motivated his subordinates, won their loyalty and affection, nurtured their creativity, and united them in a common goal. Hoover did not prescribe a precise manner for resolving a problem; he judged work by the result.[8]

Now taking the courses he craved, Hoover forged ahead in his second semester. He considered Branner's Geology I, which met five days a week, intellectual caviar. His appetite for geology was insatiable. Soon he became the class star. Hoover packed his schedule with basic science and math courses and did not branch out into the humanities until his second year. Attending lectures and debates, he was especially interested in discussions that related geology to religion, including the theory of evolution, though he never considered his scientific learning in conflict with his Quaker beliefs. Only a freshman, he was in perpetual motion, dashing from one activity to another, skimping on sleep. During the second semester, he contracted measles, which affected his eyesight and compelled him to wear spectacles for two years.[9]

The relationship between Hoover and Branner proved symbiotic. Hoover spent the summer of his freshman year as a field assistant for

Branner, surveying and mapping the outcroppings of rock formations in the Arkansas Ozarks. He then helped the professor compile the data and construct a plastic topographical map of the region, which won a prize at the 1893 World's Fair. Hoover worked mostly alone, usually on foot, enjoying the outdoor exercise, which left him fit, tanned, and $200 richer at summer's end. He lodged as the guest of local people, some of whom were moonshiners who suspected all strangers as "revenuers" but nonetheless were kind and hospitable to the young student and fed and housed him gratis. Bert scrupulously saved his paycheck, which proved essential in getting him from summer to summer.[10]

When he returned to Stanford for his sophomore year, Hoover moved out of the expensive Encina Hall and partnered with another student to supervise a cheaper boardinghouse they called Romero Hall. There, surrounded by poorer students much like him, Bert was drawn increasingly into political conversations with such new friends as Sam Collins, the oldest member of the pioneer class, Lester Hinsdale, and a young freshman, Ray Lyman Wilbur, also a transplant from Iowa with an aptitude for science who was earning his way through. Hoover's working-class friends were concerned over the monopolization of campus offices and political influence by the Greek letter fraternities, which they considered arrogant and elitist. Despite representing a minority of students, the fraternities, by voting as a bloc, employing pledges as ward heelers, and adding big-name athletes to their tickets, created a political steamroller. The unorganized, less affluent students, known as the barbarians, or "barbs," realized that they outnumbered the fraternity clique, and if they could organize, they might win elections and influence and assume control over the disbursement of funds collected by student clubs and athletic teams.[11]

Hoover's organizational skills, ingenuity, and persuasive abilities would have proven an asset to any political group. He fit in with the barb faction because he, like them, was poor, humble, relatively powerless, and upwardly mobile. Yet Hoover's character and nascent ideals also drew him to politics. His Quaker modesty and innate shyness caused some to underestimate him, failing to realize that he was a highly competitive person, a strong individualist who could nonetheless work with a team, even lead one. Even when involved in activities that brought him no personal gain, Bert obtained quiet satisfaction at winning in competition. Moreover, he was an idealist. When this idealism and his competitive streak were bound to a cause and propelled by his enormous energy and drive, he morphed into a daunting political dynamo who nonetheless remained relatively low-key, preferring to work behind the scenes. He was less a prototypical politician than he was an organizer, a task at which few excelled. At first, some were surprised by his successes and considered them flukes, yet when they recurred repeatedly, it seemed as unlikely a fluke as the same apple falling on the same man's head every time he strolled through an orchard.

Hoover's first foray into student politics involved a face-off with an elite fraternity clique that controlled athletics and the prestigious clubs. The poorer barbs, who outnumbered the "frats" and "jocks," were steamrollered, though they were the larger faction, because they were splintered. The key to the barbs winning their first serious political fray in the spring of 1893 was turnout. They had the potential voters, but could they furnish sufficient incentives to lure them to the polls? A barb known as "Sosh," for Socialist Zion, created an organization designed to overpower the fraternity faction by dint of numbers. Hoover's friend Sam Collins brought the Quaker and Sosh together. It was like striking a match to dry tinder. Sosh announced his candidacy for student body president. He and his group, now including Hoover, were considered liberals, even radicals. Since they outnumbered the fraternity faction, they focused on uniting behind a single ticket and maximizing turnout. Sosh assigned the fledgling engineer-politician to recruit the poorest, previously scorned group of students to the barb standard. Unable to afford Encina Hall, they lived in workers' shacks left from construction of the campus. They had never voted before, nor had anyone asked them to. The persistent Hoover went from shack to shack, from boy to boy, and talked to each individually. He was relatively inarticulate, yet this made him credible to the most humble students. Transparently honest, he treated them with respect. Meanwhile, freshman "Rex" Wilbur was assigned to harvest the freshman vote, focusing on Encina Hall. Both Hoover and Wilbur delivered. Although the barbs did not sweep all offices, Sosh won the presidency and they orchestrated a stunning political upset. Their newly assembled machine would need fine-tuning before the next election. Yet they were in the game for keeps, and so was Bert Hoover.[12]

Hoover's gift for organizing was not channeled exclusively, or even chiefly, into politics. He made an even larger impact on Stanford's blossoming athletic program. He donned Cardinal red and made the baseball team as starting shortstop in his freshman year. Quick, agile, sure-handed, and deft, he played the most difficult position in the infield. His playing career was cut short when a bad-hop ground ball dislocated the ring finger on his left hand, possibly even causing a hairline fracture, because the finger did not entirely heal for several years.[13]

Yet if Bert was a serviceable shortstop, he proved an outstanding manager for this team of gifted freshmen, who mowed down every amateur lineup they faced and remained undefeated at the end of regular play. Stepping up a notch, the collegians audaciously challenged the San Francisco professional team. Trailing 30–0 after five innings, the Stanford Cardinal asked that the game be called for "darkness." Hoover's job did not involve selection of a starting lineup or other in-game duties. Rather, he scheduled the games, printed and sold tickets, collected admissions, purchased equipment, and balanced the books, daunting multiple tasks. Because the field lacked fences, Hoover and his assistants circulated through the crowd collecting admissions. On one occasion, former president Benjamin Harrison forgot to pay and Hoover was the only person bold enough to approach the former chief executive and inform him that he must ante up like everyone else. Harrison smiled and handed the manager a dollar. When Bert tried to give the ex-president his 50 cents change, the Republican leader told him to keep it. Raising his voice, Hoover informed the distinguished guest that Stanford was not a charitable institution. Harrison compromised by purchasing additional tickets.[14]

Hoover also managed the Stanford football team, which like the baseball team fielded an all-freshman lineup during its first year. With barely enough players to assemble a squad, they could not conduct full scrimmages because they lacked sufficient teammates. All participants played both offense and defense, and some played every minute of every game. Although football is a fall sport, the team did not get organized until January and did not play its first game until mid-March of 1892. They challenged the established team of the University of California, Berkeley, which assumed the inexperienced upstarts would prove a pushover. The ambitious manager scheduled the game at a San Francisco stadium, which seated fifteen thousand, but he printed only ten thousand tickets, the maximum number of spectators anyone expected. Yet the Thanksgiving Day extravaganza quickly exhausted the tickets, and patrons continued to stream in. Bert, his assistants, and the Berkeley manager and his helpers borrowed buckets and washtubs from local housewives and collected admission in gold and silver coins, the currency of the day. Ultimately, it amounted to $30,000, enough to finance Stanford's entire 1893 season. Incredibly, the game was delayed for half an hour because neither team had remembered to bring a football. Bert dispatched an assistant manager downtown to a sporting goods store via streetcar. The student bought two pigskins and rushed back while the opposing team captains argued at midfield. In yet another minor miracle, the Stanford team, some of whose players were involved in their first game, upset the highly touted Berkeley gridironers 14–0 in the kickoff of what became a traditional rivalry.[15]

By the fall of 1894, the precocious freshmen of 1892 had become seniors and boasted their greatest team of that era. They had lured the inimitable Walter Camp, known as the father of college football, to coach the Cardinal. Camp believed that from tackle to tackle Stanford had the best line in the nation, more formidable than any of the Eastern powers. He used his vaunted defense aggressively to attack the opposing offense.

Most of the games were low scoring. The players were quite small by recent standards. The largest Cardinal player, the left guard, weighed 194 pounds. The largest back, the fullback, weighed 174 pounds, and the quarterback weighed 147 pounds. Berkeley also boasted an exceptional line and an elusive back in Wolfe Ransome. After Stanford's stunning defeat of Berkeley in 1892, the teams had tied during the following year, making 1894's the decisive game. During the first half, a Stanford guard burst through the line, blocked a Ransome punt, scooped up the ball, and raced for a touchdown. Stanford won, 6–0. Even more compelling was a final, three-game barnstorming tour in California after Amos Alonzo Stagg, the legendary coach, challenged the strongest team in the West to face his powerful Chicago team, the dominant team in the Midwest. Chicago won the first game at Pasadena on Christmas Day, Stanford countered with a victory on December 29, and on January 1, the Cardinal defeated Chicago at the Los Angeles Athletic Club. The savvy Cardinal had reaped a small fortune, which restored the Athletic Department to solvency, but the faculty forbade such barnstorming thereafter. Hoover, who had helped inspire the scheme, considered the limitation reasonable, although the closely bunched games had helped balance the books of an athletic department chronically in debt.[16]

At the beginning of the 1894 season, the Cardinal gridiron squad, having proven itself on the field, was on the verge of its most successful season. Yet Bert kept a close eye on the till because the team remained $1,500 in debt. Further, his Quaker principles impelled him to treat all individuals equally. The playing field, the same one used for baseball, remained unfenced, and the manager and assistant manager still circulated through the grandstand collecting admissions. Just before kickoff at one game, Hoover asked his crew if every patron had paid. They replied that everyone had, with the exception of President Jordan and his guest. Bert bounded over and informed Jordan and his companion that they must comply with the rules and pay for admission. Jordan promptly did, as did his guest—Andrew Carnegie.[17]

During his junior and senior years Hoover packed his schedule with as many science and engineering courses as possible. He took classes in geology, mineralogy, chemistry, advanced geology, French, ethics, and hygiene. He enrolled in German, but the language proved difficult. Bert stopped attending class without formally dropping it and failed the course, the only one he flunked in college. He never became fluent in any second language, though he learned to speak French haltingly. Beyond his love for science and mining engineering, Hoover selectively took humanities classes that interested him, such as history, economics, and English literature, and passed them. His retentive memory was a formidable asset in courses dealing with history and classical literature.[18]

Bert continued to splice together jobs to keep himself solvent as he scurried between classes and miscellaneous extracurricular activities. He sold his newspaper distribution business as a sophomore and began the more lucrative task of picking up student laundry for cleaning and returning it to individual rooms, employing assistants. As a senior, he added a more ambitious responsibility, importing entertainers to campus, guaranteeing them a flat fee, and retaining any remaining profits from ticket sales. Among the speakers he hired was William Jennings Bryan, who subsequently became the Populist and then the Democratic candidate for president in 1896, 1900, and 1908. Hoover was unimpressed by Bryan's oratory, which he considered more ballyhoo than substance. The recruitment of speakers and performers was a risky venture and sometimes the impresario lost money. For example, Bert lured the world-famous Polish pianist Ignacy Jan Paderewski to campus, guaranteeing him $2,000. The concert netted only $1,600. Bert offered to give the entire sum to the pianist and an IOU for the remainder. Paderewski generously declined the full amount, gave Hoover a percentage, and canceled the remainder. Years later, Hoover fed Paderewski's native Poland after World War I, returning the favor. When Paderewski thanked him, Hoover said there was no need to; Paderewski had once been generous to an indigent student.[19]

Hoover's most lucrative pay came from summer work. After mapping the Ozarks for Professor Branner in 1892, Bert spent the following two summers performing a similar task for Dr. Waldemar Lindgren, another famed Stanford geologist, and working chiefly in California's High Sierras. As he had for Branner, the fledgling engineer helped construct a topographical map of the region, received college credit for his work, and was listed as a joint contributor to the project. In the fall of 1894, he returned five weeks late for the opening of the fall semester, putting him behind in his classwork for what became the most frenetic semester of his academic career at Stanford and requiring strenuous efforts to graduate on time the following spring. Nonetheless, Hoover immensely enjoyed the outdoor work and the scenic beauty of the Sierras, which whetted his appetite to graduate and become a professional mining engineer.[20]

While mapping the Sierras with Lindgren in 1893, Hoover also mapped out in his mind a blueprint for untangling Stanford's student finances, a hodgepodge of clubs and athletic organizations resembling scrambled eggs, with little cohesion and no central oversight. Many of them, mired in debt, were compelled to disband every year, default on their arrears, and reassemble the following year. When Bert returned from his summer job for his junior year, he approached the leaders of his faction with a sweeping plan to reorganize student finances and outlined his ideas for a new student constitution. There would be several officers, with all funds channeled through a centralized treasurer, who would maintain scrupulous records. The barbs decided on a ticket of the three H's: Lester Hinsdale for president, Herbert Hicks for football manager, and Herbert Hoover for treasurer. The elections were to be held during the spring semester of 1894, the constitution ratified in a student referendum, and the newly elected students would serve for academic year 1894–95, Hoover's senior year. Bert was particularly reluctant to assume another burden because he was already overcommitted and his grades could suffer. The treasurer would be paid because of the amount of labor involved, yet Hoover said he could not accept pay derived from a constitution he himself had written. The barbs pleaded for Bert to run. He was universally respected and could balance the books, and his faction did not believe they could win without him. Hoover ran because of the duty he felt to implement his plan.[21]

The election in April set precedents. Fences were plastered with posters and sidewalks were covered with chalk. The turnout was enormous: about 85 percent of the student body voted. The barbs captured all the important offices. After a mixed result the previous year, the barbs were now the most powerful faction on campus. Hoover's stronghold remained Encina Hall, his ward, which the barbs carried decisively, complemented by the poor students in the old construction shacks, who had been brought into the mainstream of campus life. Following the election, the entire student body assembled in the chapel to debate and vote on the constitution. After a heated argument on a torrid California afternoon, the students approved the new charter, which remained intact for more than a generation. The campaign marked the pinnacle of Hoover's career as a campus politician, although he would not take office until the following academic year, when the constitution became effective. He had emerged as the intellectual leader of his faction, having demonstrated an ability in debate to strike to the heart of an issue like a dagger. Due to his shyness, he was not one of the most popular students, yet he became one of the most influential. His presence was crucial to the success of the ticket. The turnabout since the freshman year of an ironclad fraternity-athlete monopoly on offices and power was revolutionary.[22]

The pace of Hoover's life accelerated, crammed with course work, labs for Branner, student politics, odd jobs, and full-time summer employment. Although he remained reserved, Bert made a multitude of friends, often forged in political combat and athletic administration. However, his group of friends was eclectic, with more than engineers, athletes, and student politicians among them. He was admired as Stanford's most versatile student, constantly busy, able in many areas, unselfish, an individual of impeccable intellectual and fiscal integrity. Tall and thin, about five-eleven, he was usually clad in a double-breasted blue suit, which he changed frequently into yet another suit identical in style and color. He had an unlined, rotund face, and his eyes were wistful, yet snapped to attention at the sight of a friend.

During the spring semester of his junior year his stamina was tested when he contracted typhoid—the disease that had killed his father. He recovered but lacked money for the infirmary bill, so Professor Branner paid. The geology professor seemed a teacher, mentor, employer, and guardian angel rolled into one. Hoover fell behind in his studies but recouped before departing to map the Sierras with Lindgren for the last time, in the summer of 1894. Before leaving, he failed the English 1B exam once again. This left only his coming senior year to make up the deficiency.[23]

Hoover's essential adult personality had emerged, and his basic traits would vary little thereafter. Quiet, unobtrusive, craving neither credit, nor fame, nor money, he led by action. He labored patiently and assiduously, yet he received bursts of inspiration and his intelligence was complemented by his self-discipline and an unerring intuition about people. His achievements in extracurricular activities appeared surprising, given his introverted personality, yet this success was repeated consistently. He was neither flashy nor ostentatious. Those who got to know him, however, found him to be a "people person," adept at persuasion in small groups, a stimulating conversationalist, tolerant, meticulous about details, yet someone who also grasped the big picture. Contented and even tempered, he did not flaunt his views and could compromise, yet Bert was firm about principles nonetheless. When he walked across campus, most students knew him. Friends stuck to him like cement. A group of Stanford friends became the core of his later relief operations and his public career. "I believe one of the great elements in his success has been his ability to do any part of any job," a classmate explained. The classmate, a fraternity man, said that Hoover had bids from many fraternities, including his own, because they believed he would add prestige to their ranks, yet the young geologist declined for financial reasons and because he considered fraternities elitist. His later success did not surprise his Stanford friends.

Moreover, "It is worth mentioning that none of his old pals were ever jealous of him," his fraternity friend added. "This is characteristic of all those who have ever been associated with him—they are ever after boosters of Herbert Hoover."[24]

Hoover enjoyed a spectacular career at Stanford. The climax occurred during act 4, his senior year, when he fell in love. As with many things about his young life, it appeared to be a fluke, yet flukes happened to Hoover with a remarkable consistency. The Iowa-born Quaker who arrived at Stanford to major in geology fell for a woman who not only was of Quaker heritage and born a few miles from his own hometown in Iowa, but also was Stanford's first female geology major, and only the fourth in the nation. The two were equally smitten. The first love of his life, she would be the last. The beautiful, bright, athletic sorority girl with an iridescent personality had many suitors, yet she chose one of the shiest and least sophisticated with women and, superficially, among the most awkward in social situations. Meeting Lou Henry supplied the one element missing in Hoover's busy, rewarding life, which quickly became the fullest and most joyful it had ever been.[25]

Professor Branner was the maestro who orchestrated the introduction, asking Bert to help Lou ascertain the geologic era of a laboratory rock specimen. Lou already knew Bert by reputation and had been eager to meet him. He was not quite what she had expected, as he had assumed gigantic proportions in her imagination on the basis of the pump-priming Branner had done. Lou craved geology and the outdoor life as much as her paramour did. She could ride, shoot, fish, hike, camp, and bicycle and was equally adept in the wilderness or dancing in the ballroom. Despite her tomboy upbringing by a nature-loving father, she possessed all the subtle feminine graces. "She had that blush of a woman," one of her friends observed. "If she has it, she doesn't need anything else. If she doesn't, nothing else matters." Hoover recognized her qualities. "As I was Dr. Branner's handy boy, I felt it my duty to aid the young lady in her studies, both in the laboratory and in the field," he wryly wrote.[26]

As a couple they had complementary assets. Vivacious, well-read, and an articulate conversationalist with an appreciation for humor as well as for the fine arts, Lou was a fearless, adventurous woman with radiant blue eyes and a contagious grin, consistently upbeat and gifted linguistically. Bert's new paramour became fluent in five foreign tongues and in addition read Latin. She was a brilliant creative writer in genres as varied as fiction, biography, and lyrical descriptions of nature. Still, the ultimate arm of her intellectual arsenal was common sense. Her mind was comparable to Bert's, quick and deep, yet she had a nurturing, feminine grace and lacked his ferocious drive. Her passion for geology, however, was comparable. She did not want to become a professor, or the president of a woman's college, of which she was fully capable. She wanted to become a professional mining engineer like her future husband, to climb down mine shafts and judge the quality of ores, to work in the outdoors, to do what male mining engineers normally did. That was an unrealistic aspiration in her time, but she dreamed big. It was highly unlikely that a mining company would hire a woman, or that male miners, often laboring in isolated, rugged environments, among rough men whose avocation was original sin, would accept a woman as their boss. Yet during the first years of her marriage to Bert, she came as close to realizing that ambition as was possible under the circumstances, accompanying her husband almost everywhere, providing analysis and common sense, and enjoying the fulfillment of "roughing it." In those early years before public responsibilities overwhelmed Hoover, it was an exceptionally companionate marriage.[27]

Some of Lou's sorority sisters considered Bert beneath her social status, yet social status meant little to Lou, nor was she deterred by the opinions of others. In fact, she admired Hoover more because he earned his education the hard way. Neither of them took shortcuts. Certainly she had potential suitors who were wealthy and polished, who were articulate and descended from aristocratic families. Yet Lou was not a superficial person. She could see inside Bert and she understood and appreciated him as no other woman ever did. If he was a diamond in the rough, he was a diamond nonetheless, with a noble heart. He treated her with respect but not with false flattery. She admired his mind and his tenacity. Yet Lou was also fiercely independent—like Bert, an individualist. "It isn't so important what others think of you," she said, "as what you feel inside yourself." Their attraction was entirely mutual. Later, Lou told a friend that she had majored in geology at Stanford, "but I have majored in Herbert Hoover ever since." There was not an iota of competition, no one-upmanship. From the time they met until she was buried they never argued publicly.[28]

The relationship quickly progressed from the dating of rocks to the dating of couples, with hardly a rocky moment. One Friday, Bert, dressed in his best double-breasted blue suit, called on Lou at Roble Hall. With her polished social graces, Lou was more sophisticated than he was, had seen more of America, and had far more experience with men than Hoover had with women. Yet she was a freshman while Bert was a senior. Her route to Stanford and geology was circuitous. She had earned a degree in education from the California State Normal School (now San José State University), taught third grade for about a year in her hometown of Monterey, California, and then worked as an assistant cashier at her father's bank. Inspired by a lecture by the touring Professor Branner, she took the audacious step of enrollment at Stanford as a geology major, a decision supported by both her family and Branner.[29]

With only two semesters before Bert graduated, the couple telescoped their courtship while Hoover experienced the busiest year of his young life, yet the relationship continued to gain momentum. Bert became a social butterfly, at least by his standards. By the spring of 1895, the couple was inseparable. Together they attended the junior hop, the charity ball, and the senior hop. Bert thoroughly enjoyed himself and Lou helped draw out his introverted personality. They also enjoyed outdoor activities together. The new campus provided clubs that specialized in hiking, camping, and fishing. Often groups of students traveled by buggy, horse, or mule to the mountains, or explored new beaches. Hoover and Lou stuck together on field trips sponsored by the Geology Department, which enabled the pair to combine work with pleasure. Sometimes the pair strolled together, hand in hand, on the pastoral campus. Bert and Lou felt comfortable together in silence, simply soaking in natural beauty. They could communicate intuitively; there were long, contented intervals without speaking in which each could feel the other's presence. As he won Lou's heart, Hoover's horizons expanded beyond the Ozarks or the High Sierras. Before Bert's graduation in May 1895 they had probably reached a tacit agreement to marry, though Lou included caveats. She must first earn her geology degree and Bert would need a job that could support a family. Meanwhile, they would correspond and visit when possible. Unfortunately, most of their correspondence has been lost or destroyed, and they saw each other only a few times during Lou's sophomore and junior years. Bert had some doubts that he could hold on to such a desirable woman for three years, at a distance. Lou wondered if Bert might become so immersed in his work that she would lose him to his ambition. Yet the bonding proved permanent; commitment was irrevocable between them, and neither ever seriously considered another partner.[30]

The university did not penalize Hoover for returning late from his summer of mapping with Lindgren, and gave the star student eight credits for his summer surveying. He would need every one of those credits to graduate. During the fall semester of 1894, Hoover plunged into his work as treasurer, reorganizing student financing and implementing bookkeeping methods that would be adopted by his successors. He complained that administration of the athletic teams, which generated the greatest revenue but also incurred the largest debts, consumed too much of his time. Yet Hoover was so conscientious that, although he achieved his goal of slicing through the Gordian knot of student finances, his own grades suffered. The aspiring geologist was pulled in different directions: a social whirl with Lou, the mundane daily grind that combined academic work with part-time jobs to support himself, and student government. The job as treasurer required infinite patience, yet he felt that it needed doing and he earned the appreciation of his fellow students for his unselfish, unremunerated attention to the task at hand. If Diogenes had set out to find an honest man on the Stanford campus, he could have stopped by Bert's room at Romero Hall.[31]

Bert redoubled his classroom efforts, exploited his abilities to prioritize and to manage stress, and exerted every ounce of his resolute stamina. He did not compromise on his commitments to Lou, to the student association, or to his part-time jobs. Neither did he dodge any of the tough courses. During his final semester, he took history, ethics, hygiene, economics, and three geology courses. This involved a steady grind in and outside class, yet Bert thrived and reaped personal and academic rewards. He had to obtain university permission to carry an overload, yet he focused on graduating on time because he was exhausting his money. Miraculously, he passed nineteen credits, removed the conditions from the fall courses, and could add eight hours for his summer work with Lindgren toward graduation. Bert's final semester represented the conquest of mind over matter.[32]

Yet a major roadblock stood between Bert and his AB in geology: English 1B. Since failing it on his entrance exam and being "conditioned" to remove the deficiency, he had flunked the dreaded exam on every subsequent try. But another fluke soon appeared. One of Hoover's sympathetic professors—and there were many—found it incomprehensible that Stanford would deny a diploma to the most exceptional geology student it had ever produced. The noted paleontologist Professor J. P. Smith pondered how Hoover could write scientific papers with impeccable stylistic clarity, yet repeatedly fail the 1B exam. He finally solved the riddle. As a student, and later as an author, Hoover infinitely, patiently, inexorably revised his work until the meaning was precise and the prose and grammar were impeccable. He could not do this on the 1B exam because he was timed. Smith took Hoover's best paper, had him revise it out of class for grammar, spelling, punctuation, and even neatness, and brought it to the chair of the English Department. He argued that no student who could communicate so clearly, and who had satisfied his professors by writing exacting scientific treatises, should be denied a Stanford degree.

Although this was a bit irregular, the English chair agreed and scribbled "passed" across the top of the paper. It had been a close call, closer yet because Hoover could not have financed an additional semester. Stanford had a heart, and Hoover would never forget it.[33]

It would be misleading to overemphasize the magnitude of Hoover's multifarious activities as an undergraduate without also remembering the sound education the young geologist achieved in the classroom and in the laboratory. For a small, private university in the foundational stage, Stanford attracted an extraordinarily talented faculty and student body. An unusual number of its graduates became successful in law, politics, science, athletics, and a vast array of other pursuits. Moreover, many of them remained connected and reached out to one another across barriers of time and distance. The engineers were a particularly close, gifted group. Professor Branner grounded his students firmly in mathematics, geology, chemistry, physics, and civil engineering to a greater degree than most prominent professors. Though rigorous, he gave them unbounded individual attention and permitted them the freedom to explore. Inside and outside the classroom, Hoover absorbed a first-rate education and a love of his craft and of his alma mater that remained with him all his life. To some extent, before and after Stanford, Hoover was self-educated, but this education was layered upon the sound, solid schooling he received at Stanford. In his professional life, he always gave preference to Stanford engineers.[34]

On May 29, 1895, Hoover received his AB degree. He did not make the rounds to tell his friends good-bye, because he felt confident he would see them again. His idealism had been sharpened, not blunted, by his college experience, yet the practical side of Bert Hoover always remained dominant. He had set foot on the Stanford quad as an unsophisticated seventeen-year-old from a small-town upbringing, raised almost exclusively by members of his own religious sect. He was leaving his alma mater a professionally trained engineer who had forged abundant friendships that were destined to endure and were bound in common endeavors. He had learned to be efficient at managing his time and energy and had acquired an appreciation for his own leadership abilities. He had found he could be elected to office, yet he had also learned that popularity mattered less to him than making a contribution. He discovered that he could match wits with the best students in California and felt confident he could succeed in the wider world. Hoover was still naïve when he left Stanford, but he was also flexible and ambitious, and the budding mining engineer had demonstrated an ability to get along with people. Like most college graduates, he had mixed feelings. He was leaving a world he loved and entering an uncertain, larger universe.

In the late spring of 1895, the newly minted engineer stepped into a world that would challenge his wit, grit, and perseverance. The nation was writhing in the throes of the Panic of 1893, which made finding any type of engineering job almost hopeless. Yet Hoover had beaten the odds before. Those who knew him at Stanford knew that betting against him was imprudent.

THREE

The Great Engineer

I n 1893, a financial panic struck the nerve center of the American economy in the East and slowly crept westward, reaching the Pacific almost simultaneously with Herbert Hoover's graduation from Stanford. Businesses and banks failed, workers were laid off, unemployment skyrocketed, and a contagion of fear intimidated Americans from buying, investing, borrowing, or lending. As the young Hoover prepared to launch his career, job opportunities vanished. Most men with money to hire workers balked, reluctant to invest in hazardous enterprises. In normal times, Hoover's gilt-edged credentials, with the support of Professors Branner and Lindgren, would have made him the pick of the new litter of engineers. Yet, despite his network of connections, Branner could not find a single job for his protégé, the best student he had ever taught.[1]

Hoover's transition from academia to the harsh world of reality was eased by one final summer mapping the topography of California's High Sierras for Waldemar Lindgren. With money in his pockets, Bert considered working permanently for the government, which might bring security but would impose a low ceiling on his ambitions. Already he reminisced nostalgically about Stanford. In a letter to a friend written during the first summer after graduation, Bert confessed, "But this is life—the other was happiness."[2]

Then the first stage of his career arced downward when the federal bureaucracy shrank via panic-driven layoffs and he was laid off in the fall of 1895. Briefly, Hoover considered enrolling in graduate school at the Columbia School of Mines or at Johns Hopkins. Branner advised him to keep active in the field by penning scientific articles, which Hoover did, publishing half a dozen essays about mining in engineering quarterlies in the following months. Hoover's heart, nonetheless, always lay in fieldwork, and he began making the rounds in the region he knew best, the Grass Valley goldfields, to seek a job as an engineer. To his dismay, he found a college education a liability during hard times. Many mine supervisors considered college men arrogant elitists, afraid to soil themselves by hard work, unable to meld with common miners. They preferred men who rose steadily through the ranks. Accepting reality, Hoover learned to conceal his Stanford qualifications and humbly accepted a job starting literally at the bottom—as an underground "mucker," wielding a pick, pushing and loading an ore cart, working first at the Reward Mine, then at the Mayflower Mine, on ten-hour night shifts, seven days a week, for about $2.50 per day. After some initial hesitation, the miners, many of Cornish extraction, accepted him, and mutual respect resulted. Hoover bonded and learned lessons about both mining and people the hard way. In February of 1896, Bert took a daring leap of faith. Aspiring to move up, though he knew the odds were long, he quit his job and joined Tad, May, and his cousin Harriette Miles, whose father, his uncle Laban, had been an Indian agent. When he moved in, the four shared a house in San Francisco, and Hoover's family was united for the first time in many years. Bert enjoyed a brief vacation and then sought greater professional opportunities.[3]

Instead of returning to the mining fields, Bert audaciously approached Louis Janin, a French-born mining engineer employed part-time by the

Rothschild enterprises who was the most renowned consultant on the West Coast. If Bert could not obtain a position under Janin, his referral might help. Over lunch, Janin patiently explained that he had a lengthy backlog of applications and no openings, except for a typist. Boldly, Hoover accepted the clerical job, explaining that he had filled similar positions for the Oregon Land Company and had handled Professor Branner's office correspondence. He might derive valuable experience about the business side of becoming a mining engineer just as he had learned the workman's perspective by working with manual laborers at the Reward and Mayflower mines. Janin started Bert at somewhat less than he had made shoveling ore, yet Hoover believed proximity alone might open doors. Janin soon found in Hoover the same flawless execution that had pleasantly surprised Branner in his laboratory assistant. With a minimum of instructions, Bert produced a maximum of work. Janin gradually increased Hoover's responsibilities. He sometimes dispatched him to inspect mines and to temporarily manage properties. At the office, Janin asked Hoover, in collaboration with an eminent attorney, to edit and polish a legal brief for a case dealing with mining assets in the High Sierras for which he was serving as an expert witness. Hoover completely rewrote the brief, explaining that his boss and the famed attorney were starting from a false premise and reasoning to fallacious conclusions, peppering his own brief with minute, specific details. Astounded, Hoover's boss and the lead attorney asked how he knew so much about the mines in question, conceding that his arguments made good sense. Bert explained that he had mapped the region for three summers with Waldemar Lindgren and had worked as a mucker in the mines described in the lawsuit. Hoover's version was adopted and Janin won the suit. This proved the first of many surprises. Janin had opened an oyster and found a pearl. He promoted Hoover again and increased his salary to $3,000 annually. The young Stanford alumnus became a jack-of-all-trades. His chief job was to scout mines for investment potential, but he also managed mines and helped in the office as a business consultant. Though his grammar remained imperfect, Janin found Hoover's field and office reports succinct and logical and his judgment reliable. His mind could store information like a vault and he could bear a strenuous workload without stress. Janin considered him the most capable young engineer he had encountered in years, and he appreciated his humility and his selfless devotion to the task at hand.[4]

In October 1897, the prestigious British mining firm of Bewick, Moreing asked Janin to recommend an experienced mining engineer of at least thirty-five years to manage its ten gold mines in Western Australia and to prospect for additional ones. A gold rush comparable to that in California in 1849 was under way in Australia. American engineering technology was the world's best, and someone who worked for Janin would be the best of the best, the Britons reasoned. Hoover had worked for Janin for about eighteen months, and the astute consultant knew he might earn a great deal of money employing him over time. Nonetheless, he decided unselfishly that the opportunity was too great to deny the young man. He wrote a long, glowing letter strongly urging the British firm to hire Hoover, stretching the truth by stating that Bert, only twenty-three, was "not quite 35." The British firm telegraphed an offer to Hoover without even a preliminary interview. The untried engineer, who grew a beard and mustache to conceal his youth, started at $150 per week, which was equal to his monthly salary under Janin. The new position placed Bert on the fast track to making him a mining superstar. Over the long term, it changed his life, tangibly and intangibly, in profound ways no one could have predicted. Janin's generosity was a gift, a break in the direction of Hoover's destiny, which had been loping along and now leaped ahead. As in other cases in which fate was bountiful, he passed along his good fortune. His first act was to notify Tad, urging him to quit his job and to enroll in Stanford's engineering school at Bert's expense. Bert also pledged to support May.[5]

Hoover took a roundabout route to Australia, traveling east by transcontinental rail with visits in West Branch and New York, and crossing the Mississippi River for the first time. Then he embarked by steamer to London, boning up on Australia by reading books he had purchased in

San Francisco and New York. Wearing his best double-breasted blue suit, he met his new employer, Charles Algernon Moreing, whose family had cofounded the partnership in 1750. Having begun with a single mine in Cornwall, the firm now constituted an octopus with tentacles wrapped around the globe. The company controlled coal mines in Wales, the African Transvaal, and China; gold mines in Australia, New Zealand, South Africa, and West Africa; a tin mine in Cornwall; a turquoise mine in Egypt; lead-silver mines in Cornwall and Nevada; and copper mines in Canada and Queensland in northeastern Australia. Not satisfied, they scoured the globe for lucrative properties. They acted as consultants to other companies and managed specific mines for a fee. Hoover's job in Australia was to wring greater profits out of declining mines and find new ones to exploit. Communications were slow to the island continent, and Hoover would be largely on his own, with only general instructions, and would learn to improvise. Hoover and his boss hit it off at the initial meeting, with the older man commenting that the American seemed well preserved for thirty-five. They spent the weekend brainstorming at Moreing's opulent country estate. Hoover was impressed, yet also mortified, for he had glimpsed the hordes of London's poor. After a brief tour of British historic sites and the bucolic countryside, he boarded a steamer bound for the austere Australian desert he would call home for almost two years.[6]

Departing Britain on a bleak winter morning, he crossed the Channel to France, then proceeded down through Italy, crossed the Mediterranean to Egypt, plowed southward via the Red Sea, then crossed the Arabian Sea to India. The last leg took him below Java to Albany, a port town in southwestern Australia, where the passengers were quarantined for two weeks because a few had contracted smallpox. Hoover was unimpressed by some of his fellow travelers. "The Englishmen on board are a thorn in our sides," he wrote. "They are all alike, no more expression than a nail keg; all combined could not show the intelligence of an American 10-year-old." Bert found the British snobbish, bland, humorless, dull, and clannish. Perhaps the most onerous leg of the journey involved the poverty and desperation he encountered at Port Said along the Suez Canal. "As one goes up the street," he wrote, "you are followed by a swarm of would be guides and dealers in all sorts of truck." The description is vivid: "Beer sellers with tanks on their backs and a glass in each hand, boys with watches, photographs, men with cigars, women with fruit." In a long letter permeated by descriptive prose, Hooyer seemed appalled by the people desperate for Western cash at every corner.[7]

When Bert arrived at the mines in Western Australia, conditions were primitive, the heat searing. For three weeks the temperature remained in triple digits around the clock. Wind gusts blew through the outpost at Coolgardie, carrying scorching sand, which penetrated clothing, shelter, and belongings. Hoover described a landscape that was flat and bleak. The desert was monotony in triplicate: bush, bush, bush. "Some gray brown and some brownish gray." There were "no birds, no animals, no beasts except ants and flies, chiefly flies. Graves everywhere, indicating the spot his water bag became empty and warning others to bring larger bags or more bottles." At night, the men sometimes camped on the desert floor or crammed, twelve to a room, in a cheap inn where the sheets had not been changed in weeks. If a man died between stops, burial was burdensome. The sand was too shallow for a proper grave; one would have had to dynamite into the bedrock. In their haste, gravediggers sometimes buried two to a grave. One claimed to have struck gold while digging a grave and quickly abandoned the corpse.

Surface water could be found only every fifty or sixty miles. Thunder rumbled nightly, but it rained down dust with no water in it. In the vast stretches of Western Australia, it was easy to get lost, hard to be found. Often horses were supplanted by the more durable camels. Hoover sometimes used a bicycle, and later, a primitive motorcar. Unlike in American goldfields, firearms were absent, banned by the government. The population was enticed by a single obsession: gold. Thousands of prospectors poured into the goldfields, seeking a materialistic form of nirvana.[8]

The transplanted Californian longed for the lushness of Palo Alto, reproaching Australia as the most melancholy place he had ever visited.[9] Hoover found the outback utterly isolated from civilization. He was well paid, but the money was hard earned. "Anybody who envies me my salary can just take my next trip with me," he wrote home, "and he will then be contented to be a bank clerk at $3 a week the rest of his life in the United States."[10]

The elements were not the young engineer's only tribulation. Back at Stanford, he was caught in a love triangle. Bert had asked Lou Henry to marry him upon graduation in 1895, but she had rejected the offer, and he suspected she might be laying other plans. Meanwhile, another woman who might shelter marital aspirations toward him, Harriette Miles, enrolled at Stanford. It is possible Lou knew about Harriette, and Bert's sister, May, was trying to play matchmaker between her brother and Harriette. May's intercession angered Bert, who wrote her curtly from Australia to stay out of his business. He patiently explained in a letter to Tad and to Harriette herself that he felt great affection for her, but that it was not of a romantic nature. During his Stanford years, he had become overwhelmed at one point and considered dropping out, but Harriette stiffened his backbone and kept him in school, for which he was forever grateful. However, his heart remained with Lou, and if she would not marry him, he would not marry at all. Eventually, May, Tad's fiancée, Mildred Brooke, and Bert himself, via several letters, persuaded Harriette that Bert's intentions were not amorous. She then transferred to a university in Kansas, ending an uncomfortable stalemate at Stanford. In retrospect, it appears there was never any serious estrangement between Bert and Lou and that she never actually considered marrying another man. Hoover had jumped the gun by proposing in 1895, which violated the couple's agreement that before their marriage she must graduate and he must have a job at a sufficient salary and in a hospitable environment to make marriage practical. Bert was lonely and isolated in Australia, and he betrayed his anxiety as he poured out his heart to Tad. It is quite possible that the threat to his relationship with Lou existed more in his mind than in her heart.[11]

After the initial family intercession, Bert instructed May to bow out because the matter was settled. The young engineer confided to Tad that Harriette had been the kind of sister he had always wanted and that May was incapable of being. Hoover ended his letter by thanking Tad for helping to untangle his love life and by promising to hire him as an engineer upon graduation. He also wrote that he was saving money to upgrade Tad's higher education. "By next year I hope to place you in a better place than Stanford," Bert wrote, mentioning Columbia as one possibility. Later, Hoover reflected that he might have injured Harriette's feelings and feared he had been too blunt. The episode showed the rocky relationship he had with his younger sister, whom he believed consistently demonstrated bad judgment and had been too emotionally dependent on her elderly grandmother Minthorn.[12]

Isolation and loneliness occasionally flashed into passages of both anger and wit in Hoover's correspondence with his older brother, the keeper of his secrets. Tad was Hoover's umbilical cord to America, to family and friends. He mailed his younger brother American magazines and purchased and sent clothes to Hoover's specifications. Yet those who consider Hoover an emotionless robot should read the sarcasm and mildly abusive language he employed when he felt a letter from Tad was overdue. After all, Tad had more spare time than Bert, who wore himself out on the job, then, after midnight, penned long epistles to his brother, who was singularly empathetic, but simply lacked Hoover's ferocious energy. The temporary rage was born of frustration. "You seem to have taken a streak of uncommon communicativeness of late," Bert wrote, "having written 63 words in 93 days or 63/93 of a word per diem which I judge must have required plenty damn hard work, I suggest you take a vacation now and recoup for ten days or so." Piling it on, he wrote, "I fear you will damage your thorax by undue exercise," adding, "Of course, I appreciate the saving of ink and paper that you so carefully indulge." He even suggested that Tad dictate to stenographers if he found it excruciatingly bothersome to send news of home to a man whose only companions were kangaroos.[13]

Most of Hoover's work in Australia was done in the field. He traveled thousands of miles by horse or camel, inspecting the company's properties and seeking lucrative investments. Initially, his headquarters was at Coolgardie. When the railroad reached farther inland he moved to the larger town of Kalgoorlie. The great rush was ebbing. The surface veins at Coolgardie had already been practically exhausted. Bert shut down mines that were not cost-efficient and installed superior technology to reach deeper veins at other mines, importing American machines and men, including Stanford engineers. His philosophy was not to mine the surface and move on, but to install sophisticated equipment that could wring profits from low-grade ore over a long period. Kalgoorlie was more promising, with larger deposits at deeper levels, sometimes mixed with base metals, and extracting the ore posed substantial obstacles, including a lack of water for use in the mining process. Bert designed a filtration system to recycle water that was ultimately employed in most Australian mines. He practiced economies of scale, weeded out incompetent workers and slackers, yet maintained high morale by paying higher wages than most competing mines. He won the respect of the miners, who called him "Chief," although he was younger than most of them. The appellation stuck. For the remainder of his life his close friends and colleagues called him "Chief," not "Mr. Hoover," or even "Mr. President." Hoover proved a decisive and adept organizer and an imaginative manager, and he showed common sense in his judgment of the relative value of mines. In all of Western Australia, there was not an engineer of comparable skills. His firm's stock rose on the London exchange, exactly the results his superiors desired. They approved greater responsibility and an increase in salary.[14]

On one of his inspection assignments about 150 miles inland, some four or five days of hard riding beyond Kalgoorlie, Hoover encountered a small, underworked mine operated by Welshmen who called their mine the Sons of Gwalia. The Welshmen, who lacked the capital and resources to develop the mine expertly, asked him to visit their property. Hoover, impressed by the richness and depth of the veins of gold, found a miracle where one might expect a mirage. After evaluating the shaft's potential, he wired his London headquarters and recommended they purchase a two-thirds interest for $250,000 and the promise of an additional $250,000 of working capital. A half-million-dollar investment purchased solely on the basis of an untested mine and a novice engineer was a substantial risk. A mistake of this magnitude at this precocious stage of Hoover's career could have cost him his job and irreparably tarnished his reputation. Moreing was willing to take a calculated risk because he trusted Hoover's judgment, though it was based on a hunch. It was a hunch that paid off. Although Bert remained in charge of all Moreing properties in Western Australia, the senior partner hired him to manage the Sons of Gwalia mine personally and raised his salary to $10,000 annually, plus expenses and a small percentage of the gold it yielded. Bert struck a mother lode. Not only were the veins rich; they were extremely deep. Ultimately the excavation produced some $55 million in gold and continued operations until 1963. The strike, and the way it had happened, almost casually, became a legend and spread Hoover's reputation throughout the mining world.[15]

By April 1898, after less than two years in Australia, Hoover was earning a composite income of about $15,000 annually, counting salary and consulting fees, making him one of the top field engineers in the entire world. He was manager of two mines, the exponentially rich Sons of Gwalia and another gold mine nearby, and served as a consulting engineer to eight mining companies and one financial company. In the hierarchy of British mining, the consulting engineer ranked above the mine manager. At the Sons of Gwalia, Hoover served as his own consulting engineer. He earned every cent. Although he drove his men hard, he drove himself harder. The indefatigable engineer put in workdays beginning at six a.m. and ending at two a.m., working to exhaustion and barely sleeping. He thrived on hard work, and he shared his plentitude, surreptitiously putting six relatives and friends through Stanford and paying monthly stipends to Tad and May.[16]

Bert's meteoric rise, ambition, aggressiveness, and energy seemed a threat to his immediate boss in Australia, who realized the Stanford grad had outperformed him and jeopardized his own job security. Knowing the young American was being groomed as his superior, he tried to sabotage him, and they feuded. Hoover suppressed most of his resentment yet confided to Tad that he was on the brink of boiling over at times. Whether by native ability or simply by dint of struggle and stamina, he was making himself indispensable to Bewick, Moreing. Even in the home offices of the parent company, some feared him, though that fear translated into respect. Hoover was lonely, with no social outlets but work, and he confessed his angst to Tad. Of his boss, he wrote, "I know the die has been cast a long time that I should eventually succeed him. He has accidentally learned this and has plotted continuously and deliberately for many months to throw me down as a safeguard to himself." Bert was resilient and reasonably confident that he would prevail, yet he did not take his job or imminent success for granted. Philosophically, he thought big, yet was too realistic to boast or exaggerate. "I hold a good hand," he wrote Tad. "I have the confidence of my superiors. If I lose it is your future that troubles me."[17]

In a subsequent letter, Hoover was incensed over developments and less secure about his future. "Before you receive this I shall have resigned from Bewick, Moreing," he wrote his elder sibling. He was fuming with disgust that went beyond his superiors in Australia to the partners in London, whom he believed had snubbed him. He complained, "I engineered the whole Sons of Gwalia deal out of which Moreing made $2,000,000 and he never gave me a bean nor a share, damn him."[18] Meanwhile, the versatile engineer was exploring other prospects. "I have the joy of writing you of an advancement which I sometime since anticipated to you and which has now been formally made," he wrote his elder sibling. "I had some offers from another company." In order to retain Hoover, Bewick, Moreing promptly promoted him and offered him 10 percent of all profits from their Western Australian mines. He would be totally in charge of the mines in Western Australia, and his only immediate superior would be the New Zealand and Australian general director. His income would be increased by at least $4,000 annually, making him one of the highest-salaried employees in the world, beyond even his own field of mining. Precisely when a door seemed to be slamming shut, with some luck, and a great deal of effort and planning, Hoover had helped to pry open another door to wide vistas and incalculable, unanticipated adventures, and a yet closer call. Hoover had both helped and allowed events to gravitate to him. In life, in business, in love, in hitting a homer or striking out, timing means everything.[19]

Shortly thereafter, a more staggering development occurred. In early November of 1898, Hoover announced to his brother his appointment as managing director of all mines under the control of the Chinese government. He would receive a salary increase plus one-fifth of all profits from development of Chinese mines, with a stipend that included food, luxurious lodging, transportation, and a horde of Chinese servants. He would outrank everyone except the Chinese minister of mines, Chang Yen Mao, an imperial official.

Hoover was anxious to leave Australia and abandon his acrimonious relationships with administrators there. Further, the Australian climate had taken a toll. He had developed a bladder infection due to the filth and heat, and he would have been compelled to leave within six months because of health problems. "I am damned glad to get out of here," he informed Tad. "You would have to know the country to appreciate it. Nothing could be worse; my whole stay here has been a nightmare in a dozen regards." Australia had rocketed him upward in his career, yet he had endured the experience solely for professional advancement. His experience had confirmed his gifts as an engineer, yet it had tested his mettle, weakened his health, and tried his patience.[20]

It is clear in light of Hoover's experience in Australia and later, his aggressive drive, tenacity, and willingness to embrace difficult tasks, and his refusal to shrink from hard decisions and risky, direct, decisive actions, that he did, at least at the outset of his career, care a great deal about making money in a hurry, as any orphan who had always barely scraped by might have. He tried to help friends but did not pawn off freeloaders for hire by his company. He worked his men hard, himself harder, and he got results. Although he supported family and friends, he lived frugally and invested some of his money in stock. These were primarily sound investments in which he never lost substantially, but he was not averse to taking modest risks. Hoover understood that mining was an inherently risky occupation in which the odds of failure were high but the rewards of success were occasionally astronomical. He accepted disagreeable tasks and unpleasant people as part of his job. He had no illusions that Australia and China were Eden before the Fall. He wanted credit for professional advancement and was proud of his accomplishments, but he did not wallow in glory or rest on his laurels. Bright, innovative, driven, he was tough and virtually fearless, with a warm heart, a generous soul, and common sense, and he was a solid judge of people as well. As a miner and a young orphan, he learned resilience, failing occasionally and starting over without shirking fault or letting obstacles daunt him. Hoover had earned respect from his superiors and from his peers, though sometimes it was grudging respect. Bewick, Moreing considered him a jewel in the rough when they dispatched him to Australia. When he departed, he was simply a jewel.

Fortuitously, the China job, offering a more comfortable environment for a woman, would enable him to marry Lou Henry. The deal was almost closed, yet he had to consummate the details and the timing would be crucial; he would not have much time in America before departing for China. Hoover's life was moving at warp speed. The young engineer promptly cabled acceptance of his promotion to his employer, then dispatched a telegram to his informal fiancée, who had already become Stanford's first female geology graduate—with honors—earning higher grades than her betrothed. His cable was brief and enigmatic; it was not an outright matrimonial offer. Rather, he wrote, "Going to China via San Francisco. Will you go with me?" Lou interpreted this as the awaited proposal and quickly accepted. After briefings in London on his new responsibilities, Hoover steamed across the Atlantic and then crossed North America by rail. Bert went directly to Monterey and spent thirteen days becoming acquainted with the Henry family. Initially suspicious of the man who was to snatch their daughter to a land where, according to rumor, the natives might eat her, the Henrys were soon charmed by the young man with big visions. Hoover liked the entire family. Before leaving he asked Lou's father, Charles Henry, to help handle some banking affairs. The wedding was a simple ceremony, performed by a Catholic priest with special dispensation from his bishop, because there was no Protestant minister of any denomination in the predominantly Hispanic community. The Henrys had Quaker lineage but had become practicing Presbyterians since departing Iowa. During her marriage, Lou consistently worshipped as a Quaker, without formally converting, though the couple's attendance at services was sporadic. The bride and groom dressed in matching brown suits with only family present, held the ceremony in the Henry home, and then caught a train to San Francisco, where they embarked upon a voyage of discovery of each other and the world.[21]

The Hoovers sailed for China on February 11, 1899, their suitcases bulging with books about the Celestial Empire, which they hungrily devoured on the three-and-a-half-week passage, which served as their honeymoon. The young couple stopped at Yokohama, Japan, for brief sightseeing, and also inspected the shrines at Kyoto. In March, their ship docked at the mouth of the Pei-ho River near the outskirts of Tianjin (then Tientsin), a city of five hundred thousand and the most important commercial center in North China. They rented a commodious house in the foreign settlement, an enclave eight to ten blocks long on three parallel streets. The Hoovers enjoyed touring ancient Chinese sites and again they dipped into reading about China's history, culture, and philosophy. Lou began taking daily lessons in Chinese and found she had a gift for the difficult tongue, which relied on intonation to clarify meaning and included a multitude of characters. Within a year, she became fluent and could recognize more characters than her teacher, who said in 1929 that she was the best student he had ever taught. Lou became her husband's chief translator of Chinese mining books, although he had other help as well.[22]

Shortly after their arrival in Tianjin, Lou began several projects that fused her love of writing with a passion stimulated by the exotic environment. In 1900, she began writing a book-length interpretation of the social characteristics of the Chinese people, then became diverted to a history of the Boxer Rebellion, which would occur later that year. In 1901–3, she discontinued the study and resumed an earlier short biographical profile of the empress dowager. She continued to dabble in Chinese history and literature and left many projects partially complete. While in China, she contacted a New York literary agent, who accepted her as a client to write two books describing Chinese culture. She researched and wrote the studies sporadically for the next forty-three years without submitting them for publication. Still, Lou published articles, including some finely crafted biographical profiles. It is quite possible that of all modern First Ladies she possessed the most natural ability as both a writer and a public speaker. (Like her husband, she wrote all her own speeches.) Clearly, she had the creativity, sensitivity, humor, irony, and gift for graceful descriptive prose to publish professionally to entertain and inform, an unusual repertoire of talents. Yet her life was so packed with other activities, and her ideas were so numerous, that she was unable to focus on a lengthy project single-mindedly over time to complete it. This was a major disappointment, but one she accepted. Her passion for people and for life outstripped her passion to become a professional writer, and she had little ambition for fame.[23]

Lou's passion for Chinese culture and thirst for adventure were expressed in other ways. She began collecting ancient Chinese blue-and-white porcelain from the Sung, Ming, and Qing dynasties, bargain shopping in obscure antique stores, amassing an enormously valuable variety, specimens of which remain on display at the Hoover Presidential Library. She accompanied her husband on many of his extended geological expeditions into distant regions of China. In the evening, she settled down with him to read classical literature, sometimes in its original tongue, as well as Chinese history, philosophy, and geology. While camping for the night, Lou wrote descriptions of their journeys into interior regions where the villagers had never seen a white woman. Her patience in waiting for Bert in California while her fiancé was marooned in the Australian outback, and her wisdom in delaying marriage until she earned her degree in geology, both proved justified. For a woman who thrived on adventure, she had hitched her destiny to a tornado, and in China she would cheat death narrowly without flinching.[24]

Concerns about family and friends followed the Hoovers to China; in fact, they multiplied. About one month after their arrival in Tianjin, Bert and Lou learned that May had married a San Francisco plumber named Cornelius Van Ness Leavitt. Dismayed by the match, May's brothers believed their sister had demonstrated bad judgment once more because of Leavitt's meager income and apparent lack of polish and ambition. Bert's and Tad's families grew closer, but May's marriage created a permanent estrangement. Nonetheless, the Pacific Ocean failed to separate the newlywed geologists from California. Lou now joined Bert in sharing their bounty with family and friends through private, confidential philanthropy. She chipped in to help complement a scholarship fund Bert had created shortly after leaving Australia. His higher salary plus Lou's family's money helped increase the number of Stanford students they were covertly aiding, and Lou also sent money to help needy personal friends to graduate. She partially funded her sorority's new house on campus. Now Tad joined Lester Hinsdale as a funnel for funds. Unlike some philanthropists, Hoover did not wait until his fortune was made before he started to give it away.[25]

In Australia, the young engineer had lived in a hut of corrugated metal penetrated by sand swept up by the wind, with ubiquitous black flies his inevitable companions. In Tianjin, the Hoovers dwelled in an opulence that sometimes embarrassed their Quaker modesty, especially considering the destitution of the Chinese masses. This was not Hoover's idea. His boss, Chang Yen Mao, insisted that the young American would lose face if he did not display his high status in Chinese society. Chang, a former stable groom who knew nothing about mining but was an astute court politician, had risen to his position by intrigue, flattery, and bribery, manipulating the influence of his patron at court, a powerful Manchu prince. The nouveau riche Chang seldom did business before noon and his meetings sometimes dragged on until three or four a.m. Bert and Lou were attended by fifteen servants at the cost of less than one in America and were served nine-course meals at home, five courses when in the field. The couple was given five ponies, each with a groom. In addition, Hoover employed a secretary and an interpreter, on constant call. There were no telephones, but messenger boys stood on twenty-four-hour call. Besides their three-story mansion in Tianjin, the couple was furnished with another imposing dwelling in Beijing and still a third in Tong Shan near the coal mines Hoover managed. The Hoovers stood near the apogee of society in the foreign settlement, involving rounds of mandatory social revelry. Evenings included lavish dinner parties and grand balls. On some nights the men sipped cognac from crystal snifters, played billiards, and engaged in convivial conversation at the foreign club. Intrinsically egalitarian, the Hoovers had to compromise their preference for simplicity to satisfy the community. Nonetheless, some foreigners looked askance at the Hoovers' inclination to fraternize with the native Chinese, including their own servants.[26]

Bert was further distressed by the pay scale in China and the layers of petty corruption. He paid miners 10 cents per day—above the going rate—yet found their inefficiency frustrating. Chinese society, at all levels, was riddled with a tradition called the "squeeze," a bribe for doing work for which one was already paid a salary. Hoover tried to eliminate the practice by paying decent wages, but he never succeeded completely. All work was done exclusively by hand, though Hoover modernized the enterprises he ran by using Western technology. He tried to inspire the Chinese to respond to pay based on initiative and individual merit yet could not instill such foreign values. Bert did not consider the Chinese lazy; he doubted that Americans would have worked as well for so little money.[27]

China was in the throes of change during Hoover's employment: first, a brief period of modernization under the boy emperor, Kwang Tsu, followed by a reversion to reaction under the empress dowager, complicated by a convulsive upheaval under the antiforeign Boxers, culminating in chaos and mass slaughter of Christians, missionaries, and their servants. The antipathy of the Boxers was directed at all foreign influence in China. Bert's initial assignment was to modernize production and increase profitability at the Kaiping coal-mining and processing operation, in which Bewick, Moreing shared an interest under the oversight of the Chinese government. The mines were not only the largest in China; they were among the largest in the world, and they had fabulous untapped potential. Improving efficiency and profits was a relatively straightforward task for an engineer of Hoover's ingenuity. However, Chang's fate, and ultimately Hoover's, drifted afloat the shifting tides of Chinese politics. Chang felt that he had to impress his superiors in the imperial government not simply by an incremental growth in profitability through introduction of Western technology, but by quick wealth via discovery of gold mines comparable to the Sons of Gwalia. Hoover's ambitious boss was not deterred by the prosaic reality that Chinese gold mines had been worked to exhaustion over a period of centuries, and he sent Hoover on hopeless explorations to the far reaches of the Celestial Empire, at extravagant cost, a fool's errand.[28]

Hoover improved production at the coal works through infrastructure innovations and disciplined workmanship, yet most of his time was diverted to futile searches for gold mandated by Chang. China was an ancient empire in a rush. Chang could not conceive that in a country as vast as China there were not pockets of gold, and he was uninterested in base metals such as iron, copper, lead, or zinc, on which his countrymen might build an industrial economy. Each time Bert returned empty-handed, Chang dispatched him to the nether realms of the empire: to

Shandong, the Gobi Desert, beyond the Great Wall to Manchuria and Mongolia, and to Shansi and Shensi provinces. Some of the trips lasted more than two months. Hoover probably saw more of the Celestial Empire than any foreigner since Marco Polo. The scope of the expeditions and Chang's expectations for them were unrealistic. Hoover was the representative of Chang and, by extension, a reflection of the former stable groom's elevated status. Because of his eminence in China, Hoover was not permitted to streamline expeditions by limiting them to a small team of experts and fellow geologists. Instead, his excursions were the equivalent of a Mardi Gras parade in New Orleans, designed to entertain the peasants. The parade was aligned in precedence of the order of importance of the officials. One expedition began with a rail trip to the end of the line, where Hoover was met by a retinue comprised of one hundred heavily armed cavalry, a general and twenty officers together with their orderlies, government officials who read proclamations, an interpreter, a huge contingent of servants, grooms, and coolies, a cook, and mounds of luggage. The party included ten extra ponies, one hundred mules, and a hodgepodge of carts stacked with supplies. Officers unfurled flags and banners as they proceeded. The Chinese even wanted to carry the Hoovers, but the couple demurred. The cumbrous caravan crept along at twenty miles a day, even less when its majordomo stopped to inspect ancient mines. At least the pack mules were not burdened by tons of gold to carry back to Beijing.[29]

Hoover's inspection of previously worked mines seemed unorthodox to the peasants. Previous government officials had only skimmed them from the surface, but Bert actually ventured down into the shafts. Once, when Lou accompanied her husband into a dilapidated mine, the local miners grew alarmed that a woman's presence might attract evil spirits into the pit. Some villagers believed the mysterious green-eyed foreigner could peer through the rock and soil and spot mounds of gold. They crept close to see gold reflected in his eyes. Failing, they asked him point-blank. Hoover mysteriously responded that he could give such vital information only to the "superior being" at Beijing. At a monastery,

Hoover encountered hundreds of orphans adopted by the missionaries, who had been sent four mysterious oblong leather objects from America for Christmas presents. Bert led them outside and showed the children how to kick and throw them, and there followed the mayhem of their first football game.

When Bert, often accompanied by Lou, bedded down around a campfire or within a village inn, they dug into a huge collection of books that included works by Confucius, Mencius, Plato, Shakespeare, Goethe, Alexandre Dumas, Victor Hugo, Jean-Jacques Rousseau, and Émile Zola. Later he dipped into Balzac, Montaigne, Voltaire, Mirabeau, and the Encyclopedists. He read studies related to his work about British and Chinese mining and an occasional detective novel. Lou's taste for literature and history was eclectic, and she wrote an incomplete account of her travels, which she originally planned to publish. If Hoover ranked among the best-read modern presidents, Lou probably ranked among the best-read modern First Ladies. One subject that did not interest her was politics.[30]

The American engineer never found the precious metals Chang craved, yet he did confirm that China contained the greatest anthracite coal reserves in the world, some of which were already being developed at Kaiping. Over time, this represented China's best opportunity to create an industrial economy and raise its people's standard of living. Hoover made some progress in developing the potentially lucrative coal resources, but his work was barely under way before China was roiled by the turmoil of revolution. Western imperialists were slicing and dicing the Celestial Empire, carving out coastal enclaves and trade monopolies that drained Chinese resources and denied its people a fair portion of the profits. The revolutionaries, who called their clan the Righteous Fists, were known in the West as the Boxers and were motivated by hatred for such symbols of Western influence as Christianity. Christian missionaries and larger numbers of Chinese Christians were slain, sometimes burned alive, and their churches were burned and pillaged. Combining nationalistic zealotry, xenophobia, and religious mysticism, the

Boxers considered themselves invulnerable to foreign bullets, though they were sadly mistaken, and believed deceased warriors would rise to help expel the foreign devils. The empress dowager implicitly encouraged the Boxers and arrested the young emperor, and the modernization movement was curtailed. Elements of the Chinese imperial army sympathized with the Boxers. As the contagion spread in the spring of 1900, Hoover recalled his field expeditions to the relative safety of Tianjin, protected by a combined contingent of foreign troops and a larger group of the imperial army trained and commanded by European officers. Some of Hoover's Chinese servants fled, while others sought his protection. Even high-ranking officials who had worked with Westerners asked Bert to shield them, including his boss, Chang Yen Mao, now out of favor at court, and Tong Shao-yi, director of the railroads and later the first premier of China.[31]

The foreign compound at Tianjin was ill equipped to withstand a massive assault. The allied soldiers in the village, chiefly Russians, totaled about 2,300 and were lightly armed. In addition, the compound's minuscule population included some 400 able-bodied men, with some rifles and revolvers, and 300 women and children. About 5,000 Chinese imperial troops sent there to protect the village instead defected to the 25,000 Boxers, giving the aggressors a lopsided advantage. Moreover, more Boxers and rebellious regular troops poured in daily to stack the odds still further, peaking at almost 400,000 by June 23. Initially, the town lacked defensive fortifications and food had to be rationed. If ever a marriage in its early stages was tested by adversity, the Hoovers' was; the newlyweds stared death in the face. Their response to the siege reveals volumes about their courage and coolness under fire, and it solidified their rapid bonding as a couple. Throughout their lives together, Lou shared the dangers, the triumphs, and the heartbreaks of Bert's career. The Boxer Rebellion also showed a great deal about their respect for each other, their versatility, and their ability to work together as a team. Bert was never a coward; Lou lived on the edge. Yet they were also fortunate. Some equally brave souls lie buried in China.[32]

Neither Bert nor Lou ever fired a shot, yet they were prepared to. Lou, a deadeye marksman, strapped on a .35 Mauser. That first evening, the village lacked any type of fortifications and was vulnerable to a massed direct assault. As the ranking engineer, Hoover took charge, and his responsibilities rapidly expanded. He organized the men to empty the warehouses of wool and cotton bales as well as bags of rice, peanuts, sugar, and grain, which they stacked by daylight to erect a wall. Bert worked around the clock. He doused fires and created a voluntary fire department. He repaired holes ripped in the fortifications, acted as a messenger, and stood night watch. He provided the Chinese in the settlement with food, provisions, and protection. When an arrogant British officer who considered all Chinese the enemy attempted to execute them, Hoover interceded to save their lives. A river ran near the village, but the only water-purification plant lay outside the defensive wall. Nightly, Hoover sneaked out, started the motors, which attracted Boxer fire, and, with help, carted one day's supply of safe water back to the compound. Bert consolidated all food in a common warehouse, calculated the supply of daily calories required, and distributed rations to the community. Lou spotted a herd of cattle grazing in the no-man's-land between the village and the Boxers, persuaded a soldier to round them up and bring them in, and supervised the feeding and milking of cows and the distribution of milk, giving priority to infants and children.[33]

The newlyweds were so busy they rarely saw each other. Lou volunteered as a nurse at the provisional hospital, ripping up sheets for bandages and using the remaining cotton to make swabs. She commuted by bicycle, riding close to the low wall, and had several close calls. While she was pedaling, her front tire was blown off by a Boxer shell. One evening after a long shift at the hospital, Lou was playing solitaire at home, sitting in a side room. While she dealt, a shell crashed through a back window and exploded, blowing out the window and the front door. Lou continued to play impassively. Her only comment was that she could not seem to get the hang of solitaire. During the crisis, Lou chased looters from her home with a butcher knife. On another occasion, she read her own obituary in a San Francisco newspaper smuggled in by a Chinese messenger, at which she chuckled. On July 5, most of the women and children were evacuated by barge to the safety of the coast, but Lou felt her place was to remain with Bert. Earlier, some of the men had suggested shooting their wives, lest the Boxers storm the settlement and rape them, a suggestion Bert furiously rejected.[34]

The defenders of the settlement were so undermanned that at the beginning they could station only one armed sentry every hundred yards. At any time, a massed assault at weak spots in the defense would have overwhelmed the settlement. Even after relief began to trickle in, the Boxers, who also increased daily, added to their numerical superiority. The Boxers, in fact, made numerous assaults, but never in full force, and never directed at a vulnerable point. They lacked the military training and discipline to breach the fortifications and slaughter the outnumbered, underarmed settlers. The raiders were far better armed than their opponents. It is estimated that they fired sixty thousand cannon shells into the settlement. These inflicted casualties and damaged buildings but were not decisive because the artillery's trajectory lacked precision. Finally, at a point when the settlers had been worn down, with the hospital filling, and food and ammunition supplies low, the imperial army allied with the Boxers changed sides for a second time and a bloody battle of former allies resulted. Peering through binoculars, Hoover counted two thousand bodies floating in the river that flowed outside the compound. Ultimately, although the Boxers had martial zeal, they lacked martial discipline, the ability to plan, and a hierarchy of command. They constituted a disorderly band of fanatics, not an army, although if help had not arrived, they might have worn down their adversaries. They probably never realized how close they had come to exterminating the foreign settlement. Moreover, the defenders, at least the civilians, were not professional soldiers either. The trained soldiers defending them represented several nationalities, spoke different languages, and often argued.

At what point a minor miracle morphs into a major miracle is difficult to determine, but the survival of the settlement virtually intact might rank as the latter.[35]

Finally, relief arrived. Welsh fusiliers and American marines marched in with the Americans bugling "A Hot Time in the Old Town," the most welcome song he ever heard, Hoover remembered. Yet victory was not inevitable. The Boxers still retained a substantial numerical advantage. The allied commanders made a bold decision. Rather than wait to be taken by siege, they decided to take the offensive in an audacious surprise attack that would demoralize the Boxers and chase them from the field. A part of the battle would be fought on an open marsh with rugged, difficult terrain, unknown to any of the allied officers. Hoover knew the landscape better than anyone in the foreign settlement. The military men asked him to act as guide for the charge, placing him in the front ranks. As the assault began, men began dropping around Bert, and he asked for a rifle. It settled his nerves, but he did not fire it. The last thing the Boxers had expected was a frontal attack. The daring of the allied commanders and the element of surprise proved crucial. The Boxers broke ranks and fled. The battle, a calculated risk, took a great toll in casualties on the relief troops. Nearly one in seven of their soldiers was killed or wounded. The settlement was now safe, though materially decimated. Most of Hoover's possessions had been lost, destroyed, or looted, though Lou's precious porcelains and Bert's valuable book collection survived.[36]

The foreign troops dispatched to quell the Boxers inflicted a Carthaginian peace, plundering, pillaging, and raping in the wake of the fleeing Boxers. The assets of Hoover's company were seized by an influx of Europeans and Russians scavenging the spoils. The Russians occupied the mines; the Chinese themselves ripped up the railroads; even American soldiers joined the looting. China became a grab bag for looters. Hoover's mining infrastructure lay in ruins, and he prepared to depart for America, wishing China good riddance. However, Chang, seeking to regain favor at court, operating on the principle that self-preservation constitutes the first law of survival, approached the American with a deal that would salvage Chinese and British interests and provide leverage to regain title and possession of the precious Kaiping coal-mining operations. Chang proposed deeding the property to Hoover, as the representative of Bewick, Moreing, a British company, which would give him standing to sue in British courts to recover the assets from the predatory European armies. Chang correctly perceived that the Europeans would not respect the rulings of Chinese courts but would bow to decisions handed down by British courts. Further, Chang and Hoover reasoned, nations would be less likely to seize by force property that had the imprimatur of British protection. Moreing and Hoover each received substantial shares of stock, giving the British firm the controlling interest in the property. Later, the initial deed to Hoover was altered to become a lease, because under Chinese law, imperial property could not be sold to a foreigner. Hoover's share of the stock amounted to $50,000. In return, after raising investment funds in Europe, he would return to China as director of the mines, the processing plants, and the transportation network, for which he would be paid generously. Hoover's negotiations rose above the realm of mining to international diplomacy. He had to deal with difficult personalities, national pride, and competing interests, both to protect Chinese rights and to ensure the profitability of his own company. The deal required patience, perseverance, tact, imagination, and moxie.[37]

After visits to Europe and America, Hoover returned to China in early 1901 as director of the Kaiping mines and their processing and shipping facilities. En route to resume his duties in China, he dropped off Lou for an extended vacation in Japan. He pieced together the sprawling enterprise from the fragmentation that had wrenched it apart in the wake of the Boxer uprising. He imported American engineers and machinery, raised wages, minimized the squeeze but again failed to eliminate it, and streamlined production. The railroads were rebuilt, the port improved, and the cement plants upgraded; steamships plied the oceans with exports, and the efficiency of the enterprise returned it to a state of profitability, with corresponding rises in the value of the stock on the London exchange. The company's properties were sprawling, involving much more than coal mining. It manufactured cement, operated canals, and owned cargo vessels and a railway, and employed twenty-five thousand men. Hoover constructed a new harbor and new mine shafts and modernized the mining techniques. The company began to reap generous profits.[38]

Chang demanded a share in the increased profits and Hoover negotiated a compromise that raised his income and helped the suave Chinese official save face at court. A second board of directors, comprised entirely of Chinese nationals, was created to receive a greater share as profits improved and was authorized to exert a voice in policy. Unfortunately, the newly attractive stock drew foreign capital that competed with Bewick, Moreing for a controlling interest. By September 1901, the financial power of the firm had passed from Moreing and his British capitalists, who owned 38 percent of the debentures issued in mid-1901, to the Belgians, who owned 62 percent. Their Far Eastern representative, Émile Francqui, was a military man turned financier, closely connected to Belgian king Leopold II. During 1902 there was a struggle for control of the company and the Belgians gained the upper hand. Bewick, Moreing lost control of the board and Francqui traveled to China to implement a new order. Hoover could remain as mine director, he was told, but his American engineers would be replaced by Belgians. All policy decisions would be issued from Brussels. This was anathema to Hoover, who once again packed to return to California, which he planned to do ultimately, anyway. In order to retain their prized engineer, Bewick, Moreing offered him a junior partnership at the London home office with a 20 percent interest in the firm. Recognizing that this meant security, Hoover accepted. He was only twenty-seven when he left China, yet he was already a well-traveled engineer. He had been at the nexus of earthshaking events, had barely escaped with his life, and had seen China as few foreigners had. No wonder he titled the first volume of his memoirs *Years of Adventure*. As for Émile Francqui, the American would meet the autocratic Belgian under entirely different circumstances about fourteen years later. Francqui would ask Hoover for a favor—a big favor—and Hoover would perform it.[39]

The two-headed board of directors never worked well. The Europeans did not take the Chinese seriously and haughtily ignored them. Chang had two supporters on the European board, Hoover and Edmund de Wouters, a Dutchman, who argued that the two-board system had been negotiated in good faith and had sound legal standing. Arrogance would estrange the proud Chinese and could incite legal trouble. In 1903, Chang, now an aging man, sued in British court, accusing the European board of violation of the contract he had signed with Hoover. As a member of the board, Hoover became a party to the suit, as did all board members. Chang did not accuse Hoover personally of doing anything wrong, and at the trial Hoover testified in support of Chang's position. Although in later political wars charges were trumped up to accuse Hoover of cheating the Chinese, the truth was quite the contrary. Not only had Hoover defended Chinese sovereign rights; he had saved Chang's life during the Boxer uprising. Theodore Hoover explained that the best evidence of his younger brother's good faith was that Chang "made Herbert Hoover the guardian of his precious son after all the fury and contention of the legal battles was over."[40]

The Hoovers arrived in London in early November of 1901 and Bert quickly acquainted himself with the other partners. Two partners, Thomas B. Bewick and Edward Hopper, who had been Hoover's boss in Australia, had retired. The new firm included Charles Algernon Moreing, who owned a 50 percent interest, Hoover, with 20 percent, T. W. Wellstead, allotted 10 percent, and A. S. Rowe, the company accountant, with 20 percent. Hoover had to buy into the partnership for $40,000, but his net worth at the time was approximately $750,000, though not all of it was liquefiable. Moreing was involved in the business and financial end; Wellstead was a mechanical engineer; and Hoover was the technical engineer and became the company's roving troubleshooter. The firm managed some twenty mines worldwide and pursued new properties to develop, part of Hoover's job. The American remained a partner for about seven years, until he left to become an independent consultant. Bert worked primarily in the field and spent only about one-tenth of his time in London, unlike his London colleagues. While connected with the firm, he circled the globe five times by steamer. Sometimes he was away for months at a stretch; once he was absent for nearly two years. Still, the rising engineer managed to return to America every year except one until 1914, and his heart remained in his homeland. As a globe-trotting expert evaluator and investor, Hoover opened offices in San Francisco, New York, London, Paris, St. Petersburg, Melbourne, Johannesburg, and Rangoon. His informal office was wherever he happened to be, even a tent in the jungle or the desert. The Stanford alum's associates marveled at his unrivaled ability to keep track, almost solely by memory, of his business in Colorado, California, Australia, China, Egypt, Europe, the Near East, South Africa, India, Russia, Ethiopia, Scotland, Korea, and Canada. Bert's assignments required a mixture of engineering skill, financial acumen, and the ability to deal with people, including other engineers, employees, stockholders, the press, and even the general public. The American did much of his paperwork aboard ship. At each port he collected cables; he replied to them while at sea, dispatching his responses at the next stop. He maintained his diverse reading habits, consuming world literature at every opportunity and setting aside two hours nightly for pleasure reading, a habit he retained for the remainder of his life, including during his presidency.[41]

Hoover personally managed twenty mines, most of them in Australia. The first extended voyage of Hoover's partnership was to his old domicile on the island continent. By then, the gold fever had receded; many of the mines had been exhausted and shut down. Hoover was concerned about mining gold as the pillar of the company's income and persuaded his partners to diversify into base metals, which produced more consistently over a longer period and ultimately yielded greater profits. "Taking the world as a whole," Hoover said, "the gold produced costs more than it sells for."[42] Nonetheless, Hoover's rate of success with gold was higher than that of any other mining engineer of his time. In his gold mines, he drilled deeper and found veins of lower quality, yet by implementing the most modern technology and employing the best workers, he extracted greater profits from them than from the richer veins near the surface. His men trusted him implicitly and became his fanatical followers. "Completely unknown to the public at large, he was the most famous of all in his own field," biographer Eugene Lyons writes. His men worshipped him. "The best of this human crop was to follow him into his new career as they had followed him from Australia to China, from China to Russia, and back again," Lyons explains.[43] One Australian gold mine demonstrated the efficacy of Hoover's strategy. The mine produced 1 million tons of metal worth $18 million after previously having lost nearly $1 million under other management. Nonetheless, the backbone of successful mining, Hoover proved, was the exploitation of large deposits of low-grade ores, especially those needed by industry, such as copper, zinc, lead, and coal. The man who earned the title of the Great Engineer achieved fame largely by his consistency. He always thought big. Over the course of his mining career, including the time after he left Bewick, Moreing to become a private consultant in 1908, Hoover employed more than 1 million workers. At the time he retired from mining in 1914, over 125,000 men were on his payroll.[44]

Not only were these golden years for Bert's mining career; they were a boon for his family and, when they could live and travel together, a sustained adventure. Lou enjoyed soaking up exotic sights, meeting new people, exploring diverse cultures, and having the opportunity to share Bert's work. Lou, and later their two boys, accompanied him on most of his trips. Herbert Jr., born in London in 1903, accompanied his parents to Australia at five weeks, carried along in a basket. Allan, born in London four years later, went to Burma during his fifth week. Both children were registered at the American consulate, establishing their identity as

American citizens. Lou coupled her nurturing with her handling of family logistics; otherwise, her husband could not have been so single-minded in his devotion to work. She carried the children on horseback and camelback and shielded them from arctic cold and sweltering tropical heat, from rain and snow. She set up a home wherever her husband wandered. In 1907, the Hoovers rented a spacious semipermanent home in Campden Hill, London, with a distinctive red door, known as the Red House. The two-hundred-year-old structure, complete with stables, servants, and spacious, venerable living quarters in which to dine and entertain, was also the home of a menagerie of family pets, including a dog named Rags, Persian and Siamese cats, and pigeons. Still, the family's hearts remained at what they considered their permanent home at Palo Alto, near the Stanford campus.[45]

In December 1902, after returning from a mine inspection abroad, Hoover discovered a twenty-page letter addressed to him by A. S. Rowe, the firm's accountant, who had disappeared in the middle of the night. Rowe confessed that he had stolen about $1 million from the firm, a staggering sum for that time. He had engaged in reckless speculation, lost on his investments, and forged bonds and stock certificates, defrauding clients, to cover his losses. When he departed, Rowe took the remaining cash in the company's coffers. Hoover and Wellstead, who could not reach the senior partner, Algernon Moreing, who was hunting tigers in China, had to render a prompt, clear-cut decision upon which rested the future of the company. Summoning a press conference, they announced that, although their lawyers had ruled the firm a victim rather than an accomplice, and they were not legally liable, the junior partners considered the company morally liable and announced that it would pay off the bad debts completely. Upon his return, Moreing was temporarily agitated, but he soon realized that a default would have destroyed the company's reputation, driven away new clients, and forced them out of business. Ultimately, the decision raised the reputation of the revered firm, which actually attracted additional clients because of its transparent honesty. Hoover's share amounted to 25 percent, and the next three years, until the money was repaid, were a slow grind. It meant starting over. Hoover's savings had been wiped out; it was as if he were back at Grass Valley wielding a pick on his first job. Rowe was tracked down in Canada, extradited, convicted of embezzlement, and sentenced to ten years in prison. The Hoovers held no grudges. During these bleak years, Bert and Lou aided Mrs. Rowe and her four children until she divorced her husband, remarried, and became solvent. Even Rowe himself, after his release, sent the Hoovers a letter thanking them.[46]

The financial strain of recouping from the Rowe defalcation and the unrelenting stress of his work since graduation in 1895 took their toll. Hoover had been working too hard for too long, sleeping only four hours per night. In 1904, he was on the verge of a nervous breakdown and his doctors ordered him to get away from his work and his family responsibilities for a brief unaccompanied break. Hoover boarded a steamer for South Africa, where Bewick, Moreing owned mines. There, he fished, read, and tried to unwind. He slept long hours and soaked up the solitude. Still, he could not resist inspecting a few mines and negotiating several business deals near the Cape of Good Hope. The relaxation helped but did not bring total release. When he returned to London, the stress returned with the culmination of Chang Yen Mao's trial. After the settlement, in which Hoover was exonerated, the family, first Lou and Herbert Jr., followed by Bert, traveled to their favorite spot on the globe, California. There, they visited Lou's family in Monterey; stayed with Tad and his wife, Mildred Brooke, at Palo Alto, where they also attended the tenth anniversary of Stanford's pioneer class; and fished, camped, and hiked. The vacation renewed their spirits. For Hoover, nothing could compete with the grandeur of nature and the familiarity of family, fishing, and California sunshine. During his entire ninety years, this was the only period when Hoover suffered from an illness related to nervousness. For the remainder of his life, including the turmoil of his presidency, he remained extraordinarily calm and his stamina proved remarkable. Of course, it is impossible to read his mind, and it is likely that he worried. Yet he always drew upon inner strength, the resilience of Quaker stoicism, and the outdoors.[47]

During his career, the Great Engineer achieved a reputation for necromancy; he could raise deceased mines from somnolence. One of the most prominent demonstrations of that ability occurred in Australia, the site of earlier triumphs, but the mine at Broken Hill proved an exasperating, prolonged experience in frustration before resolution in triumph. It required much more than reorganization and cost-efficiency to resurrect the depleted Broken Hill mine; it took a lengthy period of trial and error, with numerous failures. Broken Hill, an exhausted silver mine, lay in an arid, trackless region of the outback. While extracting the silver, mine operators had left mounds of tailings that included zinc, but no one had discovered a method of extracting the zinc profitably from the refuse, especially considering the absence of a reliable source of water. Hoover created the Zinc Corporation, an international company, raised millions in capital, and invested heavily in new methods designed to separate the zinc from the refuse, beginning in 1905. Yet three successive techniques failed, as the stock plummeted and directors resigned from the board. Hoover was on the verge of conceding that to think big sometimes meant to lose big. Much of his own money and his reputation were invested in the mine. Finally, in 1908, his perseverance paid off. The corporation not only became profitable; its profits accelerated until it became the most lucrative zinc mine in the world, continuing production even beyond Hoover's death in 1964. The secret was a process Hoover designed called oil flotation, in which he used the capacity of zinc to float upon oil to separate the ore from the tailings. The success of the Zinc Corporation corresponded with Hoover's zenith with Bewick, Moreing and the peak of the parent company's ascendancy.[48]

Of all the mines Hoover developed, none showed more potential than an ancient silver, lead, and zinc mine deep in the steamy, nearly impenetrable jungles of northern Burma, near the Chinese border. During his early explorations, Bert unwittingly crept into a tiger's lair. Recognizing fresh tracks, he backed out prudently. On his next excursion to Burma, the daring engineer brought Lou and the boys. Both adults contracted malaria, but fortunately the children did not. During his fevered delirium, Hoover penned stacks of poetry, highly unusual for him, but the poetry passed out of his system along with the malaria infection. Like the Broken Hill mine and several others, the Burma mine took years to develop and overlapped his period as a partner in Bewick, Moreing and the time after 1908 when he became an independent consultant yet still retained an interest in some properties he had developed earlier and for which he continued to sit on the boards of directors. The Burma mine had been worked from about 1450 to 1850, when silver near the surface became exhausted. Attempting to dig deeper, the Chinese struck water, and they lacked the sophisticated equipment to cope with the seepage into the tunnels. The Chinese priority was silver, and they left half a million tons of lead heaped as refuse mixed with other metals, including zinc, copper, and antimony, which they considered waste. This slag also contained lower grades of silver, which could be separated by modern chemistry. Hoover recognized the potential of the site, yet it posed formidable geographical obstacles. He had to construct an eighty-mile rail line over two mountains, erect hydroelectric plants and a smelter, and build an infrastructure for thirty thousand workers, including housing, schools, and recreational facilities. The local tribal leader became rich, and the miners enjoyed the highest pay they had ever received. The audacious engineer began by separating the lead tailings, which provided seed money for development. On his recommendation, Bewick, Moreing purchased an interest in what became known as the Bawdwin mine, and Hoover himself bought 18 percent, violating his cardinal rule of abstaining from investing in stock in mines he managed. He became a director of the Burma Corporation in 1908, and in 1914 he became chairman of the board. The mine began producing lead in quantity in 1908.[49]

The Great War and his commitment to relief for Belgium ultimately forced Hoover to dispose of his holdings. The timing was unfortunate for Hoover because by 1913, the mine was producing enormous profits from a variety of ores, and the war made its assets even more valuable.

Eventually, the Bawdwin development became the richest silver and
lead mine in the world. The mine's expansion was a phenomenal achievement. Hoover constructed a tunnel 350 feet deep, despite the water level
that had deterred the Chinese, and struck untapped veins of silver, in
addition to the silver Hoover extracted from the slag heaps aboveground.
It was a difficult task as well because of the rugged terrain, the distance
from civilization, and the lack of a skilled workforce. Moreover, Hoover
demonstrated that he had grown beyond a mining engineer. He became
an international businessman, a problem solver, potentially a tycoon on
the scale of Rockefeller, Carnegie, and Ford. Hoover enjoyed the challenges, but money was not his main objective, and he willingly gave it
up when the time came. Still, had he chosen a different path, one wonders how high he might have risen in his chosen profession. Though
Hoover could be highly focused, over his lifetime he consummated a
multitude of ventures, many of them simultaneously. He preferred those
involving people to those involving technology.[50]

When his contract was due for renewal in 1908, Hoover sold out to
investor W. J. Loring for $150,000 and decided to strike out as an inde-
pendent consultant. Moreing pleaded for him to stay, even offering the
American the controlling interest in the firm. Business had tripled during
Hoover's seven years with the partnership, and his star quality attracted
clients. However, Hoover felt he already had sufficient money, was tiring
of the incessant travel, and wanted to spend more time in America. He
also had temperamental differences with the British senior partner, who
flaunted his wealth ostentatiously, speculated with company money, and
harbored political pretensions. Moreing, whom Hoover considered a
reactionary dilettante gliding along on the firm's reputation, had run for
Parliament as a Tory and lost. However, more than lifestyle differences
were at stake. Hoover was moving in new directions and wanted greater
latitude to pursue his own interests and become rooted in America.
He was entering the period of his career where he had risen beyond
the stage of a technician who patched up failing mines to a venture

capitalist and an international businessman who raised capital, sought prudent investments, developed them, and received commissions enduring indefinitely, which would provide a stream of income so long as the mines produced.[51]

Meanwhile, Bert's older brother, Tad, had earned his engineering degree at Stanford, worked for a London company, Minerals Separation, and struck out as a private consultant at about the same time as his sibling, with offices in the same building, which housed a cluster of Europe's leading engineers. Tad was a savvy engineer, only a notch below Bert, even though he had gotten a later start because of a deferred education in engineering. Ultimately, he enjoyed a distinguished career as an engineer and a scholar and administrator at Stanford. The brothers had much in common, including fine minds, a rugged constitution forged in the outdoors, tenacity, a gift for mechanical objects, a fascination with engineering, practicality, common sense, and sound judgment. Tad never developed the enormously successful mines that his brother found in Australia, Burma, and Russia, yet few engineers did. Tad perhaps understood Bert better than anyone except Lou. He recognized that Bert combined the gift of Midas with the grit of hard work. Yet capital and mine owners sought Hoover as a consultant not simply for his success, but also for his reputation for absolute fidelity to his word. His sterling reputation for absolute honesty, along with his engineering virtuosity, attracted more clients than he could accommodate.[52]

At Bewick, Moreing, Hoover had earned a reputation as a man who could fix problems, who could deal with people, negotiate contracts, and discover potential wealth in remote regions of the world. With inexorable energy and the drive of a locomotive, he also possessed a keen intuition about people and about ores. In a profession in which only one in one thousand mines proved profitable, Hoover experienced failures, yet his success rate was among the highest of his time, and the enormity of some of his successes more than compensated for the inevitable failures. For an investor, a bet on Hoover was a safe bet. Moreover, Hoover was adaptable to differing climates, terrains, underground formations, and types of people; he was versatile, flexible, and inventive. He viewed obstacles as opportunities and was daunted neither by men nor by nature. Perhaps among his secrets were his zest for his work and his intrinsic joy in problem solving. He never gave up, nor deserted a friend or people in need. He eventually applied these skills and traits to fields beyond engineering. All American engineers who worked abroad had higher reputations because of Hoover's place in the firmament. If they could not get Hoover himself, many entrepreneurs believed, the next best thing was an American engineer complemented by American technology. There was a high esprit de corps among the American engineers based in London, especially those housed in proximity to Hoover's office, making it the epicenter of the profession. Many American engineers who had never met Hoover opened doors by claiming to be intimates. This remained true for decades. He was a legend in his profession beyond his own time.[53]

The timing of Hoover's break with Bewick, Moreing was not coincidental. By 1908, his boys were about school age and he wanted them to be educated in America. By 1909, the Hoovers were spending more time at their real home in California. In 1912, they lived primarily in Palo Alto, San Francisco, and New York, with Hoover's chief office in San Francisco. He continued to maintain foreign offices in London and St. Petersburg, and they retained the Red House. Once Herbert Jr. and Allan were enrolled in public school at Palo Alto, Lou found herself traveling less with her husband yet commuting to Europe frequently to be with Bert. Although Hoover still set a backbreaking pace, he became marginally less peripatetic than previously. However, much of his work went on inside his head. His chief job lay in thinking. He was, in effect, renting his mind to clients. Hoover became extremely selective in his choice of customers, and the bidding price for his time was high. He retained only a skeleton staff, hiring talented young engineers on an ad hoc basis and parceling out specific assignments, relying largely, though not exclusively, on Americans. He named John Agnew, a gifted British engineer he had met in Australia, as his chief of staff. Hoover chose the project, devised the plan of action, raised the capital for development, then delegated the details to Agnew and moved on to another venture. Although the American was famed for restoring mines to profitability, he was also astute in abandoning mines that did not fulfill their promise, cutting his losses. The scope of his projects actually increased; more than ever, he thought big. Gifted engineers found it a privilege to work for him because he rarely interfered with the details of their work and his name fattened their résumés. Hoover never incorporated nor gave his company a name. The only name on the door at any of his offices was "Herbert C. Hoover." He did not advertise, nor did he need to. Bert accepted commissions or stock in enterprises rather than a flat fee for his work, which kept a torrent of income flowing for many years beyond his retirement as an engineer. This is one explanation for the fact that he lived the remainder of his life after 1914 with very little visible means of support.[54]

One of Hoover's most ambitious projects lay on the eastern rim of the Ural Mountains, which separate Europe from Asia. The vast estate—sprawling some 1.5 million acres—was owned by Baron Meller-Zakomelsky, a distant relative of the Romanoffs. For generations, some 170,000 peasants had earned a living from the forests and mines, which held deposits of iron and copper. Unfortunately, the owners lived profligately and the property had declined. After a Scottish businessman refinanced the debt-ridden estate, Baron Zakomelsky gave Hoover carte blanche to restore the region to prosperity. The American engineer found the high-grade ore depleted, and thus he designed techniques to process the remaining low-grade ore cheaply in large quantities, importing American engineers from Butte, Montana, with experience in mining low-quality iron ore. Because of the isolated location, Hoover constructed smelters near the mines, built factories to convert the metals into finished products, and laid 350 miles of railroads to deliver them to market. He restored the lumbering industry and produced turpentine, sulfuric acid, and acetone as by-products. Within a few years the once decaying outpost in the wilderness was showing profits of $2 million annually. Further, Hoover improved the lives of the peasants by paying them higher wages. He constructed schools, churches, hospitals, and theaters, believing that high morale inspires productive workers. The baron caught the reform fever and sold some land to peasants at reasonable prices. Kyshtym became a model town. The once sulky peasants developed a sense of community and professional pride. The businesses prospered until the Russian Revolution of 1917, well after Hoover's departure in 1915. Animated by class resentment, the inflamed workers expelled the managers and attempted to run the industries themselves, resulting in a collapse of discipline, a decline in technical standards, and a relapse into abject poverty.[55]

In addition, Hoover developed the massive Irtysh properties, about a thousand miles up the Irtysh River from Omsk, a remote location in Siberia. Despite the bleak setting, the land harbored rich deposits of lead, zinc, iron, gold, silver, lead, and copper beneath the surface. Hoover was particularly impressed by the rich, deep veins of coal ore. The problem was that the minerals were intermixed, and transportation was totally absent. There were no roads, rail lines, or canals. Having raised $10 million for the project, including some of his own money, he constructed a lengthy railroad, smelters, and refineries. The prodigious undertaking included unearthing and smelting the ores and manufacturing from them such diverse products as metal doorknobs, steel rails, and even steamboats to ply the Irtysh River. As at Kyshtim, he erected a model town and raised the peasants' morale. The enormous project was just on the verge of becoming highly successful when it was interrupted by the Great War, followed by the Bolshevik Revolution. The train of prosperity careened off the tracks into the abyss of chaos.[56]

At the request of the czar, Hoover also developed several remote mines previously worked by slave labor, which the Russian ruler had hidden from the world. After Hoover had witnessed the dilapidated slave camp, any illusions he might have had about the motives of the czar or the prospect for peaceful reform vanished. He had contempt for the brutal system the Russian autocracy represented, observing, "Some day the country would blow up" in a revolution. He had learned a great deal about the world during his mining career, and America looked better and better. He considered the British snobbish, the Germans arrogant, the Russian system corrupt and degraded, China hopelessly backward, and Europe aristocratically top-heavy. Long ago Benjamin Franklin had concluded that travel broadened one but did not necessarily make one a happier person. Hoover remained a tough-minded idealist who all his life admired the upward mobility in his own country over any other. After Russia, as he pondered his future, Hoover considered his alternatives and reflected that free will can be either a blessing or a curse and that life holds few certainties.[57]

Hoover's aspiration for public service began around 1910, when he asked David Starr Jordan to write a letter recommending Hoover for a position in the Taft administration. In 1912, Jordan wrote a second letter on Hoover's behalf to President Wilson, yet neither offered the prominent engineer an opportunity in public life. Hoover's desire and perceived duty to influence history had many dimensions. He always wanted to write, and he poured out his passions in heartfelt letters to Lou and Tad, eloquent in their simple, unadorned affection. At sea, he would retire to his cabin at night to write journals about his experiences. His earliest attempts to realize his ambitions as a writer were in the field of mining. He began publishing in mining journals regularly, first in America, then in Europe. Between 1896 and 1912, Hoover published almost two dozen articles on the geological, administrative, and economic facets of mining in prominent professional journals. He even suspected, and his college mentors did as well, that he might have a future in academia. Certainly some major universities might have hired him on the basis of these early publications alone. His administrative credentials would have served him well as a college president—ideally, as president at Stanford. He might well have missed his calling in academia, he later reflected, but decided instead to undertake the relief of Belgium. He had by then padded his credentials. Hoover's series of lectures, practical, theoretical, and ethical, about geological engineering at Stanford, and then Columbia, were collected and published as *Principles of Mining* in 1909. Lou reorganized, polished, and edited his prose. As a primer on the techniques of mining, it stood in the advance guard of its time. It was straightforward and accurate, with descriptive insight, drawing upon his experience. The brief study was used as a college textbook for several decades. More important to historians, the book included a chapter about the ethics of engineering. Hoover emphasized the obligations of engineers to employees and to the general public, supported labor unions, admonished businessmen that the days of laissez-faire had vanished and with them the roughshod treatment of workers, who deserved respect and decent pay and worked better when they got it. Drawing upon his experience with common laborers worldwide, Hoover concluded that well-paid workers with high morale produced more for the dollar than meagerly paid workers, who did just enough to get by. Mine administrators, and in fact employers in general, were obligated to demonstrate fairness and equity. Otherwise, turmoil would ensue, to the detriment of all concerned.[58]

Shortly after Hoover made the transition from partner in Bewick, Moreing to independent consultant, he and Lou embarked on a project that resulted in the most important book ever published by a husband-and-wife team who became a presidential couple. Lou became intrigued with the most inscrutable mining classic of the Renaissance, a codification of mining processes by a Saxon, George Bauer, writing under the pen name of Georgius Agricola. Agricola, a contemporary of Martin Luther, a physician and scientist, and one of the most learned men of his time, wrote in Latin, still the language of science. When he described mining processes that had no equivalent in ancient Latin, Agricola coined Latinate words, which had befuddled translators for centuries. Lou commenced an attempt to create the first readable English translation but was thwarted by the bastardized Latin used to describe the chemical and metallurgical procedures. Bert joined her effort by painstakingly replicating the experiments until he determined the meaning of the improvised Latin, a tedious process of trial and error. Lou, who read both Latin and German, worked from an earlier, defective German translation. The team approach solved the riddles incrementally. Earlier attempts had failed because Latin experts were not mining engineers and few mining engineers were as proficient in Latin as Lou. The couple devoted five years to their two-pronged labor of love: they loved each other and they loved their task. Lou, who had initiated the project, enjoyed challenges, both mental and physical, and was undeterred by the prospect of failure. Meanwhile, Bert continued his normal work, but the translation consumed virtually all their leisure time. The couple canceled social invitations and Hoover did not fish.[59]

In 1912, the translation was complete. For about five years it had consumed virtually all of their spare time and had almost become an obsession. The couple carried the bulky manuscript wherever they traveled and worked on shipboard. The book was published by their friend Edgar Rickard, and no expense was spared. Published in white vellum, the book duplicated the nearly three hundred woodcuts from the original manuscript. The book quickly became a collector's item, a contribution to art, science, and the humanities. No modern president, nor any of the economic titans of the age—the Carnegies, Rockefellers, or Morgans—completed such an undertaking. However, Bert could not have done it without Lou. His spouse, who possessed skills in all the relevant fields, might have done it without Bert, but she had no desire to do so. Indeed, although they were listed as coauthors, Bert usually received most of the credit, even though Lou's contributions were more essential. Hoover's contributions were nonetheless significant. He wrote copious footnotes that explained the chemical processes, an introductory biography of Agricola, and appendices that included all editions and translations in every language, as well as a bibliography of books describing mining technology to 1700. The couple dedicated the edition to the man who not only had inspired them both, but also had produced the match that lit the spark, John Casper Branner. The finely crafted book was reviewed favorably in the *American Historical Review* and was partly responsible for Hoover's appointment to the Stanford board of trustees in 1912. The couple was jointly awarded the first gold medal issued by the Mining and Metallurgical Society of America, though most people referred to Bert as the author.[60]

By the time he retired from mining in 1914, Hoover commanded an army of over 125,000 employees in an empire virtually worldwide in scope. Estimates of his wealth varied widely at different times, from $4 million to $30 million.[61] "In all the history of mining industries there have not been a dozen men in a class with him for scope of accomplishment," Eugene Lyons writes. "In his early thirties he was widely regarded in his profession as the world's outstanding mining engineer; by the time he was forty, this regard was unanimous." Lyons concludes that Hoover doubtless possessed the most composite talents of any engineer of his generation. "There were greater experts in this or that specialized branch of the field—geologists, metallurgists, power engineers, chemists, construction engineers," he explains. "These were often the specialists whom he employed and deployed and directed on thirty or forty great enterprises in all parts of the world at once." The biographer concludes, "But there were few, if any, who could compare with Hoover for all-around proficiency; for his extraordinary blend of technical knowledge, mechanical know-how, organizing ability, and business acumen."[62]

FOUR

The Great Humanitarian

Europe had not experienced a major war since the age of Napoléon. Freedom of speech and worship, the right of individuals to choose their own calling, and material prosperity were making leaping strides. Only two nations, Russia and Turkey, required passports for entry. The epoch had inspired a passion for justice, and hope for a more peaceful world appeared on the verge of realization. Herbert Hoover later remembered the era before the war as one of social and educational reform, scientific innovation, and a rising standard of living. In America, about 80 percent of the population had achieved middle-class status. Hoover himself had stood near the pinnacle of attaining the greatest fortune of any engineer in history.

Now back on American soil, Hoover waded tentatively into public service by volunteering to help his adopted state of California lure European exhibitors to the 1915 Panama-Pacific International Exhibition. He returned to Europe, lining up the British, French, and German governments to participate in the fair. Yet his efforts faltered when the outbreak of the Great War made the exposition inconsequential for European nations. Destiny had placed him at precisely a time and place that would dictate more than a detour in his life. It marked an irreversible change in direction.[1]

The war swept in with sonic speed. On June 28, Gavrilo Princip, a Serbian nationalist, assassinated the archduke Franz Ferdinand, heir to the throne of the Hapsburg monarchy. The Austrian Empire seized the occasion to settle old grudges with the rebellious upstart Serbs. Ethnically, the Serbs were Slavs, and Russia, a Slavic nation, considered itself their protector. Germany aligned with Austria, a country of Germanic people, while France sided with Russia. Nationalism inflamed both alliances as they expected to flex their military muscle, crush their enemies in a brief conflict, and emerge supreme in Europe. When Germany, flanking France's defenses, invaded France through neutral Belgium, Britain, linked by treaty to preserve Belgium's sovereignty, joined the conflict. Each side expected the other to fold, yet they were evenly matched. Within weeks, Europe was embroiled in a colossal conflict that would slay 7.5 million soldiers, maim and kill 20 million civilians, and inflict death and destruction from the English Channel to the steppes of Russia. On August 4, 1914, the day Britain declared war on Germany, the British foreign minister, Edward, Viscount Grey, predicted, "The lamps are going out all over Europe; we shall not see them lit again in our lifetime."

Hoover compared the war to "a fog upon the human race." "The world made the sad discovery that deeper in European nations than the arts of peace and human progress were age-old hates, rivalries, imperialisms," he wrote. And Europe was to drag the world down with it. The Great War became the pivotal point in Herbert Hoover's life.[2]

On Monday, August 3, a week before his fortieth birthday, Hoover received an urgent call from the American consul in London, Robert Skinner, who pleaded for him to come to his office. Americans were choking the consulate for every inch of space. Having fled the war-torn continent, thousands of tourists, teachers, and temporary workers were begging Skinner to find passage for them to return to their homeland.

Ships were tied up in port. No nation, including Britain, would accept American checks, currency, or any type of credit, without which the fleeing U.S. citizens could not obtain food or lodging. Americans were caught in a mousetrap of international intrigue. Skinner knew Hoover had not only money and influence among important Britons, but imagination and empathy as well.

Hoover rushed to Skinner's office and found the stranded Americans in a state of pandemonium. One man proposed that the group petition the U.S. government to compel the belligerent armies to cease fighting until all Americans were back on their native soil. Dismissing this as gallows humor, Hoover turned to practical matters. Quickly, he loaned gold and British pounds from his resources and those of wealthy friends and engineering associates, much of it with no collateral except a promise to repay.

Skinner soon received a call from American ambassador Walter Hines Page. The U.S. embassy, like the consulate, was spilling over with frightened Americans seeking a ship home, and, temporarily, shelter. Hoover assembled groups of volunteers, chiefly engineers, who set up tables in the spacious ballrooms of the Savoy Hotel. Working under the auspices of the American Citizens' Committee, they doled out British pounds to frantic U.S. exiles, booked passage home, and found temporary lodging. Hoover expanded operations to several smaller British ports. Lou created the Women's Committee, which replicated her husband's work among single women and those with children and no male companion. Both Hoovers calmed the nerves of the frantic escapees from the continent suddenly aflame. Lou conducted tours of museums and British castles to take troubled minds off the uncertainty that had descended upon them.[3]

Hoover had to improvise. One elderly woman insisted she would not board a vessel unless Hoover personally signed a guarantee that her ship would not be sunk by a German submarine. He signed, quipping that if the lady survived the crossing she would be grateful, and if she were sent to the bottom there would be no one left to complain. A wealthy woman went on a hunger strike because Hoover could not book her first class. He took her down to the cafeteria to discuss her complaint, where the aromas of cooking food soon tempted her to end her fast. During six weeks, the American Citizens' Committee doled out about $1.5 million to some 120,000 refugees, 30,000 of them teachers, on the honor system. All but about $300 was repaid. The U.S. government dispatched a battleship loaded with gold to aid the stragglers, but by that time most of them were already bound for America. Hoover had built a bridge across the Atlantic.[4]

Rapidly sucked into the vortex of war, Hoover attempted to unscramble his expansive mining operations from the consequences of the conflict, remaining in London long enough to sort out the complications and opportunities that were bound to arise. He presided over a vast worldwide mining empire that specialized in base metals that could be molded into cannons, shells, rifles, and all modes of transportation on land and sea and in the air. All of Hoover's mining properties stood to appreciate in value; in fact, some already had. Potentially, he might become the richest mining engineer in history if he managed his properties shrewdly.[5]

The tiny nation of Belgium—which had bravely resisted the German invasion only to be overrun and occupied—now found itself ground between the British blockade to the west and the German army to the east. The most densely populated nation in Europe, Belgium, highly industrialized and urban, had imported 70 percent of its food before the war. Now only a few weeks separated Belgium from devastating famine. A committee of Belgian engineers was attempting to scrape together food for the nation but had been thwarted by Allied red tape and German inflexibility. Ambassador Page, impressed with Hoover's compassion and organizational abilities, encouraged the committee to invite the American engineer for a meeting.

Hoover's heart was rent by the Belgian dilemma. The committee pleaded with him to chair a voluntary organization to save the besieged population, yet he was uncertain he, or anyone else, could resolve it. He knew little about nutrition, international diplomacy, and transportation, or where to find, on a consistent basis, the money and food to supply millions of hungry Belgians. He was more than an engineer, he knew, but he was not an authority in food relief.[6]

Hoover asked for time to think, and he retired to the Red House to ponder his future—and Belgium's fate. The task was unprecedented in scope and audacity. A private organization was to undertake the feeding of an entire nation for the indeterminate duration of a war, built up without an existing infrastructure, lacking personnel, commodities, or transportation. Hoover would need to obtain huge supplies of food during wartime, transport it to the Belgian borders, and distribute it from there to the Belgians with life-sustaining consistency. Just as complex, he would have to find money to purchase the food and scarce ships to transport it, and create a staff out of thin air to implement the complete scheme. He had never done anything comparable, nor had anyone else. It would be the largest private relief operation in history. It would mean relaxing the British blockade at one end and delivering food within German-occupied territory at the other. It would be a formidable feat to persuade warring nations, whose objectives were polar opposites, that saving Belgium lay in their interests.[7]

Almost immediately, problems had descended on Hoover that would require infinite patience, perseverance, imagination, and fortitude to overcome. Back in California, there was an impending change in the presidency of Stanford, and he knew he was under serious consideration. To accept the challenge in Belgium would mean forfeiting that opportunity. Chairing the committee would force him to be separated from his family for protracted periods, traversing war zones and risking his life. He felt the burden of Atlas, with the world upon his shoulders. Pacing the floor of his upstairs bedroom for several days, he contemplated his future. His Quaker conscience weighed on him. Posed against the physical and mental stress was the stark reality that millions of innocent civilians would starve if he refused the challenge to help them. Preying on his mind were the ghosts of famished children, the real victims of war. "We may count food in calories," he said in retrospect, "but we have no way to measure human misery." Looking beyond the present generation, Hoover explained, "We no longer have the right to think in terms of our own generation."[8]

Hoover decided that attempting to feed Belgium was something he simply could not refuse. He faced the prospect not with enthusiasm or exhilaration, but with grim determination that he dared not fail. Finally emerging from his personal purgatory, he descended the stairs of the Red House for breakfast with his Stanford friend Will Irwin, now a famous war correspondent, and said, "Well, let the fortune go to hell."[9]

Even before announcing his acceptance of the committee chair, Hoover cabled the Chicago commodities exchange and bought options on ten thousand bushels of wheat for delivery to Belgium. Cereals constituted a major portion of the Belgian diet, and though Hoover lacked the money, the ships, and the manpower to begin the project, he had tied down the first shipment of wheat before prices spiked.

In creating the Commission for Relief in Belgium (CRB), Hoover was entering terra incognita, setting a precedent as a "Napoleon of Mercy." At the time there was no large international organization with staff and contingency funds in place, no umbrella group such as the United Nations with an existing infrastructure to call upon contributions from its members. Neither did the United States possess such a contingency appropriation. "In more recent times the world has grown accustomed to American action to save lives and restore the fractured economies of far-off lands," George H. Nash writes. "Indeed, today, such involvement is almost universally taken for granted. One reason for this expectation, one reason for its acceptance—although few know it today—is the institution created by Herbert Hoover."[10] The CRB was to become the model for CARE and UNICEF. Hoover incubated these concepts, starting purely with his own ideas, with little time to plan and implement his scheme. He was on a treadmill of obtaining money, food, and transportation and ensuring the food's delivery to hungry mouths. At intervals, relief ran only days ahead of the Grim Reaper. The experiment might well have failed. At times it nearly did.

The Commission for Relief in Belgium, with Hoover as chairman, was headquartered in London, with auxiliary headquarters at Rotterdam, Brussels, and New York. Hoover crossed the Channel frequently, avoiding mines and German submarines. When visiting the Germans he stayed at their military headquarters at Charleville in occupied northern France. Hoover was provided with a passport, issued by no nation, under his own signature, which permitted him to traverse international borders without being stopped or searched. He owned a German document stamped: "This man is not to be stopped anywhere under any circumstances."[11] He was absolutely discreet in refusing to divulge military information to either side, though privately, his sympathies lay with the Allies. Hoover protected himself with a veil of silence and earned the grudging respect of both belligerents.[12]

Food purchased in America was shipped across the Atlantic on the CRB's own fleet of about seventy-five vessels, each sporting gigantic red-and-white banners and flying the flag of the CRB. Inscribed on each ship's sides was the identifier "CRB" to ensure its immunity from attack by German submarines, although occasionally the CRB did lose transports to U-boats. Hoover acquired food that packed the maximum nutrition and could be shipped in bulk, at the lowest cost, and was imperishable. All vessels were inspected at a British port for contraband, and then docked at Rotterdam, the nearest neutral port, where the cargoes were unloaded. The provisions were transshipped from Rotterdam to Belgium through an intricate network of canals and sometimes by rail. Within Belgium, the Comité Nationale, comprised of Belgian leaders, handled internal distribution, under the loose supervision of a skeleton staff of American volunteers. Food preparation and the serving of meals at local levels were carried out by forty thousand Belgian women, exclusively volunteers. Those who could afford to pay purchased the food at slightly above cost, with profits used to give free food to the destitute. Meals were fed at canteens, or kitchens, rather than sent to homes, in order to apportion rations. Supplies of bacon, lard, rice, peas, and beans were distributed to even the most remote communes.[13] With scientifically designed diets and no citizen turned away, the people of Belgium were probably better fed than some of the poor in New York, Paris, or London.

One of Hoover's chief incentives for aiding Belgium was his lifelong commitment to the welfare of children. To accommodate their specific nutritional needs, canteens were established to provide an additional noon meal for children and pregnant women, as well as the elderly. Before war's end, the canteens were serving some 2.5 million persons. The child mortality rate dipped below the ratio for normal times, and child health improved overall. The CRB also established a special Babies' Milk Fund to provide milk to children younger than three years. By late June 1917, there was at least one clinic and milk depot in each of the 621 Belgian communes, furnishing medicines, nursing bottles, and infant clothing.[14] Early in 1915, the CRB created a national organization for Belgian war orphans. These included children of deceased soldiers, children of civilians who had lost their lives through causes connected with the war, and children of prisoners of war. The charity gave money to families for care of relatives or, when necessary, placed the children with foster parents. The association provided an education for older war orphans that would train them for a profession after the war.[15]

Hoover's empathy for children never faltered. He witnessed many grim episodes during the war, but the only sight that moved him to tears was the suffering of the war's youngest victims. He vowed never again to tour breadlines or soup kitchens that would expose him to such anguish—a decision that, during the Great Depression, caused many Americans to draw the erroneous conclusion that their president was too hard-hearted to face the destitute.[16]

The organizational structure of the CRB was based on centralized decisions, with decentralized implementation. Working informally, Hoover dispensed with diagrams and organizational charts, took casual notes of conversations, and stored most information in his memory. He chatted with associates over lunch but seldom convened full-scale staff meetings. He selected able, idealistic assistants, including some twenty-five American Rhodes scholars, and gave them a great deal of latitude to accomplish their missions, emphasizing individual initiative and ingenuity. One man, given the task of managing an entire port, asked what his job was. Hoover told him to keep the food moving and did not elaborate. He remembered telling one assistant, "Make your own decision. You are on the ground. I'm not. You wouldn't be there if you couldn't run the job."[17]

Hoover served without pay—an example followed by most of his coworkers—and paid for his own food, transportation, and lodging. He asked no one in the organization to sacrifice more than he did. Many of his elite volunteers were fellow engineers, and a high esprit de corps formed among them. They developed an intense loyalty to Hoover, and many served in his later work in the U.S. Food Administration, the American Relief Administration, and the feeding of the Soviet Union.[18]

Hoover found diplomacy his most frustrating job. With no diplomatic standing and representing no nation, he dealt directly with kings, prime ministers, foreign ministers, generals, and admirals, arguing how the undertaking was in the self-interest of both sides, who had diametrically opposing war aims. "Very soberly and sincerely I believe no one else could have done what he has done for Belgium," journalist Edward Eyre Hunt wrote. "I believe no one else could have dealt, as he has done, as a private citizen, without title and without pretensions, with Kitchener, Lloyd George, the Kaiser, von Bethmann-Hollweg, von Bissing, Briand, Poincaré, and King Albert."[19] Initially, both Germany and Britain balked at the idea of feeding Belgium by carving a passage through their lines, considering Hoover at worst a spy for the other side and at best a half-baked idiot or a naïve do-gooder. The Germans argued that they could not abstain from torpedoing relief ships, lest they contain contraband. Winston Churchill, First Lord of the Admiralty for Britain until forced to resign in disgrace after Gallipoli, was the most obstinate of the Britons. Declaring Hoover a spy, Churchill had foreign minister Sir

Edward Grey investigate him. Grey found the charges groundless and, after long hearings, praised Hoover for his work. Nonetheless, Churchill, who called Hoover "an S.O.B.," denied the CRB chairman the right to penetrate the blockade with supply ships. Hoover appealed over his head to Prime Minister Herbert Asquith, who granted consent.[20]

When timing was crucial, Hoover took the direct route rather than the more circuitous course. "If a thing was really necessary we did it first and asked permission afterwards," he said. Often, he bought food in advance of securing funds. His audacity stunned those who did not know him. The impudent Hoover once told a British cabinet minister that he must have clearance papers immediately to ship food to Belgium. The minister replied the request was impertinent and impossible. "There is no time in the first place, and if there was there are no good wagons to be spared by the railways, no dock hands, and no steamers." Hoover quietly interjected, "I have managed to get all of these things." The minister signed the papers, commenting, "There have been—there are even now—men in the Tower of London for less than you have done."[21]

At other times, when he needed an issue resolved promptly, Hoover often went directly to the person at or near the top, rather than working his way up the diplomatic ladder. David Lloyd George, chancellor of the exchequer at the beginning of the war, initially found some of Hoover's requests brazen. When he rejected a crucial request by the CRB chairman, Hoover interrupted the eminent Briton. "For the next fifteen minutes he spoke without a break," Lloyd George said, "just about the clearest expository utterance I have ever heard on any subject. He used not a word too much nor yet a word too few. By the time he had finished, I had come to realize not only the importance of his contentions, but what was more to the point, the practicality of granting his request. So I did the only thing possible under the circumstances, told him that I had never understood the question before, thanked him for helping me to understand it, and saw to it that things were arranged as he wanted them."[22]

Ambassador Page was so impressed by Hoover's determination and persuasive powers that he wrote President Wilson a glowing report about the chairman's work. "The surplus food being near exhaustion in the United States and Canada, he now has begun on Argentina where the crop is just coming in," Page revealed. "I introduced him to the Argentine minister the other day and the minister said to me afterwards, 'Somehow I feel like doing what the man asked me to do.'"[23]

Hoover's job required heart and grit. He navigated among the governments of warring nations, maintaining his poise and equanimity, yet pushing with unrelenting determination to obtain concessions that proved vital. He preferred to deal man-to-man with each official, treating all with meticulous respect while holding his own ground. Regardless of rank, he dealt with each on a level of equality. He had the audacity to challenge tough-minded men with cold logic tempered by warm human empathy. He was patient and possessed the tenacity to wear them down.

As Hoover's accomplishments grew, so did his reputation. His diplomatic skill and audacity induced Ambassador Page to recommend him to Wilson for a position in the State Department.[24] The CRB chairman was so respected in Britain that a representative of the government asked him to become a British citizen and accept appointment as minister of munitions, promising that a title of nobility would follow. "I'll do what I can for you with pleasure," Hoover responded, "but I'll be damned if I'll give up my American citizenship, not on your life!"[25]

While neither the Germans nor the British trusted each other, they both trusted Herbert Hoover.[26] "Think of a man who could go from one war front to the other in the midst of the greatest war and greatest suspicion in history without question of any sort," Ray Lyman Wilbur said. "His own signature was his passport."[27] Hoover conferred with German generals at their secret headquarters at Charleville and never leaked the location. At Berlin, he met with Reich Chancellor Theobald von Bethmann-Hollweg and visited the foreign minister, the underminister of state, the minister of the interior, and the president of the Reichsbank. Hoover found the German military men straightlaced and dead serious. German generals were decisive and kept their word. On the other hand, they were almost inhumanly methodical and humorless.

They were easier to deal with than British civilians, however, who were subject to the caprices of politics and sometimes wavered, though British public opinion supported the work of the CRB.[28]

Hoover's most hazardous diplomatic crisis occurred when General Traugott von Sauberzweig, the German military governor of Brussels, informed Hoover peremptorily that his country had decided to withdraw permission for the CRB to operate in Belgium. Then, in an epiphany of personal anguish, the general confessed his despair over public criticism of him for ordering the execution of Edith Cavell, an English nurse in Belgium, on grounds that she had spied for the enemy. Sauberzweig exclaimed that he had been "painted as a monster all over the world because of that Cavell woman." Hoover responded that he would be considered a much greater monster if he ordered the starvation of millions of innocent civilians. Shaken, the general reconsidered, then wrote out a permit allowing the CRB to continue its work.[29]

Throughout the war, some Britons, especially military leaders, argued that the Germans, as the occupying army, were responsible for feeding Belgium. Hoover countered that the Germans would never deprive their own army—the more food they gave to the Belgians, the less they would have for themselves, and the sooner their army would collapse. They would let the Belgians starve first. Hoover pointed out that the British had gone to war ostensibly because Germany had violated Belgian neutrality. "It would be a cynical ending if the civil population of Belgium had become extinct in the process of rescue," he told Lord Grey.[30] To permit Belgium to starve would be to shame Britain in the eyes of the United States.

Hoover took a similar approach when negotiating with German officials, pointing out the importance of the goodwill of the United States, the most powerful of neutral nations. America could tip the balance in an interminable deadlock, drawing upon its unlimited manpower and natural resources. Alienating America might tempt its government to join the Allies, the Germans feared. The Germans knew the Americans would not enter the war on their side, but they hoped to keep the United

States neutral. A neutral America was, in effect, an ally of Germany. Although most American trade was with Britain, the Germans feared American manpower more because a war of attrition would demoralize their troops and wear them down. In the long run, Hoover's humanitarian arguments carried less weight than American public opinion and the military might behind it.[31]

In March 1915, Hoover was compelled to assume responsibility for feeding a portion of northern France, whose 2.5 million urban, industrialized people lived within a region about the size of Massachusetts. The Germans had invaded and seized the territory upon their penetration of France in 1914. The invaders were halted and compelled to retreat by the Battle of the Marne, but they held a portion of the area until 1918. Feeding northern France represented a different type of problem from feeding Belgium. The region had been denuded of able-bodied men, who had joined the military, and the remnants consisted primarily of women and children. Further, unlike Belgium, which had been defeated, France remained an active and formidable combatant. The general framework of CRB administration was preserved. American volunteers collaborated with a native French committee to distribute the food at a local level. The chief CRB official, Vernon Kellogg, a Stanford professor fluent in German and learned in German history and culture, resided at the German headquarters at Charleville, where he was closely monitored by the military. Although there was initial suspicion on the part of soldiers, most of them eventually supported the work of the CRB and sometimes even helped to distribute food.[32]

Hoover's mission of mercy was unpopular among a minority. In particular, Lindon W. Bates, the director of the New York office of the CRB, lost his son aboard a ship torpedoed by a German submarine as the young man was crossing the Atlantic to work as a CRB volunteer. Bates expressed his anguish by blaming Hoover, accusing him of violating the Logan Act of 1799, which prohibited negotiation with foreign powers by individual Americans lacking diplomatic credentials. Bates leaked confidential CRB documents and circulated derogatory rumors about Hoover to isolationist senators and congressmen. He found a sympathizer in Henry Cabot Lodge, the powerful Massachusetts senator who hated the president and saw Hoover as a minion of Wilson, though Hoover was, in fact, a fellow Republican. Lodge launched an investigation, and a federal court considered indicting Hoover. Fearing publicity from such an episode could wreck fund-raising for Belgium in America, Hoover rushed home to defend himself. He summoned a press conference at which he received promises of supportive articles and editorials. Ambassador Page and Secretary of the Interior Franklin Lane lined up an appointment with President Wilson for the embattled Hoover. Wilson, who detested Lodge, promised his support and appointed a committee of prominent businessmen who helped lend credibility to the CRB's effort. Hoover next called upon Theodore Roosevelt at Oyster Bay, where the men enjoyed a warm meeting. Roosevelt said that Lodge worried excessively over anything that might involve the U.S. abroad, and agreed he would restrain the senator. The gist of Hoover's argument was that he was not negotiating diplomatic agreements equivalent to treaties that would bind the United States. He did not presume to represent the United States; his actions were no more limited by statute than were those of the Red Cross. He represented a private, charitable organization performing humanitarian work. Further, the State Department had been thoroughly informed of his work all along and approved of it. Lodge was soon isolated in a sea of Hoover supporters that included the president, the cabinet, the press, public opinion, and Theodore Roosevelt, the most popular Republican. Lodge continued to grouse, but he dropped the matter formally, and Bates retired from the CRB to rest his jangled nerves.[33]

After his initial meeting with Wilson in 1915, Hoover kept in touch with the president via Colonel Edward House, his diminutive confidant. When House traveled to Europe during the war he often dined with Hoover at the Red House and used the CRB chairman as a sounding board for ideas he and Wilson had conceived to negotiate an end to the war. During House's 1915 visit, Hoover told House bluntly that he considered their scheme naïve, arguing that both sides were embittered, demanded nothing less than total victory, and desired world domination and territorial acquisitions. House returned to Europe the following year and informed Hoover that he and the president had hammered out a second peace plan. They would publicize specific peace objectives advocated by the United States, fair to all sides. America would align with the group that accepted its plan. Hoover reiterated that the second scheme was equally naïve. The blockade and bombing of civilians had driven home the war to civilians and the mutual enmity defied compromise. Hoover, although he devoutly desired peace, pointed out that the pledge lacked credibility with the Germans. The American press and the Wilson administration itself had clearly indicated their preference for an Allied victory, and the Germans would not fall for the ruse.[34]

Wilson nonetheless continued to employ Hoover as a source of information throughout the war, praising him for his "extraordinary work" in Belgium.[35] Hoover's performance also won the admiration of other observers. "Mr. Hoover is a perfect wonder," said Senator Frederic C. Walcott, "one of the most remarkable men I have ever met," terming him "a perfect genius for organization." Another associate of Hoover's concluded, "The situation in Belgium to-day is so extraordinary that if Hoover lost heart or died, in a few days the Belgians who are dependent on him would feel the pinch."[36]

The CRB was on an endless quest to raise money. The commission's charter held its members primarily responsible for debts beyond money raised, and initially the money fountain seemed to trickle rather than gush.[37] Private charity provided an initial bridge to solvency. Fund-raising drives were initiated in every state in America, in all British colonies throughout the world, in most Latin American nations, and in Japan. The most generous private donations were given by the British Empire. The CRB drummed up backing through newspaper and magazine support, dispatched public speakers, and sponsored charity dinners. Lou Hoover, a more eloquent public speaker than her husband, played a major role in fund-raising in America.[38]

Hoover campaigned diligently to attract large contributions from old associates. A New York engineering society donated $500,000, originally earmarked for constructing a new headquarters, to the CRB instead. Hoover's mining friends in Australia sent $70,000. In 1915, many private American citizens gave donations amounting to thousands of dollars, yet per capita they gave less than Canada, Australia, or New Zealand prior to U.S. entry into the war. The 220,000 Belgians living in England donated $250,000 monthly. In October 1916, Hoover obtained the assistance of Pope Benedict XV, who issued a statement supporting the raising of money for the starving children of Belgium and authorized the Catholic clergy in America to solicit funds for their aid. It was not so much the amount of money contributed by the world's people as their moral support that enabled the private relief drive to succeed. Without the pressure of world opinion, the subsidies from the Allied governments would not have been forthcoming. In addition to money, railroads and steamship lines delivered cargoes at or near cost, and groups of farmers, communities, even entire states delivered donations in kind, which included clothing and medicine as well as food, sometimes by the boxcar.[39]

It soon became evident that the CRB could not provision Belgium and northern France indefinitely purely on private donations. Hoover appealed to Lloyd George, who was noncommittal. After discussing the funding crisis with Asquith and Lord Eustace Percy, however, Lloyd George overruled the militarists and granted a $4.8 million monthly subsidy. Hoover next obtained an appointment with the French premier, who was also noncommittal. That evening, Hoover chatted with Maurice Homberg, president of a leading French bank, who asked the American for an estimate of the sum needed to supply northern France. Hoover told him it would take around $8 million. The following morning he received two checks totaling $7 million, and thereafter, money arrived regularly.

Though officially anonymous, because the French were subsidizing their people under German occupation, both sides clearly understood the source. When the needs accelerated, both the British and the French upped the ante. Through public subsidies, private gifts, and the sale of food to employed, solvent Belgians, Hoover patched together enough to tide the CRB over through each crisis, though with a slim margin of error. After America entered the war in 1918, the U.S. government took over the responsibility of financing the CRB and thereafter the organization operated on sound footing.[40]

As events in Europe worsened, the United States moved inexorably toward war. Hoover returned to New York at the end of 1916 and managed the CRB from his office there. Unfortunately, America's grip on peace was rooted in quicksand. In January 1917, Germany declared a war zone around Britain that included unrestricted submarine warfare. On February 3, President Wilson severed relations and expelled the German ambassador. Realizing it was only a matter of time before the United States joined the Allies, Germany launched a massive offensive against Paris before the weight of American power could prove decisive. Earlier, Hoover had cautioned against entry into the conflict, but he shed his inhibitions as CRB vessels were sunk. In early March, he conferred with Wilson at the White House. A week earlier a telegram from German foreign minister Arthur Zimmermann had been intercepted and decoded. It promised Mexico territory in the American Southwest if the Mexicans joined a successful war against the United States. On March 15, a revolution in Russia overthrew Czar Nicholas II and briefly installed a democratic government, providing a temporary impression that the war pitted democracy against autocracy. For his part, Hoover expected that a more convulsive, extreme leftist revolution would follow. With war imminent, he returned to Europe to consummate contingency plans already in place. When America entered the war, he would continue to direct CRB operations at Rotterdam. From there, the responsibility would pass to the remaining major neutrals, the Spanish and the Dutch, who would direct the CRB within Belgium and in northern France.

Before Hoover departed, Wilson assigned him two secret tasks. Hoover was to determine what resources would be required by Britain and France to win the war; second, he was to survey the war economies of the Allies to determine whether therein lay any lessons for America. On April 6, America declared war. His missions, overt and covert, virtually completed, Hoover headed back to his homeland.[41]

After the war, audits of the CRB's books showed not only a lack of personal profit for anyone involved, but also an incredibly low margin of overhead, less than one half of 1 percent, made possible by the donated time and resources that epitomized the mission. Today, many charities take pride if they can hold overhead to 20 percent.[42] When it closed its books as an active organization, the CRB had on hand a surplus of undistributed food, which it sold in Europe. This, combined with its low overhead, enabled the charity to finish with a surplus of about $35 million. Hoover had decided as early as 1916 that any money left over should be devoted to Belgian education, which had been virtually destroyed by the war. More than $18 million was donated directly to the universities of Brussels, Ghent, Liège, and Louvain and to other educational institutions. During the 1920s, an additional $1.6 million was given for the rebuilding of the University of Louvain. Most of the remainder was used for an educational exchange program that enabled Belgian scholars to study in America and vice versa.[43]

"When this war is over," Hoover told a group of students in 1915, "the one thing that will stand out will not be the number of dead and wounded, but the record of those efforts which went to save life."[44] Before the war he had been barely known outside his profession, yet his service in the CRB had made him a figure of international stature. Now, upon America's declaration of war, President Wilson immediately cabled Hoover to consult with him about the U.S. food supply. Based on his experience, Hoover seemed the best-qualified man to deal with the complex production, conservation, and distribution of food to Allied and neutral nations. Wilson and Hoover shared the belief that with the generous resources of America at their command, the Allies could wear down the Central Powers. The war would be won in part on the home front, and the troops and civilians who were best fed would have higher morale than their adversaries. Hoover arrived in New York Harbor on May 3, traveling that evening to Washington to consult with Wilson. Hoover's Stanford friend Ray Lyman Wilbur, now president of Stanford, awaited him onshore. "Word was sent to me that he would come on a certain boat," Wilbur remembered. "I can well remember the grey morning when his liner came in to the dock in New York City. The ship ahead of his and the one just behind had been torpedoed."[45]

Hoover spoke with the president for about an hour and did most of the talking. He had lobbied for the position and had strong support from Colonel House and Interior Secretary Franklin Lane. Yet his nomination encountered resistance. Agriculture Secretary David Houston worried about Hoover poaching on his turf. Agricultural spokesman Henry Wallace opposed Hoover, as did Henry Cabot Lodge, who objected to federal control of agriculture on the grounds that it would concentrate power in the hands of President Wilson. The most vehement opposition arose from farmers, who considered Hoover a businessman and wanted a farmer or a farm-state representative in the position who would put farm interests first.

Hoover had mapped out his plans while crossing the Atlantic. He wanted a single-headed organization, not a committee, which might quibble endlessly and conclude indecisively. He insisted that he be permitted to serve without pay and that he continue to direct Belgian relief. When the president proposed labeling him the "food czar," Hoover said he preferred the unpretentious title of "food administrator," which was less likely to offend Congress. Wilson, a former college president, was accustomed to working through committees, but Hoover helped persuade him that in wartime the committee approach lacked decisiveness and dispersed responsibility. Later, Wilson reorganized his advisers into a war cabinet, including each cabinet member and leader of a major agency with war-related responsibilities who discussed contentious issues. Wilson made the final decision on the spot. As food administrator, Hoover reported directly to the president and sat on the war cabinet.[46]

Initially, Hoover was to serve in an advisory capacity, although he was compelled to take action while the authorizing bill, the Lever bill, waddled feebly through Congress. Despite the urgency, the national legislature debated the measure for three months, while problems piled up and crises festered. During the debate, the solons were diverted into issues such as Prohibition, proposed as a device to save grain but considered by some a moral issue. Hoover testified before numerous congressional committees, impressing members with his knowledge of world food conditions. He usually spoke without notes or a prepared statement. When Senator Thomas Gore of Oklahoma questioned Hoover about the price of beans per bushel, Hoover replied that he had always bought them by the ton. As a food management expert he explained that his philosophy included a balancing of interests. Farmers and businessmen must be allowed profits or the incentive system would break down, yet he would prevent gouging to exploit the war emergency. He must supply the American and Allied soldiers, and civilians of all countries. He must protect the nation from inflation, he explained, which often accompanied wars. Inflation led to high prices, which in turn inspired demands for higher wages and led to disruptive strikes, which could jeopardize the war effort. Finally, on August 10, 1917, the bill was enacted.[47]

Hoover believed that if sacrifice was shared rather than concentrated on a single economic class, most Americans would accept it on patriotic grounds. He wanted to demonstrate the efficacy of the democratic system in wartime, to prove it could outproduce and outlast German autocracy. He had no desire to Prussianize America, either via onerous regulations or by creating a top-heavy bureaucracy. "It was a colossal educational project," Wilbur, his closest lieutenant, explained, "where a whole people had to be convinced and stimulated to act at each meal as to help with the war." Exhortation became one of the Food Administration's chief weapons, as deadly as artillery to the Germans.

Hoover also wanted to instill practical lessons about the type of government that worked with people, not against them. If he could infuse Americans with self-discipline and a sense of unity as well as the willingness to sacrifice in a common cause, the purpose for fighting the war would be realized. He had witnessed regimented systems requiring an army of enforcers flounder in Britain, France, and Germany, where the temperature of enthusiasm on the home front dipped to arctic levels. Instead, he would make persuasion and minimal regulation the lynchpin of his administrative style. His premise was that most Americans were patriotic and would react more enthusiastically if they were led rather than driven. Altruistic motives were intertwined with realistic and self-serving ones in the Food Administration's promotional literature. Winning the war quickly would prevent America's allies from being engulfed and prevent the flames of conflict from leaping the Atlantic.[48]

Following Hoover's example, the infrastructure of the Food Administration was comprised largely of volunteers, many of whom had worked with Hoover at Stanford, in the mining industry, or in the CRB. For the nucleus of the staff, he hired the sons of two presidents, Dr. Harry Garfield, president of Williams College, and Robert A. Taft, later a U.S. senator. Hoover also employed Lewis Strauss, who was later nominated to head the Atomic Energy Commission. A poor young man from a Jewish family, Strauss volunteered to work for Hoover after being rejected by the military. Beginning as an office boy, Strauss quickly became indispensable in the organization and was promoted to be Hoover's personal secretary. The men bonded and became lifelong friends.

Hoover never openly chastised a subordinate, although he did so privately. In public, he took responsibility for errors and shunned credit, helping to develop ties of trust in both directions. The Food Administration leader wanted to tap the patriotism and generosity of spirit he found in these young men, just as he had found it in his cohorts within the CRB. Like their boss, those who could afford to do so worked without pay, allowing the organization to operate on slender appropriations. His assistants took their task seriously, and their morale was high. To further motivate his staff, he showed them a cablegram from Lord Rhondda, the British food controller, stating that "it now lies with America to decide whether or not the Allies in Europe shall have enough bread to hold out until the United States is able to throw its force into the field." Time was the enemy. The Food Administration was confronted by a narrow window of opportunity for success.[49]

The Great War was America's first modern war, the first to require the mobilization of the entire population, both civilian and military, and the first major war fought abroad. Some 100 million Americans would have to throw their weight behind the war effort with a more refined degree of organization than had ever been necessary. Although a sophisticated man, Hoover had sought throughout his life to make complicated tasks simple, to define objectives, and to pursue them in a straightforward manner. As the head of the Food Administration, he directed a streamlined organization. "My idea is that we must centralize ideas but decentralize execution," he had told a Senate committee. He was democratic in philosophy but decisive in action. The Food Administration was a no-frills organization, which Hoover termed "the only war agency which wore no bells and costume jewelry." Further, he wanted to provide every American on the home front the sense that they were making a meaningful contribution.[50]

As he had at the CRB, Hoover rarely held staff meetings, and he eschewed charts and graphs. His propensity for simplicity and a direct line of authority was based on his experience in Europe, where he had watched food czars come and go in quick succession in Germany, England, and France. He utilized the same approach that had worked well in Belgium, relying on a few simple rules for the public rather than bludgeoning them with regulations. He relied on able generalists, not specialists in areas related to food. He assigned an assistant a responsibility and let him alone to achieve the desired results. His management method maximized individual initiative without micromanagement. Most assistants appreciated his trust in them and rose to the occasion.[51]

The structure of the Food Administration was relatively simple.

Hoover made major decisions and delegated implementation. A Conservation Division under Ray Lyman Wilbur and an Education Division under Ben S. Allen were also headquartered in Washington. Below the superstructure, the infrastructure included a state administrator appointed by the governor of each state, and county and municipal administrators. All of these public servants at the local level and most at the national level were unpaid volunteers. Some 750,000 volunteers served at the grass roots. The Food Administration employed women to a greater extent than any other federal agency in history and gave them a meaningful role in the battle for food, making "every housewife a warrior." The major victories would be won in American kitchens, he advised; frugality could help feed Allied soldiers and civilians as well as America's own military and its civilian population. "Ninety percent of American food production passes through the hands of our women," he explained. "In no other field do small things, when multiplied by our 100 million people, count for so much."[52]

Hoover converted conservation into a crusade to determine who could save the most. He challenged Americans as they had never before been challenged. "The question of who wins this war," he said, "is the question of who can endure the longest, and the problem of endurance, in a large degree, is a problem of food and ships to carry it in." The appeal to patriotism not only saved enormous quantities of food for export; it lifted morale on the home front. Hoover believed that by winning the war by minimizing coercion, he could vindicate the principle of democracy, although he conceded that the war required a greater intrusion into civilian society than normal conditions. His decision to focus on conservation, rather than rationing, was based on practical as well as idealistic grounds. Rationing would have been a bureaucratic nightmare that would create red tape, prove enormously expensive, and be cumbrous to phase out when the war ended. It would be ineffective because a large proportion of the American people lived on or near farms and could divert crops to their own use. Moreover, such a program would have multiplied black markets.[53]

The efforts of the Food Administration were launched amid severe handicaps. Droughts in 1916 and 1917 produced below-average harvests at the very time the Allies needed more. From a statistical perspective, the United States was left with nothing to export. Although it would be possible to compensate by increased production by 1918, in the short run, the only way to obtain a surplus to export was by conservation. To persuade Americans that conservation in small amounts by individuals would reach totals that could help the Allies outlast the Central Powers in a war of attrition, Wilbur, Allen, and Hoover himself launched nationwide speaking and publicity campaigns. Food Administration speakers, most conspicuously Wilbur, fanned out across the country, appearing even in small communities. Wilbur coined catchy slogans such as "Food Will Win the War," "Fighting with Food," and "Not Business as Usual, but Business Absolutely Unusual." In some talks he reduced war contributions to simple mathematics, such as the number of slices of bread consumed. He dramatized the role individuals and families could play and was explicit about what each person could do: buy Liberty bonds, cease eating bacon and white flour, curtail consumption of sugar, raise home gardens, can fruits and vegetables, and avoid squandering morsels. Whether at home or at restaurants, Americans were instructed to eat one helping, clean their plates, and ask for no more. About 20 million Americans signed pledge cards to abide by the guidelines and were given a sticker for their window indicating their vow to conserve.[54]

The promotional campaign employed every form of media and technology, advertising via radio, newsreels, feature films, and celebrity endorsements. From May 1917 to April 1919 the Food Administration released 1,870 press releases. Films were shown in theaters and high schools, as well as to social and civic organizations. Articles were placed in newspapers, and the Education Division dealt with specialized publications such as women's magazines, trade and labor journals, and farm weeklies. Campaigns to sign pledge cards were conducted by the Boy Scouts, the Girl Scouts, and the Camp Fire Girls. The agency even publicized the names of cheaters, seeking to shame them. Clergy were asked to deliver sermons emphasizing the serious nature of conservation efforts. Like Franklin D. Roosevelt's later effort to launch the National Recovery Administration, the Food Administration employed every avenue in order to reach American citizens and inspire a bandwagon effect. Prominent artists painted Food Administration signs, billboards were plastered, and neon signs lit the night. Some 50,000 signs were placed on railroad coaches, plus another 120,000 in streetcars. Hundreds of thousands of pamphlets and tracts were distributed to public libraries. Poets joined the crusade by rewriting popular nursery rhymes for children to chant. One observer noted, "No other agency of the government touched the home as regularly." Although the Food Administration was criticized by certain groups, especially farmers who wanted higher profits, the conservation campaign worked more efficiently than the rationing regulations of the European powers. Food alone did not win the war, but it helped.[55]

Lou Hoover played a major role in the conservation effort, delivering countless speeches to women's groups and civic organizations. She used her position as a leader of the Girl Scouts to involve the Scouts in conservation, and she established a large residence hall that provided accommodations for single young women drawn to Washington for war work. Lou also made her own household a model of conservation, or "Hooverizing," a word coined to describe her husband's admonitions to conserve. The Hoovers went well beyond the letter of the rules, eating simple fare, which was also served to guests, including government officials. Meat, sugar, and fats were minimized or excluded entirely from every meal. White bread, cakes, and pastries were not served, and wheat was replaced by buckwheat or corn cakes and corn bread made from coarse yellow meal. Vegetable oils substituted for lard and butter. No sweets were served, and all members of the family meticulously cleaned their plates and asked for no more. When the family exhausted the winter's coal supply, Lou refused to buy more. Instead, the entire family donned sweaters and light jackets and maintained a heatless home.[56]

The most essential ingredients of the diet of the Allied nations and their military men were fats, wheat, and sugar. Fats, which play an important role in human health and stamina, were obtained primarily from pork. The price of hogs, which fatten on corn, was driven by the price of corn. If selling corn directly to the public became more profitable than selling it to hog producers, shortages in pork would develop. To stabilize the markets and ensure a steady supply of both, the Food Administration negotiated agreements to establish a ratio between the price of corn and the price of hogs, which ensured reasonable profits to corn farmers and producers of pork. Hoover played no role in pegging the prices, which were determined by committees of experts, including farmers. The prices had to provide incentives yet be fair to all groups, including consumers. By a combination of price incentives and conservation, the Food Administration greatly increased the export of lard, bacon, and ham to the Allies.[57]

Hoover's task of calibrating a nutritional regime to sustain troops and civilians was complicated by the differences in the diets of Americans and Europeans. While Americans consumed more meat, Europeans' diets were comprised of a higher percentage of bread. More than half the French diet, and slightly less in Britain, consisted of wheat. Congress authorized the government to interject itself into the economy by fixing prices of essential commodities. Hoover preferred the normal law of supply and demand but considered price setting a lesser evil than shortages during wartime. Headed by Hoover's friend Julius Barnes, the Grain Corporation, which operated as a separate arm of the Food Administration, guaranteed wheat farmers $2 per bushel for their 1918 crop in order to stimulate production. The Grain Corporation helped control prices in another, more intrusive manner: it was authorized to purchase the entire wheat crop and sell it to processors at a fixed price. Sugar, a similar essential commodity, obtained chiefly from Cuba, the West Indies, the Philippines, and the southern United States, was handled in a similar manner. The Sugar Equalization Board had a government-mandated monopoly to purchase the entire sugar crop for Americans and the Allies. Antitrust laws were temporarily suspended for the duration of the war. Hoover clamped down on food processors and limited the market of wholesalers for every product for which the Food Administration set a price, attempting to prevent exorbitant prices for consumers. Violators of Food Administration policies, which were loosely enforced by committees representing trade associations, were required to pay a fine in the form of a modest donation to the Red Cross. Egregious offenders could have their licenses revoked, putting them out of business, but this rarely occurred.

In theory, Hoover disliked government intrusion into the marketplace, but he grew increasingly willing to intercede as the war progressed, although he firmly opposed socialization of any industry. In the battle over regulation versus free markets, Hoover stood somewhere near the middle, representing neither the extreme right nor the extreme left. While he had fought valiantly for priority for food ships in the bureaucratic skirmishes over scarce shipping, near the end of the war, as he envisioned the possibility of terminating the carnage rapidly, he grew more inclined to give priority to troop ships. Over the course of the war, he moved incrementally in the direction of temporary regulation, to be relaxed with victory, yet he remained essentially a pragmatist throughout the conflict.[58]

Wilson did not turn often to Hoover for political advice, though he usually listened carefully when advice was offered. When Hoover suggested that something be done to prevent war profiteering, as many businessmen stood to become rich off war demand, Wilson recommended the measure to Congress, which adopted the excess profits tax. Worried about the lack of crucial labor at harvesttime, Hoover joined farm groups to inspire legislation to exempt agricultural workers from the draft, giving them the same status as munitions workers. Following the Bolshevik Revolution of 1917, Wilson queried Hoover about a proposal brought to him by the British and the French, who wanted to invite the Japanese to invade Siberia to arrest Bolshevik eastward expansion. Hoover pointed out that the Russians and the Japanese, who had fought a war in 1904–5, were bitter rivals and that such intervention, likely to be ineffective anyway, would sow hatred toward the Western powers. Moreover, Hoover warned, if the Japanese, themselves an expansionist power, prevailed, they were likely to dig in and remain entrenched permanently. Despite Hoover's advice, Wilson sided with the Western Allies and dispatched a small contingent of American troops for the ostensible purpose of ejecting the Japanese, should they sink roots.

On the whole, Wilson liked and trusted Hoover. Although a lifelong Republican, Hoover backed Wilson's call for election of a Democratic Congress in 1918, which the president hoped would support him at peace negotiations to follow the war's end. Wilson already envisioned the mechanism of a world organization to enforce the peace, with which Hoover sympathized, though without the inflexibility of the Presbyterian president. The appeal backfired. Though Democrats carried both chambers, Congress would, indeed, torpedo the peacemaking. Hoover lost standing among isolationist Republicans, yet became the darling of some internationalists in both parties.[59]

In early 1918, the Russian Revolution fell into the hands of Bolsheviks, whose leaders pulled Russia from the war. During the spring, the Germans heaved the full weight of their armies in a risky offensive against the western front. The food front also faced challenges. Parlaying transportation, competing with shipping needed for troops, squeezing out the last remaining ounce of conservation, Hoover kept the wheat, bacon, rice, and sugar flowing to the tables and trenches of Europe. The Allies had requested 750,000 tons of wheat to tide them over through the winter months; Hoover sent 850,000 tons. With the abundant harvest of 1918, he won a close race with starvation, yet the outcome remained tenuous. Allied generals now expected victory, but not until 1919 or 1920. Hoover was forced to plan on the contingency that the war might continue for a year or more and stockpile supplies in Europe. Measured by peacetime standards, the United States was greatly overproducing. No one could predict how long American farmers could continue to meet the burden of European demands. On the other hand, if an armistice occurred abruptly, farmers would be stuck with an enormous surplus, much of it perishable. To protect American farmers, who had played such a vital role in pushing the Germans into a corner, Hoover concocted a scheme to feed the enemy and neutral nations after the war, which would simultaneously save the continent from famine and dispose of the American surplus.[60]

Meanwhile, the war machine of the Western powers inexorably ground down the Germans, whose morale was collapsing. Allied momentum was spurred by the fresh, yet untested American army, which swarmed into battle, their vigor and numbers overwhelming the weary, disheartened Germans. By mid-September 1918, with Allied commanders predicting that final victory would not occur until the following year, Hoover issued orders for mandatory conservation in all public eating places. Restaurants and clubs must serve bread containing at least 20 percent flour substitutes and could not place sugar bowls on tables or use more than two pounds of sugar per every ninety meals. Yet the pace of events outraced the Allies' understanding of them. Even as Hoover employed new plans to tighten belts, the Germans were breaking down. On September 26, four days following Hoover's conservation order, the American and Allied armies launched their steamroller offensive in the Meuse-Argonne sector, including 1.2 million American troops. On October 6, Germany yielded to the inevitability of their defeat and offered an armistice on the basis of Wilson's relatively generous terms for peace, the Fourteen Points. Wilson asked his war council, including Hoover, to submit stipulations he should include in the terms for negotiation. Hoover inserted a provision mandating the feeding of the ex-enemy and occupied nations during and after the peacemaking. Wilson included it in his set of conditions.

The armistice was formally declared on November 11, 1918, and a peace conference was set to meet at the Versailles palace, near Paris, at which the victors would dictate the terms. Hoover cautioned Wilson to remain in America, above the fray, and employ his stature as leverage, yet the president announced he would attend personally, confident of his persuasive talents. Hoover accompanied Wilson to Paris as his food adviser. With the war over, the plagues of famine and pestilence swept down like a cloud of locusts. In 1918, a catastrophic world influenza pandemic killed more people than the Great War, including Americans. More than half of the employees of the Food Administration were stricken. Bert and Lou were bypassed, but Herbert Jr. contracted the contagion, which left him partially deaf for the remainder of his life.[61]

The Food Administration had proven to be one of the great successes of the home front and further embellished Hoover's reputation. He was so efficient that during the final nineteen months of the war, neither Allied soldiers nor civilians were forced to go short on rations for a single day. Despite Hoover's antipathy for big government, the Food Administration had reached into every household in every community, inspiring cooperation between farmers, processors, shippers, businessmen, and volunteers. This vast apparatus was liquidated completely within four months of the armistice of November 11. When it closed shop in 1919, the Food Administration returned to the Treasury not only its full congressional appropriation of $150 million, but an additional $60 million in profits. Total administrative expenses were less than $8 million. The agency helped place some 28 million additional acres under cultivation. There had been no major scandals, inflation was moderate, and prices for consumers were reasonable. Throughout the war, Hoover had to balance many objectives, but the interests of Americans were paramount in his mind. He had been willing to expand government power under stress, but he wielded power as frugally as he spent dollars, and when the emergency expired, he quickly shrank the bureaucracy he had built. Throughout, he was a pragmatic idealist, something like the president he served, though perhaps less expansive in his idealism and more practical in his expectations.[62]

The home front had prospered, yet all segments did not prosper equally. Farmers wanted higher prices, but Hoover believed, aside from necessary incentives, that no portion of the population should profit excessively because of the war. After all, the excess profits tax had been partly his brainchild. Yet Hoover controlled only one sector of the economy—

agriculture and its appurtenances—and his reach was limited. The real, and legitimate, complaint of farmers was that when the war ended abruptly, they were stuck with a huge surplus, which inspired an agricultural depression during the otherwise prosperous 1920s, especially because farmers continued to produce at wartime levels once wartime demand had declined. Hoover did the best he could. Combining his characteristic altruism with his equally characteristic hard-nosed business practices, he sold large portions of the American farm surplus, almost exclusively on credit, to the Allies, the defeated powers, and the prostrate, starving nations of Central and Eastern Europe, and later, to the famine-stricken infant Soviet Union. Once again, as he had for Belgium and then the Allies, Hoover employed his power to preserve millions of lives and found vital markets for many farmers.

In 1918, while he remained in Europe, the Belgian government attempted to persuade Hoover to accept an award or decoration, but he steadfastly refused honors from Belgium and other foreign nations. The only order he desired, he said, was to be considered a friend of the Belgian people. Inspired, some Belgians suggested to their king a new award to be issued specifically, and solely, for Herbert Hoover. King Albert designed a simple medal designating Hoover as "Friend of the Belgian Nation." He was also given a Belgian passport stamped "Perpetual." The only other foreign award he accepted was the French Legion of Honor. Nonetheless, avenues, schools, and buildings were named for him throughout Europe and the United States. Many believed that Hoover, more than any other man, deserved the Nobel Peace Prize.

FIVE

Samaritan to a Continent

A great civilization had committed suicide. Four years of war had devastated a continent. From France through Belgium and the German frontier, from Poland deep into Russia, and throughout the Balkans, cities and towns lay in ruin, bridges and railroads had been destroyed, and fertile farmland had been trampled by armies. Unemployment was pervasive. Famine and disease stretched to every part of the continent, while women and children prowled the streets, scrounging for food. A political power vacuum hovered over the desiccated empires of Austria, Turkey, and Russia. The Soviets sought to expand their newly incubated ideological and territorial empire, often by fomenting revolutions amid the turmoil, where famine fed anarchy. The Allies, seeking to bludgeon the prostrate Central Powers into signing an unpalatable treaty, clamped down a food blockade that cut off not only their enemies, but also numerous neutral or liberated countries, punishing women and children as well as defeated warriors. Europe would never again be the powerhouse of military might, economic dominance, cultural inspiration, and aristocratic privilege that it had been prior to the Great War.[1]

On November 7, days before the armistice, President Wilson issued an executive order authorizing Herbert Hoover to convert the Food Administration into an international relief organization. Dispatched to Paris to take charge of feeding postwar Europe and to participate in the Versailles peace conference, Hoover left Edgar Rickard, his assistant administrator, in New York to dismantle the American aspects of the Food Administration while he expanded his responsibilities from the North Sea to the Urals in a prodigious undertaking to feed and restore Europe.[2]

The armistice of November 1918 ended the war with Germany, but it did not set the terms for peace. Within weeks of the cease-fire the victorious Allied leaders assembled at the Palace of Versailles outside Paris for the series of conferences that produced the Treaty of Versailles. Although the representatives of many real or prospective nations crowded the lobbies, the dominant power was held by the Big Four, consisting of President Wilson, British prime minister David Lloyd George, French president Georges Clemenceau, and Italian prime minister Vittorio Orlando.

Hoover was prominent among the numerous aides and advisers attached to the Big Four. His chief responsibility, however, was not orchestrating a utopian peace, but feeding, nourishing, and rebuilding a devastated continent. From November 1918 through September 1919, he wore many hats, serving as U.S. food administrator, head of the Grain Corporation and the Sugar Equalization Board, and director of Belgian relief. He was the de facto leader of the Supreme Economic Council, which reported directly to the Big Four. Hoover's numerous titles involved overlapping responsibilities. The strongest advocate of relief for the devastated continent, he wanted centralized control under American auspices because the United States provided nearly all of the food and personnel, including American soldiers borrowed from and paid for by the Quartermaster Corps, on loan from General John J. Pershing, a major backer of Hoover's objectives. Hoover wanted to dispose of the American farm surplus by selling it to the starving Europeans, on credit if necessary, until the excess from the 1918 harvest was exhausted.[3]

While Wilson sought a just peace with Germany, Clemenceau fought for the harshest sanctions and opposed any action that might indirectly aid the defeated enemy, including the feeding of nations that might trade with Germany. Thus, as the negotiations continued at Versailles, the main task of the American relief mission was to pry open the food blockade, chiefly maintained by the British navy, that denied nourishment to men, women, and children, most of them noncombatants, including virtually every nation except those aligned with the Allies. The Allied leaders, excluding Wilson, reasoned that Germany and Austria could be starved into signing a Carthaginian peace. Hoover considered such a strategy irresponsible, imprudent, and morally bankrupt. To those who argued that the Germans deserved to die, Hoover remarked, "No matter how we feel at the present moment, we must write now into history such acts as will stand to our credit in the minds of our grand-children."[4] A punitive peace would be virtually impossible to enforce and would embitter the next generation, sowing the seeds of a future war, providing a strong incentive for the defeated nations to seek vengeance and, when their turn on top came, to be meager with mercy. Moreover, the policy of intentionally enervating the defeated, neutral, and liberated nations deterred economic recovery among the victors as well as the vanquished. The economy of nations, especially the patchwork of new nations carved out at Versailles to accommodate ethnic minorities, resembled a crossword puzzle that required prudent stitching together.[5]

Hoover, better than most, understood the economic interdependence of Europe and America—the two lands must prosper or fail together. Yet men with long views were in short supply at Versailles. In December 1918, Wilson requested a $100 million appropriation for food relief; Congress approved it on February 24. Creating the American

Relief Administration (ARA) as the chief agency of American distribution of aid, Wilson added another responsibility to Hoover's portfolio of food and aid agencies by appointing him administrator of the ARA. However, Senator Henry Cabot Lodge, partly because he detested both Wilson and Hoover, had attached an amendment denying credit for the purchase of food for the former enemy powers. Germany and the vastly truncated Austrian state, both virtually penniless, were among the most food-deprived countries in Europe and verged on political anarchy animated by imminent famine. Germany had already experienced an uprising in Berlin and a Communist revolution in Bavaria following the armistice, while a Communist revolution failed in Vienna. Despite Lodge's amendment, Hoover vowed to defeat revolution and fill empty stomachs at a single blow.[6]

Since Lodge had blocked sales on credit to Germany and Austria, the Germans were forced to buy provisions partly with their gold reserve. Hoover, remaining within the letter of the law, arranged for other sales to the ex-enemies by a circuitous route. Congress appropriated funds for Britain, which in turn loaned the money to Germany and Austria. With famine and revolution running rampant in the continent's heartland, Hoover's men posted signs stating that any major public disturbances would result in the halt of food aid. During the armistice, the two major defeated powers received 42 percent of all food aid.[7]

Hoover's problems, however, were diplomatic, economic, and logistical. With the emergence of new states in the aftermath of the collapse of the Austrian, Russian, and Ottoman empires, the infrastructure within these new nations was often a scrambled muddle, which made transportation and communications challenging. Through Hoover's efforts, food seeped into the anguished areas even before the Allies relaxed the food blockade in March 1919, usually paid for from a small reserve fund made available to Wilson and residual revenue remaining in the till of the Grain Corporation, which had ended the war with a profit. Hoover also shipped food to the Near East, where the remnants of the dismembered Ottoman Empire were faltering. Selecting an experienced staff from the Food

Administration, the CRB, and the army and the navy, Hoover installed food experts in Paris to examine the nutritional needs of each nation, paying scrupulous attention to children. Wilson, through Pershing, assigned army officers from the Quartermaster Corps to warehouse and distribute food. Their salaries were paid by the military, keeping overhead low. Even while the blockade remained in effect, Hoover dispatched relief on vessels protected by the American navy.[8]

While he fought diplomatic battles in Europe, Hoover also represented the rights of American farmers, whose warehouses bulged with surpluses of wheat, cotton, corn, pork, and dairy products. Claiming they were no longer bound to previous agreements, the British and French reneged on their wartime contracts with the United States, turning instead to cheaper markets in British colonies and in Latin America. Hoover feared that an economic collapse among American farmers would trigger the failure of rural banks, widening into a larger national economic downturn. He protested that the Allies had a moral responsibility to their own ally. If they backed out, American farmers would be ruined. The next time Europeans went to war, he warned, America might be less likely to send their young men abroad to save them.

Rebuilding nations upon the ruins of Central and Eastern Europe was comparable to constructing the Eiffel Tower using an Erector set. The region seemed to seesaw between leftist fanaticism and reaction, a pendulum that oscillated between chaos and Communism. The misery and suffering that followed the war had widened the gulf between the starving masses and the extravagant elite. In Hungary, for instance, parties, rulers, and ideologies rose and fell in rapid succession. There, Hoover's ARA represented a major—perhaps the only—significant stabilizing force.

Hungary had been an enemy nation, Austria's partner in the Hapsburg monarchy. In the wake of a postwar revolution, a short-lived republic was installed. A second revolution soon followed, led by the Communist Béla Kun, dispatched from the Soviet Union to incite an uprising. Kun staged a brief reign of terror, purging and killing not only political enemies, but even some ARA men in the process of feeding children. Romania, encouraged by France, soon invaded Hungary and waged war on the divided nation. Hoover announced that food relief would be withheld until Kun was overthrown. Kun did fall, but the Romanians continued to loot the country, even seizing ARA food from children's hospitals. Another coup placed into power the archduke Joseph, a Hapsburg, who vowed to restore the prewar monarchy. Hoover, fearing the archduke would precipitate a major civil war, ordered food withheld until he was removed. Viewing his situation as untenable, Joseph abdicated. This was Hungary's eighth revolution in five months. When the 1919 harvest was reaped, Hungary became self-sufficient and the ARA mission ended. The Big Four issued an edict from Versailles ordering a blockade of Romania until it withdrew its army from Hungary. The Romanians capitulated.[9] To Hoover, food relief had offered an opportunity to combat political chaos.

Poland had been a battlefield for German and Russian armies, and it experienced some of the most grievous suffering of any country. Assured by President Wilson's declaration promising self-determination for ethnic groups, the Poles, whose homeland had been partitioned for 150 years, declared independence from their German, Austrian, and Russian overlords immediately following the armistice. American food shipments to Poland began in January 1919 and continued until the harvest of the following spring, complemented by army surplus food and medical supplies. Using charm and persuasion, Hoover was able to arrange the shipment of supplies through German-occupied districts at a time when Germany was still under blockade.

Like Poland, Finland had not experienced independence for centuries, having been part of czarist Russia. Finland regained its freedom after the Bolshevik Revolution of 1917, then plunged into civil war pitting Finns backed by Germany against Communists supported by the Bolsheviks. The pro-German faction prevailed and the Germans installed the kaiser's brother-in-law as king. Following the armistice, the Finns expelled the German pretender and created a republic. During the armistice, Hoover defied the Allied food blockade to send food to the Finns, protected by the American navy. Initially, Hoover tapped a $5 million fund controlled by Wilson to provide free meals to 35 million Finnish children. Later, he negotiated a large food loan for Finnish relief, and Finland became the only European nation to repay its debt in full. Hoover also worked through Wilson to obtain diplomatic recognition for republican Finland. The president dispatched his relief director to persuade Clemenceau. After the conversation between Hoover and the Frenchman, the Big Four issued a letter instructing their foreign ministers to extend diplomatic recognition to Finland. Largely due to Hoover's efforts, Finland formally gained standing as a free nation. Finland's grateful people coined the word *huuvere*, meaning "charity," or "loving all men as brothers."[10]

Working from an office in Paris, Hoover's ARA functioned with crisp, military precision. In place of paintings, the walls were plastered with huge maps pinpointing relief operations and identifying all ARA shipping points in more than twenty-five countries. The ARA was a streamlined, maximally efficient business with a human heart. Americans, Hoover said, had never endured genuine famine on the scale of Europe, not even during the Civil War. He lamented "the pallid faces; the unsmiling eyes; the thin, anemic and bloated children; the dead palls over towns where the children no longer play on the streets; the dull, listless movements and dumb grief of the women; the sweep of contagious diseases and the unending procession of funerals."[11] Jews were particularly grateful for Hoover's solicitude. "May I as one of 110 million Americans thank you from the bottom of my heart," wrote Rabbi Stephen S. Wise, leader of the American Jewish Congress in 1919. "I am thinking not only of your devoted help [to the Jews] in Poland and elsewhere, but your larger inclusive service which has so greatly honored the name of our country in all European lands." Lewis Strauss wrote on behalf of the Jewish community, after Hoover had publicly condemned anti-Jewish pogroms in Poland and Ukraine during 1919 and 1920, that Hoover stood up for European Jews when no one else seemed to be looking or listening. The slaughter and suffering he witnessed took a "psychic toll" on Hoover, his wife, Lou Henry Hoover, wrote. "A certain definite and very original kind of joy of life was stamped out of him by those war years."[12]

While the treaty negotiations simmered at Versailles, Hoover attempted to slice through numerous roadblocks that held starving populations hostage. In order to transport food to where it was needed, the infrastructure of the continent had to be rebuilt. The arteries of Europe—the Rhine, Elbe, Vistula, and Danube, as well as numerous canals and ports—lay in disarray. Locomotives stood stranded by intermittent strikes and coal shortages. Ethnic minorities fought pitched battles over disputed land and resources and issued a multitude of virtually valueless currencies unrecognized beyond their borders. Travel between nations was slowed by new and different gauges for railroad tracks, high tariff walls, and passport checkpoints every few hundred miles. In a region beset by a multitude of problems, Hoover's subordinates were resourceful, improvising and introducing a degree of order amid the rubble. During one of the numerous guerrilla wars that erupted, neither side would yield to the other to permit passage of a food train, yet both agreed to surrender to the U.S. Food Administration, formally handing over their swords to one of Hoover's representatives. In a race against starvation, the entrepreneurs of food distribution won—most of the time.[13]

Hoover had to attack many problems simultaneously. As usual, he decentralized problem solving by finding the best man for the job and permitting him to solve it with his own ingenuity. To help Hoover restore the continent's transportation and industry, General Pershing loaned Colonel Anson C. Goodyear, whom the general termed "the best coal man in the world." Goodyear had civilian experience in both railroading and coal mining. Sent to the rich coal mines of Czechoslovakia, Goodyear had doubled coal production in Central Europe within a month. Like Hoover's, his methods were unflagging energy, long hours, generosity, diplomacy, and self-sacrifice. Goodyear circulated throughout mines in Poland, Austria, Hungary, Yugoslavia, and Czechoslovakia. With little help, skimping on sleep, he dashed from camp to camp, offering food and fair treatment. When he discovered $25,000 in American banknotes sitting idle in an Eastern European bank, Goodyear asked Hoover if he could use it to buy the miners tobacco. Hoover consented, the miners satisfied their craving, morale improved, production rose, and locomotives began chugging.[14]

While coal powered the engine of recovery, the ARA also rejuvenated transportation and communication in order to transfer commodities and orchestrate economic recovery throughout Central, Eastern, and Southeastern Europe and the Near East. Hoover helped restore canals and railroads to service as well as rolling stock, boats, and barges. His men facilitated traffic along the Rhine, the Elbe, the Vistula, and the Danube while reestablishing telegraphic and postal communications. Hoover organized the European Coal Administration to manage coal production and distribution in Eastern Europe. He also directed the Eastern European Railway Administration, controlling and coordinating railway and canal transportation in that region. Working with a dysfunctional atmosphere that screamed for order, the ARA built hospitals, warehouses, orphanages, schools, ports, roads, and telegraph lines. It constructed thirty thousand miles of rail tracks and rebuilt barge canals along the Danube. Hoover drew upon more than fifteen hundred American engineers and businessmen from the military. Constituting the core of his rebuilding effort, his men traversed international borders, uninspected, traveling on passports signed by Hoover. Equally important, the ARA commanded legions of volunteers in local communities who labored under the direction of minute American staffs. In most nations, the United States furnished only the food and a blueprint for organization; volunteers at the local and regional levels implemented the program, minimizing overhead costs.[15]

In the summer of 1919, just as Europe's famine was almost conquered, an outbreak of typhus spread westward from Russia along the Baltic to the Black Sea, enveloping Lithuania, Poland, Romania, Serbia, and Ukraine. It was an epidemic brought on by rampant homelessness and the lack of sanitation. Typhus is borne by lice. Fats needed to make soap had been eaten, while some people had even consumed cats that carried lice. The Big Four assigned the problem to Hoover, though it did not lie within his field of expertise, and he mobilized quickly to fight the contagion that was raging rapidly toward the heartland of Europe. Hoover drew a quarantine line stretching north-south across the continent, beyond which the disease would not be permitted to spread. Borrowing a thousand specialists from the medical corps and the Red Cross, he obtained all the delousing equipment available from the American, British, and German armies, including hair clippers, soap, and portable baths. People from within the infected zone were bathed and scrubbed, their clothes burned, and their heads shaved. Only after undergoing these procedures were they permitted to cross the line of separation into safe areas. While the military furnished most of the manpower, soldiers were supervised by ARA volunteers, who planned strategy and directed operations on-site. At the height of the epidemic, some 1 million people were infected, with one hundred thousand dying weekly. Within six months, the ARA had tamed the threat.[16]

When the ARA officially expired in July 1919 and most government support ended, Hoover transformed it into a private, charitable foundation. While most aid to adults halted that summer, the feeding of children continued through the early 1920s, financed by donations from individuals, foundations, and major philanthropists. As a private group, the ARA helped supply food, clothing, and medicine for some 14 to 16 million children, chiefly in Central and Eastern Europe and the Near East. As a separate service, Hoover organized special care and food relief for 19 million war orphans. Among the major recipient nations were Poland, Yugoslavia, Czechoslovakia, Romania, Germany, Latvia, and Lithuania. Poland and Austria were among the largest beneficiaries. In addition to assisting children, the ARA continued support for special groups among the intellectual community, such as teachers, professors, writers, and artists, among whom unemployment was widespread.[17]

By the time he departed from Europe for his homeland on September 19, 1919, Hoover had delivered 28 million tons of food and supplies worth

$5.5 billion in less than a year. The United States provided 96 percent of the credit for purchases and 93 percent of the supplies. ARA staff remained in Austria, Czechoslovakia, Yugoslavia, and Poland well after Hoover left the continent.[18]

Through Hoover's relief efforts, as much as one-third of the population of postwar Europe was saved from death by starvation and disease. Moreover, some 15 million children were restored to health, giving them a chance for normal lives.[19] Hoover's work gave the war's survivors a chance for renewed vigor, peace, and prosperity. He had transplanted the aphorism that charity begins at home and expanded it to encompass a continent. In the short run, it meant survival; in the long run, it meant hope.[20] His biographer George H. Nash writes, "Herbert Hoover was responsible for saving more people than any person in history."

Aside from delivering food, rebuilding railroads, and dredging canals, Hoover had attempted to heal the wounds of war in less tangible ways. He made a valiant, if not entirely successful, effort to avert chaos and build a bridge to normality. He and his volunteers helped stem the infection of totalitarianism, at least temporarily, and gave Europe a chance to preserve and incubate democratic institutions. Hoover was sickened by the slaughter of war, as well as by the spirit of vengeance and diplomatic bungling that followed, while populations starved and nations disintegrated. Hoover feared that within a generation another catastrophic war might materialize. He believed it could be prevented, but he lamented that wisdom and generosity had died on the battlefield.

In his public career during the Great War, Hoover was single-minded but multidimensional. He devoted his energies to feeding populations, saving the lives of children, avoiding a punitive peace, and creating stability that would avert another war. In all of this he remained a pragmatic American nationalist who, once his country entered the war, exerted every effort to win it, and, once that was done, to protect American interests. He comprehended, more than almost any American of his time in public life, the autocratic nature of much of the European continent, and he knew this autocracy would inevitably be overturned by its peoples, whatever America did. He was also realistic about the embedded ethnic and nationalistic rivalries, the tradition of militarism, and the appeal of messianic doctrines that addressed genuine grievances even if they did not solve them, or solved them at too great a cost. He believed that America had a role to play in world affairs but could not dictate the outcome of global events through military might. He felt that America's best policy was to allow the European nations to work out their problems, to help mitigate them when it could, and to facilitate stability and a degree of prosperity. These goals should be accomplished by neither retreating nor intruding. The League of Nations was a tool but not a panacea. He did not believe American troops should remain in Europe, nor should the United States intervene in any European revolution. He did believe in joining the League of Nations, imperfect though it might prove to be. From relief of the anguished to treaty making, Hoover was a man with a soft heart and a hard head.

As he returned to America, Hoover wanted to temporarily withdraw from public life, enjoy the outdoors, and catch up with his family. Upon arriving in California, he announced that for the coming month he would answer no telephone calls, read no letters longer than a single page, nor deliver any long speeches. After loading their car with fishing gear, the family embarked on a vacation, yet public responsibilities compelled Hoover to return after four days. He had become a quasi-celebrity and could not in good conscience shirk duty. Lou, for her part, desired a more normal family life and began to construct a magnificent dream house she had designed herself adjacent to the Stanford campus. Originally planned as an intimate cottage, it morphed into a fifty-seven-room mansion with openings at each level to a terrace.

Hoover had refused remuneration for his relief work during the war, and now, with a diminished fortune, he pondered his financial future. After a brief interlude he opened an engineering office in San Francisco with the full intention of resuming his career in engineering, yet he never did. Interested in shaping public opinion without holding a public office, he dallied with the idea of publishing a newspaper. He purchased shares in the *Sacramento Union* and the *Washington Herald* and loaned money to friends to buy stock in the dailies. In 1919, he performed some discreet editorial duties for the *Herald* and met with the daily's managing editor and its reporters. During the same period Hoover tried, but failed, to purchase shares in the *New York Herald* and the *Baltimore Sun*.[21]

Hoover's life had reached a crossroads. Either he would return to the familiar, lucrative task of mining, or he would commit himself permanently to public life, a decision dictated only in part by his own preference. He found his opinions in demand, and he felt obligated to respond. His involvement occurred incrementally, yet the long road to politics and public service had no end. The war had produced explosive changes that disconcerted him. It had unleashed the genies of nationalism, Communism, and destructive technology that could not be rebottled. Hoover remained fundamentally a resolute optimist and a believer in gradual progress. Personal success should be linked to communal responsibility. "Character," he remarked, "is made in the community as well as the individual by assuming responsibilities, not by escape from them."[22]

Despite his desire for simplicity, the pace of Hoover's life did not slacken upon his return to America; if anything, it intensified. Much in demand to speak and write, he threw himself into explicating the issues of the day. During the fifteen months after arriving in the United States, the forty-five-year-old was constantly in the public eye, delivering forty-six speeches, penning twenty-eight magazine articles, and testifying before nine congressional committees. Meanwhile, he fleshed out his personal, political, and economic philosophy, which he later condensed in his treatise *American Individualism* in 1922.[23]

America did not emerge from the Great War unaffected by the turbulence that had rattled postwar Europe. In 1919, more than 4 million Americans participated in some three thousand strikes, aggravated by the specters of socialism, Communism, and anarchism. Such radicalism, punctuated by violence, inspired a Red Scare and an indiscriminate crackdown by Attorney General A. Mitchell Palmer, including mass arrests and deportations. President Wilson convened two industrial conferences to devise conciliatory means of settling labor issues. The first adjourned inconclusively, with no major accomplishments, generating no legislation. Yet the second was urged to take a longer, more theoretical view and develop a philosophy to accommodate the contrasting aims of capital and labor. Hoover served as vice chairman, presided at one-third of the meetings, and played a major role in writing the report. The chief innovation, largely at his suggestion, was the concept of shop councils comprised of representatives of management and labor to defuse issues at the local level before they became exacerbated. The councils would complement, but not supersede, unions, which operated at the national level. Hoover considered strikes wasteful but did not oppose them as a last resort. He also commissioned a study of waste in industry by engineering societies in which he played a leading role. He would pursue the ideas of shop councils and curtailment of waste at greater length during his tenure as secretary of commerce.[24]

Hoover had returned to America a tired and disgruntled man. Despite his misgivings about the flawed handiwork of the peacemakers in France, he now believed ratification of the Treaty of Versailles and the League of Nations was essential to cobble Europe back together. "Until peace is made, Europe cannot get back to work and production," he warned. "Until peace is consummated, none of the European countries which have been at war can borrow money; none can reorganize their internal finances; raw materials cannot be obtained; industry cannot be restarted."[25]

Hoover considered the League of Nations as vital to the successful implementation of the Treaty of Versailles and the maintenance of peace by providing international arbitration for disputes between nations. Without the League, the treaty itself would falter, national boundaries would remain scrambled, and communication, transportation, and trade would be paralyzed. During speeches in October he linked American recovery with Europe's.[26]

Once again, Hoover faced the haughty, stubborn leader of the opposition, his old archenemy, Senator Henry Cabot Lodge of Massachusetts, who opposed the creation of the League because he was concerned that American membership would diminish national sovereignty, and who fought to reject the Treaty of Versailles. Yet Hoover could not placate Wilson either. The president vainly insisted that the treaty be ratified completely intact, refusing to budge as congressional approval of it without revision diminished. Hoover, less stubborn than the president, advocated ratification with reasonable Republican reservations rather than see it fail entirely. During a nationwide speaking tour, Wilson suffered a series of strokes that left him partially paralyzed and bedridden. Their leader now sidelined, the pro-League forces faltered. Hoover joined with former president William Howard Taft and other moderates to create the League to Enforce Peace, advocating a settlement based on the belief that a compromise treaty was better than no treaty. Without ratification, America would be denied a voice in continental foreign policy altogether. Hoover was willing to accept a concession; Wilson and Lodge, poles apart, wanted a treaty only on their terms, or else a diplomatic vacuum.[27]

Hoover's support for a moderate treaty was based partly on economic considerations. Without peace, a large portion of world trade would be paralyzed, punishing America as well as Europe. Whatever one thought of European power politics, he warned, self-interest dictated approval of the treaty in revised form. Further, Hoover doubted Europeans had the backbone to enforce peace without America. He preferred full participation but reluctantly concluded that the pact could not be ratified without the diluting amendments. Hoover's readiness to bargain soon earned him enemies in Washington. He was despised by the irreconcilables of the GOP, including Hiram Johnson, Henry Cabot Lodge, and Robert La Follette, for not throwing his weight wholeheartedly against the peace pact. He was equally reviled by others in both parties for his willingness to compromise. The logjam killed the treaty, just as it had disabled and disillusioned Wilson, leaving him a shell of his former self. Hoover rebounded to fight another day.

On November 13, 1919, the League to Enforce Peace endorsed the debilitating Lodge Reservations, and Hoover reluctantly followed suit.

He appealed to the president to yield, yet received no response from the embittered recluse, who never spoke to him again. Nonetheless, the treaty was defeated in the Senate on November 19. Purists on both sides of the diplomatic divide voted against it. The Democratic Party had fractured, and the nation was left deeply divided. The treaty's defeat gratified the irreconcilables, yet history's verdict gratified virtually no one.[28]

Hoover's return to America had sparked speculation about a possible run for the White House. He was widely admired for his food relief, administrative abilities, and character, and his prominent role in the treaty fight had only increased his presidential appeal. Yet Hoover lacked the drive that propels most successful candidates. Friends and surrogates pushed forward a diffident candidate for the 1920 Republican nomination. The campaign swelled among progressive journalists, a core of devoted Stanford alums, and former food relief partners. Hoover was especially popular among college students, university faculty, women, and labor leaders, yet he made no effort to harvest votes from specific interest groups. Many of his backers were uncertain of his political affiliation, and he received support for the nomination from both parties.[29]

The bid to nominate Hoover received little encouragement from the man himself. Over the course of the primary elections, he did not campaign in a single state, nor did he deliver any political speeches designed to boost his candidacy. On several occasions, he declared that he was not a candidate and urged supporters to cease their campaign. He disliked personal attention and opposed political pandering, patronage politics, and cultivating interest groups, and he considered cutting backroom deals unethical. Hoover explained that he lacked the temperament for politics. He considered himself too sensitive to endure political smearing and believed that he could do more good outside of Washington. When a former Stanford classmate offered to promote him for president, the reluctant Hoover replied, "Consulting my own personal inclination I do not want public office." He explained, "This implies entry upon a road of self-seeking, whereas my view is that I should agitate for issues, not for myself." Some doubted his disclaimers, but Hoover knew the presidency could be a prison.[30]

Hoover attracted early support from prominent progressive journalists in both parties, including Ray Stannard Baker, Ida Tarbell, and William Allen White. Nonpartisan advocates included Joseph Pulitzer's *New York World*, and the *New Republic*, edited by Herbert Croly and Walter Lippmann. Other journalistic support, such as from the *Boston Herald* and the E. W. Scripps newspaper chain, seemed willing to back Hoover as the candidate of either party. On December 27, 1919, *The Saturday Evening Post* wrote that Hoover's dearth of political ambition was refreshing and would make him a better president.

Hoover seemed all the more attractive because there was a power vacuum in each party. Wilson wanted a third term, which was impractical politically and impossible due to his health. None of the wannabes stirred much genuine enthusiasm. Therefore, early in the primary season, at a time when Hoover's political loyalty was uncertain, the Democrats courted him tirelessly. Some advocated pairing Hoover with New Yorker Franklin Delano Roosevelt on the Democratic ticket in the hope that their youth and kinetic energy would stir voters. Roosevelt himself sought to recruit Hoover for such a ticket. On January 2, 1920, FDR wrote diplomat Hugh Gibson, "I had some nice talks with Herbert Hoover before he went west for Christmas. . . . He certainly is a wonder, and I wish we could make him president of the United States. There could not be a better one." Yet Hoover believed he would be hitching his fate to a lost cause. Nonetheless, when Roosevelt was nominated for vice president on the Democratic ticket, Hoover wrote generously, "If you are elected you will do the job properly."[31]

The longer Hoover could remain above the fray, his best-informed advisers knew, the better his prospects. The moment he declared a party allegiance, the deference given him would vanish and political attacks would begin. Yet it was unrealistic to believe he could remain uncommitted indefinitely and win a major party nomination without exerting himself and personally directing his own campaign. The GOP

Old Guard was unlikely to permit his nomination, preferring a more pliable man such as Warren Harding or an utterly predictable candidate like Calvin Coolidge. Republicans did not believe they needed Hoover on the ballot to win. Disenchanted with Wilson's leadership in the controversy over the Treaty of Versailles and the domestic turmoil of 1919, the nation was likely to vote against the incumbents, which would make a Republican victory relatively easy with a nominal candidate.[32]

On March 30, 1920, Hoover made clear his party affiliation by wiring a supporter in California that he would not repudiate a campaign being waged for him in the GOP primary in that state, although he would not actively campaign. His chief objective was to discredit his major opponent in the primary, arch-isolationist Senator Hiram Johnson, an irreconcilable enemy of treaty ratification. Hoover had been a member of the Republican Club of New York from 1909 to 1917 and had cast his only presidential ballots for Republican William McKinley in 1896 and Bull Moose Republican Theodore Roosevelt in 1912. His family and most of the communities in which he had been raised in Iowa and Oregon were predominately Republican. Entering the primary was a risk for Hoover; losing his home state would be an embarrassment. Moreover, Johnson controlled a slickly oiled political machine capable of steamrolling opponents. Johnson polled about 370,000 votes to some 210,000 for Hoover. It was not a bad showing for a novice politician against a grizzled veteran, and it did seriously cripple Johnson's chances of capturing the nomination. However, Hoover did not win a single delegate, and his embryonic campaign was virtually stillborn. Both men were wounded by the outcome.[33]

Hoover's backers entered him in several later primaries, yet his campaign never gained traction and he garnered few delegates. Beginning in late May, Hoover's enthusiasts traveled to Chicago for the GOP convention. By then, command of the campaign had been handed off to George Barr Baker, a close associate of Hoover from New York. The engineer himself did not attend the conclave. There was a great deal of excitement surrounding Hoover in the galleries, and his friends, such as

William Allen White, hoped a stampede among the delegates might develop in the likely event of a deadlock among the front-runners, General Leonard Wood, former Illinois governor Frank Lowden, and Hiram Johnson. The predicted deadlock materialized, yet overnight the party chieftains resolved to nominate Senator Warren G. Harding of Ohio. Harding's chief recommendation was that nobody hated him and nobody feared him. A glib politician, Harding was not a polarizing figure and stood to help the GOP in the swing state of Ohio.

Hoover polled a paltry nine and a half votes on the final ballot. He was not seriously disappointed by the outcome, and likely his friends were more downcast than he was. Hoover conferred with Harding after the nomination and attempted to persuade him to back ratification of the League of Nations with reservations. Harding appeared to agree, but he wavered after talking with opponents of the League. During the campaign he straddled the issue, suggesting that possibly a new type of organization could be created, less objectionable than the League, which the United States might join, a scheme that was promptly forgotten. As a practical measure, Hoover supported Harding, destined to be a certain winner, whose Democratic opponent, Ohio governor James M. Cox, had an uphill battle against public weariness with Wilson's stubborn refusal to compromise over the League of Nations and his insistence that America play a guiding role in world affairs. Harding's campaign slogan, "Back to Normalcy," resonated with voters. On the remote chance that Cox upset Harding, the Democrat would inevitably face a Republican Congress in which he could never muster a two-thirds majority to ratify the treaty. Deliberately or unwittingly, Hoover had impressed Harding, which would open doors for him to take a cabinet position.[34]

FDR biographer Patrick Renshaw notes the effect that timing had on Hoover's reputation. "Had he won as a Republican in 1920, it is intriguing to think counterfactually for a moment," Renshaw writes. "Presumably, he would have presided over the prosperous 1920s and left office in March 1929 one of the most admired and successful presidents in history."[35]

Certainly in 1920 no one could have foreseen the election of 1928, much less the stock market crash of October 1929.

Hoover's party loyalty, his standing as a gifted administrator, and Harding's personal respect for him led to an invitation to join the new cabinet as secretary of commerce. Hoover accepted, conditional on his being given a voice in everything that dealt with national or international commerce, sometimes overlapping the departments of other cabinet officials. Harding relied on him heavily. Early in his tenure, Hoover became involved in a greater humanitarian undertaking than the feeding of Belgium and postwar Europe, providing sustenance to the fledgling Soviet Union, which was teetering on the brink of starvation. At Versailles, Hoover had attempted to lift the food blockade on the Soviet state clamped down by the Allies, and also to provide food relief through the vehicle of Norwegian Arctic and Antarctic explorer Fridtjof Nansen, acting as Hoover's proxy. The Allies had intervened in the Russian civil war, backing the White Army opposed to Lenin's Bolsheviks, and the Communist leader was suspicious of their motives. The Allies were reluctant as well; France initially blocked transmission of the offer to Lenin. Hoover ghosted all the correspondence signed by Nansen and masterminded the overtures for the Norwegian, a figurehead with no diplomatic experience. The efforts to provide food relief to the Communist state foundered upon the shoals of dogma. The Western nations insisted on a truce in the Russian civil war. The embattled Soviet leader snubbed that stipulation and coupled his rejection with a diatribe against capitalism, which made food relief both ideologically and logistically awkward at that time.[36]

By 1920, the Russian civil war was winding down and Hoover's place in Harding's incoming cabinet provided a forum to dispatch unilateral relief furnished by the United States. By this time, conditions in the former Russian Empire had deteriorated from hunger to outright famine. Early in 1921, reports reached America that a torrid drought, compounding the destruction of the Great War, revolution, civil war, and the collectivization of agriculture, had devastated the Soviet state. The broiling heat and lack of rain rivaled Dante's inferno. There was not even seed corn for planting, because the peasants had eaten it, so the coming harvest would be minuscule. There were few draft animals, because the farm families had eaten them as well, and had also devoured their pets, including rodent-killing cats. The dogmatism and brutality of the Bolsheviks contributed to the misery. They had ruined the economy and wrecked the infrastructure of men and machines needed to perform skilled labor, employing policies based more on dogmatic political theory than on realism. Mines and factories manufactured 75 percent less than before the war. Railroads carried less than 7 percent of prewar freight. Once an exporter of foodstuffs, the one-party nation could now not feed itself. Suffering increased throughout the Communist state but was most severe in the Volga Valley and in Ukraine. Foreign investors avoided the Soviet Union as inexorably as the pestilence perpetrated by nature and men fastened its grip.[37]

In July 1921, the celebrated Russian writer Maxim Gorky directed an open letter to the Western nations pleading for aid for his struggling country. When Gorky's letter fell into Hoover's hands, it had reached perhaps the only man in the world capable of providing adequate nourishment to Bolshevik Russia, an international pariah that had already threatened invasion of Poland and the Baltic nations and had fomented Red revolutions throughout Europe, most conspicuously in Hungary and Germany. Hoover exemplified the experience, the heart, the skills, and the will to feed the needy. Moreover, as an influential figure in the American government, he could tap the world's most bounteous food supply, unravel red tape, and overcome logistical obstacles to speed provisions to their destination. Hoover found Communism offensive, nor did he sympathize with the previous czarist regime, but he disliked starvation more. He must persuade the American people, his own government, and the Bolsheviks that the task of collaboration was worthy and doable and that diametrically opposing ideologies could somehow find common ground.

When some Americans objected that aiding the Soviets might clamp the iron grip of the dictators upon their nation, he exclaimed: "Twenty million people are starving. Whatever their politics, they shall be fed."[38]

Walter Lyman Brown, the chief ARA official in Europe, opened negotiations with Maxim Litvinov, the English-speaking assistant people's commissar of foreign affairs, at Riga, Latvia, to consummate an agreement in mid-August 1921. Hoover insisted that the Soviets release all American political prisoners held in Russian dungeons. The Soviets complied. Brown stipulated that the ARA must operate under its normal ground rules, some of which were alien to Bolshevik dogma. The Soviets must permit ARA volunteers free movement, exemption from search, and immunity from arrest. Food would be distributed solely on the basis of need and Russian assistants hired on the basis of merit alone. These conditions were difficult to implement, because nothing in the Soviet Union was done on the basis of need or merit. The ARA would pay for food and transportation to the Russian borders. Within Russia, the Soviet government would pay for storage and transportation. In addition, $10 million of czarist gold the Bolsheviks had seized must be contributed, funding a small portion of food purchases. The gold was given reluctantly, because much of the czarist reserve was being used to finance revolutions throughout Europe. The ARA pledged to avoid participation in any political activities within Soviet Russia. On August 20, Brown and Litvinov signed the Treaty of Riga, defining the dimensions of the ARA's authority in Russia. Although the Soviets fudged on some provisions and the two groups elbowed for power, for the most part, both sides complied. There was less friction at the top level than among lower-level party functionaries and ARA volunteers.[39]

Russia's agricultural infrastructure had disintegrated under the burden of the Great War, subsequent droughts, the civil war, and the forced collectivization of farms and incitement of class warfare against wealthy peasants, or kulaks, who possessed agricultural expertise, during the period of war Communism in 1920–21. War Communism was supplanted by Lenin's pragmatic retreat to limited capitalism under the

New Economic Policy of 1921, a necessity detested by the doctrinaire Bolsheviks. Ideologically, the peasants were defined as mere paraphernalia to the urban working class, the nexus of pure Marxist theory. Yet theory uncomfortably fit reality. More than 80 percent of the Russian population was rural, and by 1920 the working class, the theoretical vanguard of orthodox Marxism, numbered as few as 1.2 million amid a population of 150 million. The constant upheavals and diminution of the peasants had devastated the countryside. Shipments of grain from the rural areas shrank drastically. Moreover, strikes of recalcitrant workers, peasants, and transport operators, bickering for the crumbs of spoils, paralyzed the economy at the precise time the arid heat baked the dry fields.[40]

Two observers assigned by Hoover inspected the countryside and reported on conditions. Dr. Vernon Kellogg, a Stanford professor and prolific author who had worked with Hoover in the CRB and Food Administration, sketched the suffering he witnessed in graphic prose. "They sit there waiting to die," he wrote. Kellogg described human scarecrows and children huddled on a blanket with their mother, begging for food, of which she had none to give. James P. Goodrich, former governor of Indiana, was also dispatched to analyze conditions. Goodrich wrote that the regions threatened with famine went far beyond what had previously been reported and affected entire families. Hoover had initially planned to concentrate on the feeding of children, but unless adults were fed too, they would perish and, with them, their dependents.[41] Conditions in the cities were grim, with children already dying of starvation. Reports from the Volga described famine on a massive scale. Later expeditions to Ukraine, not a part of the Riga agreement, found a comparable extent of starvation.

To head the ARA mission to Russia, Hoover selected Colonel William N. Haskell, a serious professional military man who had directed relief in Armenia. A West Point graduate and a veteran of the Great War, Haskell emanated an aura of authority necessary for dealing with Russia's often unhelpful regime. Haskell's report was dire. "The whole situation in Russia at present seems to be that everything is old, broken, worn-out, gutted," he wrote, adding, "Nothing works and everybody seems to be milling about in a semi-dazed condition with only one thought in mind, that is, where are they going to get food to eat, shelter, and clothing."[42]

Haskell was shocked by his findings on a tour of the Volga Valley and reported that 10 million peasants faced starvation in Ukraine. Poor crop yields and displaced peasant farmers were not the only missing links in the food chain. Haskell cabled to Hoover: "Railroads hanging together, roadbeds unrepaired, derailed cars ditched. Thousands [of] cars deteriorating on sidings where rails and ties had been removed from under them." Workers and farmers were burning rail ties to warm their homes during the frigid winter. Further, just as trainloads of food lay halted on the Trans-Siberian Railroad, the Volga River froze, eliminating an alternative method of moving provisions. With most horses slain for their flesh, camels were pressed into service. Some food was carried on the backs of humans, often women. In regions where no food arrived, people survived on grass, weeds, acorns, twigs, bark, and roots, even resorting to cannibalism.[43]

Eyewitness accounts confirmed rumors that the law of the jungle ruled the land. "In 1921–1922, when parents killed their children, and children killed their little brothers and sisters, eating the flesh raw and salted, they proved to have gone mad and become beasts," a Russian writer related. Two doctors reported that cannibalism was prevalent, joined in by entire families. During the winter of 1921, a woman was discovered devouring her husband's dead body. When authorities sought to remove the man's corpse, she screamed, "We won't give him up, we will eat him ourselves, he is ours." A Russian university professor reported in November 1922, "Families were killing and devouring fathers, grandfathers, and children." He explained, "Ghastly rumors about sausages prepared with human corpses were common." An American volunteer reported that the punishment for cannibalism was to lock up offenders and leave them incarcerated until they died of starvation.

One ARA veteran was confronted by a man who had eaten his children before the eyes of his starving wife. "I shall eat her tomorrow," he boasted; "she is too weak for any protest and could only grumble." In the city of Samara, in the heart of the famine section, authorities found ten butcher shops selling human flesh. One father relished the eating of his two small children, remarking that the "children's flesh tasted sweeter than pork."[44]

Strong and forceful, Haskell made enemies among the Soviets, as well as among veteran ARA volunteers accustomed to a more informal, less top-down approach. Yet he held the mission together and proved resourceful and resolute. Firm yet fair, he ran a streamlined, efficient organization that made the most of meager resources and American volunteers spread thin over vast distances.[45]

The ARA men sent to Russia were hardened veterans of the European ARA, where they had served as supervisory personnel. Both compassionate and determined, they constituted the core of the organization and were fiercely devoted to Hoover. Some of the fieldworkers were borrowed from the armed forces. All of them operated under the most rugged conditions, mentally and physically, of any ARA assignment, and they faced its most ambitious and challenging mission. "Trying to kill people may sound more exciting than trying to keep them alive, but don't believe it so," one explained.[46]

The volunteers hit the ground ready to work. Every delay meant lives lost. ARA supervisors were dispersed to establish food kitchens, originally for children, soon extended to feed adults, throughout the famine regions. The American personnel were stretched thin within the districts, some of which were as large as European countries. Once in place, the ARA men used local people to carry out the feeding in each community. The ARA program began modestly in September 1921 by feeding 200 children in Petrograd. By October there were 68,598 feeding stations, and by February 1922 more than 1 million children were being fed. By August, the program served 4,173,339 children and 6,317,958 adults, reaching about 10 million people overall. Like most of Hoover's programs, the ARA's work in Russia was decentralized and relied heavily on 120,000 local Russian volunteers who operated 15,700 kitchens. The scope of the undertaking dwarfed the CRB role in Belgium. Moreover, the greater distances, the dysfunctional railroad system, and the harsh climate made the rescue effort incomparably more complex.

If Haskell held the organization together within the Soviet Union, Hoover was the glue internationally, and his credibility lent a public face to the relief effort. He kept the money flowing from Congress, the public, and philanthropic foundations, which in turn kept the food arriving. As the secretary of commerce, he was crucial to the morale of his own men and commanded respect, sometimes grudgingly, from the Bolsheviks. "We cannot quit for Hoover's sake," Haskell said repeatedly. Hoover's presence was a calming factor; Haskell's administrative style could be abrasive. As chairman of the ARA, Hoover did not micromanage the organization within Russia, but he made the final decisions. Moreover, Hoover's stature in the world community was a powerful tool and sometimes intimidated the Bolsheviks, thwarting confrontations that might have necessitated a withdrawal.[47]

In postwar Europe, the foremost political problems the ARA had experienced arose from the turmoil and instability of the region, coupled with inexperience and incompetence in high offices. Now, in the Soviet Union, problems included outright sabotage and a fear of outsiders that verged on paranoia. The Bolsheviks had no intention of permitting the ARA a free hand or major credit. They found it difficult to conceive of anyone distributing food without some political agenda—after all, everything in Russia was done on the basis of a political agenda. The Bolsheviks did not want impartial feeding, nor did they desire staffing based on ability. The Soviet bureaucracy proved an exasperating bottleneck. The Cheka, or secret police, constituted the most persistent troublemakers. Haskell telegraphed Hoover in October 1922: "Every move we make scrutinized by Cheka. . . . Our agents constantly watched." The Cheka

created a shadow organization to monitor, infiltrate, and claim credit for
ARA accomplishments.[48]

Kremlin leader Vladimir Lenin alternated between support for the
ARA—which he needed to preserve his country, and possibly even his
own grasp on power—and his predilection to wage indiscriminate class
war on all capitalists. He wrote a comrade that "as for the Hooverites,
we must shadow them with all our might. The weakest must be compromised by scandal, chiefly employing liquor or women." He confessed his
embarrassment over accepting aid. "Without joy and contentment do
we accept the gifts of the American benefactors. The bread of alms is
not sweet. We know it well; you pay the most for charity." In fact, relief workers were feeding hungry children and showed little interest in
politics.[49]

Lenin was brutal and manipulative, yet after overcoming his initial
paranoia, he became one of the more pragmatic among his comrades,
proving capable of making short-run concessions in order to preserve
the revolution. An opportunist, Lenin was eventually converted to the
view that the ARA might help him salvage his country's economy. Temporary compromise was a viable means to an end. He considered America the only nation that had emerged from the Great War with substantial
financial resources to make significant investments in the Soviet Union.
In a note to a Kremlin colleague, Lenin observed, "*Hoover* is a real plus."
Several days later, he added, "Agreements and concessions with the Americans are super-important to us; with Hoover we have something worth-
while." He considered the ARA an avenue to trade and diplomatic
recognition from America that the Bolshevik leader considered keys to
the long-term success of his party and country. Hoover was not averse
to a degree of mutually beneficial trade, but he consistently opposed diplomatic recognition on the grounds that the Soviet regime was duplici-
tous and antithetical to American democratic principles.[50]

Haskell was realistic about the role American relief might play in the
survival of the Bolshevik regime, writing Hoover that although he considered food relief necessary on a humanitarian basis, it would have no

effect on dislodging the men in the Kremlin, who had "a strangle hold on Russia," even though the government "lacks support and confidence of the people. No opposition party dares raise its head." The unpopularity of the Bolsheviks and the possibility that relief might help them complicated Hoover's task of prying money from Congress or raising it through charity drives, yet the commerce secretary forged ahead.[51] To Americans who voiced concerns that feeding Russia might make it more difficult to uproot the totalitarian government in power, Hoover responded, "We must make some distinction between the Russian people and the group that have seized the government." He elaborated, "I think you will need to separate in your mind the 200,000 Communists in Russia from the 150,000,000 Russian people."[52]

Russian relief dwarfed any of Hoover's previous relief actions. Food was not the ARA's only contribution to the health of the Soviet people. It also fought epidemics of typhus and, to a lesser extent, cholera and other infectious diseases. Some of the ARA volunteers contracted typhus; a few died. The ARA conducted delousing campaigns and inoculated more than 8 million people against contagious diseases. It distributed $8 million in medical supplies and $1.5 million in clothing, and it provided seed for the 1923 crop. By the late summer of 1923 the corner had been turned. The debilitating drought ended and a bountiful harvest ensued. Hoover continued to feed children even after the harvest. He planned to raise funds in America to continue feeding adults on a limited basis, but after the Soviets negotiated contracts to export their own grain to Finland, Germany, and Italy, over his protests, Americans refused to contribute more money for Russian relief and Congress balked. The end of Russian relief closed an epoch in Hoover's life. He had distributed $3 billion in American aid within Europe and Russia since 1914. It is estimated, conservatively, that he saved about 20 million lives, including 9 million children.[53]

The Great Humanitarian was revered in the nations he had freed from the shackles of hunger, including Bolshevik Russia, where he was lionized by the Russian masses and many intellectuals, another distressed group to whom he had offered succor. Even the Soviet government was fulsome in its praise, presenting Hoover with a scroll "in the name of the millions of people saved" and proclaiming that the Russian people "will never forget the help given them." Maxim Gorky composed a personal letter to the American stating that "your help will be inscribed in history as a unique memory of millions of Russians whom you have saved from death." Nonetheless, as the Cold War grew frigid, Hoover received incrementally less space in Soviet history books. In the last editions he read before his death he had become a spy for the bourgeoisie.[54]

Hoover's acts of personal kindness are as impressive as his international philanthropic accomplishments. Shortly after returning from Europe at the end of the Versailles conference, he was driving down a curved, narrow mountain road in the West with his friend journalist Mark Sullivan, when they sighted an old roadster perched at the edge of a ravine. They stopped to ask if they could help, and the owner replied that his car would never run again. Hoover asked him how much the machine was worth. The man replied that it was worth at least $35, maybe $50. Hoover paid him $75. Then all three men pushed the car over the edge of the cliff and watched it tumble down.[55]

On another occasion, Hoover was driving in Northern California when he picked up a young hitchhiker. The youngster explained that he had left his home in Memphis and driven a car to California for a used-car dealer. Unable to find work, he had been forced to pawn his belongings. He was hungry and ill clad. After buying him dinner, Hoover gave the teenager $100, making him promise not to reveal the source of the money. Hoover also furnished a card with the name of a friend who might give his new acquaintance a job. The following day, the youth appeared in a store and tried to buy new clothes. The salesman proved suspicious and tried to inveigle from him the source of his large bill, but the youngster was recalcitrant. Finally, he said that it had been a gift from Herbert Hoover, which the salesman considered a suspicious story. The police called Hoover, who confirmed the gift and said it had been his wish to keep the source secret. The young man found a job and ultimately became a high official at a California oil company.[56]

After the Great Engineer morphed into perhaps the greatest secretary of commerce in history, he was noted for his kind treatment of everyone who worked for him, as was the case when he became president. Upon his retirement, a Commerce Department chauffeur recalled his boss's generosity. "Hoover never would let you work for him overtime without some compensation," said George L. Lee. "And there was no time-and-a-half then, you know, so it came out of his own pocket." He added, "When I had to take him home and he saw that I had missed dinner, he'd bring me into his house to eat. And he used to pay his other chauffeur extra money to bring the chauffeur's salary up to what Hoover called a decent wage." The man elaborated that the commerce secretary was "very considerate to poor people."[57]

SIX

Secretary of Commerce, Locomotive of the Economy

Warren G. Harding was a man aware of his own intellectual limitations. As president-elect, he assembled the best minds in the Republican Party to staff his cabinet. Aware of Hoover's astute grasp of issues and people, and his prodigious organizational skills from his role in feeding Europe, Harding sought Hoover as a key adviser as well as administrator.

Despite the need in Washington for Hoover's skills, the private sector was reluctant to give up such an enterprising engineer and businessman. In 1920 the Guggenheim family, owners of the world's largest metallurgical empire, offered him a contract with an annual income of at least $500,000. Despite the enormous sum, Hoover decided duty meant more than money and chose to join Harding's cabinet at $15,000 per year. Yet securing congressional approval for the position required delicate negotiations. Hoover's appointment encountered opposition from a conservative clique of senators who considered him progressive, independent, and an internationalist tainted by service in Woodrow Wilson's cabinet. Conservatives instead wanted Andrew Mellon, a billionaire businessman from Pennsylvania who embodied fiscal orthodoxy and laissez-faire. Harding, who excelled at compromise, offered a quid pro quo: he would condition-ally invite both Mellon and Hoover to join his cabinet, but no Hoover meant no Mellon. The senatorial bloc caved.

The president-elect offered Hoover his choice of Interior or Com-merce; Hoover picked Commerce, a relatively new and obscure cabinet seat. Hoover's opponents believed the forty-six-year-old political upstart would be buried in his new position, but they underestimated Hoover, who never thought small. Accepting the job, he attached conditions—which Harding accepted—demanding a voice in all matters that con-cerned the economy, regardless of departmental jurisdiction, meaning he would inevitably tread on the jurisdiction of his jealous peers. Upping the ante even more, he insisted he be permitted to gobble up agencies that seemed afloat in the morass of the bureaucracy, and he pressed the president-elect to increase the personnel and the budget of the Com-merce Department. Harding admired Hoover's boldness. Here was a man of action, a veritable Caesar of bureaucracy, who was, nonetheless, an efficiency expert. These arrangements unofficially made Hoover "sec-retary of commerce and undersecretary of everything else."[1]

As president, Harding handled political situations personally while delegating matters of substance to intelligent men with good judgment. Given free rein, the young commerce secretary flourished under the com-mander in chief's indulgent leadership. Hoover drafted speeches and exec-utive orders for the president and offered advice on patronage, including jobs outside his own department and government positions in the West-ern states. Harding trusted his judgment, and although their personalities and lifestyles differed, their relationship was cordial. Harding brought to Washington a set of cronies who advised him politically; thus, he was not dependent on Hoover for political guidance. Yet Hoover contributed to initiating two of the administration's most significant accomplishments shortly after taking office. His lobbying for disarmament contributed to

the Washington Naval Conference, and he helped shape legislation creating the Bureau of the Budget as an independent agency.

Hoover, for his part, relied on the president's political finesse to
smooth relations with other cabinet members. During Harding's time in
office, Hoover refrained from criticizing the president, though he disapproved of the bootleg liquor and poker parties Harding enjoyed with his
"Ohio Gang" in the sanctity of the Executive Mansion. A believer in
working within the system, Hoover hoped that despite the chief executive's odious companions, as commerce secretary he could add rectitude
and a voice of reason to the administration. Ostensibly calm, Harding
was in reality a chronic worrier. Nonetheless, "Harding encouraged me
in everything I wanted to do," Hoover said later. "I never knew him to
give a promise he did not keep." By 1923, the commerce secretary would
emerge as one of the president's most influential advisers, helping shape
Harding's political strategy for his 1924 reelection campaign.[2]

As secretary of commerce, Hoover took a sophisticated but humane
view of the U.S. economy. As biographer Kendrick Clements notes,
"Philosophically, he believed in limited government and volunteerism,
but temperamentally, he inclined to government activism and strong
leadership."[3] Hoover intended to balance the interests of capitalists, labor,
and consumers, mitigate poverty, ease the hard edges of competition,
and help raise the standard of living for all Americans. Especially concerned with the status of the working poor, he envisioned a safety net
for the indigent, but one that was not wholly constructed and implemented by the government.

Taking a large view of what had been a modest office, Hoover was
soon an octopus at the center of government, his tentacles probing into
every nook. Every important component of the executive branch seemingly had an umbilical cord attached to the Commerce Department. He
generated ideas and dispatched his assistants to every American state
and to far corners of the globe to implement them. Hoover devised a
well-rounded, all-inclusive program aimed at each major sector of the
economy. Commerce quickly became the most efficient department in

the cabinet, perhaps in the entire government. Hoover performed many duties that fell between departments or within other departments, or were outside of government entirely, chairing numerous government and quasi-government committees and commissions. Among his committees were the Colorado River Commission, which planned a dam on the river at Boulder Canyon, ultimately named the Hoover Dam. He continued to administer the American Relief Administration and planned a seaway to connect the Great Lakes with the Atlantic Ocean via the St. Lawrence River. The necessary pact with Canada was not ratified by Congress until the Eisenhower administration.[4]

By the end of 1921, Hoover had established himself as one of the dominant members of the administration. He was well prepared for cabinet meetings. Direct and decisive, he listened patiently but intended to have his way. He did not enjoy confrontations, yet he did not back down. While he got along with most of his fellow cabinet secretaries, he seemed destined to conflict with Andrew Mellon, who had accepted the position of secretary of the treasury. Nearly two decades older than Hoover, Mellon had less energy and spoke little, engaging in few direct conversations with his counterpart at Commerce. Both favored a small, streamlined government, yet Mellon inclined toward laissez-faire conservatism, while Hoover tilted toward Theodore Roosevelt's dynamic progressivism. Naturally, they clashed over tax policy. Hoover favored lower income taxes to spur economic expansion and consumption, yet higher estate taxes to shrink large, unearned fortunes over several generations. Mellon, he thought, was too defensive on behalf of the wealthy. Harding often sided with Mellon.[5]

Yet Hoover's disputes with the mild-mannered Mellon were sedate compared with his smoldering feud with Secretary of Agriculture Henry C. Wallace. Intelligent yet easily angered, Wallace championed farmers and believed everything concerning agriculture fell within his purview. He resented Hoover's encroachment on what he assumed was his turf. Hoover considered it his responsibility to promote trade and marketing of all American products, including agricultural commodities, especially

exports. While Wallace represented a single commodity, Hoover's interests encompassed the well-being of the economy as a whole. Wallace was
also far more liberal than Hoover, especially on tariffs, taxes, and farm
legislation. The chief point of contention between the two men became
the McNary-Haugen Bill, proposed by the Western Farm Bloc, an alliance of farm-state senators and representatives, which advocated that
the federal government guarantee a high domestic price to farmers, purchase surpluses beyond domestic needs, and dump them abroad at a
loss, with taxpayers footing the bill. Hoover considered the proposal
impractical. Low farm prices were due to chronic overproduction, he
charged, and the McNary-Haugen Bill would encourage infinitely greater
surpluses, aggravating the problem. Moreover, he pointed out, foreign
nations would not permit America to dump cheap produce on their markets, undercutting their own farmers. They would raise tariffs on U.S.
imports, and trade wars would rocket. Further, the farm surplus was so
great that buying the full amount would bankrupt the federal government. Hoover preferred the solution of organizing farm cooperatives
with the assistance of government loans and technical aid. Farmers could
buy and sell as a bloc and store nonperishable products in warehouses,
releasing them gradually to prevent flooding the market at harvesttime.
According to Hoover's plan, farmers should diversify by planting specialty crops, such as fruits and vegetables, rather than depending on a
handful of staples such as wheat, corn, and cotton, which saturated the
market during productive years. Farmers should retire depleted lands
and plant cover crops to prevent wind and water erosion. Had Hoover's
advice been fully implemented, the infamous Dust Bowl of the 1930s
might have been mitigated. Hoover also championed the Capper-
Volstead Act of 1922, which exempted farm cooperatives from antitrust
laws, which Wallace also backed. The commerce secretary helped
inspire the Agricultural Credits Act of 1923, which created twelve inter-
mediate credit banks to loan money to farmers, who must live on credit
between harvests. The only economically realistic solution, mandatory

crop controls, was politically unrealistic because farmers and their representatives in Congress blocked passage of such legislation. Wallace's death in 1924 removed Hoover's most scathing rival from the cabinet. His successor, William M. Jardine, was a Hoover supporter and advocate of farm cooperatives.[6]

Hoover was the cabinet's pivotal figure in seeking resolution of the severe economic recession of 1921–22. The downturn was partly a result of the difficulty of readjusting to a peacetime economy. American farmers kept producing at wartime levels and overproduction caused prices to fall. International trade fell during the first years of peace because European nations, winners and losers alike, were exhausted and broke. Since America's first major panic in 1837, the federal government had avoided intervention in downturns, relying on Adam Smith's "invisible hand" to correct recessions. Yet it was Harding's administration, not FDR's, that first attempted to harness federal power to solve economic slowdowns in a systematic albeit modest fashion. Hoover was instrumental in prodding the administration to take action. Tens of thousands of American citizens had declared bankruptcy, and more than 5 million were unemployed. Secretary Mellon believed that slack labor and inefficient use of capital must be purged from the sick economy to promote recovery, which was the approach followed during previous slumps. Senator George W. Norris of Nebraska, a progressive on some issues, was even more critical. "We had better let God run it as in the past and not take the power away from Him and give it to Hoover," he carped.[7] Hoover agreed that the economy must be stripped of waste and inefficiency, but he was also sensitive to the plight of jobless Americans. Borrowing from his own experience, he proposed to Harding that he appoint and undertake a President's Conference on Unemployment to suggest methods to alleviate the issue.[8] Harding asked him to recommend the appointees, and the commerce secretary drew upon one hundred leaders from business, labor, government, and academia. Hoover chaired the sessions, which met for three weeks in September and

October 1921. As the commerce secretary preferred, it adopted a decentralized approach. The body appointed local employment committees and urged states, municipalities, and the federal government to undertake work on planned repair and public works projects immediately rather than postponing them, including construction of roads, buildings, bridges, harbors, and national forests. Private businesses, which possessed far more resources than the government, were asked to expedite work. A permanent Committee on Civic Emergency Measures, chaired by Colonel Arthur Woods, coordinated the implementation at the national level. Hoover considered the construction industry the balance wheel of the economy, and priority was given to quick start-ups. Seasonal work was expanded throughout the hard winter months to even out employment throughout the year. The government established job exchanges at the state and local levels to match the unemployed with available positions suited to their skills. Hoover also encouraged job sharing so that fewer persons would become totally unemployed. He theorized that countercyclical spending by the government could help mitigate the business cycle, accelerating the tempo during hard times and scaling back during runaway booms. He advocated the maintenance of a permanent pool of money at the federal level, but a bill for such a fund sponsored by William S. Kenyon failed. He also urged the Federal Reserve Board to adapt its rediscount rate to the state of the economy in order to avoid booms and busts. Further, Hoover's Commerce Department revved up its activities related to compiling statistics useful in economic forecasting such as unemployment, inflation, production, surpluses in agriculture and industry, and import-export data. He commissioned studies by leading social scientists to determine where the economy seemed headed and where resources might be most productively allocated. Turning to his relief experience, he mobilized private charities to feed, clothe, and provide medicine for the needy and to raise funds for them.[9]

Harding also employed Hoover as chief troubleshooter for the ailing industries of the 1920s, most conspicuously coal and railroads, which teetered on the brink of failure. The businesses were interconnected:

locomotives gulped coal, while railroads transported the product to market. The price of one depended on the price of the other, and a gain for one seemed to be a loss for the other. Both industries were overbuilt. Too much coal had already been mined to provide full-time employment for miners, and too many railroads engaged in cutthroat competition with one another. Virtual monopolies that had been pieced together during flush times by empire-building capitalists, coal and railroads faced a similar eventual fate: technological obsolescence. Oil would soon replace coal, while motor vehicles would supplant railroads. At best they would lose their dominant roles in the economy. Like farming, both industries had been prodded to produce at full steam during the war and were left with depressed demand afterward. Owners tried to squeeze profits out of low wages for workers, while workers threatened to strike without wage increases. Hoover's job was to construct some agreement that would keep the national economy humming. He hoped the railroads could salvage their stability by reorganization and consolidation, but he found any specific plan opposed by some companies or vetoed by the government. The conflict peaked when rail workers struck in 1922. Attorney General Harry Daugherty, without consulting Hoover, crushed the strike by obtaining a draconian injunction, of which Hoover disapproved. Meanwhile, the coal miners simply extended their contract for a year while the U.S. Coal Commission conducted a study designed to implement reforms, postponing their day of reckoning. The mines produced and the trains rolled, but no one was entirely happy with the outcome.[10]

In the steel industry, Hoover spearheaded a movement to curtail working hours from a twelve-hour day and seven-day week to eight hours and five days. Men with higher morale work more efficiently, he insisted, and he wanted laborers to have additional time to spend with their families and for recreation. Steel barons argued that firing down the furnaces would be ruinous, dampening America's competitive edge with foreign steel. The commerce secretary persuaded Harding to invite the industrialists to the White House, where he and the president attempted to persuade them to reduce hours. Instead, the steelmakers appointed a committee to study the issue and delayed for a year. Choosing to employ political and public pressure rather than seeking legislation, Hoover leaked to journalists letters he had written to the owners over Harding's signature, and the newspapers berated the stubbornness of the steel titans. At length, the public relations campaign and the president's prestige forced the steel mill proprietors to back down during Harding's rail trip west in 1923. Hoover inserted a passage in Harding's Tacoma speech publicizing the new agreement, lest the operators renege on their promise. The breakthrough was a signal accomplishment for Hoover.[11]

At the Commerce Department, Hoover had transformed a hodge-podge of jumbled agencies into an efficient machine. He infused his department with a sense of pride and purpose that made Commerce the most dynamic workplace in the cabinet. Finding that he lacked adequate staff, Hoover hired two secretaries and three assistants with his own money, giving them a combined salary greater than his own. He utilized his management skills to reorganize, formulating three divisions: for industry, for trade, and for transportation and communication. His mission was to help facilitate business and trade, provide vital statistics, and harness new technology utilizing a maximum of voluntary cooperation and a minimum of coercion. During his tenure, the number of Commerce employees increased from 13,005 to 15,580, and appropriations from $28 million to $37 million annually, largely due to the addition of new bureaus and tasks. At the same time, he vowed to reduce wasteful overlap and excessive expenditures.[12]

Hoover made the Bureau of Foreign and Domestic Commerce the centerpiece of his department, organizing it along commodity lines in order to stimulate trade. To manage the bureau he hired his friend Julius Klein, who expanded its duties and infused its employees with a clear purpose and a sense of determination. Whereas other bureaus reported to Hoover's assistant secretary, Klein's bureau reported directly to Hoover. Klein created an independent statistical division to gather, collate, and disseminate data helpful to businessmen and exporters. Some fifteen commodity sections were created to study trends and to advise on marketing and the purchase of raw materials. Within the Bureau of Standards, Hoover created a Division of Simplified Practice, which became the core of his system to standardize industrial parts, reducing cost and enhancing marketing. After initial studies, leading producers within a field met under the rubric of their professional associations and adopted voluntary specifications for their products. Most changes were simple, invisible, and based on common sense. Hoover pursued the process industry by industry and reduced redundancy in products as varied as aircraft, wool blankets, hardware, men's suits, rubber boots, and automobile tires. One study found forty-nine styles and sizes of milk bottles with tops necessitating twenty-nine sizes of caps. An investigation reduced the sizes of bottles to nine and the sizes of caps to one. Standardization of concrete blocks reduced the cost by 25 percent, which produced greater profits and lower prices. Auto parts designed to last longer saved consumers $15 million per year. Commerce experts studied materials discarded as waste in the industrial process and found uses for them. A conservationist at heart, Hoover introduced a new element in conservation beginning with the raw material and ending up with the finished product. No one had thought, for example, of conserving trees by making the use of the harvested lumber go further. By the end of 1928 the standardization program was saving industry an estimated $600 million annually, which translated into higher profits and reduced prices for consumers. The program did not tamper with aesthetics, only with technical modifications, most at the micro level. The engineer's passion for efficiency extended to the federal government itself. Hoover created a Federal Specifications Board to unify the diverse specifications of the departments scattered throughout government. This resulted in centralized purchasing, which reduced costs to the government and enabled manufacturers to satisfy management demands. Commerce helped reduce paperwork in the federal government and in private industry by standardizing forms and eliminating duplication. The department expanded its scope during every year of Hoover's tenure. In 1925 the Bureau of Mines and the Patent Office were transferred from Interior to Commerce. In 1926 Hoover induced Congress to create an Aeronautics Division within Commerce, followed by a Radio Division in 1927.[13]

Hoover took a personal interest in encouraging American homeownership. Believing that single-family homes with lawns offered the most nurturing environment for raising children, Hoover sought to reduce the cost of housing, promoting the cause through publicity. He created a Housing Division within the Bureau of Foreign and Domestic Commerce and utilized the same process of simplifying and standardizing the hidden facets of home construction that he had applied to other industries. The bureau disseminated model zoning codes and plans for reasonably priced, attractive houses. The commerce secretary also believed an increase in home construction would stimulate the economy and might aid employment by eliminating seasonal labor. He devoted more energy to construction, with an emphasis on building homes, than to any other industry. In addition, he worked through the private organization Better Homes in America, which promoted homeownership, serving as president or chairman of the board from 1922 through 1934. The organization's forty-five hundred local chapters offered tours of model homes and lobbied for cost reductions. It also helped draft building codes and issued a manual for homeowners. During the Coolidge years, the commerce secretary turned to the task of making homes more affordable to middle-class families by reducing the interest rates on mortgages and stretching them out over a longer period. Most bank loans at the time were limited to five years or fewer and covered less than half the cost of the home. Interest rates were exorbitant, ranging from 12 to 15 percent. By 1927 Hoover had implemented a program to piggyback mortgages and helped reduce the interest rate to about 6 percent.[14]

As an internationalist in a nation inclined toward isolation, Hoover played an extensive role in foreign affairs during the 1920s. With Harding's blessing he advocated for U.S. entry into the World Court, a modest step up onto the international stage, yet the Senate balked at ratifying the treaty. Hoover also served on the presidentially appointed Dawes Committee—named after its chair, Chicago banker Charles G. Dawes—whose task became to reevaluate war debts owed to the United States by its former allies, which were linked to reparations paid to the Allies by the defeated former Central Powers, assessed as blame for initiating the war. America's loans had been made from money appropriated by Congress, and thus only Congress could annul them. Yet this was a political impossibility. The loans had been financed by bonds purchased by American citizens. If the debtor nations did not pay them, the bondholders would have to be repaid by the American government by raising taxes; in essence, Americans would have had to pay themselves for bonds they had already purchased. Realizing the principal was inviolable, Hoover advocated reducing the amount by lowering the annual interest rate and stretching out the payment period. He wanted to couple this concession to an agreement by the Europeans to partially disarm, which would reduce their financial burden. Additionally, he proposed dealing with countries individually and linking debt obligations to a nation's ability to pay. The central framework of Hoover's ideas was adopted by all three Republican administrations during the 1920s and codified in the Dawes Plan of 1924 and the Young Plan of 1929. As president, Hoover promulgated the debt moratorium of 1931 as the only feasible alternative to imminent default. Although Hoover's lenient terms were economically feasible, they were politically impractical in Europe, where the war debt was unpopular and reparations aroused hostility among Germans.[15]

Throughout the 1920s, Hoover also wrestled with the issue of American private loans made to foreign nations, primarily in Germany and South America, at unrealistically high interest rates. American bankers were tempted because the returns were far greater than any investments they could obtain in America. Frequently, American bankers used the money deposited by their clients to make the loans. Not only did this drain capital needed for American expansion; it was highly improbable that the

exorbitant interest plus the principal could ever be repaid. The tantaliz-
ing quick profits were an exercise in wishful thinking. Many bond issues
floated by municipal or regional governments abroad constituted sums
larger than the total value of all public and private assets within their
jurisdiction. Unable to meet the interest payments when they fell due, the
foreign borrowers issued short-term notes at still higher rates, pyramiding their loans to postpone the day of judgment. Hoover warned that the
debtors were already virtually bankrupt, with little or no security. Further, some money was spent recklessly to fuel an arms race and to support extravagant social programs without imposing higher taxes. The
commerce secretary advised repeatedly that the loans were speculative.
Nonetheless, American bankers considered any federal intervention meddling in their affairs. Ultimately, as Hoover had predicted, the foreign
bankers defaulted en masse, dragging down American banks with them
and contributing to the Great Depression. By that time, Hoover was president and was roundly blamed for the very catastrophe he had been one
of the few sufficiently prescient to foresee.[16]

On July 20, 1923, President Harding embarked on a transcontinental
railroad tour that he hoped would provide relief from the stress of Washington and help him assess his prospects in the West for reelection in
1924. He invited Hoover, who was fishing with his family in the Sierras,
to join the party at Tacoma. From there, they boarded a ship for Alaska,
where Hoover inspected fisheries and Harding delivered goodwill speeches.
Harding's mood grew increasingly morose as the trip progressed. The
chief executive played bridge incessantly to forget his worries and coaxed
Hoover into joining the games. Later, the agitated president invited
Hoover to his cabin and confided that he had learned of scandals within
his administration, including one involving his friend Jesse Smith, in the
Justice Department. After Harding had informed Smith that he would be
arrested, Smith had burned his papers and committed suicide. "If you
knew of a great scandal in our administration," the president asked
Hoover, "would you for the good of the country and the party expose it or
would you bury it?" Hoover advised him to reveal the details and avoid a

cover-up. He pressed for details, but the president became withdrawn. "In all the history of this government," Harding confessed, "there have been only three cabinet officers who betrayed their chiefs, and two of them are in my administration." The reference was to Attorney General Harry Daugherty and Interior Secretary Albert Fall, both parties to the Teapot Dome oil swindle. The sordid details that would emerge after Harding's sudden death were to bring his reputation crashing down. During the return voyage, the president's vessel had a minor collision with an accompanying destroyer. Belowdecks, the depressed Harding blurted out that he wished his ship would sink. If this was a death wish, it was destined to be fulfilled.[17]

Back on the mainland, the president was drained by an endless succession of speeches and glad-handing receptions. During a major speech in Seattle Harding became disoriented, clutched the podium, and nearly collapsed. Hoover picked up the president's fallen papers, arranged them in proper order, and, gamely, the chief executive completed the address, but his health worried his associates, who canceled the remainder of his itinerary and rushed him directly to San Francisco, where he could receive rest and serious medical attention. The president's personal physician, a marginally competent Ohio crony, Dr. Charles E. Sawyer, diagnosed the problem as exhaustion complicated by eating tainted crabmeat. Two days of bed rest would suffice for total recovery. As Harding's train sped southward to his final destination, the president was indeed overly stressed and increasingly irritable, although the problem was not food poisoning. Dr. Joel E. Boone, a navy physician, told Hoover that Harding's condition was serious. Upon receiving Boone's advice, the commerce secretary cabled his Stanford friend and physician, Dr. Ray Lyman Wilbur, to assemble a group of heart specialists to meet the party at San Francisco. Wilbur and other physicians correctly diagnosed a heart attack and, over Sawyer's objections, prescribed two months of absolute bed rest. Harding temporarily rallied and his spirits brightened at San Francisco's Palace Hotel, where Hoover had taken an adjoining room. On the evening of August 2, Harding's wife, seated by his bedside, read him an article about himself from *The Saturday Evening Post*, as the chief executive seemingly gained strength. Suddenly, the president became bathed in sweat, and the Duchess, as she was known, rushed from the room, screaming for doctors. By the time they arrived, the president was dead. Wilbur signed the death certificate, attributing his demise to heart failure.[18]

Hoover promptly telephoned Secretary of State Charles Evans Hughes, the senior cabinet member, and asked him to contact Vice President Calvin Coolidge, then visiting his father in Vermont, and request that Coolidge have himself sworn in as president. Harding's body was borne across the country by train as mourners lined the tracks and loudspeakers broadcast the deceased's favorite hymn, "My Redeemer Liveth," as a dirge. Unknown to the public were the scandals rumbling like a volcano within Harding's administration, which would destroy his reputation following the interment of his body in his hometown, Marion, Ohio. Hoover disapproved of Harding's associates and the president's laxity in restraining them and had considered resigning, but he believed he could add integrity to the administration. Moreover, Hoover knew that Harding was shocked and betrayed when he learned of the Ohio Gang's corruption. "People do not die from a broken heart," Hoover said, "but people with a bad heart may reach the end much sooner from great worries."

Across the continent in Vermont, Vice President Calvin Coolidge, a tight-lipped man popularly called "Silent Cal," was sworn in as Harding's successor. No sooner had his term begun than scandals lingering from Harding's reign descended upon the White House. They included kickbacks in return for the leasing of government oil properties at Teapot Dome, Wyoming, and Elk Hills, California; thefts from the Veterans' Bureau; and malfeasance in the Justice Department by the custodian of alien property, who filched assets seized by the government from enemy aliens during the war. Many of those implicated were Harding's friends, such as Attorney General Daugherty, who had managed Harding's presidential campaign. On January 27, 1924, President Coolidge announced that he planned to bring to justice those guilty of wrongdoing in the Teapot Dome and other oil lease scandals during the Harding administration. He said he was appointing independent counsels, men of high reputations, drawn from both parties, and that anyone found guilty would be punished. The law would be enforced, illegal contracts would be voided, and the public interest would be protected. Coolidge appointed special prosecutors promptly and, after some delay, fired Daugherty, who escaped incarceration because of two hung juries. Interior Secretary Albert Fall was not so lucky; he was convicted of accepting bribes. Several Harding associates and poker buddies averted prison by suicide. The new president appointed Harlan F. Stone, subsequently chief justice of the Supreme Court, as Daugherty's successor. When Stone asked Hoover in 1924 to recommend an honest man to clean up Washington corruption, Hoover suggested J. Edgar Hoover (no relation). Other seamy aspects of the Harding administration trickled and then gushed out. Harding had apparently fathered a child by his mistress, Nan Britton, and reputedly had had other affairs. Though he was so well liked by the public during his presidency, Harding's reputation plummeted. Today his name is synonymous with presidential scandal.[19]

Cantankerous, archconservative in politics and lifestyle, and quaintly reclusive, Calvin Coolidge took a minimalist approach to government. He espoused common sense, emphasized thrift, advocated low taxes, and was penurious with money, both his own and the public's. Feeling that it was prudent for government to leave well enough alone, Coolidge avoided precipitous action. "If you see ten troubles coming down the road, you can be sure that nine will run into the ditch before they reach you and you will only have to deal with one of them," he predicted, ironically for a man who had succeeded Harding. Coolidge was a thoroughgoing conservative in religion, in the economic and social order, and in fishing; he fished with worms, much to Hoover's consternation.[20]

Although he was far less gregarious than Harding, the new president's serious nature and rectitude provided a welcome contrast to the crass crudity and outright larceny of Harding's companions. A man with few social intimates in Washington, he had warmed to Hoover while still serving as vice president. Coolidge admired Hoover's mind and the breadth of his knowledge and respected his sound judgment and common sense. Both were men of few words in public, yet they each had a puckish sense of humor and enjoyed each other's company. Both were eminently practical men. While Coolidge displayed a folksy style and common touch that were astutely glamorized by his press agents, he recognized that behind the scenes Hoover possessed savvy political judgment, and the commerce secretary soon became the president's chief adviser on patronage in California and the West. Coolidge was far more provincial than Hoover. He did not know the country, much less the world, nor was he intellectually curious.

Coolidge often invited Hoover to come alone to the White House for an evening of "chatter." Grace Coolidge was her husband's opposite in temperament, vivacious and chatty, and she and Lou became close friends, remaining so for the rest of their lives. For the most part, the Coolidge-Hoover team functioned smoothly. Hoover gave the chief executive his complete loyalty. The president referred many problems outside of Commerce to Hoover and asked him to write executive orders, which he signed, and speeches, which the chief executive delivered without editing. In 1924 Hoover was one of the key strategists in mapping out Coolidge's campaign.[21]

Despite their predominantly sound relationship, Coolidge at times worried that his commerce secretary might become a rival for the 1924 GOP presidential nomination. Hoover sometimes overwhelmed him with ideas, and he constantly prodded the penny-pinching Coolidge for greater appropriations for the Commerce Department. The inscrutable chief executive once said of Hoover, "That man has offered me unsolicited advice for six years, all of it bad." As Martin Fausold, a Hoover presidential biographer, observes, "The remark, of course, was outrageous. In fact, the opposite was true." If Coolidge felt irritated at times by Hoover, it might have been because he felt overly dependent on his younger cabinet member. Yet Coolidge badly needed Hoover, whose boundless energy helped compensate for the lethargy of the president. Coolidge was not lazy, but he suffered from unsteady health. His chronic indigestion required naps after lunch, and he battled depression aggravated by the death of Calvin Jr., who died from an infected blister developed while he was playing tennis at the White House. The president's health and melancholy factored into his decision not to run for reelection in 1928. Personal traumas aside, Coolidge badly needed a man of Hoover's probity and versatility. Further, Hoover did not seek political power and allowed Coolidge to bathe in credit whenever he could persuade the press to praise his boss.[22]

Although occasionally uncomfortable with Hoover, Coolidge would have been much more uncomfortable without him. Unlike that of Harding, an experienced politician on the national level who brought to office a circle of cronies he could lean on, Coolidge's ascendency was sudden and unexpected, and he lacked Washington connections. Coolidge had not run for president and had been propelled into prominence chiefly by the timeliness of the Boston police strike and his vigorous response to it. Coolidge and Hoover were alike in important ways. Both were simple, direct, and unpretentious, had sprung from rural roots, and were socially inhibited. Yet, privately, they enjoyed intimate conversations, especially with each other. They and their wives melded well as a group. Despite gossip, rumor, and speculation, there was never any serious possibility that Coolidge would dismiss Hoover from the cabinet. There was an element in their relationship that was symbiotic. On one occasion, when he believed he had hurt Hoover by stating that he would not appoint him secretary of state, should the position become open, the president publicly made amends. For his part, Hoover was aware of the president's sensitivity, and Hoover was properly deferential. He deliberately remained in the background despite attempts by the press to glamorize him, and rarely, if ever, disagreed with Coolidge directly, much less publicly. Coolidge gave full latitude for free expression at cabinet meetings, but he made final decisions, and once an issue was determined, he expected the cabinet to present a united front. He doubtless would have dismissed any official who openly defied him. In this respect, Coolidge was not a weak president.[23]

As commerce secretary, Hoover dealt with virtually every new form of technology that appeared during the 1920s. Perhaps the most glamorous was radio. The Great War had accelerated the development of radio communication between ships at sea and armies in battle. After the war, broadcasting soon outgrew a military monopoly and stations proliferated, with virtually no government regulations. Amateurs (among them Herbert Jr.) and commercial and political broadcasts created a cacophony of noise as they overlapped frequencies. When Hoover asked a sixteen-year-old amateur broadcaster how he and his friends protected their frequencies, the teenager reluctantly conceded that they beat up the offenders. Within the government, turf wars raged between the Navy, Post Office, and Commerce departments over which would be assigned responsibility, and Coolidge decided that it was most appropriate for Commerce. He convened voluntary meetings of industry representatives and assigned frequencies for each station, although he had no legal authority to enforce them. More powerful stations were free to drown out weaker ones. Still, Hoover persisted, holding a series of these conferences every year from 1921 through 1927, until Congress finally created a Federal Radio Commission, which included members representing different sections of the country appointed by the government. Hoover predicted an exciting future for radio if it could be properly coordinated, avoiding monopoly and furnishing safeguards against unscrupulous demagogues. He had hoped that radio would focus on education and news, and he wanted to ban advertising, though that proved futile.[24]

Enforcement of the 1927 bill was vested in the Commerce Department, and Hoover dispatched an undermanned staff of inspectors throughout the country to ensure that broadcasters remained within their assigned frequencies. The flamboyant evangelist Aimee Semple McPherson broadcast from her powerful Los Angeles station, disregarding her designated wavelength, and her sermons meandered over the airwaves. After requesting several times that McPherson confine herself to her assigned wavelength, the commerce secretary shut down the station. She fired back a telegram. "Please order your minions of Satan to leave my stations alone. You cannot expect the Almighty to abide by your wave length nonsense," she wrote. "When I offer my prayers to Him, I must fit in with His wave reception. Open this station at once." Later, McPherson relented. Subsequently, a small religious sect in southern Illinois traveled to Washington to obtain a wavelength, gaining an audience with Hoover and the administrator of the radio division. The group informed the commerce officials that they had sold all their property and received $200,000. They were planning to construct a gigantic broadcasting station to inform Americans that the world was doomed to end within a few weeks. Hoover suggested that rather than building a new station they could reach more people promptly, an important imperative, by using their money to purchase blocks of airtime on existing stations. After all, their station would be worthless once the world came to an end.[25]

America's prosperity during the 1920s was energized by technological marvels, some made possible by inventors such as Thomas Edison and Henry Ford, both friends and admirers of Herbert Hoover. The vibrant economy was driven by electrically lighted homes, telephones, motion pictures, and automobiles; the latter quite literally propelled the economy forward down country lanes and city avenues. Hoover was a booster of all of these innovations and facilitated the development of several of them. Together, they transformed America. While Hoover was amplifying radio during 1927, he also became the first American public official whose face, along with his wife's, was transmitted by infant television from his office in Washington to the headquarters of the American Telephone and Telegraph Corporation in New York. Hoover considered picture broadcasting a pathbreaking achievement, although telecasting on a commercial scale did not materialize until after World War II. At Commerce, Hoover eased the task of inventors by eliminating paperwork needed to, acquire patents and accelerating the process.[26]

Captivated by technology, Hoover envisioned a great future for aviation in America, a nation of vast distances with many people and products to transport. Once commercial flight became faster and more reliable than railroad travel, he knew, it would quickly supplant rail for long-distance passenger service. In the short run, it could speed delivery of freight and mail, while pilots who gained experience in commercial flight would become valuable military assets. Within the Department of Commerce Hoover created an Aeronautics Division, which raised standards for airline safety, including the training and licensing of pilots. America, which lagged behind Europe in aviation at the beginning of the 1920s, soared past the Old World by the end of the decade. Hoover employed the leverage of airmail contracts as an indirect inducement for rapid, reliable development. The Bureau of Standards conducted research on air transportation, and the commerce secretary obtained a $2.5 million grant from the Guggenheim Foundation for research into air travel. Hoover plotted out routes from New York to San Francisco via Chicago, and envisioned air trade with Latin America. He promoted the achievements of aviation pioneers such as General Billy Mitchell, who sought better air defenses; Admiral Richard E. Byrd, who flew over the North Pole in 1926; and Charles A. Lindbergh, who in 1927 became the first person to traverse the Atlantic while piloting solo. Hoover brought a child's delight and a visionary's anticipation to the future of the airways, and he was determined that America would lead the world in aviation during peace and war.[27]

During the 1920s, the automobile was rapidly winning the race for dominance of transportation. Yet the nation's infrastructure was unprepared for the impact of millions of primitive cars and trucks clanking along dusty roadways. Mounting accidents and fatalities, as well as urban traffic congestion, concerned Hoover. Commencing studies of automobile and highway safety, he convened meetings of experts and public officials and encouraged them to adopt voluntary guidelines in the absence of authority to enforce laws affecting intrastate transportation. At the outset, most roads were unlabeled, with few posted speed limits and little uniformity. Hoover recommended standardized shapes for signs, speed limits, safe highway dimensions, and other measures. Most states and major cities adopted the codes following a National Conference on Street and Highway Safety convened at the Commerce Department during the spring of 1924. Hoover studied methods of reducing accidents, including zoning laws to minimize city congestion, wider streets to permit ample parking, and the location of shopping centers with spacious parking lots outside the hearts of municipalities. He suggested construction of highway arteries bypassing downtown areas, widening of avenues to ensure pedestrian safety, pedestrian isles, traffic circles, designated unloading spaces, elimination of taxicab "cruising," and the prediction of areas of urban growth in order to anticipate density of automobile traffic. In these insights, as in other attempts to manage new technology, Herbert Hoover was on the cutting edge of his times.[28]

Hoover considered water America's greatest natural resource. "Every drop of water that runs to the sea without yielding its full commercial returns to the nation is an economic waste," the commerce secretary explained. His objective was "the coordinated long-view development of each river system to its maximum of utilization."[29] He suggested that the government cease thinking about "single power sites, single land projects, single navigation improvements, or local flood controls," and instead construct "large interconnected systems of trunk lines from [the] seaboard with great feeders from our lateral rivers."[30] He envisioned a system of waterways linking the Great Lakes with the Gulf of Mexico, Pittsburgh with Kansas City, and Chicago with St. Paul. He wanted to connect the Great Lakes with the Atlantic Ocean and the Upper Mississippi River with the Gulf.[31]

Paying particular attention to waterways, Hoover initiated major advances in national planning. Water resources lay in every region of the nation, including the basins of the Columbia, the Colorado, the

Missouri, the Ohio, the Tennessee, the Great Lakes, and the St. Lawrence. Of twenty-five thousand miles of possible inland waterways, only
seven thousand were navigable. Hoover believed that dredging and
widening rivers for commercial traffic should be funded by the federal
government with aid from the states, and that the central government
should contribute to flood control. With 20 million acres of potentially
arable land too dry to cultivate, the government, he insisted, should also
assist in irrigation programs and recover the cost by charging farmers.
The situation became more complex when generation of electricity from
waterpower was involved. Hoover believed the national government
should build hydroelectric dams but allow private capitalists to generate
and distribute electric power. Where the electricity was a natural by-
product of dam construction or irrigation projects, it was acceptable for
the government to generate power, which it should sell to private utilities. The money paid for the rights to the power would reimburse the
government for building the dams. The commerce secretary did not
want the federal government to be directly involved in selling electricity
to consumers. He felt this could be done more effectively with less political favoritism by private utilities. Hoover did not believe the government should compete with private companies in selling power. It would
set a dangerous precedent because firms in any business could not compete efficiently with the government. The central government could operate at a loss and bill the hidden cost to the taxpayers, while individual
companies could not. Thus, some taxpayers would be benefiting at the
expense of favored regions. In instances where the power could not be
distributed profitably by individual companies, Hoover was willing to
permit the government to do it. Hoover was the first federal administrator, while secretary of commerce, to integrate a large-scale program of
planning. On his agenda, which still required approval, were a huge dam
at Boulder Canyon on the Colorado River, the Grand Coulee Dam on the
Columbia River, an Intracoastal Waterway, and the St. Lawrence Seaway linking the Great Lakes with the Atlantic Ocean via the St. Lawrence River. Many of Hoover's water projects arose from his desire to

help farmers find cheaper transportation to markets and to irrigate and reclaim arid land. President Coolidge was sparing in his support for appropriations, but all of the major projects initiated by Hoover during the 1920s were ultimately completed.[32]

Aside from the St. Lawrence Seaway, the most prolonged negotiations dragged out over Hoover's plan to construct a mammoth dam at Boulder Canyon on the Colorado River. President Harding appointed Hoover as the federal representative on a commission representing the six states designated to apportion water from the dam's reservoir. The water was coveted by the dry desert states, especially the largest, California, which many feared would seize the lion's share. Secretary Wallace, Hoover's cabinet nemesis, opposed such irrigation on grounds it might exacerbate the agricultural surplus, as did Hoover's California archenemy, Senator Hiram Johnson. With the required unanimous agreement near, Arizona balked, followed by California. The deadlock remained unbroken until 1929, after Hoover had become president, and construction stretched until after Franklin Roosevelt assumed office. At the groundbreaking, Interior Secretary Wilbur christened the structure "Hoover Dam." In a vindictive act, FDR's interior secretary, Harold Ickes, renamed it Boulder Dam. Agreeing that Hoover had originated the dam, the U.S. Congress, backed by new president Harry S. Truman, restored the old name, Hoover Dam, in 1947. Much progress was made on waterway and dam development during Hoover's tenure at Commerce. He was disappointed, however, that President Coolidge declined to approve developments on the San Joaquin and Sacramento rivers on fiscal grounds and refused to proceed with development of the Columbia River.[33]

Hoover also became involved in a potential water development project at Muscle Shoals, Alabama, on the Tennessee River, which the government had purchased to produce nitrates for ammunition during World War I. The site also could be used to generate electricity in a backward region and to supply fertilizer for farmers. Hoover, Harding, and Coolidge preferred private development, but there was no consensus in Congress for any specific plan. Henry Ford offered to lease the site for one hundred years but encountered strong opposition and withdrew his offer. At Hoover's suggestion, Coolidge appointed a commission, including some members proposed by the commerce secretary, to study the issue. The group reached no definitive conclusions, and the site, still undeveloped, caused a political brouhaha during the engineer's term as president.[34]

As commerce secretary, Hoover waged a war on waste that was related to his commitment to frugal, farsighted use of natural resources to ensure their perpetuity. Forests, lakes, rivers, and even the oceans around us did not have to be entirely undisturbed, he believed, but they must be managed prudently. In the mid-1920s, he lamented that "two thirds of the original primeval forests of the country have been cut" and that "timber is now being cut at a rate four times faster than the replacement through new growth." He observed that "between the cutting of the forest and the final use of the wood nearly sixty-five per cent of the total volume was previously lost." Hoover became one of the first prominent Americans to link the harvesting and processing of natural resources through the entire industrial process to their ultimate consumption.[35]

As an outdoorsman, Hoover flourished in the replenishment offered by forests and mountains, lakes and streams. The most fervent political outdoorsman since Theodore Roosevelt, Hoover was elected president of the National Parks Association and proved a formidable fund-raiser for the park system. He exhorted Americans not only to preserve forests and parks for posterity, but also to enjoy them. Protecting forests and wildlife necessitated more than planting trees; it meant planting a love of nature in the hearts of those who used the nation's parks.[36]

In addition to his role with the National Parks Association, Hoover served as honorary president of the Izaak Walton League, which celebrated recreational fishing. As commerce secretary he sought to preserve both sport and commercial fishing, a crusade he continued as president. He took a personal interest in the Bureau of Fisheries, previously a reservoir for deadwood bureaucrats, and installed career experts as committed to preservation of species and their proliferation as he was. Hoover used the coast guard to prevent the slaughter of seals in American waters by Japanese fishermen, and he sought legislation to prevent oil pollution in coastal areas. In Alaska, a territory where legis- lation was unnecessary, he helped save the salmon population from extinction and restored the declining stock of halibut. Off the Atlantic Coast, he conserved salmon and sturgeon, sorely depleted, and sought to replenish crab, lobster, oyster, and clam fisheries. He restocked fresh- water game fish, growing fingerlings to the survival point in hatcheries before releasing them.[37]

Beginning in the early 1920s, Hoover's Bureau of Foreign and Domes- tic Commerce spearheaded an effort to break attempts by foreign cartels— often colonial powers whose colonies exported a valuable raw material—to manipulate prices of resources vital to American industries. The most troublesome for Americans was the British quasi-monopoly on raw rub- ber produced by their colonies in the East Indies. By limiting rubber production and creating artificial scarcity, Britain increased the price of rubber, used chiefly for automobile tires, from 20 cents per pound in 1922 to $1.21 per pound by 1925, a cost to American drivers that Hoover estimated at $900 million per year. The coffee cartel, controlled primar- ily by the Brazilian government, raised the price of coffee beans from 13 to 30 cents per pound between 1924 and 1925. Other smaller cartels were intent on gouging their way to prosperity by commandeering com- modities such as long-staple cotton, sodium nitrate, and potash. The common thread in these international cartels was that they held a vir- tual choke hold on scarce resources and exercised tactics that forced the selling price far beyond the cost of extraction. On practical grounds, such monopolies undermined international trade, establishing prices purely by manipulation. In the long term, Hoover feared these monop- olies would inject governments into the natural law of supply and demand, bankrupting many nations by the gouging of a few, and risk inciting trade wars and, in the long term, even military wars.[38]

Hoover's Bureau of Foreign and Domestic Commerce dealt with cartels by applying leverage exercised through a variety of tools. Under a law initiated by Hoover and enacted by Congress in 1922, the bureau searched for new sources for the raw materials. For example, in its quest for potential sources of rubber, Commerce sent experts to explore the interiors of Brazil, Mexico, Colombia, and East India, attempting to stimulate competition. In addition, Commerce encouraged industries to employ substitutes, reduce waste, practice conservation, and develop synthetic alternatives. Public opinion was mobilized through the press and radio. Hoover attempted to organize American importers in a solid front against foreign monopolies. Through trade associations he helped to persuade American manufacturers not to bid against one another. He advised American bankers to avoid loaning money to international monopolies, although he did not advocate direct government action to prevent it. Eventually, Hoover triumphed in his most important battle. The British Empire's rubber price fell back to 20 cents per pound, and in April 1928 the British government announced that it would abandon its quota on rubber. Philosophically, Hoover believed that world commerce would flow healthily when prices were set by supply and demand, not by government autocracy. An internationalist in foreign affairs, he was a nationalist in domestic policy who made American consumers his foremost priority.[39]

After a steep yet brief decline in 1920–21, the American economy grew steadily, almost explosively, throughout the decade, fueled by consumerism, tax cuts, and Hoover's campaign against waste, as well as a host of new inventions that lit homes, brought entertainment to mass markets, and put the nation on wheels. The annual reports Hoover delivered in the form of a statistical abstract summarizing the state of the economy at the beginning of each fiscal year bore out the nation's economic growth. By 1926 the United States enjoyed the highest standard of living in the world, and the highest in its own history. The prosperity was attributed to President Coolidge's hands-off approach to business and Treasury Secretary Mellon's tax reductions. On January 1, 1928,

Hoover reported that the economy appeared stable as the nation entered the new year.

Despite the nation's unprecedented opulence, fears about the mania driving investments developed in Hoover's mind during the decade. He did not have a specific timetable for an end to the boom, nor an idea of the scope of the inevitable downturn. Still, he took on the distasteful task of belling the economic risks epitomized by Wall Street stock speculation and the Federal Reserve System's easy money policies. The commerce secretary issued some mild public warnings, but he worked primarily behind the scenes, aided by friends in key positions, such as Senator Irvine Lenroot of Wisconsin, chair of the banking committee, and Adolph Miller, Hoover's closest friend on the Federal Reserve Board. Following the 1922 recovery, the boom in building became so robust that Hoover feared it would soar dangerously high, initiating a meltdown. In March 1923 he advised President Harding to warn that construction was overexpanding. The president concurred, but he warned that a publicized statement from the chief executive would be risky. Instead, Harding signed a memo written by Hoover, which was sent out to contractors on Commerce Department stationery and reprinted in the *New York Times*.[40] Later, in his predictions for 1926, Hoover cautioned against economic recklessness. Speculation in real estate and on the stock market ran rampant, creating inflation. Installment buying was overextended, and some sectors of agriculture performed feebly, leaving many farmers deeply in debt. Turmoil threatened labor-management relations.[41] "What we need is an even keel in our financial controls," he wrote. He began a series of steps to mold public opinion and government policy, advocating, if necessary, a small decline sooner rather than a cataclysm later. In a 1927 *New York Evening Post* article, Hoover wrote that an extensive study showed "that peace-time slumps in business were the direct result of booms, so that the boom and not the slump should be the object of attack." He emphasized tools the government could use, including management of credit and currency, statistical projections, and a reserve of public works to ramp up or curtail construction in order to mitigate the business cycle.[42]

Privately troubled, Hoover lobbied the Federal Reserve Bank and its branches to escalate their rediscount rates, making it more expensive to borrow cheap dollars, which were fanning the wildfire of speculation. His confederate, Senator Lenroot, wrote the governor of the Federal Reserve on November 23, 1925, expressing alarm that both the central bank and the Federal Reserve Bank, located at the nexus of a buying spree, were feeding the frenzy with easy loans and had not heeded his appeals to rein in speculation. Lenroot, speaking for himself and Hoover, wrote that circumstances resembled the chaos prior to the recession of 1921, and he fulminated against lenient lending charges, concerned that the New York stock market was becoming overheated. He noted a *New York Times* article explaining that interest rates were being kept artificially low to facilitate a flow of gold from America to the Bank of England, which offered higher-interest returns to investors in its bonds. This was intended to help the British remain on the gold standard, but the result might be to pull the economies of both countries down together. D. R. Crissinger, the chairman of the Federal Reserve and an old Harding friend, conceded that some of Lenroot's reasoning was correct but that the Bank of England's security was vital to world financial stability and that the Fed's cheap money policies did not threaten America. A rapid exchange of letters ensued, some written by Hoover for Lenroot. The governor of the powerful Federal Reserve Bank of New York, Benjamin Strong, who exerted dominant influence on Wall Street, proved as unyielding as Crissinger to the warnings of Hoover and Lenroot. The American economy survived the threat of 1925, but by 1927, market mania had developed a self-perpetuating momentum. The central bank and its New York branch, as well as most regional banks, adhered to the cheap money policies, but four regional banks heeded the appeals and raised rates. It was too late. The hemorrhaging had spread beyond Wall Street into the arteries of commerce. The market would survive another tumultuous year, but the crash Hoover had tried so strenuously to avert would strike in October 1929. By then, Hoover would be president. His worst fears had materialized. The man who had done perhaps more than any other to ward off the crash would be blamed for it both in his own time and in posterity.[43]

In 1927, as the stock market hurtled toward disaster, the forces of man and nature appeared to combine to wreak havoc. Awash in temporary prosperity, the nation would soon be deluged by the Mississippi River. Rain drenched the heartland from August 1926 through the following summer, swelling the Mississippi's extensive tributaries to the west and the east, overloading the great river itself. The river was protected by a series of levees, most constructed by the states, but they proved no match for the gushing waters. By the spring of 1927 the Mississippi was unable to contain the overflow, and every state south of Illinois, especially Louisiana, Arkansas, and Mississippi, braced for a calamity. President Coolidge appointed Hoover, known for mastering emergencies in Europe, to cope with the greatest natural disaster Americans had yet faced. "We are humble before such an outburst of the forces of nature and the futility of man in their control," Hoover lamented.[44] Embarking from his Memphis headquarters, he traveled throughout the South in a Pullman railcar loaned to him by the Illinois Central, remaining in constant communication with hundreds of assistants. His train often rolled over rails covered by water, the crew unable to determine the depth or damage to the tracks, risking their lives. From the bluffs at Memphis overlooking the Mississippi, Hoover gazed down at the water rushing downstream, sweeping away animals and dwellings in its path. "Do you realize . . . what this means?" he asked a nearby reporter. "It means that at this moment the volume of water passing Memphis is ten times greater than that pouring over the Niagara cliffs when the Niagara River is at maximum flood state."[45]

The Mississippi not only leaped over its banks; it crashed through or tunneled under containment levees, creating crevasses or breaks in the earthen walls, spreading yellowish muddy water over millions of acres, sweeping away homes and barns, immersing entire towns. Altogether,

more than 25,000 square miles of farmland and small towns were inundated and about 750,000 persons required evacuation or food and medical care. About half lived in quickly constructed resettlement camps
occupying high ground, often levees that remained intact. More than a
million chickens drowned, along with 9,000 mules and horses, 26,000
head of cattle, and 127,000 hogs. The Red Cross saved the lives of 271,000
animals isolated on high ground by feeding them until the water receded.
As the U.S. government had no contingency fund for natural disasters,
Hoover assembled resources from the army, the coast guard, the Army
Corps of Engineers, the American Red Cross, state and local governments, and legions of volunteers. Hoover's initial task was to save the
marooned. His makeshift rescue fleet consisted of coast guard cutters,
private yachts and skiffs, motorboats, enormous paddle-wheel steamers
loaded with small boats, and a thousand craft built on the spot from
crude sawmill lumber, propelled by a thousand purchased outboard
motors and manned by volunteers. The flood brought out the best in
some. Bootleggers lent their swift, maneuverable boats and their navigating skills to the massive rescue efforts. Army and private planes soared
overhead, spotting survivors clinging precariously to trees and rooftops,
and radioed the locations to the nearest boats, which plucked them from
peril. Before Hoover assumed control, between three hundred and four
hundred died; afterward, less than half a dozen.[46]

With most of the stranded saved, Hoover and his crew raced ahead
of the flood to evacuate farms and villages before the muddy waters
arrived. In each threatened community, some ninety-two throughout
the valley, Hoover organized a committee of local citizens to rapidly
build a refugee camp atop high, solid ground to house displaced residents. Hoover himself designed the layout, each impromptu village following the same basic model, including army tents with wooden floors,
drainage, running water, electricity, lighting, and fire protection, and
amenities such as schools, churches, and stages for plays and concerts.
The Red Cross provided food, clothing, outhouses, sanitation, and inoc-
ulation against infectious diseases. Wild animals such as deer, rabbits,

turkeys, and quail shared the levees with domestic animals, sometimes aided by humans. All were welcome except snakes.[47]

In the Deep South camps were usually segregated; in the upper South they were more often mixed, yet the need for speed sometimes trumped local customs. In general, morale was high. At several camps, blacks complained of discrimination; Hoover appointed Robert R. Moton, Booker T. Washington's successor at Tuskegee Institute, who in turn appointed an all-black committee to investigate the claims. The Moton committee issued two reports, concluding that abuses had occurred yet were isolated, not general. The group attributed most of the problems to local whites, especially planters who wanted to ensure the return of their sharecroppers and tenant farmers to the plantations once the waters receded. Some local Red Cross committees, composed exclusively of whites, tried to sell blacks food provided by the National Red Cross, rather than give it away, as they had been instructed. Many blacks were grateful to Hoover for his efforts toward fairness, and a group in Pine Bluff, Arkansas, later presented him with a loving cup as an expression of their gratitude.[48]

Among large cities, only New Orleans, nestled in a bowl that dipped lower than the Mississippi, with portions even lower than the Gulf of Mexico, was seriously threatened. Rainwater had to be pumped up over the levees and into a system of spillways that snaked above or below the city, channeling the water directly to the Gulf and relaxing the pressure against the levees. Because the break of a levee at any point reduces the pressure at other points, city and state officials decided to sacrifice sparsely populated St. Bernard and Plaquemines parishes below the city to prevent a break at thickly populated New Orleans. Over several days, thirty-nine tons of dynamite, some planted by a scuba diver at the base of the targeted levee, produced a sufficient crevasse to almost wholly submerge Plaquemines and St. Bernard. The New Orleans business community had promised to compensate the farmers and fishermen ousted by the flood, but their pledge was only partly fulfilled. In the aftermath of the great disaster, Hoover lobbied to obtain federal protection for communities lining the nation's avenue to the Gulf, and he received much of what he requested. He had to tread lightly, however, for Coolidge was reluctant to embark on expensive public works.[49]

As the floodwaters receded, Hoover expressed gratitude for all who had pitched in to save not only themselves, but their neighbors as well. "I suppose I could have called in the whole of the Army," he remarked. "But what was the use? All I had to do was call in Main Street itself." Hoover was proud of the effort of his countrymen.[50] Though he never attempted to dissuade federal aid, he welcomed help from all quarters. According to historian Bruce Alan Lohof, "the lessons of the flood experience are that Hoover was a personable and popular fellow, that he operated with ease and spontaneity at the grass roots, and that he displayed considerable acumen in public relations." Although Hoover admired self-sufficiency, Lohof concludes, the commerce secretary "expended considerable time, energy, and initiative on the task of making the central government function."[51]

Hoover's performance along the Mississippi padded his political résumé at an opportune time. A poll of newspaper editors voted the flood as the greatest story of 1927, eclipsing even Charles Lindbergh's solo transatlantic flight. For an entire month, the *New York Times* ran daily front-page stories about the deluge. Hoover was featured in hundreds of articles and appeared in magazine stories, Sunday supplements, newsreels, and radio broadcasts. The *Idaho Statesman* featured an article entitled "Hoover to the Rescue," stating that "America is sold on the organizing and directing genius of Hoover."[52]

The disaster along the Mississippi provided Hoover with his first exposure to Southern racism, poverty, and the peonage system. Troubled by the injustice he witnessed, he tried to do something to alleviate its harsh edges. Many plantation owners were willing to sell their overextended plantations, which were mired in debt and overly dependent on a single, labor-intensive cash crop. Determined to give tenants an opportunity to earn economic independence, Hoover sought to obtain a pool of money from private philanthropic foundations for loans to white and black tenant farmers to buy small parcels carved from the old plantations. Each parcel would include housing, equipment, implements, and animals. Profits from interest paid by the borrowers would be used to expand the program, and, gradually, more tenants and sharecroppers would be lifted out of the peonage system each year. Yet Hoover was unable to obtain the necessary funds to launch the program, and his reforms foundered. He had now seen firsthand human heartbreak in America, as well as in the Old World, and knew it would take time and patience to overcome. He did not know how much time, or how much patience.[53]

SEVEN

Into the White House

I n the summer of 1927, President Calvin Coolidge, escaping from what the pale Vermonter considered the upper South's torrid heat, took the entire season to relax away from Washington and fish near Rapid City, South Dakota. Journalists followed like lemmings yet found few morsels of news. Herbert Hoover, enjoying a respite after his exhausting work in the Mississippi Valley, was also vacationing in the West, at one of his favorite retreats: the annual Bohemian Grove encampment beneath the California redwoods, an invitation-only mecca for the wealthy and famous who enjoyed the camaraderie, scenic beauty, and skits featuring all-male, bawdy satire. No political storm clouds appeared on the horizon for either man. The GOP, the majority party, was united. The campaign of 1928 loomed, but incumbent Coolidge appeared a shoo-in for reelection. The president had long since smothered the scandals of the Harding era, and the economy seemed robust and expanding. Meanwhile, Hoover bubbled with fresh ideas to propel the nation's wealth to even greater heights of economic opportunity. For the time, both men rested.

At about noon on the drizzly day of August 2, 1927, nearly nineteen months before the end of Coolidge's term, some thirty reporters who had accompanied the president for a sleepy vacation assembled for an impromptu press conference in the mathematics classroom of the local high school. Coolidge, already waiting, said curtly, "The line forms on the left." As they filtered by the president, he handed each a slip of paper with a single sentence, typical in its brevity, earthshaking in its content. The sentence read, "I do not choose to run for President in nineteen twenty-eight." If Coolidge's purpose was to keep the reporters, and the nation, guessing, he succeeded. The wording was curious. What did "I do not choose" mean? What was his rationale? Why was he closing the curtain without a final act, or at least taking a bow? The reporters, hoping to flesh out their stories, prodded the president, yet he retorted only that that there would be no further comment on his part.[1]

Coolidge's declaration struck like a thunderclap at the Bohemian Grove. Everyone, including Hoover, knew that the announcement automatically made the commerce secretary the front-runner for the 1928 GOP nomination. Yet he remained noncommittal, as Coolidge's cryptic wording seemed to leave an opening for a draft. Hoover repeated ceaselessly that he enjoyed the Commerce Department and preferred to remain there under Coolidge's benevolent tutelage. Coolidge deserved a second term, he insisted, and could win one. Hoover parsed his words as carefully as the president did, saying nothing that could be considered disloyal, nor anything that would appear to advance his own candidacy.

Republican Party regulars were dismayed by Coolidge's sudden withdrawal and attempted to discern whether his decision was final. Many believed that, although the president would not campaign for renomination, he would feel obligated to accept a draft if the GOP offered it to him. The business community and conservatives, who considered Coolidge the bedrock of prosperity, were most disturbed, fearing a more activist president might meddle in their affairs. "Coolidge is a known quantity politically," explained one party regular. "He plays ball with the organization. And he stays put. I'm not so sure about some of these other fellows." The Old Guard formed virtually a solid phalanx in favor of drafting the incumbent at the convention, even if he made no attempt to clutch the nomination. Publicly, Hoover stated that the president should be renominated; privately, he admitted to Coolidge that some of his friends were urging him to run but that he would much prefer to remain in the cabinet under the president.[2] While journalists attempted to ascertain the intentions of the White House occupant, an astute political observer wrote, "Whether Calvin meant it or not, I believe he is fairly out of it. The country has in a large measure accepted the statement at face value, and the active candidates will occupy the field without much elbow room remaining."[3]

Shortly after Coolidge's abrupt withdrawal, Hoover's close friend ex-congressman James H. MacLafferty, also an intimate of Coolidge, visited the First Family in Yellowstone National Park, where they were vacationing. MacLafferty told the president that many people in California regretted his decision. "Well, it is much better not to want to run and to have them want you to, than it is to want to run and them not want you to," the president reflected. Mac told Coolidge that with him out of the race, the West Coast would go for Hoover, and Coolidge nodded his assent.

On December 6, Coolidge met with the Republican National Committee, stating that they should respect his wishes and begin to seriously seek another candidate. Meanwhile, other pretenders to the nomination revved up campaigns. Most were favorite-son candidates who lacked influence beyond their own state or region. They could be spoilers, but none were likely to win the nomination. Party bosses hoped for a deadlock similar to 1920's, which would enable them to supersede Hoover and handpick another malleable candidate. Soon numerous Republicans were testing the waters, among them Senators Charles Curtis of Kansas, Guy Goff of West Virginia, George Norris of Nebraska, James Watson of Indiana, and Frank Willis of Ohio as well as Vice President Charles G. Dawes. A majority of delegates could not be assembled by winning primaries at that time, although such victories might win publicity. Most delegates were appointed by state committees, governors, legislators, or other means. Of all the candidates, Hoover was the only one with a national following at the grassroots level, and for that reason he was the most electable in the general election. He had won fame for his relief work in both Europe and America, as well as his productive tenure as commerce secretary. Although he had made enemies by serving in the Wilson administration, backing the Treaty of Versailles, and opposing the McNary-Haugen plan, no one seriously doubted his ability, his honesty, or his capacity to get things done. The fact that he had never held an elective office was rarely considered a liability during the campaign.[4]

Every time Hoover probed Coolidge about whether he should enter the race, the president deflected the question without either firm approval or disapproval. In February, with the Ohio primary pending, Hoover asked the chief executive directly. Did he intend to enter in Ohio? Coolidge replied tersely, "No." Pressing the matter, the commerce secretary asked whether he thought Hoover himself should enter. "Why not?" replied Coolidge without enthusiasm, probably due more to the man's laconic temperament than to any ill feeling. Ohio would present a legitimate challenge to Hoover's presidential prospects. Opposing a popular local, Senator Frank Willis, whom Coolidge did not like, Hoover might well have lost the vote, yet Willis died a month before the primary. While Hoover did not demonstrate great vote-getting ability, he had finally declared himself a candidate for president. It was also now clear that Coolidge himself had no intention of staging a campaign, yet a few conservatives remained hopeful he might accept a draft. As Hoover accumulated delegates, however, the draft movement began to lose momentum.[5]

Ohio had settled the issue that Hoover was, indeed, a candidate, but long before the commerce secretary made it public, an underground campaign had gotten under way. Hoover backers had learned from the 1920 effort how to build from the grass roots and overcome the opposition of entrenched bosses. Hoover clubs began at Stanford and spread nationwide. He drew heavily upon supporters in the journalistic community. His friends William Hard and Will Irwin, both well-known writers, published biographies that humanized Hoover, while numerous reporter acquaintances wrote glowing articles. In addition, Hoover was popular in academia, including among professors, students, and academic administrators. The president of Yale publicly endorsed him, as did Ray Lyman Wilbur, now president of Stanford. Although support was swelling, Hoover did not appoint a campaign manager. Instead, Hubert Work, Coolidge's interior secretary, coordinated operations at the national level. Below him were regional campaign directors in the Northeast, the Midwest, the West, and the South. Close personal friends Ogden Mills and Edgar Rickard managed the campaign in New York State. Yet while Hoover directed the efforts from behind the scenes, he did not wage a public campaign. Even in states where he entered primaries, he did not stump for support. In fact, Hoover did not deliver a single overtly political speech during the entire primary season. It was clear that he was seeking the job, but he much preferred the appearance that it sought him.[6]

Despite his public reticence, enthusiasm for a Hoover candidacy continued. Michigan Republican leader Justus S. Stearns was asked by the *Grand Rapids Herald*, "What are we going to do for a presidential candidate since Mr. Coolidge has kicked the chair from under us?" Stearns replied, "Nominate a better one. Hoover!"[7] Henry Ford, an ardent Hoover backer, said of the engineer, "He knows the working man's point of view," adding, "Hoover can bring capital and industry together."[8] Senator George H. Moses of New Hampshire, a political admirer of the commerce secretary, explained the dynamics of the Hoover campaign. "He has not said so, but we are making a candidate of him. He is attending to his job as secretary of commerce, but we are carrying him to the people."[9] Another U.S. senator, Frederick H. Gillett of Massachusetts, said that Hoover "has the gift of infecting his subordinates with his own energy and inciting in them the most strenuous loyalty; he has an unblemished character, and, in my opinion, is extraordinarily equipped to make a great president."[10] Former president William Howard Taft and former New York senator Elihu Root counted themselves among Hoover's prominent supporters.[11] He also won ringing endorsements from famed inventor Thomas Edison and from Hollywood moguls Louis B. Mayer and Cecil B. DeMille.[12] The advertising impresario and bestselling author Bruce Barton toiled for Hoover, even offering him free lessons on how to polish his speaking style, which Hoover declined.[13]

No issue dominated American life during the twenties more than the federal ban on alcohol, which had become law with the ratification of the Eighteenth Amendment in 1920. In February 1928, during the Ohio primary campaign, Senator William E. Borah of Idaho, a passionate defender of the ban, mailed a questionnaire to leading GOP contestants to determine their position on Prohibition. A light drinker, Hoover had abstained during Prohibition on the grounds that he favored obedience to the law. He believed Prohibition had increased industrial efficiency but was impractical without concurrent state enforcement. Hoover did not complete all of Borah's questions, and he attempted to tread a middle path. "Our country has deliberately undertaken a great social and economic experiment, noble in motive and far-reaching in purpose," he wrote. "It must be worked out constructively."[14] (Almost every historian who has quoted this well-known passage has omitted the final sentence.) Hoover stated that in the short run he opposed repeal of the Eighteenth Amendment and supported attempts to enforce it, but he did not comment on possible repeal of the Volstead Act, which carried out the amendment, and also declined to recommend a Prohibition plank for the party platform.[15]

Hoover drew solid support from numerous constituencies. He had enthusiastic backing from women because of his support for women's suffrage, children, relief, recreation, and better housing. The Scripps Howard newspaper chain, which had backed La Follette in 1924, now supported Hoover. Many European ethnic groups, including Poles, Czechs, Yugoslavs, Russians, and Germans, were grateful for his help to their native lands during the Great War.[16]

The South posed unique complications. The region controlled about

one-third of the delegates needed to nominate the candidate, yet Southern delegations comprised large numbers of blacks, who, denied suffrage
by state law, were ineligible to vote in general elections. To appease black
delegates en bloc might alienate whites whose votes would be needed to
win, yet to discriminate against them might lose the support of Northern
blacks, who were eligible and voted largely Republican. Southern politics was boss dominated and riddled with corruption. Some delegations,
called "black-and-tans," included both races, while "lily-white" delegations were entirely Caucasian. Sometimes contesting delegations of mono-
lithic or mixed-race varieties challenged for seats, which were settled by
the credentials committee at the convention. Hoover carefully avoided
personal involvement and his lieutenants pragmatically backed the delegations solidly committed to the commerce secretary, who enjoyed a
distinct advantage in the region where citizens of all races fondly recalled
his service during the Mississippi Flood of 1927.[17]

The nomination process on a state-by-state basis was a greater obstacle
to Hoover than a single nationwide referendum would have been, as the
general election clearly indicated. Hoover remained on the job at Commerce, skipped some primaries to avoid annoying powerful favorite sons,
and did not campaign actively even in those states in which he did enter.
Hoover's showing was mediocre, but he did not hurt his chances while his
friends lined up delegates in the nonprimary states through more conventional tactics. Hoover lost to Frank Lowden in Illinois, Lowden's native
state. James Watson edged Hoover in Indiana and Guy Goff beat him narrowly in West Virginia. In Indiana, the strong support of the Ku Klux Klan
that helped Watson top Hoover there probably aided him in other states.
The engineer lost to Senator George Norris in Nebraska, where Norris
was a favorite son, and also in Wisconsin, where both candidates were
outsiders. Hoover carried California and New Jersey unopposed and topped
weak opponents in Michigan, Maryland, and Oregon. The commerce secretary did not enter the Massachusetts primary, yet won a whopping 85.2
percent of the vote with write-in ballots.[18]

In May, Hoover trekked to Coolidge's office for one final attempt to approach the president. He told Coolidge he had about four hundred votes for certain, almost enough to guarantee a first-ballot victory for the nomination. But if Coolidge wanted to be drafted, he was welcome to all of Hoover's ballots. As penurious with words as he was with pennies, the incumbent replied, "I think if you have 400 delegates you ought to keep them." This was about as effusive as Coolidge ever got. It marked the passing of the scepter. Approaching the final stages of the campaign, the president, although he did not overtly help Hoover, generously removed any final impediments to his nomination. Coolidge discouraged his own supporters from entering him into the race. In May he declined to appear on the Wyoming ballot and in April he refused to enter the Massachusetts primary. Coolidge bluntly told two of his supporters, "I have studied it all over and have finally concluded that I do not want the nomination." Shortly before the convention, Secretary Mellon and National Committee Chairman William Butler instructed their home-state delegates from Pennsylvania to vote for Hoover. This was enough to ensure a first-ballot victory.[19]

The Republican convention convened on June 12, 1928, at Kansas City and remained in session for four days. Hoover had already obtained commitments from 476 of the 545 delegates needed for nomination. Prior to the conclave, the commerce secretary and Senator Borah had hammered out a draft platform, which was adopted in substance by the platform committee. Hoover's most formidable challenger, Lowden, withdrew from consideration after the platform committee rejected inclusion of his major objective, the McNary-Haugen plan, which guaranteed price supports for farmers. The hard work of the Hoover team triumphed. They had assembled a virtually unbeatable first-ballot nomination as the final opposition to Hoover melted away at Kansas City. There would be no deadlock, no smoke-filled, boss-dominated coronation in 1928. Hoover had carved out a consensus. The only member of the Hoover family to attend was son Allan, who served as a page. The commerce secretary canceled his appointments and directed his campaign by telephone from Washington.[20]

The commerce secretary listened to the proceedings by radio at his Washington office. On June 14, when the evening nominations were made, family and close friends huddled in the library of the Hoover home to hear the announcement over the airwaves. Neighbors gathered in the drawing room, and a few reporters awaited the outcome in the dining room. Hoover had selected a California friend, John L. McNab, to deliver the nominating speech, but he read only a few sentences before the convention floor and the galleries erupted into a demonstration for Hoover that continued for twenty-five minutes. When order was restored, McNab described Hoover's life as a series of epic achievements. "If the American people a quarter of a century ago had set out to prepare a man for the presidency, they could hardly have devised more apt experience than Hoover's," McNab said. Afterward, the nominating of other candidates resumed, followed by the balloting, which resulted in a comfortable first-ballot victory. Hoover won 837 votes, Lowden 74, Curtis 64, Watson 45, Norris 24, and Coolidge 17. Most of the votes for other candidates came from Midwestern states. In his home, Hoover showed little emotion before the assembled well-wishers and reporters, except to smile and kiss his wife, and withheld immediate comment from the press. On June 15, the delegates nominated for vice president Senator Charles Curtis of Kansas, an elderly conservative expected to help attract votes in the farm belt. For the first time in American history, both nominees on a party ticket had been born west of the Mississippi River. While Hoover did not choose Curtis, he consented to his nomination.

George Moses notified Hoover of his nomination for president by telegram, and Hoover accepted by return cable, stating that he would strive to maintain the high standards of rectitude set by Coolidge. The president responded with a cable backing Hoover in what were for Coolidge glowing terms. He wrote the nominee that "your great ability and your wide experience will enable you to serve our party with marked distinction." The vigor of Coolidge's message mattered enormously. The GOP was closing ranks behind its ticket.[21]

On June 26, the Democrats met at Houston, where seats on the floor and the galleries were segregated, and nominated their only serious candidate, Alfred E. Smith, who had won four two-year terms as governor of New York. Though Smith's background was as prototypically urban as Hoover's had been rural, both were self-made men. While Hoover's chief assets were his superb mind and his ability to forge lifelong friendships, Smith was a more natural politician, gregarious, opportunistic, a political professional who had risen through the ranks, who knew politics intuitively but lacked a polished formal education. Temperamentally and intellectually, there was a gaping contrast; one man's strengths were the other man's weaknesses. Al Smith had begun as a fish peddler and ward heeler for New York's notorious Tammany Hall machine, which thrived on patronage, and he tolerated the degree of corruption necessary to grease the political wheels. Neither well-read nor erudite, he was rather provincial, ignorant of both world affairs and even those of much of his own nation west of the Hudson. With his New York brown derby, cigar, and East Side accent, which grated on the ears of Midwesterners, he could not persuade Western farmers that he understood their problems. Smith was a better, more convivial public speaker than Hoover, a good mixer, with a magnetic personality, yet he fidgeted before the stationary microphones of that day, which caused some words to be mangled, especially via radio. Except for his urban style, which he flaunted, and his Catholicism, as well as his desire to repeal Prohibition before it had yet grown widely unpopular, his generally conservative views, especially on business, might have appealed to many conservatives. Indeed, some of the Democrat's positions were distinctly traditionalist; he disliked women's suffrage, the expansion of government, and extensive regulation of business. As Martin Fausold points out, "In many respects, Hoover was the more liberal and progressive candidate in 1928."[22] On the whole, however, the men were not far apart ideologically; neither roamed far from the political mainstream of their time, and each might be considered center-left. Their chief differences were in style and personality. The glad-handing, ebullient New Yorker, who chose as his theme song "The

Sidewalks of New York," might have given the impression that his philosophy lay to the left of Hoover's, but these differences were largely superficial.[23] Hoover was much better known nationally and internationally than Smith, and both candidates were men of integrity who never deliberately said a false or unkind word about each other, although some of their less-principled subordinates embraced a win-at-all-costs philosophy. Moreover, Smith's chief enemy was neither Hoover's stature nor his own provincialism, but the deceiving glow of the Coolidge-era prosperity. Voters were to ultimately vote their pocketbooks in 1928. As one analyst explained, "No one will shoot Santa Claus."[24] Phrased differently, mammon was a powerful ally.

Now focused on the general election, Hoover applied his virtuosity in organization to his campaign, as did his legion of friends. He did not appoint a special campaign committee but instead delegated the task to the Republican National Committee, chaired by his most respected political consultant in the cabinet, Interior Secretary Hubert Work. After Coolidge declined to run for another term, Work had been the first cabinet member to endorse Hoover. A conservative Westerner, Work helped forge ties with Old Guard Republicans. With the Progressives already backing Hoover, the GOP was more united than at any time since the split between Theodore Roosevelt and William Howard Taft in 1912. Work's task was to implement strategy devised by Hoover. As in most previous Hoover operations, policy was centralized and execution decentralized. Regional campaign managers focused on local issues, fund-raising, and turnout, operating under the rubric of Hoover and the central committee. Within each region, volunteers were organized on the state, county, municipal, and ward levels. Like the CRB and the ARA, the campaign organization resembled an octopus with many tentacles but a single head. Work considered overall prosperity more important than parochial or interest-group issues. Hoover emphasized farm problems to a greater degree, especially cooperative marketing. He was confident of his support in the West and portions of the East, yet he considered the Midwest a battleground where farmers had not fared as well as most groups during the prosperous 1920s. Many farmers still blamed Hoover for urging them to maximize production during the Great War, only to have prices plummet when the war ended suddenly. Nonetheless, most did not consider New Yorker Al Smith a plausible alternative.[25]

American political tradition—until Franklin D. Roosevelt shattered it in 1932—held that nominees were not officially informed of their designation until a party of official representatives visited them at their homes and personally notified them of their selection. For Hoover and his wife, who still considered Palo Alto their permanent home, this required a transcontinental trek by rail. Along the ride west, he visited briefly with Vice President Dawes in Chicago and paid homage to President Coolidge at his fishing lodge along the Brule River in Wisconsin. While the men fished, Coolidge with worms, Hoover with artificial flies, the nominee angled for a more important prize—Coolidge's public endorsement. Afterward, the two quiet men attempted to chat, seated in rocking chairs on the porch of the lodge. Coolidge joked that Hoover would not hold up his end of the conversation but conceded that his commerce secretary was a better fisherman.[26] Coolidge gave his imprimatur to Hoover's campaign and said he would render some help, but he intimated that he wanted Hoover to remain in the cabinet a bit longer to finish some incomplete projects. As they resumed their rail journey west, Lou received a telegram that her father, Charles Henry, was seriously ill, followed by a second telegram informing her of his death. She retired to a private car to grieve. Her husband continued to greet crowds along the way, but the passing of Lou's father had dimmed the spirit of the trip. Hoover canceled a celebratory parade at San Francisco and the couple went directly to the chapel at Stanford for a memorial service for Charles Henry.[27]

After arriving in Palo Alto, Hoover went about his chief task of drafting and revising his acceptance speech. A scrupulous perfectionist, he was the last president to craft his own speeches, not only in the White House, but throughout his life. In composing his address, Hoover attempted to express his ideas accurately and with little embellishment.

As a speaker, he tended to mumble, speaking into the microphone in a flat monotone voice with little use of inflection. Never prone to exaggerate, he minimized his own accomplishments, a virtue in ordinary people but a vice among politicians.

Before an audience of seventy thousand students, professors, alums, friends, and news media personnel, Hoover stood on a small platform in Stanford's cavernous stadium, which he, as a trustee, had been influential in constructing. Beyond Palo Alto, between 34 million and 40 million people listened via radio, or later viewed the address on newsreels at theaters. He spoke directly into the microphone; his words carried clearly, and he expressed gratitude for the opportunity to serve.[28] "In no other land could a boy from a country village without inheritance or influential friends look forward with unbounded hope," he said.[29] Hoover's address synthesized ideas and programs he had advocated for years. His tone was philosophical, his content broad and general, including passages denoting moral and spiritual uplift. Hoover praised his party, especially Coolidge for facilitating prosperity, but prudently omitted Harding. He indicated, however, that his administration would move at a brisker pace. Foreseeing that religious prejudice would inevitably creep into the campaign, he tried to preempt it. "I come of Quaker stock," he reminded listeners. "My ancestors were persecuted for their beliefs. By blood and conviction I stand for religious tolerance both in act and in spirit."[30] He also believed in racial equality and opposed the model of status based on class. "Equality of opportunity is the right of every American—rich or poor, foreign or native-born, irrespective of faith or color," he explained. As commerce secretary, he had worked to ensure prosperity, yet economic plenty was merely a means to a higher purpose, he elaborated. "Our party platform deals mainly with economic problems, but our nation is not an agglomeration of railroads, of ships, of factories, of dynamos, or statistics," he continued. "It is a nation of homes, a nation of men, of women, of children."[31]

On the campaign trail, Hoover defined the economic beliefs he had developed over a lifetime of private enterprise and public service. He believed in limited regulation, stating that fair competition must be encouraged and monopolies dismantled when salutary. The federal government's most important function in regard to the economy was to allay the boom-and-bust cycle and alleviate downturns. In agriculture, he vowed to make farming as prosperous as other occupations by providing moderate protective tariffs on select products, waterway development, and more effective marketing through cooperative farming. In labor, he upheld workers' right to strike and called for legislation that would curtail the use of injunctions in labor disputes. Falling back on his reputation as an effective administrator, he called for a reorganization of the government by function, with bureaus and agencies that overlapped to be consolidated and unnecessary ones eliminated altogether. He vowed, if elected, to launch a massive public works program that would include waterways, highways, and public buildings, projects that would alleviate unemployment. Estimating the cost at $1 billion, he did not promise either tax cuts or additional debt reductions. He called for enforcement of Prohibition and advised those who opposed the Eighteenth Amendment to work for repeal rather than to flout the law.[32]

Hoover was a strong proponent of women's suffrage and insisted women could contribute to a higher moral tone in politics.[33] As commerce secretary, he had worked for better homes and improved recreational opportunities, and as a national candidate he supported education and believed that strong families were crucial to the success of America. Hoover had been involved in movements to improve the quality of life of children for decades, and as president he would continue to advocate for children, asserting, "The greatness of any nation, its freedom from poverty and crime, its aspirations and ideas, are the direct quotient of the care of its children."[34]

Prosperity, Hoover believed, could best be preserved in a peaceful world.[35] Intending to make world peace a cornerstone of his foreign policy, he pledged to cooperate with the League of Nations, though not to join it, and was prepared to disarm America's military to the extent that other nations would disarm.

One passage in the speech came back to haunt Hoover: "In America today we are nearer a final triumph over poverty than in any land. The poorhouse has vanished from among us," and he added, "We have not reached that goal, but given a chance to go forward, we shall, with the help of God, be in sight of the day when poverty will be banished from this nation."[36] At the time, it might have been true that no nation had ever enjoyed such prosperity as America experienced during the 1920s. Still, Hoover took too much for granted in suggesting it would continue unimpeded, and he inadvertently provided ammunition later turned on him by his critics. His words were to prove ironic years later when the nation lay prostrate beneath the burden of the Great Depression.

Throughout the nation, press reception of the Republican's address was mixed. The *New York Herald Tribune* emphasized the speech's patriotic commitment to American values, while the *Mobile Register* considered it "a genuinely human document." The *New York Times* observed that the GOP nominee considered farm relief a more important priority than Prohibition. While the *Chattanooga Times* carped that Hoover had said nothing unexpected, the *Indianapolis Star* found his speech thoughtful and practical. The *Cleveland Plain Dealer* believed Hoover spoke directly to the common people rather than to the politicians. The *Louisville Courier-Journal* stated, "It differs from other Republican speeches, not in substance, but in spirit; in the elevation of its tone, in imaginative color, in pervasive idealism."[37]

Between August 11 and November 2, Hoover delivered only six major addresses, but he held numerous local meetings and greeted crowds from the rear platform of his campaign railroad car. On his return trip to the East from Palo Alto, Hoover delivered an address at his birthplace, West Branch, Iowa, presenting his program for agriculture and praising the rural way of life, including the central role of the family. Back east, he spoke at Newark, New Jersey, where he discussed the use of public works as a device to even out the business cycle and mitigate unemployment, as well as the creation of mediation methods to resolve labor-management disputes. At Elizabethton, Tennessee, a Republican enclave in the upper

South, he discussed enforcement of Prohibition, use of cooperative marketing for farmers, and the need for a clean campaign, disavowing bigotry. Returning to the Northeast, the GOP candidate spoke at Boston, where he emphasized tariff protection as a major element in the Republican economic program. At New York's Madison Square Garden, in the heart of his opponent's bailiwick, Hoover focused on issues government should avoid, such as competing with private business in the sale of electric power. Before an unexpectedly receptive audience, he advised that Prohibition should be given a fair trial before a rush to judgment. He did not condemn alcohol on moral grounds, but he advised that repeal, not disobedience, was the proper antidote to a failed social experiment. In his final major address, in St. Louis, on his return to Palo Alto to vote, Hoover emphasized the necessity for peace and equability between labor and capital.[38]

In a campaign pitting the first Quaker nominee of a major party against the first Catholic candidate, religion inevitably became an issue, though both contenders attempted to avoid it. Some Democrats claimed that no one of Hoover's faith could be a credible commander in chief because all Quakers were pacifists. Hoover pointed out that several of his Quaker uncles had served in the Civil War and that his own father had volunteered yet had been rejected as too young. He reminded voters that he had supported American participation in the Great War. In addition, some political opponents charged that he was ineligible for the presidency because he was a British citizen, having lived in London during much of his mining career. Hoover retorted that he was an American citizen by birth, had certainly not renounced his U.S. citizenship, and had never voted anywhere but in the United States. Another frequent assertion was that as food administrator, Hoover had cheated American farmers in order to provide low food prices to the Allies. The candidate patiently explained that he had tried to balance all interests, that he had compelled the Allies to honor their agreement to buy the full 1918 harvest when they tried to renege, and that after 1918 he had disposed of much of the U.S. farm surplus as relief for Central and Eastern Europe and the Soviet Union. At least one charge against Hoover was pure fabrication. Designed to hurt his chances in the South, rumors were circulated that Hoover had danced with a black woman while in Mississippi during the Great Flood of 1927. Actually, Hoover could dance only awkwardly, if at all. He pointed out that he had been in the small town where the alleged incident occurred for only three minutes and had never left his railroad car.[39]

The smears against Smith were predictable, yet repeated ceaselessly, often in furtive whispering campaigns, sometimes openly. Many Protestants believed Catholics owed their first allegiance not to their country but to the pope in Rome. The issue was closely linked to Prohibition, which was supported more ardently by Protestants, who pointed out that wine was used in the Catholic mass. Although the Democratic platform was dry, Smith openly opposed Prohibition, and Hoover received the endorsement of many Protestant churches because of the Prohibition issue. Hoover publicly denounced all defamatory propaganda drawn to his attention. In late September, he stated, "Nor can I reiterate too strongly that religious questions have no part in this campaign." He further explained, "There are important and vital reasons for the return of the Republican administration, but that is not one of them." The following day he restated, "The glory of our American ideals is the right of every man to worship God according to the dictates of his own conscience."[40]

Smith's aggressive attacks on those who resorted to the use of religion in the campaign probably backfired. Rather than bringing him sympathy, his outrage drew attention to the matter and did not seem presidential.[41] The Catholic issue hurt Smith primarily in the South, and while it might have changed some individual votes, it did not determine the outcome. Not until 1960 was another Catholic, John F. Kennedy, nominated by a major party. Coincidentally, he was matched against another Quaker, Richard Nixon.

Hoover came to believe that his colleague from the Wilson administration, Franklin D. Roosevelt, was not simply campaigning against him, but had stooped to circulating personal slurs and embroidering falsehoods, which the Republican considered a betrayal. Roosevelt wrote to Hoover's colleague Julius Barnes and attempted to convince him that their common friend would make an unfit president. FDR wrote that "high ideals and a forward-looking policy—not only for this country but for the world—would stand as little chance under Mr. Hoover as they have stood under President Harding, Mr. Coolidge and Mr. Mellon." The message angered Barnes, who wrote that "this letter, I am frank to say, greatly surprises me and disappoints me." Barnes added that the letter "falls below my previous estimate of your character and your ideals." Barnes went on to say that he had known Hoover for many years, had never known him to be incompetent or unethical, and intended to vote for him.[42] Barnes's rebuttal did not restrain Roosevelt, who continued to direct invective at his former friend. Shortly before Election Day, FDR told an audience that Hoover was an elitist who disdained the common people, though Roosevelt's own ancestry and education were far more aristocratic than Hoover's. "There is such a thing as too much engineering," he added.[43]

On Election Day, Hoover, along with Lou, Allan, and Herbert Jr., voted at the Stanford precinct, which Hoover carried 450–10. That evening, the family and about fifty local friends awaited election returns in the spacious Hoover mansion near campus, where running totals were posted on a chalkboard. Hoover sat quietly, puffed on his pipe, and remained composed. Months earlier the university had booked an outdoor performance by the great composer of marches, John Philip Sousa, and his seventy-piece band. When it became obvious that Hoover would win, the band marched to the Hoover home, clogging the streets with two thousand jubilant students, for a brief serenade that included the national anthem and the Stanford alma mater. The usually stoic Hoover greeted the students from a portico and shed tears. He retired at about eleven thirty and was awakened about half an hour later by a telegram of concession from Al Smith. Hoover informed reporters that there would be no speeches and no comments about cabinet selections until they were made. "In this hour there can be for me no feeling of victory or exultation," he said in his first statement to the press on the day after the election. "Rather, it imposes a sense of solemn responsibility of the future and complete dependence upon divine guidance."[44]

Numerous pundits had predicted a Hoover victory, but not the scope of it. He carried forty-two states, with 444 electoral votes to Smith's 87 votes and eight states. Hoover overwhelmed the Democrat with 58.1 percent of the popular vote in one of the most decisive victories in American history up to that time. Incredibly, Hoover won five former Confederate states, usually Democratic bastions. Smith won only Massachusetts, Rhode Island, and a tier of resolutely Southern Democratic states in the "black belt," South Carolina, Georgia, Alabama, Mississippi, Arkansas, and Louisiana. Though he had appeared a strong candidate and an energetic campaigner, Smith proved weak in every region, even where Democrats had won easily in previous contests. The defeat was nationwide and conclusive. Hoover, a more sedate, restrained campaigner, had won wet states, corn belt states, Southern states, and states that sympathized with Smith because of his religion, most by large margins. The only genuine national issue was prosperity and the desire to maintain the status quo. "Mr. Hoover, after all, was better qualified for the Presidency," the *Washington Post* wrote. The magnitude of Hoover's victory made a political comeback for Smith unlikely.[45]

The morning after their victory, the Hoover couple rose early and celebrated in a typically subdued manner, strolling the foothills and meadows near Stanford where they had courted as geology students. With the strain of the election dissipating, they walked hand in hand for an hour. Returning, the president-elect plunged into thousands of congratulatory cables from well-wishers. Most would be answered by secretaries, but a few required personal responses, among them memos from Vice President Dawes and Vice President–Elect Curtis.[46] Hoover knew his life would never be the same. Already, he was losing some of the privacy he craved. During his interlude as president-elect, Hoover confessed his fears privately to his friend Willis J. Abbot, the editor of the *Christian Science Monitor*: "My friends have made the American people think I am some kind of superman, able to cope successfully with the most difficult and complicated problems. They expect the impossible of me and should there arise in the land conditions with which the political machinery is unable to cope, I will be the one to suffer." Hoover knew that his reputation had outgrown him and that it invited a backlash if things went wrong.[47]

Despite his postelection apprehension, Hoover turned his focus toward planning his administration. His contacts with Latin American diplomats during his tenure as commerce secretary whetted his appetite to improve trade and diplomatic relations as president. He decided that a goodwill trip to Latin America would be the first major item on his diplomatic agenda. No president-elect had previously taken such a prolonged voyage to other nations. By leaving the country, Hoover also avoided upstaging Coolidge in Washington and evaded the hordes of patronage seekers pursuing him. Having campaigned to make world peace the centerpiece of his diplomacy, he decided to start in the Western Hemisphere. Hoover departed from San Pedro, California, on November 19, 1928, aboard the battleship USS *Maryland*, accompanied by his wife, a small group of advisers, and a party of reporters. Hoover paid his personal expenses, except for use of the battleship. The ten-week tour included Honduras, Peru, Chile, Argentina, Uruguay, and Brazil. Aboard ship, Hoover relaxed on deck, reading detective novels and Westerns as well as books about fishing. He and Lou joined the sailors in watching a treasure trove of Hollywood movies loaned by director Cecil B. DeMille.[48]

The incoming president considered the voyage his first step in a reorientation of American policy toward Latin America. He delivered some twenty-five short speeches, including one in each major capital. The centerpiece of his program was that he intended to inaugurate a new approach to the United States' relations with the Southern Hemisphere, renouncing imperialism and economic domination. American troops would not intervene in the hemisphere to collect debts or even to protect American lives, and he promised to withdraw all American troops remaining in Latin America. He vowed to upgrade the quality of the diplomatic corps assigned to Latin neighbors. No longer would ambassa-dorships be assigned as political sinecures or patronage rewards. Rather, able career diplomats, usually native speakers, would be assigned. He prom-ised to settle all disputes peacefully and to inaugurate airmail delivery between the hemispheres. In nation after nation, Hoover labeled his ap-proach the "Good Neighbor Policy," a strategy that would be continued by Franklin Roosevelt. As part of the new overtures, he inaugurated ex-changes of professors and students between the Northern and Southern hemispheres. Perhaps Hoover's sincerity, humility, lack of pretense, and respectful attitude helped ensure more stable relations in what had been a turbulent part of the world.

After his return from Latin America, Hoover spent time in Florida as a guest at the estate of the department store mogul J. C. Penney. There, Hoover held appointments with party leaders and fished. He visited Thomas Edison and chatted with Al Smith, also vacationing in Florida. The recent adversaries became friends who found each other's company mutually pleasant.

As the twilight of the Coolidge era dimmed and the dawn of the Hoover years beckoned, the nation felt refreshed, facing the future with confidence. Yet Coolidge prosperity was stumbling. The adrenaline that had propelled Wall Street and powered the engine of the economy was soon to receive a jolt that would forever change Hoover's life and reputation—as well as the fortunes of a generation.[49]

EIGHT

Getting a Grip on the Presidency

As Herbert Hoover prepared to take the oath of office, the American public's expectations for their new president rose. The *New York Times* noted that "the country is ready as it has seldom been for audacious leadership, [and] the chance for coincidence between the man and the hour seems almost too good an opportunity to waste. . . . Everyone agrees, critic and friend, that he is the best qualified President we have had for decades."[1] The *San Francisco Chronicle* chimed in, "No other American has ever had the breadth of experience which Herbert Hoover brings to the task confronting him."[2] Novelist Sherwood Anderson observed that the incoming president was possibly the most respected man in America and had "never known failure."[3] Only occasionally did anyone dampen the euphoria. Shortly after Hoover's inauguration, *The Outlook* observed, "He is regarded as a miracle worker. That is his misfortune. He will be required by his masters, the people, to do the impossible."[4]

Hoover seemed oblivious to the deluge of attention. As his inauguration approached, he spent much of his time at his home on S Street in

Washington, DC, surrounded by family, including Herbert Jr., with his wife and two babies, and Allan, a Stanford senior. On his last day as a private citizen, Hoover ate a hearty breakfast and perused the newspapers, deterred from a relaxing drive into the countryside by a rainstorm. His most comforting thought was that the campaigning was over and he could soon get to work.[5]

On Inauguration Day, a morning drizzle gave way to a downpour that drenched his motorcade as it crept along Pennsylvania Avenue, cheered on by thousands of celebrants. Rain pelted Hoover's face as he leaned forward to kiss the Bible, opened to the Sermon on the Mount, his favorite passage. His speech, delivered in his typical monotone, reached the largest radio audience on record at that time. For all the distractions, and the president's low-key delivery, the content was meaty, with a positive tone, including tributes to Coolidge and passages of moral and spiritual uplift. The longest portion dealt with maintaining peace in a world still impacted by the Great War. Excessive armaments wasted federal dollars and escalated tensions while bringing no additional security, Hoover insisted. He would settle disputes with other nations amicably and work to resolve differences without meddling in their affairs. In addition, the new president announced that to protect American agriculture he would summon Congress into a special session limited to two items, farm relief and moderate tariff increases. He promised to appoint a commission to investigate law enforcement, including Prohibition, and announced plans for public works, waterways, government reorganization, and improvements in public health and education. Although bursting with progressive ideas, Hoover had sliced fat from the speech, making it one of the shorter addresses for a modern president. Following the ceremony, the First Family changed into dry clothes in their quarters at the White House before Lou presided over a large tea. Hoover, who did not dance, skipped the Inaugural Ball, sponsored by Vice President Charles Curtis, attending a small charity benefit instead.[6]

The White House, muddled under Harding, somnolent under Coolidge, now became the heartbeat of government activity, blazing with action.

Commandeering the desk used by Woodrow Wilson, whom Hoover admired for his high ideals, the new president had a telephone installed, the office's first. Whereas previous presidents had utilized one primary secretary, usually male, Hoover had three, who were assigned responsibilities according to function and met each morning to plan the day's work. The president outlined objectives, giving his secretaries flexibility to take the initiative and accomplish their goals. Each man shared his leader's traits of resolve and probity. Walter H. Newton had served in Congress, as a political liaison with Capitol Hill, on the Republican National Committee, and with government agencies as well as with committees and commissions. A shrewd politician, he gathered political intelligence about pending legislation and helped steer bills through Congress. Lawrence Richey, a former Secret Service agent, had worked for Hoover at Commerce and was close to the president personally, the only one of the men who fished with Hoover. Richey handled the president's personal correspondence and managed the office, and also took on personal assignments, such as political intelligence. George Akerson, a former Washington correspondent for a Minnesota daily, became press secretary, a position he had held previously during the campaign and at the Commerce Department.

Although not among the group of secretaries, French Strother, a former associate editor at *World's Work*, contributed research to Hoover's speeches and fact-checked, though he left the president's prose alone. One of Hoover's closest friends, Edgar Rickard, returned to private business following the campaign and handled the president's personal finances. Hoover's fortune had dwindled from both investment losses and personal generosity, and during his years in office his outside income rarely exceeded $40,000 annually. He customarily declined a government salary as president and paid his own expenses, including those covering White House entertainment.[7]

In consolidating his cabinet, Hoover had assembled men of strong executive experience. Two were holdovers from the Coolidge administration, Labor Secretary James J. Davis and Treasury Secretary Andrew Mellon. Hoover appeased the business wing of the party with Mellon,

yet he also installed men who would faithfully implement his own policies, such as Ray Lyman Wilbur as interior secretary. Henry L. Stimson,
who held influence in the Republican Party and had previously served
as governor-general of the Philippines, was chosen as secretary of state,
though Hoover would often prefer the advice of Ogden Mills, an assistant secretary of the treasury, and William R. Castle Jr., the undersecretary of state. The secretary of war, James W. Good, had served as a
congressman from Iowa and held a seat on the House Appropriations
Committee. He served only eight months in the cabinet before his death
and was replaced by Patrick J. Hurley. For navy secretary, Hoover named
Charles Francis Adams, scion of a family that had produced two presidents, and later lamented not appointing him as secretary of state.
Hoover deemed Attorney General William D. Mitchell, a Democrat who
had been Coolidge's solicitor general, quite able. Walter Folger Brown,
who had worked for Hoover at Commerce and shared his boss's interest
in government reorganization, was selected for postmaster general, and
Arthur M. Hyde, former governor of Missouri and an old friend of
Hoover's, was appointed as secretary of agriculture. Robert P. Lamont,
an engineer and businessman, was appointed as secretary of commerce.
Hoover later said he regretted the choice because Lamont lacked initiative and imagination.

While legislation originated with the president or Congress, the cabinet worked at a tactical level, fleshing out, refining, and implementing
policy. At meetings, cabinet members usually reached a consensus on
major questions and then closed ranks before announcing programs,
which was usually left to Hoover. Assembling weekly, they vetted the
most significant topics, and everyone was encouraged to contribute. No
written minutes were taken. Hoover worked without notes, drawing
upon his precise memory.

The Hoover administration's first eight months were a whirlwind of
reform that indicates what might have been accomplished had the Great
Depression not intervened. There had been a paucity of meaningful
domestic reform for nearly a generation. Wilson's second term had been

preoccupied with the war, while Harding was unfit to engineer reform and Coolidge opposed it by principle. Hoover, however, moved rapidly, implementing new policies and issuing executive orders that laid the foundation for legislation. He planned conferences to study child health care, conservation, and law enforcement, and he commissioned studies on recent social and economic trends to explore his ideas for social and economic improvements.[8]

Over Andrew Mellon's objections, Hoover urged legislation graduating income taxes more steeply, placing a lower burden on the poor and middle classes. He expanded civil service throughout the government and worked to expand the acreage of federal parks and forests. To head the federal prison system, he recruited Sanford Bates, a veteran prison reformer, who made the system more humane, emphasizing rehabilitation and the potential for parole, treating women and minorities more fairly, and reducing overcrowding. Hoover canceled oil leases on federal lands, which had been perpetrated during the Harding scandals, and he instructed Walter Newton to compile a plan to reorganize the federal bureaucracy that could be translated into legislation.[9]

Three months later Hoover requested a law creating a strong Federal Power Commission to regulate interstate transmission and rates of electricity. He also sought to regulate railroad rates and to reorganize and stabilize the banking system. Hoover believed in firm and fair regulation of business and was a long-established opponent of monopoly, which he believed strangled competition and drained dry the incentives vital to productive free enterprise. He placed the interests of consumers above the profits of businessmen. During his tenure in the White House, the Justice Department instigated antitrust suits against such leading industrial giants as Radio Corporation of America, General Electric, and Westinghouse. In fact, more antitrust suits were filed under Hoover than under any previous president. During the 1932 presidential campaign, Franklin D. Roosevelt would even advocate relaxation of Hoover's stringent regulation of big business.

Hoover used the moral leadership of the presidency to protect the nation's most vulnerable citizens, including children, women, Native Americans, and African Americans. During the 1920s, he had been instrumental in founding the American Child Health Association, and he remained their most visible advocate in the White House. For many years he supported a constitutional amendment outlawing child labor, which was passed by Congress but never ratified by the states. He embraced causes important to women, including suffrage and women's participation in politics. Hoover sought to improve the well-being of Native Americans, nearly doubling appropriations for the Bureau of Indian Affairs and appointing administrators sympathetic to their needs. Native American health and educational facilities were improved substantially, and Interior Secretary Wilbur became a leading proponent of the preservation of native traditions, religions, crafts, and lifestyles. In race relations, Hoover invited black educator Robert R. Moton to lunch in the White House and increased appropriations for Howard University, a federally funded black college in Washington, DC. In addition, the president gave more urgency to labor reform, defending the right of labor to organize and to strike if necessary.[10]

One of the most contentious issues throughout the 1920s was the enforcement of Prohibition. Hoover doubted the law's enforceability and questioned its constitutionality.[11] Nonetheless, Hoover considered it his duty as president to implement all laws as a matter of principle, and he became the only chief executive of the Prohibition era who made a good-faith effort to stiffen enforcement. The most certain way to ensure the repeal of an unpopular law, he felt, was to enforce it strictly, motivating citizens to advocate for repeal.

Viewing Prohibition as a law enforcement issue, he moved responsibility from the Treasury to the Justice Department, placed agents under civil service, and discouraged the use of firearms so as to protect innocent bystanders. Eventually, his reforms led to the FBI's arrest of the nation's most notorious mobster, Al Capone, on charges of income tax evasion. Privately, the president believed that the dry era was doomed.

The chief problem in federal enforcement was that federal officials could intercept and prosecute only interstate commerce. States were responsible for bootlegging committed within their own borders, but they possessed neither the will nor the resources to arrest and incarcerate offenders. An army of agents was needed to impose the amendment, the president felt. Despite his reluctance to discuss the problem openly, Hoover spoke with GOP leaders to persuade them that the law was impractical.[12]

Hoover's concern with law enforcement extended beyond Prohibition to comprehensive legal, judicial, and prison reform. During his inaugural address he had pledged to form a commission to study these problems and recommend solutions. On May 29, 1929, he appointed a Commission on Law Observance and Enforcement chaired by President Taft's former attorney general, George W. Wickersham. The commission thoroughly probed numerous aspects of the legal system and wrote a series of detailed reports, but its findings had little influence on public policy.[13]

Shortly after his inauguration, Hoover met with House and Senate leaders to discuss the agenda for the special session. His first priority was farm relief, he explained, followed by a slightly increased tariff to protect farmers against the low cost of foreign labor. American farmers, who made up 30 percent of the population, had not shared in 1920s prosperity, when supply outweighed demand. Hoover had sought to restore that balance as commerce secretary, yet now he intended to go further. He wanted to reduce transportation costs of farm products by reorganizing railroads for efficiency and creating a waterway system for bulk traffic. A system of farm cooperatives, operating via loans and technical advice from the government, would help individual farmers combine, akin to industrial enterprises. They could pool their resources to negotiate down the goods they bought and bargain up the produce they sold. Aided by loans, they could construct grain elevators to keep nonperishable crops off the market, releasing them incrementally rather than flooding the market and depressing prices at harvesttime. A Federal Farm Board of eight members, appointed by the president along commodity lines, plus the agriculture secretary as an ex officio member, would provide technical and organizational expertise, yet the individual commodity-oriented cooperatives, pyramided from the local to the national level, would be owned and run by farmers themselves, who would formulate policy. It was not ideal for farmers—the solution was incomplete—but it was an improvement. These attempts to nationalize farming without stepping beyond constitutional boundaries made common sense, especially when combined with Hoover's schemes to diversify farming and phase marginal lands out of cultivation and plant them with cover crops.

Ironically, the chief opposition to the measure came from farm-state senators the tariff was intended to benefit, such as Smith Brookhart of Iowa and William E. Borah of Idaho. Fashioning themselves "Progressives"—conservative Republicans termed them "insurgents"—they often voted as a bloc against administration policies, focusing on legislation related to their farm constituents. Individuals such as Borah were spellbinding orators who attracted headlines out of proportion to the significance of their small electorates, some less populous than a single big-city ward. Insurgents countered Hoover's plan for cooperative marketing conflicted with a plan to pay export debentures on farm products, which would increase exports and raise farm prices to a higher level than collectives. Hoover complained that most of the debenture payments would go to middlemen rather than to farmers, exacerbating overproduction, and also precipitate trade wars when Americans tried to undersell foreign nations on their own domestic agricultural markets. The debate grew more heated than Hoover had expected, an eruption of political gamesmanship directed at a new president who wanted to be a collegial leader, not a bully. In the end, Hoover got what he wanted in the farm bill, minus the proposals he opposed. The president signed the Agricultural Marketing Act on June 16, 1929. During ordinary times, it might have mitigated the toil of American farmers, but it was not destined to function during ordinary times.[14]

If the farm bill had been a struggle, the tariff sparked outright war. Hoover had conceived a moderate tariff on farm goods to help protect farmers from lower pay scales for farm labor abroad. Yet the chief problem in agriculture was not foreign competition, but oversupply. Mandatory crop limitations were the only certain solution but would have been difficult to enforce.[15] In addition, tariffs, which involved many commodities and regional interests, were the richest source of pork in Congress. Congressmen demanded favors and horse-traded with other leaders in return for higher rates to satisfy their own constituents. Hoover attempted to remove politics from the equation with his intention to appoint a powerful Tariff Commission to raise or lower rates without congressional oversight, but for parochially oriented congressmen, the more politics in the tariff, the better.[16]

In this first session of his term, Hoover did not believe it would be necessary to summon individual congressmen to the White House to lobby them, much less offer them patronage plums for votes. Previous presidents had done this only rarely, with little success. Rather, Hoover focused his efforts on party leaders, certain committee chairmen, and the officers of the House and Senate, as well as small groups of congressmen. Aides and members of the Republican National Committee conveyed the president's wishes further.

The final measure, known as the Smoot-Hawley Tariff, had become almost an afterthought by the time it passed in June 1930, long after the stock market crash of October 1929 had stolen its thunder.[17] In the end, the bill did more harm than good. Hoover's Tariff Commission did not prove a powerful tool in ameliorating high rates. What's more, though the Senate had attached 1,253 amendments to the House measure, it had been stripped of the Farm Bloc's debenture. Perhaps most important, the levy impacted only 4.2 percent of American trade. The diminution in foreign trade in later years stemmed largely from diminished purchasing power worldwide. Neither did it incite trade wars. Other nations had leapfrogged America in erecting tariff walls.[18] Still, Hoover would have been wise to veto the Smoot-Hawley Tariff, and wiser yet not to have introduced the issue at all.

As the Smoot-Hawley debates raged, President Hoover again attempted to implement his agenda of bold social reforms. On September 28, 1929, Hoover invited a group of life insurance executives to the White House to discuss a new program to provide old-age pensions for American workers. Essentially an early draft of Social Security, Hoover's reforms differed in several respects from the program enacted in 1935, and in some regards might have been superior. Premiums would be paid yearly in a lump sum of less than $500 beginning at birth, with parents or guardians assuming the responsibility until their child became a wage earner. At the age of sixty-five, a citizen would begin receiving $50 per month. Premiums paid by those who died prior to age sixty-five would be placed in a pool and used to supplement funds available to other retirees. Those in the system would receive a flat fee; there would be no graduated scale based on previous earnings. Only those who actually needed the stipend would receive money, excluding the wealthy.

Extensive research by government staffers and private social scientists had preceded the meeting. Some of Hoover's associates traveled to Europe to investigate retirement programs there. A corpus of actuarial data was drawn from the information furnished by Hoover's Research Committee on Social Trends. The conferees agreed to build in a system to adjust income to inflation. In this plan, unlike the plan enacted in 1935, the government would not have been permitted to borrow from the fund. Unfortunately, the president's meeting with insurance executives was ill timed. Planned during the prosperous 1920s, Hoover's program was impossible to implement during the difficulties of the 1930s. Hoover and the insurance companies soon postponed the program until the return of better times. He hoped to complete the project during a second term.[19]

Hoover had also devised a strategy for public and private cooperation to insure workers against unemployment, a complement to Social Security with many of the same features. Under his plan, the states would distribute the stipends, which would be derived from annuities sold to workers or en bloc to businesses by the major life insurance companies. While at the Commerce Department, Hoover made headway in stirring interest in the plan, and several studies were produced by social scientists employed by the Metropolitan Life Insurance Company, demonstrating that such a program was feasible. The state legislature of New York, where the major life insurance companies were located, disapproved of the plan, as did the American Federation of Labor and the National Association of Manufacturers. After he became New York governor in 1928, Franklin D. Roosevelt also expressed reservations. The idea was eventually thwarted by the onset of the Great Depression. During the 1920s, when most people were employed, insurance companies had difficulty selling unemployment insurance. By the 1930s, the unemployment problem had swollen to such dimensions that no private company was willing to invest in marketing such securities. Nonetheless, this marks another example of the degree to which Hoover was more often ahead of his times than behind them.[20]

Indeed, the Great Depression was to prove to be the greatest crisis Hoover would face as president. Wall Street, a narrow thoroughfare in lower Manhattan framed by towering buildings, had become the symbol, if not the sole substance, of American economic might. Thanks largely to America's financial prowess, the United States had emerged from the Great War as the world's largest creditor, the hub of technology and banking, and the leading industrial supplier. Wages rose steadily while unemployment fell, creating the world's highest standard of living. In the lush years from 1922 to 1929, America's economy had reached a height of prosperity unknown to previous generations. Pockets of poverty still existed in the South, the Appalachian uplands, and other rural areas, yet the nation's economic future appeared bright. President Hoover appeared to have waded into a swiftly flowing economic stream. Neither he nor anyone else appreciated that it was filled with piranhas.[21]

The centerpiece of Wall Street was the New York Stock Exchange, a neoclassical temple where stocks and bonds were traded. On the trading floor, corporations, employing brokers as middlemen, sold stocks to investors, who in turn could resell their stock to third parties. As the nation's economy strengthened after the war, stock trading flourished. Theoretically, a stock's value was based on the issuing company's present, or even its future, value. Yet throughout the decade, many investors engaged in speculation, the act of acquiring stock not for its value, but to take advantage of price fluctuations. Speculators were intent on profiting from a timely resale of stock rather than on making an investment in a business. Thus, speculation could often drive the price of a stock up out of proportion to its actual value. During the bull market of the 1920s, speculation became the norm on Wall Street, with some speculators amassing tremendous wealth. During this period, about 15 million Americans, many of whom had no experience in business, waded into the stock market. Some observers believed the nation had entered a new era that replaced the boom-and-bust cycles of the past with permanent prosperity. Yet many industry leaders watched the trading and speculation with growing concern. By July 1929, some of the nation's most eminent businessmen—including Joseph P. Kennedy, Bernard Baruch, and Herbert Hoover—began to quietly divest themselves of stocks. What concerned the advance guard of the business community was that a psychology of anxiety had begun to grip the business world.[22]

On September 3, 1929, the Dow Jones Industrial Average, the yardstick of Wall Street's performance, reached 386.10 and closed at 381.17. Although no one perceived it at the time, the Dow would not equal that peak for more than twenty-five years. The market gyrated wildly throughout September, falling only to recover. In October the trend plunged steadily and steeply downward. On October 23, some 16 million shares were dumped, and for some stocks no buyers could be found at any price. About $4 billion was lost that day as confusion reigned on the NYSE trading floor. Most believed this decline, like previous crashes, was temporary. President Hoover refused to comment directly on the market, saying only that the economy as a whole was sound. On October

25, a group of prominent bankers, attempting to slow the market's death spiral, pooled their money and bought falling shares, providing a temporary respite. Yet they had little faith in their own hedge, and at the end of the day they secretly placed some shares back on the market. On Tuesday, October 29, there was a devastating sell-off of 23.5 million shares. Since September 1, the value of shares had declined by $18 billion. Some people, such as Secretary Mellon and British economist John Maynard Keynes, proclaimed the losses salutary because they would purge the economy of unsound businesses, leaving only the healthy ones. In the wake of past crashes, the federal government had not acted, and there were few calls for action now. Congressmen pondered the political implications of the sell-off, blind to the long-term effects on the nation. The hemorrhaging continued, and by mid-November the market had lost some $26 billion, about one-third of its September value.[23]

Despite the staggering financial loss, no economist or historian has been able to establish a direct cause-and-effect relationship between the crash and the ten-year Depression that followed. Just as easy credit facilitated the crash but did not render it inevitable, Wall Street's failure did not make a global, decade-long Depression inevitable. Initially, it seemed the panic would pass. By the end of 1929 the crash seemed like an aberration, or at least a normal adjustment to overvalued securities, the downswing of a pendulum that had swung too high. During the first half of 1930, planning for the London Naval Disarmament Conference was the major news story, not the deepening economic Depression. No major bank or company had failed. Even in hindsight, it is possible to interpret the stock market as simply a barometer that measures one index of business activity, rather than a cause that predetermines activity. Most expected the business decline to emulate the Harding recession of 1920–22, when the unemployment rate peaked at 5 million. Yet following the October 29 crash, jobless estimates show a downturn that initially moved at a slower rate, from 2.7 million in 1929 to about 4 million in mid-1930.

The catastrophe, however, was worldwide, not simply American made. The Great Depression was actually a series of segregated yet interconnected events in different parts of the world. The London market, which experienced stock speculation similar to that conducted in New York, had crashed a month prior to the Wall Street disaster. The National Bureau of Economic Research showed that eleven nations preceded the United States into the Depression, and eight others were destabilized approximately simultaneously.

James T. Shotwell, a social and economic historian, observed that the Great War had been the chief precipitating factor for the worldwide downturn. "Indeed, it is hardly too much to say that the world-wide economic depression is the last battle of the World War itself."[24] The war had seen prices for natural resources such as metals and foodstuffs soar by 146 percent. When the conflict ended, prices fell, but the enormous debts incurred had to be repaid. Adding to the balance were trade restrictions, defaults on gold payments by struggling governments, and hoarding of precious metals by private citizens. During the first years after the war, trade was driven by a need for replenishment, and the world's producers were slow to overtake demand. This inspired temporary prosperity at the cost of long-term stability and steady, even growth. In America, demand raced ahead of supply, but ultimately supply caught up.[25]

In Washington, President Hoover quickly recognized the dangers of the crash on Wall Street. Fearing that it represented more than an ordinary slump, he "determined that the Federal government should use all of its powers." In an attempt to arrest the deflationary spiral before it could fasten its grip on the economy, Hoover scheduled a series of private conferences with leaders from various sectors of the economy. In the first meeting, held at the White House on November 19, the president, along with cabinet members, convened with railroad executives, who agreed to maintain and even accelerate maintenance and the laying of tracks. They also agreed to avoid wage cuts in exchange for no-strike pledges from unions. On the morning of November 21, in a discussion with business leaders, the president exacted promises to avoid wage cuts and layoffs and, if necessary, to reduce the workweek in order to spread employment. This was crucial to preserve consumption, which powered the economy. Any reductions would have to come from profits, not jobs—Hoover did not consider labor a commodity to be liquidated. Some twenty-two executives agreed to implement Hoover's requests to maintain wages at current levels. Before adjourning, Henry Ford guaranteed to grant wage increases to 150,000 employees of the Ford Motor Company. On November 22, the president summoned a meeting of leaders in the building and construction industries. They agreed to maintain their building schedule to save jobs. The following day he telegraphed all forty-eight governors and the mayors of major cities, urging them to expedite the pace of the public works to avert unemployment.[26] They agreed.

Soon after, Hoover met with labor leaders, who agreed to abstain from wage-increase demands and from striking. William Green, the president of the American Federation of Labor, concurred that wages should be stabilized at least until 1930. As a result, real wages, for those sufficiently fortunate to retain their jobs, would have more purchasing power due to deflated dollars. Next, Hoover met with the directors of the Farm Board, who attempted to stave off a collapse of the commodities market, and chairmen of the federal land banks, along with the leaders of national farm organizations. Hoover then conferred with leaders of the public utilities industry, who agreed, with the exception of the insolent Samuel Insull, to cooperate with the president's program. Hoover asked his former assistant from the Food Administration and the Commerce Department, Julius Barnes, to create an executive committee of businessmen who could exert pressure to ensure that the agreements were implemented. On December 5, 1929, Barnes assembled the National Business Survey Conference in Washington, consisting of four hundred leading industrialists and financiers, to brainstorm about stabilizing business and enforcing the president's guidelines. Meanwhile, Hoover opened the spigots of credit. The Federal Reserve System combated deflation by reducing its rediscount rate to member banks and by undertaking open-market operations. It also began to reject rediscounts to banks that used loans to finance speculation.[27]

Such actions as persuading employers to preempt unemployment and stabilize labor relations had never before been attempted during a decline. Hoover was largely successful in eliminating strikes; his administration presided over a time of unusual labor peace. The prodding had tangible as well as psychological effects. Power companies increased their construction by $110 million over the previous year, while rail companies boosted theirs by $345 million and gas companies by $428 million above 1928. Moreover, the telephone and telegraph companies spent substantially more on repair and expansion. Altogether, the conclaves resulted in more than $1 billion in additional capital expenditures. Stocks also regained some of their lost ground. From mid-November through the final conference in early December, industrial stocks regained nearly three-fourths of their diminished value.[28]

While encouraging private efforts, Hoover also launched large-scale public works at the federal level. In January 1930 he authorized the initiation of work on the Boulder Dam costing $60 million, and asked Congress for $500 million for the construction of public buildings. In addition, $75 million was authorized for work on highways. Hoover stated that it was the responsibility of the federal government to partially take up the slack in construction during hard times. Since his tenure as secretary of commerce he had advocated such a rainy-day fund. Congress agreed, sometimes grudgingly. The chief criticism on Capitol Hill was not that Hoover was doing too little, too late, but that he was overreaching, attempting too much, too soon. Historian Robert Sobel noted that in 1929 Hoover "proved a more activist president than any since the wartime activities of Wilson and Lincoln." Sobel added, "Indeed, no peacetime president since Jefferson had done more to expand the power of the presidency in that one year."[29] "No one in his place could have done more," the New York Times wrote that spring. "Very few of his predecessors could have done as much." The *New York Herald Tribune* described the president's leadership as "cool and superlative."[30]

Some historians argue that both Hoover and, to a greater degree, Franklin D. Roosevelt prolonged the Depression by meddling in the economic cycle. Hoover himself was fiscally conservative in comparison with Roosevelt, but temperamentally he was an activist and was disposed to alleviate human suffering. Well-read in history and having lived and worked abroad, he also knew that economic desperation inspires political instability that often culminates in totalitarianism. Hoover did not believe that government alone could legislate or spend its way out of a depression. Yet his first priorities following the crash were to preserve social order and alleviate suffering. Still, Hoover considered it ill-advised to create a government bureaucracy that would prove perpetual after the emergency ended. He preferred decisive policy implemented by decentralized means that tapped voluntary goodwill at the grass roots.[31]

His presidency still young, coping with the shock of the stock market crash and the nation's downward spiral into depression, Hoover now faced a contentious appointment to the U.S. Supreme Court. On February 9, 1930, Chief Justice William Howard Taft resigned his seat due to ill health. The same day, Hoover announced the nomination of Charles Evans Hughes, one of the most distinguished Republicans. Hughes, a former governor of New York, had served on the Supreme Court for nearly six years before resigning to become the GOP candidate for president in 1916. Defeated by Woodrow Wilson, he later served as secretary of state under Harding and Coolidge. There were no blemishes on his record, nor any scandals in his closet. Yet opposition to Hughes hardened among the insurgent Republican clique along personal and ideological grounds. Some of the criticism of Hughes, impassioned if not unbiased, was indirectly aimed at Hoover. The insurgents, in alliance with some Democrats, claimed that Hughes was an opulent, conservative elitist, a crony of the aristocracy, and an attorney for big corporations who would orient the Court to the right. Hughes, they asserted, was an effete intellectual who did not understand dirt farmers, had never soiled his hands, and flitted among the corporate boardrooms of the Northeast. Aligned against Hughes were such GOP mavericks as Robert La Follette Jr. of Wisconsin, who had not voted for GOP legislation a single time during Hoover's term; George Norris, who had supported Al Smith in 1928 and had cast only one vote for a Hoover measure in the Senate; Hiram Johnson, the president's old archenemy still smarting from Hoover's sidetracking of his bid for the GOP nomination in 1920; and Hoover's new archenemy, William E. Borah, a silver-tongued though bellicose orator. Nonetheless, the insurgents and their Democratic allies could generate more noise than votes due to Hughes's impeccable character and distinguished record. Ideologically, Hughes could not be pigeonholed. He was not actually a conservative but a moderate liberal who had cleaned up New York City, defended Socialists expelled from the New York legislature for their beliefs, and refused to permit party bosses to map out his 1916 campaign against Wilson. Ultimately, Hughes's nomination prevailed 56–26 in the Senate. Eleven of the dissenters were Republicans.[32]

Hoover's next battle over a Supreme Court appointment occurred not long afterward and proved even more contentious than the polemics over Hughes. On March 8, 1930, Edward Terry Sanford, the only Southerner on the bench, died. The president wanted to replace him with another Southerner, particularly one from a circuit court district that had gone unrepresented for numerous years. Attorney General Mitchell perused possible nominees and recommended forty-four-year-old John J. Parker of North Carolina, a state Hoover had narrowly carried in 1928. Despite his youth, Parker was considered fair and highly intelligent and received endorsements from six former presidents, as well as the sitting president, of the American Bar Association. Although a Republican, Parker received the backing of ten Southern Democratic senators and seven Democratic governors. The jurist, who had never held elective office, had served as a special assistant to the U.S. attorney general under Coolidge from 1923 to 1925 before being elevated to the Federal Fourth Circuit Court. Opposition arose from two powerful interest groups, the

AFL and the NAACP, both of which believed Parker might prove inimical to their interests. The AFL pointed to a case in which Parker had voted with the majority to uphold the legitimacy of a "yellow dog" contract requiring job applicants to pledge not to join a labor union as a condition of employment. Parker argued that he was not antilabor; he had merely followed judicial precedent. The Supreme Court had upheld a similar contract and any contrary lower court ruling would be summarily overturned. Nevertheless, the AFL mobilized its membership to exert pressure on industrial state senators to oppose Parker. The NAACP launched a campaign against Parker as well, arguing that no white Southerner could be a fair judge. Moreover, in 1920, while running for a state office, Parker had reputedly denied being an integrationist when baited, though any white Southerner with hope of winning would have been forced to respond as such in a state in which the voting public was exclusively white. Moreover, some senators, and their constituents, did not want a truly independent thinker on the bench who examined the evidence case by case and voted on its individual merits. While Hughes's stature had enabled him to overcome the opposition, Parker had neither the stature nor the experience.[33]

The GOP insurgents alone could not block Parker's nomination; they could only make it ugly. Yet many Republican regulars who normally backed the administration joined the objectors. Senators representing states where the AFL or the NAACP wielded considerable clout resorted to self-preservation over loyalty to the president. Concerned with their own reelection prospects if they defied these potent interest groups, they weighed the odds and calculated that they had nothing to gain by voting for Parker. Meanwhile, Parker remained silent, considering it improper to lobby for a Supreme Court appointment, though he issued a letter defending his record. A more aggressive effort by Hoover might have tipped the scales in his favor. He did persuade several wavering senators, but on May 7 Parker's nomination was defeated 41–39. If the president had persuaded one more senator to vote for his nominee, a tie would have resulted, permitting Vice President Curtis to cast the deciding vote and ensuring the confirmation. It was a major setback for Hoover; such a defeat had not been inflicted on a president since the second administration of Grover Cleveland thirty-six years earlier.[34]

Though humiliated, Hoover maintained a dignified silence. The *New York Times* pointed out the hypocrisy of Southern Democrats, themselves white supremacists who voted against Parker to embarrass the president, even if it made a fellow Southerner the sacrificial lamb.[35] The *Minneapolis Journal* took aim at Senator Borah. "The Borahs of the Senate want no Supreme Court appointee whose opinion on a controversial subject will be formed after he has examined the subject," the daily wrote. "They want a man whose opinion in a given controversy they can pretty well guess in advance."[36] An editorial in the *New York Herald Tribune* punctured the Senate's cynical rhetoric: "An argument might have been made that the president should have appointed a more experienced jurist. A counterargument could have commended Parker as one of the ablest members in the circuit court system. Yet neither argument was made." Instead, the paper continued, the Senate "seemed chiefly intent on demonstrating once more its ability to rank among the pettiest deliberative bodies in the world."[37]

Following the Parker setback, the president nominated a safe successor, Owen J. Roberts, a Philadelphia attorney who had spent most of his career in private practice and had won every case he argued before the Supreme Court. He was one of two attorneys, along with Atlee Pomerene of Ohio, who had been appointed counsel for the government by President Coolidge to prosecute the oil scandals that had occurred during Harding's administration. After the bitter fight over Parker's nomination, Roberts, a moderately conservative Republican, was confirmed by the Senate within one minute after his name was presented to the upper chamber, without even a roll call.[38] Nearly two years later, Hoover again faced a Supreme Court nomination battle, yet fortunately this one fared as easily as Roberts's had. On February 15, 1932, Benjamin Cardozo, a liberal Jewish Democrat from New York, reached the bench with negligible opposition. Cardozo had not been Hoover's first choice—he had intended to appoint Attorney General Mitchell to the slot and move Patrick Hurley to Justice, but Mitchell was lukewarm about the idea. Hoover had been impressed by Cardozo's intellect and impressive service on the Wickersham Committee and felt he could be easily confirmed. Roberts and Cardozo both had noncontroversial stints on the Supreme Court and joined the ranks of distinguished jurists.[39]

NINE

Holding a Finger in the Dike

President Hoover had hoped October 29, 1929, would mark the end of America's economic dive. Instead, it was only the beginning. The upswing he expected in the spring of 1930 did not occur, and during the summer conditions worsened. Ahead lay a bitter winter. On the heels of the stock calamity came unemployment, and along with it declining production and deflation. The market, which had once seemed to have no top, now appeared bottomless. In September 1929 the Dow Average reached 381.7. By the end of October it staggered down to 247.6; by April it edged upward to 257.3; then it was down to 196.1 by January 1930 and finally to 116.6 in January 1932, the last full year of Hoover's term. At their lowest point, stocks declined to 85 in late 1932.[1]

As the Depression deepened, many realized that hard times would last longer than the 1921–22 recession had. Because the market slump was paralleled by soaring unemployment, which would leap to almost 25 percent before Hoover left office, many people believed the crash caused the unemployment and other symptoms of the Depression, and they blamed the Hoover administration for all the hardship. The president was chastised for his earlier optimistic efforts to buoy the spirits of the people, and the press grew nasty and increasingly personal. As the fall 1930 congressional elections approached, GOP political prospects dimmed.

Hunger, if not starvation, became commonplace throughout the nation. Despite the condemnation of the president's response, Hoover's critics were still not united behind any program to address the hunger crisis. The chief political issue seemed to be whether relief should be funneled through private charities and the states, or from the top down from the federal level. The chief executive pointed out that the private and local levels had an existing efficient infrastructure and more experience, all of which could be mobilized rapidly and distributed equitably and would skim less overhead than an unwieldy, quickly cobbled-together federal bureaucracy.[2]

Hoover had demonstrated this local approach in his work with the CRB, the ARA, and the Food Administration. Traditionally, the distribution of food, clothing, and shelter for those in need had been conducted by churches, temples, the Red Cross, Community Chests, the Salvation Army, and numerous other groups specifically designed to aid the needy on the basis of public donations. The chief executive felt he could stimulate their work without usurping it. The President's Emergency Committee for Employment (PECE), from October 1930 to its end in April 1931, made significant improvements by complementing the work of private charities. For example, charitable spending in New York rose from $9 million in 1930 to $58 million in 1932. Private charities exclusive of the government-inspired philanthropies expanded their donations from $4.5 million to $21 million over the same span. Direct relief was not the only item on Hoover's agenda, only the most urgent one. He planned to wage the war against the Depression along all fronts but did not intend to indulge in overkill, whether rhetorical, which he considered demagogic, or financial, because resources were finite.[3]

By the fall of 1930, unemployment had increased to about 5 million, leaving one in every nine workers jobless. Hoover responded by appointing Colonel Arthur Woods as chairman of PECE. Following the war, Woods, a former New York City police commissioner, had helped place returning veterans in jobs and had played a major role in orchestrating the 1921 Conference on Unemployment. Thirty leading citizens comprised an advisory committee, and some three thousand local committees were created to assess the needs of their communities. Woods was thoroughly dedicated. On a single day, he telephoned the governors of forty-five states and ascertained their needs for the coming winter, as well as resources on hand. His preliminary survey showed the highest pockets of unemployment existed in the industrial cities of the Northeast and Midwest. Woods appointed divisional representatives who traveled within their geographical regions and reported on needs and efforts being made. The central office collected information, devised strategies for stretching out employment, and assisted local authorities in planning distribution of relief. The local committees also undertook a house-by-house survey of necessities and local resources available. The vast majority of governors declined federal assistance. The local reports showed that many companies were complying with the president's requests. They promised to rehire when the economy improved, and they offered loans, grants, and free or subsidized shelter when available. There were many contributions in kind, including food, clothing, fuel, medical care, rent, and loans. This aid mitigated ill feeling against employers. The Woods committee encouraged small local projects as well as larger ones. It launched a program to inspire Americans to make home repairs and asked the states to approve some $450 million in state bonds that would create construction jobs. Woods requested a congressional appropriation of $750 million in grants to the states, though Hoover, who felt Congress would reject this enormous sum, reduced it to $150 million, and Congress cut it even further to $117 million. At this point, unemployment was still around the level of the Harding recession. Walter S. Gifford, president of American Telephone and Telegraph, resigned from the committee, discouraged by the lack of progress. He was succeeded in the spring of 1930 by his able vice chairman, Fred Croxton. In August 1931 PECE's responsibility and a portion of its personnel were transferred to the President's Organization on Unemployment Relief (POUR) under Gifford's leadership. Gifford appointed a committee of one hundred prominent leaders of business, labor, and industry to his advisory board. Subcommittees under Fred Croxton, Owen D. Young, and James R. Garfield planned expansion and coordination of relief.[4]

As the Depression swirled downward like a whirlpool, Hoover might have felt the world settling upon his shoulders. Legend holds that one group of ancient Greeks believed the earth rested on the back of an ancient turtle. Once, when someone had the audacity to ask what lay beneath the turtle, a precocious wit responded that it was "turtles all the way down." As the Depression worsened, it might have been appropriate for the chief executive to fear it was "Hoover all the way down." The president had numerous critics in Congress, but until the election year 1932 approached, there was no interconnected, positive program in opposition to his plans for combating the economic downslide. Initially, the president preferred to handle direct relief at the local and state levels. Local officials knew the needs of their people best. Decentralization avoided adding another layer of bureaucracy between the people and the benefits; it was swifter and more efficient. In addition, it was less likely to be politicized and to generate the type of scandals that had occurred under the Harding administration. Hoover did not believe in trading relief checks or federal jobs for votes and feared that this would happen on a massive scale on the federal level, as it had already happened in some large cities. Nor did he believe that federal aid would be distributed impartially. On February 5, 1930, he praised a group of Community Chest fund-raisers he had brought to the White House and lauded their selflessness. "Their great purpose," he said, "is the handling with large vision of the obligations of a whole city to its less fortunate residents." The president said the Community Chest provided skill in fund-raising as well as freedom from prejudice.[5] The administration sent out cabinet officers and the president himself to participate in fund-raising for private charities. These drives raised hundreds of millions of dollars and continued throughout Hoover's tenure. The National Association of Community Chests and Councils ended its 1931 drive on Thanksgiving Day with 131 cities having raised $45,694,387.[6]

Despite reservations, Hoover was willing to have the federal government step in and convert from loans to direct grants if his grassroots approach proved insufficient. But he wanted to try decentralization first, to determine whether or not it was practical. He considered decentralized government democratic. He did not want to increase his own power or that of the executive branch at the expense of state and local governments and individual citizens. His experience in relief efforts had demonstrated that decentralization worked well. Moreover, as a profound idealist reared in a Quaker environment, where all men were literally considered brothers, and having lived worldwide and immersed himself in American history, the president believed that the American people were the most generous people in the world and would take care of their neighbors. Hoover's reputation as a humanitarian sprang from the moral concept that giving not only helps the needy; it ennobles the giver. "A cold and distant charity which puts out its sympathy only through the tax collector yields a very meager dole of unloving and perfunctory sympathy," he wrote.[7] Federal money, on the contrary, meant federal control and some inevitable corruption. Hoover wanted to avoid that if possible. If it became necessary, it would be at best a necessary evil. In 1930 he did not know whether such a contingency would materialize. But his plan was to start with the least drastic remedy and escalate until the problem was solved. "This is not an issue as to whether people shall go hungry or cold in the United States," he explained. "It is solely a question of the best method by which hunger and cold should be prevented."[8] Hoover's fears about public welfare contained at least elements of truth. As historian David Kennedy points out, "He knew that once government aid began, it was likely to create dependency." For any type of government program or contribution, the demand inevitably exceeds the supply, because the demand is infinite.[9] In the twenty-first century, with an extremely widened safety net that would awe Americans of the 1930s, people still go hungry in America—and worldwide.

The subsequent failures of the New Deal to end the Depression and of twenty-first-century administrations to end the Great Recession have made Hoover a prophet. His empathy for human suffering was clear, but for Hoover, decentralization was more than a matter of ideology; it was common sense. Further, he was dubious about the proposition that a government solution existed for every problem. "Economic depression cannot be cured by legislative action or executive pronouncement," he said. "Economic wounds must be healed by the actions of the cells of the economic body—the products and consumers themselves." Still, Hoover ultimately became the most activist president in hard times until 1932 because he felt he had no choice. He said on February 3, 1931, that if state and local resources proved insufficient, "I am willing to pledge myself . . . I will ask the aid of every resource of the federal government."[10] Secretary of State Henry L. Stimson said that Hoover planned to summon a special session of Congress to provide for relief in 1931 if state and local resources proved inadequate. The president himself stated unequivocally that "I am willing to pledge myself that if the time should ever come that the voluntary agencies of the country together with the state and local governments are unable to find resources with which to prevent hunger and suffering in my country, I will ask the aid of every resource of the Federal government because I would no more see starvation amongst our countrymen than would any Senator or Congressman."[11]

Hoover employed every weapon in his fiscal and humanitarian arsenal to combat the Depression, in a multifaceted approach. The Fed, now in agreement with the president on fiscal policy, slashed its rediscount rate during the stock decline, yet fear kept both borrowers and lenders at bay. Both preferred to retain their liquidity rather than take even moderate risks. Near the beginning of 1930 Hoover signed a $160 million tax cut designed to stimulate spending shortly before Christmas. The reductions were highly graduated. Taxes on small incomes were sliced by 66 percent; those on larger incomes, 4 percent; and corporate income levies were pared down by 8.33 percent. Hoover cut taxes while still balancing his initial fiscal budget, including higher appropriations for the Departments of Labor, Commerce, and Agriculture. He reduced appropriations for the army and hoped to save money on the navy by commencing implementation of the London Naval Treaty, then under negotiation. He hoped to redirect funds saved by arms reductions into social and economic programs that would spur domestic growth.[12] Throughout about thirteen years of the New Deal that succeeded Hoover, there was not a single tax reduction intended to stimulate production, commerce, and consumption, although there were several tax increases, whereas billions were devoted to public works.

Unemployment quickly became the president's primary concern. He confessed that "the Presidency is primarily an employment agency to find jobs for 12,000,000 people." As fall and winter approached, the president stepped up a part of his relief package. A major public works program was presented that would not only employ Americans, but result in an enormous array of highways, public buildings, dams, waterways, parks, and beautification projects. Placed where the work was most badly needed, without political considerations, the programs were intended to remunerate the government over time, when possible. For example, farmers would receive loans to build grain elevators in order to sell their produce at peak market value, then repay a part of the loan from their profits. In addition, compensation flowed back to federal coffers from toll roads and bridges, dams that generated and indirectly sold electricity, and buildings that were rented. Some of the projects that were not directly remunerative simply delivered better services to the people, the recreation, and the beautification of Washington, DC.

The federal government provided the impetus, the expertise, and the leadership for these projects, yet in contrast to later federal reactions to economic downturns, Hoover considered the national government a partner with the states and with private enterprise in a coordinated, mutually beneficial effort. The federal government, for example, made obtaining credit easier, to facilitate home construction and business expansion, and the Commerce Department continued to disseminate statistical data as it had done during the 1920s. Hoover still believed that one of the lessons learned from the earlier downturns was that the construction industry was the balance wheel of the economy. While the public works program was masterminded by the president, its implementation relied upon a cabinet committee chaired by Commerce Secretary Robert Lamont and secretaries Davis, Wilbur, Hurley, Hyde, and Eugene Meyer, chair of the Federal Reserve Board. Hoover gave only general directions and left the details of the work to the committee. Beginning in 1930, Hoover initiated the largest public works program in history. The year following the crash, despite some trepidation, construction work in all sectors totaled more than $1 billion above normal. Federal construction alone amounted to $2.4 billion during Hoover's administration. "I do not accept the fatalistic view that the discovery of the means to restrain destructive tendencies is beyond the genius of our people," the president said.[13]

In the longer run, Hoover planned a systematic approach to building projects that lasted well into the future. The administration subsequently added thirty-seven thousand miles of highways and began to construct the Golden Gate Bridge at San Francisco. The federal highway budget doubled between 1930 and 1931 and the number of workers employed on highways nearly tripled by the end of the Hoover administration. Construction began on the scenic Skyline Drive in Shenandoah National Park in Virginia, maximizing hand labor. Workers were employed in national parks and forests in path and trail building, reforestation, and fire prevention. Hoover established federal land banks to reduce farm foreclosures and home loan discount banks to protect homeowners from foreclosure. To aid farmers, Hoover persuaded the Interstate Commerce Commission to order railroads to reduce rail rates for water and forage. More waterway work was done under Hoover than under any other president, a major theme in his public works program, generating jobs in every region. The integrated concept included navigation, flood control, generation of electricity, irrigation, and an interior barge canal system providing cheap transportation for bulk commodities. The federal government had already established a Division of Construction within the Department of Commerce. However, the president often was ahead of Congress in his attempts to increase federal authority to combat the Depression. When Hoover presented legislation to consolidate all federal public works in a Department of Public Works with cabinet status, Congress defeated the measure. By late 1931 Hoover was only beginning to hurtle down the tracks. His head bubbled with additional ideas for thwarting the hard edges of the Depression. Yet many of the more ambitious measures required congressional approval, including greater appropriations, and doubtless some unbalanced budgets, anathema to conventional wisdom. The Founding Fathers built a democracy more adept at preventing abuses than at moving with dispatch during emergencies. It was encumbered with checks and balances and was not built for speed, as Hoover quickly learned.[14]

On December 2, 1930, Hoover delivered his State of the Union address to the 71st Congress with an overview describing his principles of government and the direction in which he wanted to lead the nation. He followed up two days later with his budget address, which was more specific. Upbeat yet restrained, eager to lead yet respectful that his role was to lead, not herd, the president urged an acceleration of government compared to the Harding-Coolidge era, with greater spending and measures designed to nip the Wall Street disaster in the bud. He called for an income tax reduction; prompt completion of work on the tariff left over from the special session, which was creating business uncertainty; reform of the banking system; railroad consolidation; creation of a powerful Federal Power Commission; and extension of civil service to postal employees. He vowed to strive for prison reform, greater economy and efficiency, increased public works, and reorganization of the executive branch.[15]

Herbert Hoover was a fledgling politician thrust into the nation's highest political office, and he felt uncomfortable with the artifice of politics. It is possible to be good at something one does not enjoy, but it rarely comes easily. What drove Hoover to public life was a sense of duty and his belief that the higher the position, the more good he could accomplish.

Though facing America's greatest crisis since the Civil War, Hoover was matched with one of the more contentious Congresses in memory. The Republicans controlled the House and reliably voted with the president. Yet in the Senate, while the GOP held the majority, they did not hold control. Forty-two conservative Republicans clashed with fourteen Progressive Republicans, who frequently voted with the thirty-nine sitting Democrats. Most Progressives were independents who carried individualism to an almost eccentric degree, leaping headfirst into virtually every fray. Troubling all waters, they were significant more for their aggressiveness than for their numbers, as well as for their freewheeling, uninhibited rhetoric and their mercurial temperaments. While the Democrats and Republican regulars voted with their respective blocs, the insurgent Progressives voted unpredictably. They considered Hoover, whose political roots had been sunk as a Theodore Roosevelt "Bull Moose" progressive, as too liberal, perhaps even a radical, a protégé of TR and Wilson.[16]

Though the Wall Street crash occurred during the first session of the 71st Congress, the crisis did not inspire a proliferation of anti-Depression legislation. Senator Robert Wagner, however, became one of the most aggressive combatants against the downturn, often in sympathy with Hoover's objectives. The Democrat from New York initiated legislation to improve the gathering of statistics dealing with unemployment, which Congress passed and Hoover signed. The senator also sponsored a bill earmarking $150 million for public works, which became law, although Hoover knew that additional money would be needed. At times Wagner advocated greater appropriations than the president considered wise. A third bill designed to create unemployment exchanges was vetoed on the grounds that such a federal system already existed. The two men traveled along parallel tracks, but at different speeds.[17]

In addition to economic issues, Congress skirmished over stipends for veterans and reorganization of the Veterans' Bureau. Hoover urged Congress to reorganize the bureau in the interest of efficiency and better service, and he received much of what he wanted. The president removed the Veterans' Bureau from the Interior Department and consolidated all veterans' affairs under a single agency, the Veterans' Administration, which included the Veterans' Bureau, the Pension Bureau, the National Soldiers' Home, and the veterans' hospitals. Five new veterans' hospitals were completed during Hoover's administration. No comparable expansion had taken place since the Civil War. The chief executive encountered problems in dealing with veterans of the Spanish-American War, however. Veterans' lobbyists wanted to include all vets of the war, including those with as little as a single day's service, wealthy veterans who did not need stipends, and those whose disabilities related to their own conduct, such as contraction of venereal disease. The bill erupted into a political volcano. The veterans' lobby voted to defeat any congressman who opposed their version of the bill. Hoover vetoed the more generous version and was sustained by the House. A new, scaled-down law passed both houses easily. This was one of only two bills Hoover vetoed during the 71st Congress.[18]

One of the more contentious issues during the 71st and 72nd Congresses, regional in scope but national in repercussions, concerned a series of nitrate dams and potential fertilizer plants constructed along the Tennessee River in Alabama at a site known as Muscle Shoals. The complex, used to make explosives during the First World War, was no longer needed for munitions, but Senator George Norris of Nebraska, whose own constituents stood to gain or lose nothing by development of the site, wanted the federal government to erect a network of dams to generate electricity for the people of the region. Norris, who hated his fellow Republican in the White House more than any other man in the Senate, was obsessed with Muscle Shoals. In 1923, when Henry Ford offered to lease the site to manufacture fertilizer, Norris had disrupted the project. He feared and detested big business, believing the powerful monopolists would gouge their customers. In contrast, Hoover protested that government bureaucracy, corruption, favoritism, and patronage would undermine the scheme, effectively making Muscle Shoals a corporation with a board of directors consisting of the entire membership of the U.S. House and Senate. Perhaps more important, Norris's plan would discourage private incentives to develop other hydroelectric sites and retard progress overall, because no independent concern could compete with the government. Congress could dip into its till and use taxpayer money collected nationwide to benefit consumers, in carefully chosen parts of the country, who would employ political leverage to lure projects. There was a bit of truth as well as an element of paranoia in each argument. The feud was political and personal, not purely pragmatic. The only difference was over means, not ends. With significant goodwill and artful compromise the problem could have been finessed. But neither rival would budge one centimeter.[19]

Beginning during the summer of 1930, an intense heat wave scorched more than twenty states. In the Ohio, Missouri, and Mississippi valleys, stretching east to Virginia and west to Montana, as well as to the entire Southwest, crops wilted, rivers ran dry, and forest fires raged. Arkansas experienced a span of forty-three days in which the temperature stood above one hundred degrees for all but one. Hoover quickly assembled data from the Agriculture Department and convened a national conference of governors in Washington. The president appointed a national committee to cope with the crisis, chaired by Agriculture Secretary Arthur Hyde. Each governor appointed a state committee, and below each were county and local committees. Hoover established the major priorities of the committees: to maintain public health, to minimize the loss of livestock, and to sustain farm families.[20]

During the inferno of 1930, the Red Cross took up the task of providing food, spending $10 million and sustaining some 2.5 million people. The government focused on rebuilding the economic infrastructure and providing credit and work relief in the crippled regions. Hoover negotiated a 50 percent rate reduction by railroads serving the affected states, which now imported corn and water in bulk. The Federal Farm Board provided $47 million in loans to devastated farmers, 75 percent of which was repaid. Due in part to this aid, there was no mass slaughter of livestock and many farm cooperatives were saved from bankruptcy. Congress appropriated $122 million for highway work in the distressed area, employing chiefly local people. The president accelerated work on waterways, dams, and flood control in the affected states.

Eventually leading to the notorious Dust Bowl of the 1930s, the drought's effects were exacerbated by the fact that it occurred during the Great Depression. With national resources already stretched thin, the president faced massive hardship in many areas simultaneously. Congress debated the amount and type of assistance for two months before enacting an appropriations measure. Powerful senators threatened to hold Hoover's legislative agenda hostage unless he increased appropriations for drought relief in their states, and also tried to pad drought relief with pork-barrel bills. Senator Joseph T. Robinson of Arkansas demanded a large appropriation in the form of a grant to the Red Cross. The Red Cross rejected the offer on the grounds it would compromise their independence as a private organization and undermine their fund-raising. Hoover argued that such an appropriation would invite demands from other politicians during a global financial crisis during which resources were limited.[21]

The fall congressional campaign of 1930 brought the first significant electoral test of Hoover's presidency. In virtually every state, the main issue was Herbert Hoover, who served as a proxy for the weak economy. The Democratic National Committee produced an unrelenting stream of speeches, pamphlets, and radio addresses, which were not only effective in the short run but began the process of embedding Hoover's place in history as an inept, uncaring president. James M. Cox, the Democratic candidate for president back in 1920, blamed Hoover for the stock market crash and added that the Republicans had aggravated conditions by their uncaring arrogance. The GOP, he argued, had then sealed the fate of the Republic by imposing the Smoot-Hawley Tariff. Senator Hugo

Black of Alabama added that the prostrate nation had run out of patience waiting for recovery while Hoover dithered. As the opposing parties tried to pin the labels of "Big Spenders" and "Do Nothings" on each other, Hoover did not campaign in the field, preferring to work through surrogates, but he did dispatch the cabinet to campaign, especially in close states. The Republican National Committee also campaigned in crucial states, as did members of the president's staff and his personal friends. The GOP accused the Democrats of playing politics with human misery and charged that the Democrats could not point to a single law that they were responsible for enacting or repealing during the recent session. Still, Republicans were blamed for the overall downward slide in the economy. During the month prior to the balloting, stocks declined 10 to 15 percent.[22]

The returns of early November showed a virtual tie between the parties. The Republicans suffered serious, though not unexpected, defeats, losing eight seats in the Senate and bringing their total down to forty-eight. Yet some senators officially recorded as Republicans were in fact Western independents who routinely voted Democratic. In the House, which the GOP had controlled prior to the election, each party now held 217 seats, with one Farmer-Laborite who usually voted with the Democrats. In effect, the Democrats were to control both houses. Yet they lacked a titular leader and could not agree on a consistent program to deal with the Depression. They found themselves in the awkward position of having the clout to block or alter Hoover's program but the inability to enact one of their own. This would test the ingenuity of both parties as they strove to relieve the Depression with one eye on the next election.[23]

The short session of the 71st Congress commenced in early December 1930, concluding on March 4, 1931. Prior to the sessions, Democratic leaders met with Hoover and agreed to cooperate when possible in order to avoid the necessity for a special session, which would further destabilize business. Among the Democrats forming the coalition were former presidential candidates James M. Cox, John W. Davis, and Alfred E.

Smith, along with Senate leader Joseph T. Robinson and House veteran John Nance Garner. The leading Democratic Party officials, John J. Raskob and Jouett Shouse, also cooperated. Hoover established his priorities, calling for an additional $100 million in public works—adding to the $500 million already appropriated—plus $30 million for drought relief. Over the longer term, he recommended railroad consolidation, revision of the antitrust legislation, reform of federal power regulation, and restraint on spending. He urged fiscal restraint in order to avert tax increases, which would deter business expansion. Despite his admonitions, Congress enacted a bill permitting vets to borrow up to 50 percent of their Great War bonus, due to mature in 1945, and overrode Hoover's veto. Ironically, in looking ahead, Franklin D. Roosevelt, who had been reelected as governor of New York by a whopping 750,000 votes, consistently protested against the federal government's overspending and unwarranted deficit extension.[24]

In his opening address to the short session on December 3, the president warned that the fight against the downturn had entered a new, more serious stage and that victory would be neither quick nor easy. Hoover placed the Great Depression in an international context, explaining that its origins lay partly in a speculative bubble in America that had diverted capital and enterprise from constructive investments. Yet, he continued, "had over speculation in securities been the only force operating, we would have seen recovery many months ago." The roots were deeper, and they stretched worldwide. Production had fallen below the appetite for consumption, and there were shortages in capital and raw materials globally as national economies writhed to recover from the wounds of the Great War. Political agitation and revolutions toppled tottering regimes in Asia, Russia, Europe, and Latin America, precipitating worldwide financial turmoil, which had affected America. The world had grown increasingly interdependent, rising and falling in unison. The American government could mitigate the effects of the global collapse, but it was unrealistic to imagine that America could completely overcome the debacle independently. "Economic depression cannot be cured by legislative action or executive pronouncement," Hoover argued. "Economic wounds must be healed by the actions of the cells of the economic body—the producers and consumers themselves." A capitalist, consumer-driven economy could not be restored by government spending alone, he cautioned. In a relative sense, "our unemployment has been far less in proportion than in other large industrial countries." Hoover explained that he had a commitment to minimize the suffering, "to see that no deserving person in our country suffers from hunger or cold." The U.S. government had contributed by embarking on the greatest program in history involving construction of waterways, harbors, flood control, public buildings, highways, and airports. He wanted to expand the program prudently without an increase in taxation, which would mean a counterproductive decrease in private employment and consumption. The government could only redistribute wealth; it could not create it. What it gave to some it must first take from someone else.[25]

Near the end of the short session the mood of cooperation was declining. Some Democrats were critical of their own leaders, who had promised to assist the president at the beginning of the session. Hoover was losing control of his own party, too. The independents opposed him on principal and personality. Some, like Borah and Norris, tenaciously held out for regional cure-alls not supported by a majority of the Senate or most of the American people. The insurgents played a "rule or ruin" game. There were serious stylistic differences between the president and many veteran politicians as well. Even the regular Republicans, his nominal allies, wanted special favors in return for allegiance. They groused that the president did not play by the expected rules of rewarding friends and punishing foes; he did not play hardball.[26]

Hoover, perhaps motivated by his Quaker principles, wanted to stand above the fight, but this was impractical. He wanted congressmen to vote on logic and principle, but they were more interested in getting reelected. His refusal to deal in the grittier aspects of politics gave them the impression that he was weak. They could not conceive of a president who wanted to locate public works in areas of the greatest need for

employment rather than trade them for votes. The congressional wing
of the party often placed political expediency over fairness and jostled
for pork-barrel projects in their own districts at a time when money was
tight and need was widespread. Few thought in national terms. Hoover
placed principle above his own political expediency, and he paid a political price.

While navigating the rocky shoals of Congress, the president also had
to juggle international diplomacy. In 1929, he began planning to amend the
agreements of the Washington Naval Conference of 1921, which had set
limits on construction of battleships among the major naval powers. The
president sought to expand the treaty to include all smaller vessels except
submarines, and he called for a conference to include Britain, America,
Japan, France, and Italy, the major sea powers. Preceding the conference,
which convened in London in early 1930, he invited the new British
Labour prime minister, Ramsay MacDonald, also an advocate of naval
arms control, to a preliminary summit conference at Washington. Mac-
Donald arrived on October 4, 1929, was feted as a celebrity at New York
and Washington, and talked one-on-one with Hoover at the president's
idyllic retreat, Camp Rapidan. The two men found common cause while
sitting at opposite ends of a log beneath the fall foliage, adjacent to the
gurgling, trout-rich river. America and Britain, with no conceivable reason
to go to war, were nonetheless engaged in a naval arms race that stretched
dollars and pounds sterling thin during the early days of the Great Depression. The Japanese were also eager to reach an agreement; the French and
Italians decided to attend the conference in London more reluctantly, and
ultimately they did not sign the agreement. France demanded as the
price of its signature an alliance with the United States, meaning a de
facto alliance against Germany, which Hoover knew the American people and their Congress would never accept. On December 7, 1929, Mac-
Donald issued the call for the London Naval Disarmament Conference,
which convened in mid-January of 1930. Its work accomplished the last
serious progress toward disarmament prior to World War II. The Senate
procrastinated over ratification but finally approved the document 58–9

at a special session in July 1930. The agreement marked a diplomatic coup for Hoover and the cornerstone of his defense policy of disarmament, saving billions of dollars and drawing the United States and Britain closer. Hoover had also set a milestone of summit diplomacy, marking a new era in which American presidents would meet their foreign counterparts face-to-face rather than via letters, exchanges through ambassadors, or transatlantic telephone calls.[27]

Just as the London Naval Treaty was a long-term negotiation that required a great deal of preparation over an extended period, Hoover knew that confronting the international financial crisis would require extensive global cooperation. In mid-1931, the American economy was stagnant, but not appreciably worsening, until it was affected by events from abroad. Virtually every European nation was deeply in debt, with a shaky economic and political infrastructure, having failed to recover appreciably from the Great War. In early May, Austria and Germany proclaimed a customs union, which abolished trade barriers between the two nations. The move was designed to bolster the staggering econ-omies of both countries, perhaps averting political anarchy, yet such a union was forbidden by the Treaty of Versailles. Britain and France, which had largely dictated these provisions in the treaty, vetoed the merger. The crushing of the credit and tariff agreement led to a run on the German mark and the collapse of the Kreditanstalt, which held about half of the deposits of Austria. Both Germany and Austria were in imminent danger of panic and a political revolution producing a totali-tarian dictatorship.[28]

The punitive provisions of the Treaty of Versailles fastened on the defeated powers by the victors were coming home to roost, and the shad-ows of a dark future crept across the continent. The Allied nations owed war and postwar debts to America, which they could pay only if they received reparations owed them by Germany. Neither bloc of countries could pay without bleeding the other dry. It was politically as well as economically impractical to keep the promises made in the wake of war. Hoover hurriedly devised a high-stakes plan to provide a respite: he proposed a one-year moratorium on all intergovernmental debts, both war debts and reparations, during which period a permanent solution would be negotiated. The French, who wanted to cripple Germany if not decapitate their potentially powerful rival, initially blocked ratification but finally yielded. Hoover summoned a special session of Congress, at which the Senate ratified the moratorium 69–12 following ratification in the House by 317–100 on December 22, 1931. By this time, Britain had already left the gold standard, on September 21, and the pound sterling, the primary standard for ordering the world's trade, had become a victim of the Depression.[29]

Hoover's debt moratorium was only a respite, not a permanent solution. The debtor nations had a little more than a year to sort out their finances. A second problem existed. The Hoover moratorium pertained solely to debts between governments, primarily war debts and reparations. In addition, European and Latin American banks had pyramided high-interest loans based on bonds and securities issued by private banks and loan institutions offering such deliciously high interest rates that they drained American capital into risky investments that were, in fact, a glorified Ponzi scheme. When payments for short-term, high-interest loans approached, the borrowing institutions postponed the day of reckoning by issuing yet higher-interest loans based on a longer term. Many such bonds were issued by municipalities and state governments in Central and Eastern Europe and some in Latin America. Their common element was an effort to lure capital based on capricious interest rates destined to produce ultimate ruin for everyone concerned, including the investors and depositors of those foolish enough to invest in such inflated securities. Through an international consortium of private financial institutions, Hoover was able to iron out through several conferences, confirmed at Basel, a one-year standstill agreement, which did for private investors what the debt moratorium did for governments, that is, to create a breathing spell for them to untangle their finances and to minimize their losses. The public debts—war debts and reparations—were still unsettled at the time Hoover was succeeded by Franklin D. Roosevelt in March of 1933, and ultimately only tiny Finland repaid its war debts to the United States in full.[30]

While the Great Depression continued to deepen despite Hoover's debt moratorium, a trail of diplomats made the pilgrimage across the Atlantic to seek the favor of the president. In November 1931 Hoover met with Dino Grandi. The dashing, charismatic foreign minister of Italy was fluent in English and only thirty-six, and he charmed the American press and public. With no major issues dealing with trade or diplomacy between the United States and Italy, Grandi's visit was largely ceremonial. A rising star in Europe, he represented an important nation then in the process of shifting its military and diplomatic orientation. In their discussions, Grandi and Hoover agreed to form a common front in favor of disarmament at the upcoming Geneva conference, and they concurred that France would pose the major obstacle. Grandi himself was gaining favor in Europe as a prophet of peace, while at home, Benito Mussolini, who was pivoting toward militarism and aggression, viewed him as a potential rival. Grandi's visit to America, measured by public opinion on both sides of the Atlantic, was a success—perhaps too much of a success for his own good. Shortly after Grandi returned to Italy, Mussolini, somewhat jealous of Grandi's growing renown, sacked him, as well as three other ministers and eleven undersecretaries, consolidating power in his own hands, manhandling opposition, and throwing overboard his former foreign minister's experiment with small-stick diplomacy. Il Duce now held three cabinet positions in addition to being premier: foreign affairs, home affairs, and commerce. The doves of peace were giving way to the hawks of war.[31]

On October 22, 1931, French premier Pierre Laval arrived in New York, then took the train to Washington, where he met Hoover on the following day at the White House. After a state dinner, the leaders, joined by interpreters, talked until after midnight. The American president privately told the Frenchman that he believed France had supplanted Britain as Europe's greatest power, primarily because of its more robust economy. Militarily, too, France was Europe's greatest power so

long as Germany remained disarmed. The chief agreements were economic. Laval promised to help his American counterpart remain on the
gold standard, yet he made no progress when he attempted to persuade
Hoover to scale down French war debts. Only Congress could do that,
Hoover explained, and France could better afford to pay than any other
nation. Hoover pressed for disarmament, but Laval ruled that out unless
the United States would sign an alliance with France. Hoover responded
that alliances do not prevent wars; they merely expand their size when
wars erupt. When Laval departed, the leaders knew what to expect.
They liked and respected each other and understood the political reali-
ties in France and America. Yet neither side would budge much until the
Second World War was imminent. On October 26, Laval returned to
New York, where Al Smith escorted him to the top of the Empire State
Building. The Laval visit was long on symbolism and ceremony and
short on substance, but it bolstered Laval's image at home and somewhat
reassured Hoover that Laval would stand fast with him on gold.[32]

While Hoover attempted to resolve economic and political problems
in Europe, the vast Pacific was erupting into violence. The conflict had
started decades earlier in Manchuria, a semiautonomous province claimed
by China, Russia, and Japan due to its rich resources and potential for
expansion and economic development. In September 1931, Japan occupied the key city of Mukden after claiming that the Chinese had planted
explosives that destroyed a portion of the South Manchurian Railroad,
vital to the Japanese. The incident was clearly a Japanese hoax; shortly
after the purported blast, an engine and railroad cars safely traversed the
purported gap created by the explosion. But in the wake of the phony
sabotage, Japan began expanding throughout Manchuria. The League of
Nations investigated the supposed bombing, deliberated, and debated.
Secretary Stimson, backed by Hoover, argued that Japan's aggression violated the League Covenant, as well as the 1922 Nine-Power Treaty signed
at Washington whereby the Pacific powers guaranteed the territorial
integrity of China. Japan had also violated the 1928 Kellogg-Briand Pact,
which outlawed war as an instrument of national policy.[33]

Herbert Hoover was born in West Branch, Iowa, on August 10, 1874. He is pictured here at age three, his posture virtually identical with portraits of him taken when he was an adult.

The Hoover children posed in a photographer's studio in West Branch, 1888 (*left to right*): Theodore "Tad"; Mary "May"; and Herbert.

Hoover met his wife, Lou Henry, while studying at Stanford University. She is pictured during her student years, at work in Stanford's chemistry lab in 1895.

All photos courtesy of the Herbert Hoover Library.

Hoover's international relief campaign during World War I provided sustenance for Europeans in war-torn regions, including these Belgian children gathered in their school for a meal in 1915.

Bread and soup arrive at a canteen in Belgium in 1916 as part of Hoover's crusade to feed the hungry in a Europe disrupted by warfare and blockades.

Hoover poses with his catch off the coast of Seward, Alaska.

Herbert Hoover confers with Minnesota Congressman Walter H. Newton while visiting Minneapolis in 1926. After becoming president, Hoover appointed Newton as his personal secretary.

Raging waters sweep past an isolated country house during the floods that devastated Mississippi in February 1927. Hoover directed rescue and relief operations in the inundated region.

Standing in the center, Hoover is greeted by the citizens of Pine Bluff, Arkansas, in August 1927. They were grateful for the assistance they had received from Hoover's relief committee after the flood that ravaged their town earlier that year.

ABOVE: Hoover and his wife, Lou, sitting in the yard of their Stanford home in the summer of 1928.

LEFT: In the heart of Iowa's corn belt, a Hoover campaign worker decorates a tall stalk of corn with a likeness of Iowa's native son during the 1928 presidential campaign.

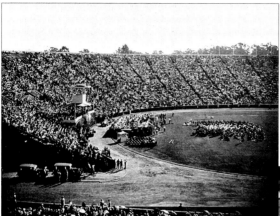

On August 11, 1928, the day after his birthday, Hoover addresses the crowd at the Stanford Stadium and accepts the Republican nomination for the presidency.

During the 1928 campaign, Hoover visits a schoolhouse in his hometown, West Branch, Iowa, accompanied by his wife, Lou.

During the 1928 presidential campaign, Hoover and Lou returned several times to West Branch. They are seen here riding in an open car down Main Street.

After winning the 1928 election, President-elect Hoover embarked on a tour of Latin America, including this stop in San José, Costa Rica. During that trip, he promised a Good Neighbor Policy toward Latin America, a phrase later borrowed by the Roosevelt administration.

President-elect Hoover and his wife continue his 1928 Latin American tour. He is shown here being greeted at the pier in Amapala, Honduras, by Honduran officials and U.S. diplomats.

ABOVE: Hoover delivered his inaugural address during a rain shower from the East Portico of the Capitol on March 4, 1929. It was the first inauguration recorded on a talking newsreel.

LEFT: Hoover poses with the world's most famous aviator, Charles Lindberg, and the flyer's wife, Anne, on August 15, 1930.

ABOVE: Hoover and his wife attending Quaker services at the New Friends Meeting House in Washington, D.C., April 1931.

RIGHT: Hollywood star Mary Pickford presents Hoover with a ticket to a movie industry–sponsored charity event for the unemployed on November 12, 1931.

Hoover marked the bicentennial of George Washington's birth with an address to a joint session of Congress, February 22, 1932.

On July 28, 1932, World War I veterans encamped in Washington, D.C., riot after a bill to pay them a bonus for their service was rejected by the U.S. Senate.

ABOVE: Hoover meeting with African-American leaders on the White House steps on October 1, 1932. Hoover carried the black vote overwhelmingly in the 1932 presidential election.

LEFT: After his defeat in the November 1932 election, Hoover enjoyed himself on a Florida vacation. An avid fisherman, Hoover reeled in an impressive catch.

In the last days of his presidency, Hoover plays a final game of "Hoover Ball" on the White House grounds. The game was played by throwing a medicine ball back and forth across a net.

Hoover delivers a farewell speech marking the end of his presidency at the National Republican Club's Lincoln Day Dinner at New York's Waldorf Astoria Hotel on February 13, 1933.

Hoover shares a limousine with President-elect Franklin D. Roosevelt on Inauguration Day, March 4, 1933.

Hoover returned to the spotlight by addressing the Republican National Convention in Cleveland's Public Hall, on June 10, 1936. His speeches at the Republican nominating convention became a tradition that continued into the final years of his life.

Hoover and his wife, Lou, share a love seat in their Stanford home, circa 1940.

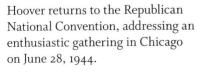

Hoover returns to the Republican National Convention, addressing an enthusiastic gathering in Chicago on June 28, 1944.

In 1949 Hoover spoke by radio of his role as the chairman of the Hoover Commission. Appointed by President Harry S. Truman, Hoover was charged with devising proposals for streamlining the administration of the federal government.

In this 1950 family portrait, Hoover is posed with his son Allan (*left*) and grandson Andrew (*center*).

As state delegations parade past the podium, Hoover prepares to address the Republican National Convention in Chicago, July 8, 1952.

On July 23, 1953, Hoover accepted President Dwight D. Eisenhower's appointment to chair a second Hoover Commission to make further recommendations for revising the administration of the federal government.

Herbert Hoover enjoying a shipboard vacation with his son Herbert Hoover Jr. off the Florida coast, February 1953.

The Hoover family gathered in West Branch to celebrate the former president's eightieth birthday in August 1954.

Hoover relaxes in the Waldorf Astoria suite that had long been his East Coast home. The photo was taken in 1960, four years before his death.

Hoover poses with President Harry S. Truman at the dedication of the Hoover Presidential Library in West Branch, Iowa, on his birthday, August 10, 1962.

Opposed to the belligerence but aware that provocation might invite war, the president instructed Stimson to issue a statement condemning the Japanese for their violation of international law. Hoover hoped the stigma of international opinion might be sufficient to deter further aggression. Stimson fleshed out Hoover's idea, adding language threatening economic sanctions. The president overruled Stimson and edited out the veiled threat, believing sanctions were more likely to lead to war than to preserve the peace, a scenario that transpired under his successor. America had no vital interests in the Far East, Hoover explained, and the military was not certain it could win a land war on the Asian continent, nor win a naval conflict in less than five years. The hand that pointed a pistol, Hoover advised Stimson, must be prepared to pull the trigger.[34]

Stimson's note, which was dispatched on January 7, 1932, and published the next day, did include a new wrinkle. What became known as the Stimson Doctrine stated that the United States would deny diplomatic recognition to any territory seized by force. Yet the declaration had no discernable effect on the Japanese, nor did world opinion deter the island nation from further conquests. The fighting soon accelerated, and Japan created the puppet state of Manchukuo in Manchuria as a Japanese-dominated province. Further, the island warriors carried the war beyond Manchuria, bombarding Shanghai, the first civilian bombing of World War II. The incursion at Shanghai alarmed the Western powers, most of them imperialists themselves. There was a large foreign settlement at Shanghai and the British had more than $1 billion invested there. Meanwhile, the League of Nations was moving on the diplomatic front. With the permission of both the Japanese and the Chinese—in fact, the Japanese had initiated the idea—the League created a fact-finding mission. The chief defense of the Japanese, which had some validity despite its underlying imperialistic motivation, was that China was not a nation in the modern sense but a conglomeration of warlords constantly slaying their own people, who could not protect property such as the crucial South Manchurian Railroad. The Lytton Commission investigation dragged on until February 1933, when it issued a report condemning the Japanese as aggressors, a predictable conclusion. Japan responded by withdrawing from the League. Japan pulled out of Shanghai but maintained a viselike grip on Manchuria. The League, and the United States, had proven impotent, and their denunciations only hardened the Japanese, though it stigmatized and isolated them. Yet in practical terms, the real estate of China would have swallowed would-be protectors just as it would have engulfed the Japanese, who would have become acculturated. The story of Manchuria and the Stimson Doctrine became a sad one after hindsight of the endgame lay in focus. Yet, ironically, once his long career ended, Stimson considered the volleys of words he fired against the invaders of Manchuria his greatest diplomatic accomplishment.[35]

TEN

Fighting the Depression

As the 72nd Congress opened, both parties looked forward to the 1932 presidential elections. The outcome of the 1930 congressional elections made it more difficult to blame Hoover for the deepening Depression. After deaths and subsequent new elections in some districts, the Democrats ended up with a slim majority in the House, which enabled them to elect as Speaker John Nance Garner of Texas. The Republicans organized the Senate with a bare majority after a long standoff during which Progressive Republicans divided their votes to prevent any candidate from receiving a majority. Finally, Bertrand Snell of New York was elected to lead the upper house, defeating John Q. Tilson of Connecticut. The Democrats approached the session without a single national spokesman and with no leader by consensus. They decided to wait for Hoover to propose legislation and then to caucus over how to respond. Both houses were splintered, as in the previous, 71st, Congress, by a bloc of mostly Western mavericks who called themselves Progressives, yet, lacking a national program, were more appropriately insurgents, concerned primarily with protecting the interests of their agricultural constituents. They often voted with the Democrats. Divided government during the course of the worst depression in the nation's history left each party chained by the idiosyncrasies of the other. The chief imbroglio arose over whom to blame if legislation stagnated, which, in fact, it did not, at least not to the degree expected. The Democrats walked a tenuous tightwire; they did not want the Depression to end on Hoover's watch; but neither did they want to be so obviously obstructionist as to receive blame themselves. The Democrats struck a wildcat well of ready cash, but it spurted from a single source: the party's national chairman, John J. Raskob, chief owner of General Motors, who financed the Democrats almost single-handedly and thereby gained a dominant role in determining policy and candidates. Not since Mark Hanna bankrolled William McKinley had a business magnate bet his fortune on politics.[1]

The 72nd Congress marked the second phase in Hoover's war on the Depression, and he took the offensive with the most ambitious legislative agenda of any president to that time. He also grew far more assertive in pushing through his unified, integrated, holistic healing balm to the economic infection. From beginning to end, he strove to dispose as well as to propose, talking regularly with influential congressmen, the GOP National Committee, and anyone who might pave the highway to passage, including members of the opposition. He did not dislike Garner, and they struck a number of deals, although he did not entirely trust him either, especially because the Texan coveted his party's presidential nomination. Garner usually limited his interference with Hoover's bills to amending or delaying them, not defeating them outright. He was a savvy politician with no inclination to damage his own presidential aspirations. Congress did not assemble until December 8, for Hoover's State of the Union address, and then the chief executive bombarded it with a succession of subsequent messages on specialized topics including the budget, foreign relations, law enforcement, and reorganization of government. All speeches were read to joint sessions by the House clerk, as was the tradition at that time, and then congressmen were given printed copies.

Thus, the formal reading of the messages was less important than the study of the content by the legislators in their offices. During the formal reading they lolled in the lobby or cloakroom, where they smoked, gossiped, and occasionally commented on the task ahead. Some were intimidated, or at least made uneasy, by the fusillade of legislation and its scope. The Republican insurgents wanted Hoover to spend more, especially on agriculture, while most Democrats wanted less spending.[2]

The president was both a fiscalist, who wanted to expand the money supply, and a monetarist, who wanted to increase spending via public works. While Hoover had severe reservations about opening the Pandora's box of insatiable demand and limited supply that outright doles would create, he had no reservations about work relief on a larger scale than had ever been attempted. The centerpiece of his economic program was the Reconstruction Finance Corporation (RFC), a government corporation for loaning money to banks, businesses, and railroads to prevent failures and stimulate trade and commerce, especially construction. Before Congress convened, the president had experimented with the National Credit Corporation, a fund of $500 million, which he prodded large private banks to create, to be made available to prop up weaker, smaller banks in danger of being swept away by the undertow of bank failures. The venture failed for several reasons. The fund was too small to make a major impact, and the bankers were wary of risking their own liquidity by making loans to failing banks. The proposed RFC was more expansive and more expensive, had the weight of the government behind it, and went far beyond the mission of bolstering banks. It remained an integral fixture in the American economy throughout the subsequent New Deal era. The RFC also had antecedents in the War Finance Corporation of World War I, created by the Wilson administration to help stimulate war production. It was resurrected briefly during the Harding recession of 1921–22.[3]

Second on the president's agenda was the Glass-Steagall Act. Its chief purposes were to save the gold standard, stabilize exchange rates, maintain wages, and increase the money supply, because only gold-backed dollars could circulate. The gold standard was severely stressed. Hoover instructed the Treasury to pay gold for currency, as required by law, and the precious metal was simultaneously depleted by foreign creditors and by Americans, who consequently hoarded it, diminishing money in circulation. The chief executive could not reveal at the time how close the nation was to defaulting on the gold standard, for fear of inciting panic. The mechanism by which the legislation worked was relatively simple, at least superficially. It permitted a portion of paper currency to be backed by certain types of Federal Reserve notes, in essence expanding the supply of gold. The psychology, given the circumstances, was providential. All the Hoover economic proposals were like interlocking puzzle pieces. The chief executive asked for a system of home loan discount banks to save homes from foreclosure and for additional capital to fund federal land banks to make low-interest loans available to farmers. He called for reorganization of failing railroads, legislation to reorganize the executive branch, and authority to lease Muscle Shoals for private development to revitalize the region. The Chief wanted to be frugal and called for a moderate tax increase to bring the soaring deficit under control, though he was willing to tolerate modest deficits. He requested legislation to make assets of closed banks available to depositors and for the legalization of branch banking. The Chief requested a widespread program of public works to be spread throughout the country, strategically placed where unemployment was greatest. He said he would follow up by designating specific public works. He also called for increased restrictions on immigration to save jobs for Americans and for labor legislation that would prohibit the use of injunctions to outlaw strikes. No one else in either party proposed such a sweeping program. There was urgency in the president's series of messages. There were some things he cautioned against: no direct doles, no general revision of the tariff, no further benefits to veterans, and no repeal of antitrust laws.[4]

Shortly after his series of addresses the chief executive summoned a large group of congressmen to the White House to explain the rationale behind his program and to ask for their aid. Although action was essential, this was no time to panic, he cautioned. He had already submitted some sixty-three major and minor bills for their thoughtful consideration. Hoover pointed out that progress had been made in public health. There were fewer ill and dying than during normal times. The president indicated that he hoped for additional progress in arms reductions, which would liberate funds for job-creating domestic public works. During his series of talks the president had requested additional money for law enforcement but had taken no stand regarding Prohibition, an issue increasingly dividing the nation, especially within the Republican Party. He felt that precious resources must be husbanded and targeted where they could do the most good, and he eschewed demagogic or emotional tangents. The Californian observed that the hardship was real, yet in a relative sense America was faring better than most of the world and was virtually self-sufficient in raw materials. The chief executive also urged Congress to consider consolidating all public works into a single Department of Public Works in the cabinet. He repeatedly emphasized the importance of railroads, especially for farm products, and warned that their bankruptcy would disrupt transportation. For the foreseeable future, they remained vital. Hoover prioritized his legislation for the congressmen, emphasizing the need for prompt action on the Glass-Steagall Act and the RFC. The suffering, as well as the potential bounty of the land, would have to be shared. Hoover strove to cultivate a conciliatory atmosphere. Indeed, through March, the 72nd Congress was less divisive than the 71st Congress had been and the period was the most productive of his presidency, despite the forthcoming election. Hoover proved an effective bipartisan leader over the course of the 72nd Congress and usually ended up achieving about what he wanted in the general form he wanted it. At the end, the landscape did not lie littered with shipwrecked legislation, though the Depression stubbornly persisted. Hoover's defenders argued that without his exertions it could have been worse. In fact, in many places, it was.[5]

Congress moved relatively expeditiously to enact the RFC. The only significant opposition came from Progressives, who based their resistance on class arguments. Senator Fiorello La Guardia of New York termed the loans to salvage banks a "millionaire's dole" and the Western insurgents wanted more money for agriculture. La Follette and Burton Wheeler passionately opposed the bill, though their own constituents stood to benefit. Hoover explained that he was more interested in saving depositors than in rescuing banks. However, when banks failed, depositors lost their savings. Congress deleted specific provisions, such as placing a limit on the amount that could be loaned to large banks, and permitting loans to bankrupt banks to repay ruined depositors. Senator Carter Glass of Virginia, who took paternalistic pride in the Federal Reserve System, which he had helped create, balked at some of the provisions. The president appeased most of his critics. He permitted Democratic leaders, Garner in the House and Robinson in the Senate, to appoint one member each to the board of directors, which was bipartisan, divided equally by party affiliation. Reaching out to farm interests, Hoover accepted an amendment permitting the RFC, through the secretary of agriculture, to loan up to $50 million to farmers. Another amendment permitted the new agency to loan money to railroads upon permission of the Interstate Commerce Commission. The chief executive named Federal Reserve governor Eugene Meyer to chair the RFC board and former vice president Charles G. Dawes to become president of the new agency. Hoover, later depicted as a passive archreactionary by some critics, actually wanted more power vested in the new federal agency than Congress was willing to authorize. Some major magazines condemned the measure as a step toward socialism. Without question, creation of the RFC marked a landmark shift toward a more powerful government. The bill included a total appropriation, in direct money and bonds, of some $2 billion, the largest relief bill passed by Congress up to that point. Over time, the agency would operate for eight years and loan $50 billion. Hoover believed the aphorism that necessity is the mother of invention and that serious emergencies require unorthodox approaches. The spirit of urgency and willingness to compromise stood out more than the decibel level of the Progressive dissenters. The RFC bill proved that bipartisan cooperation was possible and that Congress could act during an emergency. On January 22, Hoover signed the bill he had dispatched to Congress on December 7. It passed the Democrat-controlled House by 335–55 and the Senate by 63–8. In the Senate, where only five Democrats and three insurgents voted nay, the body invoked cloture several times to speed the process. Nonetheless, as one journalist observed, thousands of banks could have been saved from failure if the measure had been enacted two years earlier. However, Hoover remained convinced that his approach, as pathbreaking as it might be, remained within the parameters of restoring old, permanent jobs rather than making the economy the tail of a dog embodied by the federal government.[6]

A lesser yet nonetheless important facet of Hoover's program was an appropriation of an additional $125 million for the federal land banks, which supported mortgages on farm properties and homes, some already in default. The appropriation passed Congress and was signed on January 23, 1932. The additional capital helped farmers keep their land and enabled homeowners to remain in their homes while preserving the liquidity of the local banks that held the home and land mortgages as collateral. The funding drove home another peg in the president's plan to ease credit and deter deflation, one of the chief ogres intimidating recovery. The land banks complemented the role the Federal Reserve played for larger commercial banks. Complementing the land banks were twelve home loan discount banks, which discounted home mortgages. These institutions also supported smaller savings banks, insurance companies, and savings and loan associations. The Federal Home Loan Bank bill proposed on November 13, 1931, by the president was not approved until July 1932, near the end of the session. The delay caused the failure of thousands of banks and homes lost to mortgage foreclosures.[7]

In the fall of 1931 the U.S. economy was staggered by another crisis after Britain left the gold standard on September 21. For generations, the

British pound sterling, backed by gold, had been the glue of the world economic system. Gold maintained exchange rates and controlled the amount of currency in circulation. After Britain abandoned gold's backing, many felt it would become impossible for importers and exporters to plan ahead, especially those marketing perishable products. The prospect frightened businessmen into paralysis. European investors, fearing America might jettison bullion-backed currency next, began to drain the U.S. Treasury. France alone withdrew about $790 million in gold. By the end of 1931, some 2,294 American banks had failed, double the number of failures the previous year. Americans holding gold certificates withdrew the metal, and the rash of bank failures inspired panic withdrawals by depositors of currency, who hoarded their cash. There could be no wage stability or industrial recovery under such deflationary pressure. By the winter of 1932 the United States possessed only $430 million in bullion, with $1.3 billion outstanding to creditors. Hoover acted vigorously, warning Congress that it must enact legislation expeditiously to save America's gold standard. Meanwhile, the Treasury paid out gold on demand to foreign and domestic creditors presenting gold bonds or certificates. The president did not reveal publicly how little remained to meet obligations, yet the payments helped calm the world financial community. The drain slowed, and some of the bullion began to flow back on the reassurance that America was a safer haven than most alternatives. Yet unless Congress enacted a permanent solution, the wolf at the door would remain famished.[8]

To resolve the issue, Hoover devised a plan to permit the backing of currency and government gold obligations with certain types of extremely reliable paper, known as "eligible currency," as was already done in some countries. This would, in effect, stretch the supply of gold, making it back a larger sum of currency. Economically, the problem was largely psychological. If people considered the scheme reasonable and trustworthy, it would work. The proposal was certainly feasible from an economic viewpoint. The bigger problem was political. Hoover knew he had to persuade a Congress controlled primarily by the opposing party, during a presidential election year, to pass legislation that would doubt-less help the nation but also might help Hoover's presidential prospects. To accomplish this he recruited Democrats respected for economic acumen, Carter Glass of Virginia in the Senate and Henry Steagall of Alabama in the House, to sponsor the measure, known as the Glass-Steagall Act. Both Southerners were more conservative than Hoover, especially Glass, who embraced a phobia of large banks. Yet the president massaged egos and did not seek to hog credit. He had to compro-mise, because he preferred a more vigorous approach than his chief sponsors. Moreover, the Progressives, as usual, railed against the bill, claiming the president pandered to millionaire bankers while neglecting the poor and hungry. Hoover reacted cautiously, discreetly pointing out that when banks failed, depositors lost their money. Eventually, what became the Glass-Steagall Act navigated the legislative shoals successfully and Hoover signed it on February 27, 1932. It was among the most important acts of the Hoover administration, and the timing was cru-cial. To Wall Street, bankers, and many businessmen, the measure was even more important than the RFC. It helped restore a degree of busi-ness confidence, at home and abroad. Now only America and France, of the major powers, remained on gold. It is small comfort to say things could have been worse, yet they could have been. Hoover demonstrated patience and political finesse but received only a limited amount of credit. In fact, as his legislative achievements mounted during the win-ter and spring of the 72nd Congress, blame mounted simultaneously. As the 1932 campaign approached, the rival parties increasingly resembled the Donner party.[9]

Along with its blockbuster legislation such as the RFC and the Glass-Steagall Act, the 72nd Congress enacted a multitude of lesser bills. For example, on February 16 the House adopted the Lame Duck Amend-ment, already passed by the Senate, shortening the long interregnum between the election and inauguration of a president from early March to January 15. This permitted a more rapid transition of power, because a defeated outgoing president operated in a power vacuum during the

long waiting period and the newly elected incoming president was officially powerless.[10]

The division between the branches of government during a presidential election year, occurring in the midst of the nation's worst domestic
crisis, left the ship of state virtually rudderless at times, and when political
paralysis resulted, the reaction was to blame the opposing party. The
Democratic leadership, headed by Garner in the House and Robinson in
the Senate, was, on the whole, more conservative than Hoover. Garner
and Robinson were Southerners, and a large bloc of their supporters had
Southern roots. Unified on the objective of defeating Hoover, from 1930
through 1932 the Democrats sought to destroy the president politically.
The Democratic National Committee employed poison-pen journalist and
playwright Charles Michelson to write scathing diatribes against Hoover,
which were delivered in Congress by Democratic politicians and planted
in the *Congressional Record* and in Democratic newspapers and popular
magazines. Hoover was accused of being insensitive to human suffering,
of consorting with millionaires to foist the Depression upon the nation, of
delighting in the plight of the hungry, and of cackling maliciously while
Wall Street crashed. In addition to blaming the president for the Depression, Michelson belittled Hoover's achievements during the Great War
and as commerce secretary. The scorn was bitter and personal, some of it
pure invention. The Progressives, many of them nominally Republicans,
were often comparably abusive. Hoover refused to respond. He believed
that if he did the right things, the politics would take care of itself. In his
later years, Hoover said he had forgiven all his former enemies except
Michelson. Garner, who fought Hoover to win at all costs, later became
an admirer of the ex-president, writing, "If he had become president in
1921 or 1937 he might have been ranked with the great Presidents." He
added, "Today, I think Herbert Hoover is the wisest statesman on world
affairs in America. He may be on domestic affairs, too."[11]

Perhaps more time and rhetoric were devoted to balancing the budget during the 72nd Congress than to any other single issue. Many politicians, as well as the American public, believed sound government

required a balanced budget. Yet businessmen, and many consumers, opposed any tax increases—unless they fell exclusively on someone else. Every congressman who favored higher taxes or budget cuts in general opposed any that affected his constituents or powerful interest groups such as veterans, government employees, or labor unions. The president was troubled. Congressmen pledged themselves to balanced budgets and then voted against tax hikes or for projects that made that objective impossible. Some $2.5 billion of the $4.4 billion in government expenditures was earmarked for fixed expenses. The Depression had scoured a $2 billion hole in government revenues. Hoover was satisfied to settle for a less-than-completely balanced budget during hard times. He called for $1.6 million in tax increases. Part, but not all, of the remainder could be recouped by slicing fat. He submitted a bill for streamlining government by reorganization and paring, which was rejected. When he proposed placing government employees on a five-day week, with no pay for the day off, Congress initially balked but ultimately gave way. Hoover believed expenditures should be targeted, while some congressmen considered them Christmas presents for constituents. The president agreed to take the blame for reorganization that dismantled unpopular programs, but Congress mistrusted the chief executive to shelter their constituents' booty. As the session wound down, the government was trapped in a vise. Tax receipts had fallen by 50 percent, while spending for job-creating public works had soared. Unemployed people paid few or no taxes while they soaked up relief. At one point a grand bargain seemed in the works for a national sales tax, which gained support in both parties but faltered. The final version of the economy bill passed the Senate rancorously on June 8, 1932, the House concurred on June 28, and the president signed the final measure on June 30, only days before the session adjourned. The measure empowered the president to implement some reorganization, but only following the November presidential election, after which many expected him to become a has-been. Estimates of final savings trimmed from the budget were about $130 million, falling far short of the $300 million Hoover had requested.[12]

While Hoover's most important programs marched through the legislative chambers, several senators and representatives proposed relief programs that would expand federal involvement, though most had a short shelf life. In principle, Hoover agreed with strengthening the RFC, which he wanted to make the engine driving economic recovery by creating jobs and lubricating business and banking with credit. Realizing that private charity was failing to completely fill the necessities of the people, he was now amenable to spending a small amount for doles funneled through the states, allotted on the basis of prioritizing according to the local unemployment rate. Though he was still unconvinced that federal dollars could meet all needs, Hoover's willingness to spend outpaced that of most legislators, who wanted to move prudently at this point in the Depression, although most lusted for additional federal public works in their own districts. A small group considered the president overly penurious. In February 1932, two liberal senators, Edward P. Costigan, a New York Democrat, and Robert M. La Follette, a Wisconsin Republican, cosponsored a measure to provide $75 million in direct relief to be channeled through the states, which was handily defeated. Next, three Democrats, Hugo L. Black, Thomas J. Walsh, and Robert J. Bulkley, also submitted a $75 million bill for doles distributed by the states, but this bill, too, was defeated. Senator Robert Wagner's more grandiose measure authorizing the RFC to issue $1.5 billion in bonds to finance public works was quickly axed, as was his similar $500 million bill. Clearly, there was no consensus. Journalist Walter Lippmann joined the chorus of those who cautioned against spendthrift programs as a quick fix.[13]

The contest for scarce federal dollars and a fair means of raising and distributing the money heated up in late spring once the battle of the budget had ended. Senators Joseph T. Robinson and Robert Wagner had plans with which Hoover partially agreed. All of them concurred that work relief was preferable to doles and that the projects constructed should be useful and, if possible, self-liquidating. The president objected to Wagner's technique of financing by a bond issue and distribution by population, regardless of the unemployment rate, designed to court vote-rich constituencies.[14] However, in the latter phases of the session, the president's chief rival in devising an acceptable measure was the opportunistic Garner. Hoover complained that many congressmen wanted to convert the RFC into a pork-barrel factory designed to make risky loans to companies domiciled in their districts. An old-fashioned spoils politician, Garner loaded his bill, introduced in late May, with provisions for special interests, trolling for votes. The president pointed out that when such unreliable companies defaulted, American taxpayers would be stuck with the debts. Garner retorted that the entire RFC was no more than a pork-barrel factory.[15]

Over the course of the skirmish, several versions of the Garner bill evolved. Hoover vetoed Garner measures that passed Congress on June 6 and June 11. The initial bill contained provisions for hundreds of public works scattered throughout the country, many of them post offices, to be built chiefly by mechanical labor, concentrated in middle-class, vote-rich areas of medium unemployment. Hoover contended that Garner's public works would employ only 100,000 of a pool of 8 million jobless, none of them in permanent jobs. Garner proposed that all RFC loans be handled directly by the small RFC board of directors, which would overwhelm the six members, bypassing private banks, which had much greater resources, and effectively putting independent banks out of business. Further, the chief executive desired to focus on remunerative public works that would provide some permanent jobs and repay the costs of construction and maintenance over time, such as toll highways, tunnels and bridges, docks and harbors, dams for generating and selling electricity, and trees that could be planted and later harvested. Hoover framed a bill of his own, which included most of these provisions, but it was killed in a House committee. Congress was deadlocked; the need for legislation was urgent; the nominating conventions had met, Garner had been chosen for vice president on the Democratic ticket, and adjournment lay only days away. With the help of Senators Robinson and Wagner, Hoover and his allies cobbled together a last-minute compromise deleting most of the objectionable provisions in the Garner bill and giving Hoover most of what he wanted. One troublesome provision remained. The clerk of the House, with the consent of the Speaker, could publish the names of banks that had received RFC loans. This might ignite a run on banks by panicked depositors. Hoover did not believe the provision would be used—it was too patently self-destructive. Ultimately, the Emergency Relief and Construction Act of 1932 was passed by the House on July 14 and by the Senate on July 16, and Hoover signed it on July 21.[16]

The bold step failed to save Hoover politically, and recovery would take time. It was subsequently undermined by Garner's publication of recipients of RFC loans, fueling a runaway banking panic during the winter of 1932–33. Yet the law itself stood as a Mount Everest–sized testimonial compared to some of the previous, less vigorous attempts to lift the economy. It showed how far Hoover was willing to go and how far he had come, and it left a blueprint for his successors. In fighting this final battle over a desperately needed landmark measure, Hoover had proved his mettle. Both firm and flexible, a seminal thinker, he had grown into an accomplished legislator, working under unforgiving dead-lines and enormous stress. Yet there was no gloating in the White House in July 1932. Whether America would emerge from its economic collapse as Europe was doing, and whether the president faced a Waterloo at the polls, remained to be seen.[17]

For a divided Congress functioning in an election year during hard times, the 72nd Congress had remarkable achievements to its credit. Unemployment relief from self-liquidating public works projects totaled about $700 million. Other important bills were enacted, including ones limiting uses of injunctions for labor disputes, reorganizing procedure in federal juvenile cases, and rendering kidnapping a federal crime. Yet much time had been lost in endless debates, even as banks collapsed and mortgages fell due. Congress, and the president, could have done more and acted more expeditiously. Bankruptcy reform was not passed until after the 1932 election and budget reform was not enacted until June 1932. Congress failed to act on railroad reorganization. Nonetheless, with his program fleshed out, Hoover felt the pieces were in place for recovery. Long-term confidence, however, had not yet been achieved. Perhaps without the inflammatory oratory of the campaign that followed, the national economy might have lifted off, for there were glimmers of recovery, especially in the stock market, during the summer of 1932. But the economy remained fragile, and fear threatened to upset the delicate balance. The foremost accomplishment of this productive session was the RFC, which hurled $5 billion into the vortex of the Depression. The Glass-Steagall Act helped stabilize world currency exchanges. Near the end, Hoover and Garner became fierce antagonists, as the savvy Texan injected the rhetoric of class war into the clash. As recovery inched forward, yet buckled amid the scathing invective surrounding the campaign, progress continued throughout much of the world. The United States remained potentially the world's mightiest nation, but the glimmer of a sunrise in the summer of 1932 proved merely a firefly in the night.[18]

President Hoover spent more time seeking a solution to farm poverty than to any other issue during his tenure. A Jeffersonian in his view of the yeoman farmer, Hoover—like historian Frederick Jackson Turner, one of his contemporaries who shared many of the president's beliefs— considered the family farm the crucible of democracy. If democracy were to survive, farming would have to change, but farming was so ingrained in the roots of American traditions that the family farm as an institution must endure. Hoover proposed to amalgamate farms not by selling off small plots but by connecting them into cooperatives in which independent farmers acting in unison could practice economies of scale. These farmer-owned cooperatives were to resemble a pyramid, with the base at the grass roots. Hoover had evangelized for such a cooperative movement while secretary of commerce, and by the time he became president the movement had grown rapidly.[19]

In light of the spike in rural poverty caused by the Great Depression, Hoover renewed his push for a holistic farm program based on cooperatives. Hoover's program was interlocking. Cooperatives would provide better negotiating power on the marketplace, in selling and purchasing.

The key features were warehouses and grain elevators, constructed with government loans, which could store nonperishable crops and allow them to be released gradually rather than flooding the market at once, competing against one another. Hoover's wide-ranging program also included reduced rail rates, a system of inland waterways for bulk traffic, and a St. Lawrence Seaway to connect the hinterlands with the Atlantic. Hoover urged farmers to diversify rather than overproducing staples such as wheat, corn, and cotton. Some agriculture advocates viewed exports as the solution. Yet, abroad, prices were lower, due largely to cheaper labor overseas, and foreigners would not buy at the high American prices. Unfortunately, the simple cure-alls evoked more political pizzazz than Hoover's more scientific program. The Farm Board created during the 1929 special session enjoyed substantial success in recruiting members to the cooperative movement, and by October 1929 more than one-third of farmers belonged to co-ops. During the winter of 1930 the board began purchasing bales of cotton and bushels of wheat to prevent them from overwhelming the market and driving down prices ruinously. Gradually, the stabilization program expanded, yet farm prices still continued to plummet. Prices never reached a level where the board could recoup its original purchase price, and the board ended up selling at a loss, negotiating cheap foreign sales, and using the surpluses for disaster relief or giving them away to the Red Cross. By October 1931 wheat prices had fallen an additional 29.5 cents per bushel in a single year. Farmers suffered more than city people financially but ate a more plentiful diet. Industrial unemployment drove two hundred thousand people back to the countryside in 1931 alone, despite grim conditions in rural regions. The Farm Board proved a valiant experiment, but the law of supply and demand defeated efforts to legislate it out of existence.[20]

Among the most infamous episodes of the Great Depression was a march of some twenty thousand veterans to lobby for immediate cash payment of a bonus for their service in the Great War. During the Harding administration, legislation was enacted to pay them $3.4 million twenty-five years later, when many of them would approach retirement age. The government placed $112 million yearly into a fund, supporting bonds that would mature in 1945. However, with the Depression, the vets demanded immediate cash payment, not at the 1932 value, but with future accrued interest at the 1945 value. Hoover felt sympathy for the veterans and had been a better protector of their interests than any recent president, constructing twenty-five new veterans' hospitals, extending pensions for many disabilities not related to combat, and consolidating the Veterans' Bureau and the veterans' homes into the streamlined Veterans' Administration, which provided prompt and efficient care. Hoover should have been the most popular recent president among veterans. In 1931 Congress passed over Hoover's veto a bill loaning 50 percent of the value of the bonds to veterans immediately but did not appropriate any funds, conveniently blaming Hoover for the lack of money. Not all veterans were impoverished; in fact, some were wealthy. The president supported legislation that would pay needy veterans alone, but the vets insisted on all or nothing. The issue heated up in 1932, an election year. In January 1932, Representative Wright Patman, a Texas Democrat, submitted a bill to pay the veterans' bonus in full, based on $2.4 billion in unbacked greenbacks. Hoover pointed out that this would make it impossible to help many of the truly needy nonveterans. However, Congress was aware that the truly needy were not an organized voting bloc glamorized by military valor. Hoover was labeled stingy and unpatriotic. The president pointed out that the cost of the plan, $2.4 billion, was more than half the entire national budget of $3.7 billion. Basing the payment on unbacked currency would devalue the worth of all assets, including salaries, bonds, and the veterans' own pensions. It would create chaotic inflation and disrupt exports. Commodities produced by Americans would be worth less and banks would fail. There would be no faith in government credit.[21]

Meanwhile, unemployed veterans journeyed from the West Coast, picking up supporters along the way. Traveling from town to town, from state to state, by foot, auto, truck, or train, and sometimes transported by local police and civil authorities to keep them moving, some twenty thousand eventually set up ramshackle camps just across the District of Columbia line on the Anacostia Flats. A few camped out in abandoned buildings scheduled for demolition along Pennsylvania Avenue. Some men even brought along their families. Hoover provided army tents, food, and milk for young children covertly, lest he inspire other disaffected groups to march on Washington. The throng's purpose was to lobby for passage of the Patman bill. The House passed the measure, but it was rejected soundly by the Senate, 62–18. Had it cleared both chambers, Hoover's veto pen awaited. Hoover never doubted that many of the veterans were sincere, honest, patriotic Americans who believed in their cause. Yet among them were agitators, including a handful of Communists, who wanted to exploit the situation and inflame the public in order to destabilize capitalism. After the Senate defeated Patman's bill, all but some five thousand of the veterans departed, and Congress, at the president's request, appropriated money providing full rail fare home. Congress adjourned and left Washington. The stragglers now lacked a tangible reason to remain in the capital. At the orders of District of Columbia commissioners, the district police attempted to evict the squatters in the abandoned buildings along Pennsylvania Avenue. A scuffle erupted, and two veterans were killed by a capital policeman after one of them tried to seize his revolver. The district commissioners asked the president, in writing, to mobilize a contingent of the army to remove the veterans from all of Washington. Hoover instructed his immediate assistants, Secretary of War Patrick J. Hurley and Chief of Staff Douglas MacArthur, to use minimal force, including nightsticks but not rifles. On his own authority, Hurley decided that the outnumbered troops would be endangered, and he armed them with rifles. Assisting MacArthur were Major Dwight D. Eisenhower and Major George S. Patton. With MacArthur commanding, only tear gas was used; no bullets were fired; and there were no deaths or serious injuries. The army drove the retreating men, who called themselves the Bonus Expeditionary Force, to the district line at the Anacostia River, where Hoover had ordered MacArthur to stop. MacArthur halted for dinner and rest, then crossed the bridge as the campers fled. Accounts vary as to whether the troops, the campers themselves, or both, burned the camps, already in ruins. After returning, MacArthur received two stern tongue-lashings from an irate Hoover, who also rebuked Hurley for going beyond his orders.[22]

Democrats and opposition journalists inflamed the issue, and FDR allegedly gloated, "This will elect me." Yet in reality, while the episode hurt Hoover marginally, it had occurred near the beginning of the presidential campaign season. The unfortunate affair might have changed some individual votes, but it is unlikely that it changed a single electoral vote.[23]

ELEVEN

Democracy Is a Harsh Employer

There was no more telling symptom of the malaise that afflicted America in the months leading into the 1932 election than a soup kitchen in Chicago where unemployed men in threadbare suits and caps were photographed by news reporters as they lined up for sustenance. The kitchen was a gesture of philanthropy by America's most notorious criminal, Al Capone. The perception that gangsters were filling the vacuum by assisting the public while the federal government did little would plague Hoover throughout 1932. With the booming economy of the previous decade in shambles, and radical voices on the left and right calling for a new social and economic order, many prognosticators believed that almost any Democrat could defeat Hoover. Yet the Republicans were without a viable alternative. Hoover had deliberately avoided entering most primaries in order to avert an embarrassing defeat in the West. Twelve delegates listed Coolidge as their first choice, yet the former president preferred retirement. Lacking the consensus to unite behind another candidate, the Republicans fell into inertia, gambled on the advantage inherent to incumbent officeholders, or hoped that voters would remember Hoover's long-standing record of public service. There was little doubt that Charles Curtis would be Hoover's running mate if he desired the nomination, though some of his friends wanted to elect him senator from Kansas, a position he was more likely to win.

The Republican National Convention gathered at the Chicago Stadium from June 14 through June 16. Polled on the issues, delegates to the convention overwhelmingly cited the economy, an issue boding ill for their nominee. Prohibition remained an important issue, second only to the economy, but the GOP was fiercely divided among itself. Rather than call for outright appeal or for continuing the policy, their platform called for each state to decide the question for itself. Although Vice President Curtis was a strong "dry," Hoover considered drinking not a moral issue but ultimately an issue of personal choice. He felt that as long as Prohibition remained the law it should be enforced, and his efforts to step up enforcement led to the conviction of Capone for tax evasion. By contrast, Franklin D. Roosevelt had moved from a "damp," or willing-to-compromise, position on Prohibition to a "wet" advocacy of repealing the Eighteenth Amendment. Among the GOP delegates in Chicago was a growing sense of defeatism, a sense that, given the wretched economy, any GOP candidate faced inevitable defeat. The widespread unpopularity of Prohibition presented yet another problem. An American presidential election is primarily a referendum on the state of the country, an axiom almost as certain as the law of gravity. In 1932, the resentment of the voters was palpable.[1]

In late June, Franklin D. Roosevelt broke with tradition by accepting his party's nomination at its national convention in Chicago. His nine-hour flight from Albany added urgency and a dash of modernity to his campaign for the White House. Hoover considered FDR's descent upon Chicago as grandstanding. He had followed custom by not attending his party's convention, and he delivered his acceptance speech later, on August 11, his birthday. The reception was much better than might have been expected, given the doubtfulness of victory. The audience of five thousand at Washington's Constitution Hall cheered enthusiastically, inspired as they rarely were by a Hoover address. If he could have reached this level of animation more consistently, the reserved Quaker would have been a more popular president. Despite the widespread public perception that Hoover would be unable to vanquish the Depression, he might have campaigned more successfully if he had shared FDR's ability to make people feel better about themselves. Of course, the crowd at Constitution Hall already supported him; he was not seeking converts, and yet the enthusiasm also extended to professional journalists covering the event. "There was sudden realization of his steadfastness, his patient courage, his quiet strength," the *New York Herald Tribune* wrote. "He had given himself gallantly in what might prove to be a losing cause on both the political and the economic front, but there was no question that he had given himself."[2] At least briefly, the address rallied the spirits of the GOP across the nation. "The speech will have a tremendous and permanent effect in stabilizing the thought of the people," Henry Ford said. "I think all of our citizens are proud of our president today." R. R. Moton, the black educator who served as president of Tuskegee Institute, added, "There has been no address or state paper since Abraham Lincoln's second inaugural address that compares with it."[3] Some journalists observed that they saw empathy in the president they had not known existed. "It was straight from the heart," another daily explained.[4]

Despite Hoover's showing that he could make a rousing speech, his second term was anything but assured. The GOP remained the majority party, yet it was splintered and demoralized by the Great Depression. Many Americans, out of work and struggling to feed their families, felt that any change in the White House would be a change for the better. Unlike Hoover, Roosevelt grasped intuitively that the election would be determined by emotion, not intellectual persuasion; by the belly, not the brain. The man the voters liked best would win. The one they hated most would lose. The Depression gave the challenger a long head start. In desperate times people seek change; they are willing to take risks; on impulse the prevailing party can be tried and convicted simply for being there at the time a disaster occurred. Although Hoover addressed the nation by radio, he used it merely as a megaphone to reach a larger audience. Roosevelt had a keener understanding of the nascent medium's potential to simulate a personal conversation with his listeners. Yet some analysts agreed with Hoover and considered FDR weak, ill informed, too eager to try to please everyone, and a mediocre intellect.[5] Hoover quipped that the chief obstacles he had to overcome to win were "10,000,000 unemployed, 10,000 bonus marchers, and 10-cent corn."[6]

Hoover underestimated Roosevelt and believed he would be the easiest Democrat to defeat. He assumed FDR would find it impossible to do the work of the presidency from a wheelchair. Also, he derided Roosevelt as long on style but short on substance, calling FDR's promise to give a job to every unemployed American "cruel" for building false hope. Hoover and Roosevelt had been personal friends, or at least convivial acquaintances, until FDR turned on Hoover during the 1928 campaign. As a result, the president considered Roosevelt fickle and unprincipled, with a win-at-all-costs ethical code. Nonetheless, the Depression, not Roosevelt, was the real enemy. Under ordinary circumstances Hoover would have been a strong candidate, but these were unusual conditions. One supporter of Hoover summed up the dilemma of the GOP. "It was natural to claim for the Republican Party the great prosperity of 1928, but unfortunately it is equally natural to lay at its doors the misfortune of 1932." He explained that FDR was a more formidable opponent than Al Smith, whose Roman Catholic faith Protestants viewed with suspicion and whose links to Tammany Hall lent him an unwanted aura of big-city corruption. "Although infinitely inferior in mentality to Smith, Roosevelt has a pleasing personality; a good voice; a good appeal as a speaker, without any of the disqualifications of his opponent since religion is not an issue. . . . All he really has to do is to capitalize on the present discontent, and let that current bear him in." The writer's advice was that Hoover should be bold and assertive, frame pithy, catchy slogans, and take the offensive. He should emphasize the challenger's lack of qualifications and lack of viable alternatives to the Hoover program, placing the Democrat on the defensive.[7]

Republicans had not faced so grave a challenge for a long time. Money was an enormous problem for the GOP. The party eventually patched together about $2.5 million, more than the Democrats, but less than the $4 million they had spent in 1928, during booming times. Ironically, the Democrats spent less in winning in 1932 than they had in losing in 1928. The parties were fairly evenly matched in total spending, though the Republicans had a slender edge. Hoover and the best orator on his campaign team, Ogden L. Mills, paid for radio time out of their own pockets. The president was forced to spend a good deal of time raising money to keep the campaign solvent, finally obtaining a pledge of $500,000 from J. P. Morgan on the condition that Hoover raise matching funds. The president found the money, which lasted through the end of the GOP campaign.[8]

In mid-September, the returns in Maine, a rock-ribbed, reliably Republican state that voted in advance of most state elections in November, dumped a dose of cold reality on Republicans' hopes of carrying New England. Maine residents elected only their fourth Democratic governor since the Civil War, and two of three Democratic representatives won. There were no local issues; the election was considered a referendum on the economy. "No Maine election in modern times has appeared so ominous to Republican Presidential prospects," the *New York Herald Tribune* concluded. The results helped ignite the president's campaign, although he still did not campaign on a nationwide scale as Roosevelt was doing.[9]

The contrast in strategy was clear. Throughout the summer and fall Roosevelt barnstormed the country. Although he used a wheelchair, he carefully concealed his disability from the general public and refused to be photographed on crutches. Hoover did not plan his first major speech until October 1, believing speeches before that date were forgotten. Rather than campaigning personally, he planned to rely on surrogates and to avoid campaigning west of Des Moines. Ogden L. Mills, not the president himself, would shadow Roosevelt and refute the challenger's allegations. Hoover's aides warned that though farmers were angry, heartland votes were crucial, but the president was slow to respond. He was reluctant to leave Washington, where he was working on a program to end the Depression. Campaigning had little interest for him. He conceded that the West and the South would be carried by Democrats, and he felt his best option would be to cobble together an electoral majority in the Northeast, New England, the Mid-Atlantic States, Indiana, Ohio, and Illinois.

The Des Moines speech on October 4 was only Hoover's second since his acceptance speech on August 11. The president's press secretary, Theodore Joslin, had suggested Kansas City would be better, but Hoover insisted on speaking in the state of his birth. As his train traveled west from Washington, Hoover polished his address until the last minute. The parade from the train station to the coliseum, where the speech was delivered, was watched by 125,000 onlookers, who provided a rousing reception. Hoover, moved by speaking in his native state, rose to the occasion, delivering his remarks, which dealt specifically with agriculture, with vigor and emotion. Congratulatory telegrams poured in afterward. Joslin considered the effort at Des Moines the best speech of the campaign. "I have never experienced one like it before and I have traveled with Wilson, Harding, Coolidge, La Follette, among other Presidents and would-be Presidents," Joslin remarked.[10] Later that night the president informally discussed his Iowa boyhood with journalists, regaling them with off-the-record stories, showing a human side the public rarely witnessed. He was relaxed and among friends. Hoover reminded old friends, acquaintances, and reporters of his rural roots and his love of agriculture, but the election was now only five weeks away and much of the agrarian heartland was already lost. The defeat in Maine had galvanized the Republicans, but the Democrats had a head start and the mood of the country was sour. It was, Hoover sensed, too little, too late.[11]

Hoover was confronted with an almost entirely negative campaign waged by his opponent and his surrogates, who accused him of feeling no sympathy for the suffering of Americans and denounced his economic policies for causing the Depression. Roosevelt, who had once expressed admiration for Hoover, now held him responsible not only for sinking the ship of state, but for sinking it in a sea of red ink. In a campaign speech, FDR called for reducing the federal budget "not less than by 25%." Like Hoover, he believed in balanced budgets, although he never achieved one as president. Roosevelt made few promises with specific content. He vowed to help people but was vague on specifics. He pledged to preserve sound money but did not define "sound money."

Roosevelt needed only to exploit already existing discontent that was steaming over. He tried to be all things to all people without alienating anyone. Lamentations about the "Hoover Breadlines" for the hungry and the "Hoovervilles" for the homeless that sprang up in big cities helped make political capital of human misery. They also covered up the fact that the Democrats had few plans of their own to improve conditions. Lies were told about Hoover. Drew Pearson, writer of the syndicated newspaper column "Washington Merry-Go-Round," depicted the president as a man who was rude to his wife and habitually lost his temper, and who as a boy had peddled worthless land by duping settlers as a mere office boy for his uncle's Salem land company. But that was the least of Hoover's crimes, according to Pearson. He claimed that Hoover also swindled the unwary during his mining career. Moreover, he employed Chinese coolies as virtual slaves to mine for him and chained them to a stake in the hot sun for a full day to discourage strikes.[12]

For most of the campaign Hoover kept his peace. Only once, in his address at Fort Wayne, Indiana, on October 4, 1932, did he attempt to even partially respond. "During my public life, I have believed that sportsmanship and statesmanship called for the elimination of harsh personalities between opponents," he said. "I shall now say the only harsh word that I have uttered in public office," he explained. "When you are told that the President of the United States, who by the most sacred trust of our nation is the President of all the people, a man of your own blood and upbringing, has sat in the White House for the last three years of your misfortune without troubling to know your burdens," he continued, "without heartaches over your miseries and casualties, without summoning every avenue of skillful assistance, irrespective of party or view, without using every ounce of his strength and straining his every nerve to protect and help," he concluded, "without using every possible agency of democracy that would bring aid, without putting aside personal ambition and humbling his pride of opinion if that would serve—then I say to you that such statements are deliberate, intolerable falsehoods."[3]

In his Fort Wayne speech, Hoover also refuted the imputation that the worldwide Depression had originated on his watch, due partly to the Smoot-Hawley Tariff, and that he personally had perpetuated it. The chief executive discussed at length the Depression's origins. He cited the destruction of the Great War, the harsh treaties imposed on the defeated nations, the expenses of large standing armies, which weighed down the European economies, revolutions in Russia and China, overproduction in agriculture in many parts of the world, and a general attitude of malaise. These developments had heaped calamity upon calamity. The downturn was more complex and deep-rooted than the American stock market crash or the Smoot-Hawley Tariff. In fact, the Depression had begun abroad before the American tariff was even passed. The highly respected Bureau of Economic Research stated that the Depression had begun in eleven nations with populations totaling 600 million prior to its origins in America. The president then paused and asked why no Democrat had predicted the Depression. "I did not notice any Democratic Jeremiahs." The president slammed home that the insinuation that his administration had fomented the Depression was woefully ignorant or deliberately designed to sow political blame. He might have gone further and added that the Democrats had not proposed any solutions to the Depression, either. They wanted people to believe that if Hoover disappeared, the Depression would evaporate. Roosevelt might make complex problems appear simple, but that did not make the reality of the problems any simpler.[14]

Slander is endemic in American political campaigns, but in 1932 it reached epic proportions, destroying the image of one of the kindest men ever to occupy the White House. Some Americans were willing to believe even the most scurrilous whispers about Hoover, given the depth of the economic crisis and his image of cold detachment. During the campaign, a rumor spread implicating the president in the kidnapping of the Lindbergh baby. (Charles Lindbergh was actually a close friend of Hoover.) The fiercely loyal Lou exclaimed that after hearing the bombastic hyperbole that had smeared her husband she would have voted against him herself, had she been sufficiently gullible. Some of Roosevelt's closest advisers found the lies difficult to stomach, and several prominent New Dealers later admitted so. Raymond Moley, who subsequently broke with Roosevelt, grew to like and appreciate Hoover's skills and honesty. Rexford Tugwell, like Moley a Brain Truster and a Roosevelt speechwriter, admitted in 1974 that much of the substance of the New Deal's programs had been borrowed from Hoover. FDR's first vice president, John Nance Garner, also became a Hoover convert in later years and regretted the vindictiveness of his attacks.[15]

One of the first supporters Hoover recruited to speak on his behalf was ex-president Coolidge, who remained popular among many Republicans, although his reputation had lost some of its luster. Coolidge, resentful of the Democratic criticism, was anxious to speak, yet his health had declined and he could not travel extensively. In early September *The Saturday Evening Post* published an article by Coolidge strongly backing his former commerce secretary. Coolidge had additional incentive, because FDR had blamed Coolidge for countenancing the conditions that led to the Depression during his administration with his laissez-faire philosophy toward business interests. Coolidge wrote that Hoover had done a superb job as president, had the Depression almost under control when factors abroad pulled the world economy down in 1931, and had performed his duties better than any other world leader of his time. Coolidge reiterated that message in a speech to twenty thousand responsive Republicans at Madison Square Garden on October 11, carried nationwide via radio. He delivered a second national radio address directed at getting out the vote on election eve, the same evening Hoover delivered a related talk.

Initially, Hoover planned to deliver only three or four major speeches, yet during the final six weeks of the campaign he reached out to all sections of the nation. He believed in his policies and was persuaded that they were working. He felt he could help lift the nation out of the doldrums of the slumping economy, given a second term. To elect Roosevelt would delay recovery and might encourage the imposition of a leviathan government. If Hoover were defeated, he felt certain his policies would be abandoned. He feared the prospect of reckless experimentation and unwise concentration of power in a Democratic administration. He believed Roosevelt's plans were poorly conceived—indeed, barely thought out—and would result in bureaucracy, not prosperity. Hoover would have preferred to remain in Washington and work on the nation's problems, but now he forced himself to play a more active role in his own campaign. None of his loyal supporters had his national credibility. Some of his best orators, such as Senator Borah, had broken with him, and Curtis was no longer popular in the party because of his bone-dry position on Prohibition. Hoover knew he must still rely partly on surrogates, but he continued to write his own speeches. He felt it was necessary to travel more than he had intended to and utilize radio as much as his meager budget would permit.[16]

During October, Hoover's team saturated the Midwest with speakers, including cabinet officials, congressmen, and other high-ranking GOP spokesmen. Treasury Secretary Ogden Mills, an eloquent upstate New Yorker who was a neighbor of FDR and the most effective orator in the Republican arsenal, made the most grueling tour, trekking all the way to California to shadow the Democratic candidate and rebut his speeches. Altogether, the GOP put some 260 speakers into the field during October to refute FDR's charges, defend Hoover, and outline the Republican program. Mills and Indiana congressman Will R. Wood led the attack in the Midwest, where they compared the substance of Hoover's agricultural program with the vague promises of the Democrats.

The Republicans depicted Roosevelt as a candidate with a pleasing personality who lacked both a program and principles. Wood, in particular, attacked the Roosevelt claim that Hoover was an extravagant waster of federal dollars. Wood said the only increase in expenses was for construction work needed to provide the unemployed with jobs. FDR had claimed that the current administration had spent the most money in history without mentioning the jobs created by the federal construction. Wood pointed out that the Democratic House had denied the president the authority to thoroughly reorganize the government in the interest of economy. Roosevelt had condemned the president for pyramiding "bureau upon bureau," yet the only additions made, such as the RFC and the home loan bank system, had enabled the government to combat the Depression and save homes, banks, and farms.[17]

Addressing the Republican State Convention at Detroit and reaching the nation via a national radio network, Mills defended Hoover's record and assailed Roosevelt for lacking "any indication of having a program to lead the American people out of this valley," contrasting Hoover's integrated plan with Roosevelt's "intellectual lassitude." Mills resisted ad hominem attacks but criticized FDR's skeleton program of vague platitudes point by point.[18] On October 12, Senator Henry D. Hatfield of West Virginia accused FDR of taking a hypocritical stand on the tariff. Noting that the Democrats had accused the GOP of logrolling in enacting the Smoot-Hawley Tariff, he struck back. Hatfield insisted that "they propose a system of reciprocal tariffs wherein treaties will be entered with some forty-eight different foreign nations, and they ask the American people to believe that in the making of these treaties there will be no log-rolling or bartering." The following day, at Chicago, Ogden Mills asserted that Roosevelt blamed Hoover for his actions yet had presented no package of his own. Mills cited Hoover's massive programs of public works, job creation, relief, mortgage protection, and home and business loans and charged that the Democrats offered nothing specific. "Governor Roosevelt has no answer," he declared. Secretary of War Patrick J. Hurley charged that Roosevelt's tracing of the Depression solely to American roots was a historical distortion. The calamity and its origins were world-wide and the Depression had taken effect in some countries before leaping the Atlantic to America. FDR himself had had the tools to prevent or mitigate the stock market crash and major bank failures and had not exerted them, he claimed. The U.S. Supreme Court had ruled that banks and the New York Stock Exchange operated in intrastate, not interstate, commerce. Roosevelt, not Hoover, had the responsibility to regulate them, and he had not done so.[19]

At a speech in Cleveland, Hoover focused on economic problems, including unemployment and the tariff. He continued to defend his policies, yet he urged his countrymen to think beyond the material aspects of life and, even in their suffering, to view material possessions as a means to wholesomeness and a happy home rather than as an end in themselves. Hoover spoke to twenty-four thousand people at the city auditorium and to a nationwide radio audience. He was warmly received, yet the crowd was less enthusiastic than that at Des Moines, where he was on native turf. Along the way he made several short speeches from the rear platform of his train. Now in a fighting mood, the incumbent had decided he must be more assertive in defending his administration and not leave all the work to his surrogates. The president denied that the Smoot-Hawley Tariff had incited the Depression. It increased the general duty only 2.2 percent, and two-thirds of American products were nondutiable, he explained. Once more he emphasized that it was simplistic to attribute the Depression to a single event in a single nation. Shortly after his Cleveland address, Hoover spoke in Detroit, where he took the offensive, charging the Democrats with condemning his ideas because they lacked original ideas of their own. Virtually all of Hoover's criticism of the Democrats was directed toward them as a party and their policies, however, and he rarely employed personal invective. He challenged Roosevelt, who was avoiding the issue, to take a clear stand on the veterans' bonus and said he did not intend to make Prohibition a campaign issue.[20]

After the Detroit speech, Hoover devoted several days to public matters in Washington and to writing his next major address, scheduled for Indianapolis. From a strategic perspective, the Indianapolis talk was the high point of the campaign.[21] This wrap-up, whirlwind tour included brief speech stops in Maryland, Delaware, and Pennsylvania. The president exhibited Democratic propaganda that was being employed against him that mocked some of his most important accomplishments. He displayed flyers distributed by the Democratic National Committee with banner headlines reading "How President Hoover has failed children." Another stated, "His real interest in the Nation's children may be gained by his recorded effort to emasculate and disrupt the Children's Bureau." Another was entitled "The Bunk of the Home Loan Bank."[22] On his return the chief executive spoke for half an hour in Philadelphia. Then he headed to Baltimore and Wilmington, Delaware. The president whistle-stopped through several coal and industrial states, devoting special attention to the hard-hit mining districts, and conferred with United Mine Workers president John L. Lewis.[23]

Although by early November Hoover accepted that his chances for a second term were remote, those final days before the election saw him revitalized. As he returned to the East, which he considered his base, he planned to make one final effort in New York City, his October 31 speech at Madison Square Garden. Hoover had said from the beginning that he must carry New York to win the election, and he vowed to make a supreme effort there. In each of his previous speeches, the president had emphasized a single theme. Now, in his New York speech, he attempted to weave the strands into a common theme, provide moral uplift, and explain how his philosophy differed from his opponent's. En route, the chief executive delivered a speech to seventy-five thousand GOP partisans at Newark. He dwelled on business conditions, which he said had been improving since his debt moratorium and standstill agreement. He indicated that there had been an upswing in most economic indices since midsummer.[24]

The crowds that lined the streets to Madison Square Garden were enthusiastic, and Hoover hoped the mood indicated a shift in his direction.

The audience inside the Garden was massive. Some twenty-five thousand people had to be turned away for lack of seats. In his address, Hoover attacked Roosevelt's philosophy of government, which, he complained, was built from the top down rather than from the grass roots. FDR would build layers of bureaucracy through which the average citizen must meander. Bureaucracies are self-perpetuating and wasteful, Hoover pointed out; they represent their own interests rather than those of the people. Above the bureaucracy stand the politicians, whose objective is to keep their own jobs by doling out favors, not to the neediest, but to those most likely to vote for them. Such a model for government is unwieldy and does not have the best interests of the common people at heart. This election, Hoover stated, represented a difference not merely between two candidates but between two philosophies of government. Hoover continued to hammer away at the contradictions in Roosevelt's public pronouncements, seeking to contrast his policies with FDR's. He attacked his opponent for pandering to the popular mood rather than delivering substance, and he defended his own economic program and personal character against the attacks that had been made on him. A few days before the election, in Springfield, Illinois, Hoover accused his rival of pledging one type of tariff policy in the East and the diametrically opposed position in the West. Roosevelt could not be trusted to keep his promises, Hoover warned.[25]

Maintaining a vigorous pace through Election Day, Hoover spoke by radio to his home state of California, where polls showed him trailing, and announced that he would cross the country by rail to vote in Palo Alto. Along the way he made twenty-eight speeches from the rear of his coach and major addresses at Springfield, Illinois; St. Louis; St. Paul; Salt Lake City; and Elko, Nevada. The president conceded to his staff that only an unlikely rapid improvement in the economy could carry him to victory. Before departing the White House, he spent three arduous days writing his speeches in longhand, with minimal input from associates. He tried to be upbeat but realistic. Along the way, the president reached the point of near exhaustion, stumbling over words and almost collapsing on the platform at St. Paul. He spoke haltingly and his voice was weak. He repeatedly lost his place in the manuscript and struggled to complete the speech.[26] In Washington, a dismayed Theodore Joslin listened to Hoover's address by radio. "The President was absolutely punch drunk tonight," Joslin wrote in his diary after speaking with Hoover over the telephone. "The content of the speech was good," explained Joslin. "But the delivery of his speech was terrible. Hoover's speech didn't help him any in the circumstances. It is too bad for we were hoping it would swing Minnesota and perhaps North Dakota."[27]

Not every address showed the wear and strain of campaigning. Speaking in St. Louis, Hoover was combative and assertive. The president blamed Roosevelt for the nasty tone of the campaign, saturated with distortion and innuendo. Hoover defended his record and said the Democrats could not escape a share of the blame for conditions that instigated the implosion of the economy. "I submit that some of the greatest leaders amongst the boom promoters of this period belonged to the Democratic Party, and the Democratic candidate himself assisted actively in promotions." He added that "the Governor in his speeches conveys the impression that as President I should have stopped the boom. He does not prescribe the method by which I should have stopped it." Finally, he said, "If the President had attempted to stop that boom, one of the persons he would have needed to warn is the present Democratic candidate."[28] The president also rebutted the Democratic argument that charged him with sole responsibility for the Depression by pointing out that Democrats had offered few tangible alternatives of their own.[29] Logic was on Hoover's side, but emotion was on FDR's side. Hoover's train continued westward to Salt Lake City, where he addressed ten thousand in his final major speech, then to the small town of Elko, Nevada, where he delivered his last radio address. Then it was off to Palo Alto. At Stanford University, where classes were dismissed for Election Day, Hoover addressed two thousand students who had gathered to support him. The Hoovers cast their votes at the Stanford Union. The president carried the precinct easily. He retired to his home nearby, where family and old friends waited by the radio and listened to the returns until early evening.

The homeward journey had been difficult. On his return to California to vote, Hoover's train was halted because a vandal was spotted pulling up spikes, hoping to derail the engine. The man was arrested. In Nevada, Hoover was pelted with eggs, and the state's governor refused to greet him. With morbid humor, a man cabled Hoover: "Vote for Roosevelt and make it unanimous."³⁰ Once a beloved world-renowned figure, Hoover was no longer termed the Great Engineer or the Great Humanitarian except in mockery. The stereotype that replaced his heroic status was the personification of the Great Depression, which, ironically, he had labored tirelessly to alleviate. The modest Quaker has often been depicted by historians as glum, dejected, defeated, eager to depart the White House and release his burden. Just the opposite was true. He was eager to win a second term because he felt certain the Depression was almost over. On November 8, the American voters denied him that opportunity. Roosevelt carried 42 states, winning 472 electoral votes and 57.4 percent of the popular vote. Hoover took only 59 electoral votes and 39.7 percent of the popular vote. It was a resounding renunciation of his administration. At nine thirty p.m. Hoover conceded defeat as calmly as he had accepted victory four years earlier.

In the weeks that followed the election, major newspapers tried to explain Hoover's presidency in perspective. Considering his decisive defeat, most major dailies demonstrated respect, even praise. One common sentiment was that anyone who had found himself in Hoover's position would have been hard-pressed to do better. The *Washington Post* agreed with the president's own assessment that the American economy was reviving from its slumber in 1931 when the European economic crisis plunged it into a coma. "Mr. Hoover," the *Post* observed, "has earned the gratitude of the country for his services. He has battled with gigantic and unprecedented forces of destruction, without sparing himself." The *New York Herald Tribune* wrote that in his "resolute self-sacrificing devotion to the 'American System' Mr. Hoover proved himself a great

President." On the other hand, the *Chicago Tribune* accused Hoover of incubating socialism in America.[31] As for the judgment of history, it was then too early to ascertain whether he would be labeled with an epitaph suited for ruining the country, or apropos the first Jeffersonian Republican. He still had more than a quarter century to make a difference and to write much of his own legacy.

The long interregnum between the voting in November and Roosevelt's inauguration on March 4, 1933, was one of the most contentious in history. During the interim between the election and the swearing in, the nation was in limbo. Hoover was the last president to experience the long transition as a lame duck. The Twentieth Amendment, which ended the period on January 3 for Congress and January 20 for the president, did not take effect during his term. Although he still had the legal mandate to govern, he was deprived of meaningful power. The interlude between the inauguration and the election had created a difficult transition during earlier administrations, but the tense nature of the Hoover-Roosevelt transfer of power occurred during a precarious time. While en route to Washington by train, two days after the election, Hoover addressed a long telegram to Roosevelt, outlining the intention of America's Great War allies to cancel or reduce their war debts to the United States in light of the worldwide economic downturn. Hoover wanted to work with Roosevelt to craft a bipartisan response. Roosevelt agreed to meet with Hoover but refused to take action, declaring that the problem needed to be sorted out by the outgoing administration. Congress, rudderless, meandering, and lacking guidance, balked at even the most mundane request from the outgoing president and blocked confirmation of even low-level government appointees. Hoover was president in title only; the ship of state lay beached. Seldom was the transfer of power between an outgoing president and his successor as awkward or acrimonious. This was not because of any lack of vital executive business. Roosevelt said he would not act or comment until attired in the requisite authority of president. When Hoover talked, the public appeared deaf.

A logjam of business piled up in Congress and in the executive branch. Roosevelt instructed Democrats not to vote without instructions from him, but he issued few specific guidelines except to kill Hoover bills and appointments. Almost the entire four years of Hoover's administration had been frustrating, but the interregnum proved the most frustrating. At least during previous crises he had been in charge. Now no one was in charge. The stressful interregnum was characterized by a series of dilemmas that included a banking panic, acute unemployment, unsettled economic issues with Europe, a decline in world trade, and a fiscal crisis punctuated by uncertainty over the future of the gold standard. Hoover turned to Roosevelt, who rejected every overture. Some of FDR's advisers believed the outgoing president wanted to trap the governor into pursuing his discredited script. By March 4, Inauguration Day, the men were bitter and remote.[32]

Rumors gathered that the new president planned to devaluate gold-backed money or abandon the gold standard entirely, which provoked the greatest bank panic of the Depression, eclipsing 1929 and 1931. House Speaker Garner recklessly published the names of banks that had received RFC loans, which started a panicked run on those banks. Exchange rates became scrambled, destabilizing foreign trade. Roosevelt resolutely refused Hoover's request to spell out what steps he would take about banks and the currency despite the tide of bank failures sweeping the nation. Hoover and some of Roosevelt's most trusted advisers warned him that this would inspire turmoil in financial markets. The incoming president seemed content to let the economy drift for the remainder of Hoover's tenure. Banks and repositories were drained of assets and toppled like children's blocks during the disorderly interlude. Congress and the people would not follow Hoover, and FDR would not lead. The longer the power vacuum lasted, the worse conditions became. Some three-fourths of the withdrawals occurred during the week before FDR's inauguration, more than half during the final three days. It constituted a far greater economic catastrophe than the crash of 1929.

Roosevelt's intentions remained inscrutable. The president-elect sneered at federal interventions, arguing that he "could see no reason why he should save these bankers," ignoring the stark reality that when banks failed, depositors were left penniless.[33]

The next installment of World War I debts would overlap the Hoover-Roosevelt administrations. Foreign debtors wanted to negotiate reductions during the Hoover administration for payments due during the Roosevelt administration, but the incoming and outgoing presidents could not agree on terms, or even conduct a serious discussion on the subject. Hoover, Roosevelt, and their aides met for two major discussions, but Roosevelt wanted to wait until he became president to deal with the issue. Hoover argued that by that time it would be too late because the deadline would have passed and the debtor nations would have defaulted. The outgoing and incoming administrations also discussed the rash of bank failures. Both sides believed some form of bank holiday might be necessary to avert a total collapse, but time ran out before they could agree on details. Roosevelt consistently refused to negotiate any tentative agreement until he was actually president, and every proposal foundered on that obstacle. Under the existing circumstances, almost any clarification of intended policy would have been stabilizing, yet there were none.[34]

Hoover and Roosevelt took different approaches to their meetings, usually with one or two advisers present. Hoover wanted straightforward negotiations resulting in decisive commitments, while Roosevelt preferred pleasant chats during which not much business got done. The two men had common friends, one of whom confided that the New Dealers wanted economic conditions to decline to their lowest point before the new administration took office. Using that valley as their barometer, they could measure recovery against the period when the Depression bottomed out—Hoover's interregnum—and use those gloomy statistics in future comparisons. Even with the election over, the politically minded FDR wanted to wring every political advantage out of the failing economy.[35]

Roosevelt was an intuitively adept politician, while Hoover was no politician at all, simply a public servant with a set of objectives he wanted to achieve. While Hoover's presidency was scrupulously planned, Roosevelt's was made up off the cuff, characterized by a weak cabinet but strong advisers. Roosevelt did not initiate most of his own policy; he waited for business to be brought to him and let others flesh out the details. He procrastinated endlessly and changed his mind and his set of advisers often. He frequently borrowed from others (including Hoover), often without attribution. Raymond Moley, an early Brain Truster, commented that to conceive of the New Deal as "the result of a unified plan was to believe that the accumulation of stuffed snakes, baseball pictures, school flags, old tennis shoes, carpenter's tools, geometry books and chemistry sets in a boy's bedroom could have been put there by an interior decorator." Moley made these observations in retrospect after breaking with Roosevelt and leaving the New Deal. Those who saw FDR up close were often not as impressed with his intellect as those who saw Hoover intimately.[36]

Inauguration Day on March 4, 1933, was a chilly affair. Hoover and Roosevelt rode together in an open car to the Capitol for the swearing-in ceremony but barely exchanged words. Afterward, Hoover and his family departed Washington for New York. He planned to return to his beloved California for a quiet life in retirement, perhaps dabbling in engineering and farming, writing, continuing his work with charities such as the Belgian-American Educational Foundation and the Boys Clubs of America, and becoming more involved in Stanford affairs. However, although he was relieved of official responsibilities, his pace never slackened.

Hoover lost the 1932 election primarily because of the woeful state of the economy more than anything he did or did not do. Like all mortals, he had human foibles and made mistakes. His most fateful mistake was choosing politics as a profession. He was an introvert in a profession that rewards extroverts. He did not enjoy mixing with crowds, shaking hands, or making small talk and could not communicate emotionally to

the masses. Hoover enjoyed solitude, unusual for a politician. He was
honest to a fault, reluctant to pander or employ patronage in elections.
An orphan, reared in modest circumstances in small frontier villages,
he sympathized with the downtrodden but could not connect with them
in speeches before large audiences. He did not enjoy the public relations
aspect of politics and gave little grist to the media mills. He could not
dramatize himself or his policies. Even in 1932, after he had spent the
previous decade in politics, the political process remained alien and
unnatural to Hoover. He expected private charity to do a job that even
the entire state and federal governments could not do adequately. He
viewed hunger in America as merely a larger version of that in Belgium.
He held few lasting political grudges, but those few were intense and
obvious. His sense of humor was too subtle for large crowds. Simply put,
he lacked political skills. He wanted to win GOP nominations without
campaigning for them. Yet if he had been nominated in 1920, when both
parties wanted him, he would have presided over the prosperity of the
1920s and might have gone down in history as a great president.

Hoover made specific errors as well. He should have opposed the
Smoot-Hawley Tariff. Mandatory crop controls would have been preferable to his system of cooperatives if they could have been enforced. He
should have clamped down sanctions on Japan when the island nation
invaded Manchuria, though the Japanese might have conquered additional territory to obtain raw materials. Idealistically, Hoover relied too
heavily on world opinion to deter aggression. This approach had no
teeth. He should have compromised with Senator George Norris to begin
development of hydroelectric power in the Tennessee Valley. He should
have lobbied Congress more aggressively, including distribution of patronage. Hoover was not pursuing a fool's errand; his methods had worked
in the past. He was too intellectually honest for the times, which were
saturated with hypocritical intrigue. What might Hoover's place in history have been if he had never run for president at all? He was virtually
unsurpassed as a humanitarian and an administrator.

Hoover's good deeds and sharp mind, his generosity and his sincerity outweigh these faults, and his mistakes constituted errors in judgment, not mortal sins. He was both human and humane, and if he does not deserve a spot on Mount Rushmore, he does not deserve to be pilloried as the scapegoat of the Great Depression either. History is more complicated than that.

TWELVE

Challenging the New Deal

"I knew from the experience of all public men from George Washington down that democracies are fickle and heartless," Hoover reflected on his thrashing in the 1932 presidential election. "When the ultimate bump came, I was well-fortified to accept it philosophically . . . for democracy is a harsh employer." America had welcomed him home as a conquering hero following World War I, elected him president by a landslide in 1928, and defeated him overwhelmingly only four years later. Tad would later recall that his brother's ascension to the presidency was the worst event in the lives of their family, causing a great deal of discomfort without compensating gratification. Herbert Jr. suggested that his father and his family would have been better off had he simply returned to America after the war and rested on his laurels. "If the might and dignity of a lion may be judged by the crowd of jackals yelping in his train," Herbert Jr. reflected, "Herbert Hoover may look with complaisance on his following." Despite his disappointment, Hoover held a hopeful, perhaps naïve belief that he might eventually persuade the public that the election of Roosevelt had been a mistake.[1]

Immediately following the inauguration, Lou traveled to California with Herbert Jr. to finally spend time in her dream house. Meanwhile, her husband embarked with Allan for New York, where he had numerous loose ends to tie up. Exhausted, Hoover slept twelve hours undisturbed at his Waldorf suite the first night, then drove to Connecticut the following day to visit his devoted friend Edgar Rickard, who had handled Hoover's financial affairs during his presidency. On March 6, the ex-president issued a terse statement urging the nation to cooperate with the new president's bank holiday, though privately he had doubts about the total closing, which he considered overkill. He believed in closing only troubled banks and permitting sound banks to continue operation. His view was confirmed when most banks reopened almost immediately. The legislation enacted to rectify abuses might do harm to sound banks, he feared.[2]

On March 7, his energy refreshed, Hoover rose early and reviewed his personal financial situation, finding sufficient assets for him and Lou to continue comfortably at a reduced standard of living. He transferred some investments from bonds to stocks, which stood to appreciate along with Roosevelt's currency inflation, and deeded his Rapidan fishing camp to the federal government for the use of future presidents. Falling into a routine of activities and appointments, which delayed his return to Palo Alto, he met with admirers, investment counselors, and charitable trusts he represented, such as the American Child Health Association, the Boys Clubs of America, the Belgian-American Educational Foundation and the American Children's Relief Association. Finally, after several busy weeks, he boarded a train for California. Several hundred well-wishers gathered at the station to say good-bye.[3]

Lou had their home ready by the time her husband arrived in Palo Alto, and they spent several months relaxing. "It was a release not only from political pressures but from the routines of twelve to fourteen hours of work seven days a week," he explained. For the first time in memory, he slept without an alarm clock. He and Lou read newspapers and listened to the radio while dining on a leisurely breakfast. They

hired a team of secretaries to answer the twenty thousand friendly letters that poured in, signing the responses personally. Hoover puttered
with engineering projects with old colleagues. His friends secured for
him a seat on the board of the New York Life Insurance Company, which
brought extra income. When he was greeted at home by the governor,
the mayor, Stanford students, and old friends, his subdued wit emerged.
In his last address before going into temporary political retirement, Hoover
quipped, "You will expect me to discuss the late election. Well, as nearly
as I can learn we did not have enough votes on our side." This was the
Hoover his friends knew.[4]

Initially, unchained from telephones and no longer tied to secretaries, he enjoyed a sense of liberation. For the most part he was his own
boss, setting his own pace. The typical day began with a stroll along
Fraternity Row accompanied by two pets, a police dog and a Norwegian
elkhound, before he returned to his study, where he passed the hours
surrounded by his books, journals, and projects. With Lou he traveled
thousands of miles, visiting wilderness regions, cities, factories, and
slums. He combined fishing expeditions with exploration, heading down
rural roads at breakneck speeds. He roared into Reno and Grass Valley,
where he and Lou visited the old Comstock mine, and sped down to his
son Allan's home in Los Angeles. In his first major excursion, the ex-
president covered eight thousand miles in ten weeks. Most people he
encountered were friendly. Yet Hoover's nature demanded satisfying,
productive work. He wanted to remain active, useful, and immersed in
public affairs. He would never again be a completely contented man.
Quakers are a determined people, and Hoover was not simply purpose-
ful; he was driven. His interest in Stanford, and specifically the War
Library, consumed him. He opened avenues to influential friends, and
to Stanford streamed a steady traffic of endowments, funds for special
projects, and rare books. He resumed a more active role in the affairs of
Stanford, the Huntington Library, Mills College, the Carnegie Institute,
the Boys Clubs of America, the American Children's Fund, the Belgian-
American Educational Foundation, and other committees. "I am engaged

part-time in making a living in farming and mining on such moderate scale that keeps me out of the haunts of capital and enables me to reject offers of corporations and of radio and press or platforms for cash," he wrote Henry L. Stimson, his former secretary of state.[5]

Palo Alto might have seemed idyllic, yet it was also tame for a man of Hoover's drive and ambition. Finding the local newspapers insufficiently meaty with political news, he was soon devouring thirty national papers daily, receiving them via airmail. Not content to leave their old life behind, the Hoovers traveled extensively on the East Coast and rented a part-time apartment in the elite Waldorf Towers to be near the intellectual, political, and philanthropic action. For more than a year after his involuntary retirement, the elder statesman refrained publicly from partisan political statements, but privately he formulated plans to redesign the GOP as a clear, definitively conservative alternative to the New Deal, which was moving leftward at warp speed.[6]

By early 1934, the ex-president was hard at work on a book that critiqued the "statist" and collectivist ideologies sweeping the globe, such as Communism and Fascism, and he included the New Deal. Hoover rejected a $25,000 offer to publish a serialized version in *American Magazine* in lieu of a $10,000 offer from *The Saturday Evening Post*, in which it would reach more readers. The manuscript was boosted when adopted by the Book-of-the-Month Club. However, the publisher decided to pair its publication with a book defending the New Deal written by Secretary of Agriculture Henry A. Wallace. *The Challenge to Liberty* was published on August 10, 1934, Hoover's sixtieth birthday. He felt a sense of release; he had gotten his views off his chest. However one might disagree with his viewpoint, the book's intellectual honesty is transparent. Hoover did not mention the New Deal by name, simply by implication. It was also an indirect attempt to answer the critics of his own policies by demonstrating that he had maintained a nation free of coercion.[7]

In *The Challenge to Liberty*, the Chief dealt with the causes and consequences of the Great Depression. Hoover believed that even if regimentation could resolve the Depression—which it could not—it would be purchased at the cost of liberty. He called his slender volume "the gospel according to Palo Alto." He believed the American System had been designed for peace and the Depression had been caused by the Great War and its aftermath. It was a worldwide phenomenon, not solely an American invention, and its solution must be found in international remedies. Regimentation would only curtail production and consumption, and bureaucracy would weigh down the economy with ponderous regulations and deter creative innovation. Hoover did not consider the feeding and shelter of the needy inherently collectivist. Americans had always taken care of those in need. The New Deal was dangerous because it usurped local responsibility and concentrated power in the federal government. People receiving direct relief from the government feared losing it if they did not vote for the party in power. There was further danger that the government could distribute relief as a form of patronage.[8]

In some respects, *The Challenge to Liberty* was an elaboration of Hoover's 1922 philosophical treatise, *American Individualism*. By early October the volume had become a bestseller. To spread his creed, the ex-president purchased and gave away thousands of copies. Hoover's friend William Allen White, a fellow product of the Progressive movement, explained that the former president opposed the New Deal's methods, not its goals. In a review of the book, Professor Wesley C. Mitchell of Columbia cautioned that it would be improper to label Hoover either a reactionary or a radical; he occupied a middle ground. Still, there was no doubt that he stood to the right of the New Deal. Hoover believed that the New Dealers had kidnapped the word "liberal." The ex-president himself might best be described as a nineteenth-century classical liberal or a progressive similar to Theodore Roosevelt or Woodrow Wilson.[9]

Hoover realized that no nation could have both absolute liberty and absolute security. Although firm on bedrock principles, he compromised on implementation and over specific solutions to practical problems. The engineer planned carefully, but the artist in him could improvise and he accommodated and anticipated human error. The man who was at home roaming the fields and forests never underestimated the power of imagination. Without it, pure logic faltered. Emotion fueled him; he was no robot. A practical man, he considered drive more important than intelligence, common sense more important than a gilt-edged education.

The administrator's belief in waste reduction was not a technical fetish. His work with the Boys Clubs of America demonstrated that he detested human waste as even more obnoxious than industrial waste or despoliation of natural resources. Although he was a careful analyst who believed in order, the idea of a planned society was anathema to him. Order did not mean regimentation. He disliked all forms of totalitarianism and authoritarianism and revered individualism. Rather than view Hoover as an archetypical conservative or liberal, it is more realistic to appreciate the changes in his philosophy as he aged and the circumstances changed. It is more accurate to describe him as an individualist than to pigeonhole him as the apostle of any doctrine.

Hoover spent the Roosevelt years as an outsider looking in, working as a critic, writer, and speaker. He was, nonetheless, the single most influential Republican strategist, writer, and speaker, as well as a formidable fund-raiser. Hoover was profoundly embittered by his treatment by FDR during the 1932 campaign, and by what he considered Roosevelt's economic naïveté and political ruthlessness, and his criticism ranged from the satirical to the sardonic. Hoover condemned as unrealistic FDR's narrowly nationalistic approach to the world and the Depression. The ex-president believed the worldwide Depression could be resolved only by cooperative, international recovery, not by an every-nation-for-itself mentality. Later, Hoover condemned Roosevelt for going too far in the opposite direction, for letting the needs and priorities of other nations guide American foreign policy at the expense of domestic interests. He saw Roosevelt moving the nation toward war. When the Nazis attacked the Soviets, Hoover proposed to hedge diplomatic bets rather than immediately siding with the Soviets, because he viewed both ideologies as equally odious.[10]

During this period, Hoover honed his writing and speaking skills. His style grew increasingly erudite, and his speeches, books, and articles are sprinkled with epigrams. Speaking before small audiences, he let his natural, nuanced humor show. Though he employed secretaries and research assistants to check facts and perform clerical duties, Hoover's style remained inimitably his own, and it improved. He worked at it doggedly and daily. In 1940, Professor Elmer E. Nyberg of the New York University School of Commerce, who had made a study of the speaking ability of prominent public speakers, wrote in the New York Times that "Herbert Hoover has improved as a speaker more than any man in public life and at the present time leads all possible Presidential candidates in the content of his speeches." He rated Hoover an A-plus in oratory, while President Roosevelt, whom he graded an A-minus, had lost ground, wrote the professor.[11]

Hoover was a man on a mission, determined to right the listing ship of state and prevent it from sinking into a quagmire of unconstitutional laws and procedures. He viewed the New Deal jobs programs as naïve in an economic sense and a vote factory in a political sense. It was FDR's largesse with government money to targeted interest groups, not his success in conquering the Depression, which was borderline, that explained the New Deal's electoral victories. The people were duped into following a primrose path because the jobs were only temporary. They would end when the appropriations expired or the projects were completed. At the end of it all, the country would be worse off than before, mired in a sinkhole of debt left to future generations and future presidents to pay. Moreover, while Roosevelt spent billion upon billion on public works to generate temporary jobs, it never occurred to him to cut taxes, stimulate the private sector, and restore old, permanent jobs. Hoover wrote with passionate eloquence and improved in the process. This period brought out the hidden writer in him. Perhaps all he had ever needed was the time, the practice, and the cause. As an ex-president, he commanded a forum.[12]

Hoover was relentless and determined. He pointed out that Roosevelt's

sympathy for the poor was feigned. His humor and his ideas were borrowed, like some of his programs. Roosevelt even plagiarized some ideas
from Hoover while simultaneously claiming that Hoover had done nothing. The nation was on a treadmill of deficit spending, appropriating more
and more to remain in essentially the same place. At the rate recovery was
progressing, everyone on the planet would be dead by the time it occurred.

Hoover regarded Roosevelt as animated by a mixture of unmitigated
ambition and political savvy, yet considered the president jumbled in his
witches' brew of economic theories, which he barely comprehended: a
short-run politician with an eye on the next election, offering the nation
slogans and platitudes, fiddling while the nation was consumed in an
economic wildfire. Roosevelt was an all-or-nothing leader. Like many
charismatic leaders, the New Yorker was better at inflaming emotions
than he was at solving real-world problems. Grasping at straws of ideas
from all directions, he would pile them up until they broke the nation's
fiscal back. He pretended to care about the common man, but what he
cared about was their votes. Yet because the New Deal morphed into a
much larger bureaucracy with the coming of the war, a time when no
one questioned the need for big government, and FDR's death virtually
coincided with the end of the war, the bureaucracy built for back-to-back
emergencies was never completely dismantled and many equated the
bureaucracy itself with prosperity and expected the government to guarantee prosperous times permanently. The circumstances created a system of dependency. The crutch would not be discarded after the leg had
healed.[13]

In many respects, Hoover and Roosevelt were opposites. Hoover had
a firm grasp of economics, both practical and theoretical, whereas Roosevelt's perception of economics resembled a dalliance—he would flirt
with an idea and then move on. His approach was glib. Hoover, in contrast, took ideas seriously and mulled them over before attempting to
leap a canyon. He could be decisive but was not prone to snap judg-
ments. He wanted to use power to achieve a practical result yet revered
spiritual values and cared little for the vanities of political fame. His

attachments, to ideas and to people, were lifelong. Roosevelt jettisoned friends if doing so became politically expedient. Both men could be stubborn. Hoover could be obstinately self-righteous; however, he spurned flattery, whether sincere or otherwise. The Iowa orphan had worked with his hands, something the former governor had never done. Until he became president, there was nothing in FDR's background to foreshadow greatness; Hoover had already been one of the most famous men in the world at the time of his election. The Great Engineer wanted a slimmed-down, efficient, gazelle-type government. Hoover was profoundly religious, though not an ingrained churchgoer, and had a philosophical respect for tradition, especially for the American political institutions, with carefully designed balancing of powers.

Two men, two sets of ideas, one anchored in a firm historical foundation, the other filching ideas ad hoc. Roosevelt had the attention and the heart of the nation. Hoover, repudiated, fought patiently, relentlessly, hoping to influence contemporary opinion and legislation, but also arguing before the tribunal of history. The winners of political wars, like the winners of military wars, write the histories. In that sense, Hoover was on the losing side of history. But in the realm of ideas, and the long-run repercussions of policies, Hoover left an abundant and thorough written record of his philosophy.

Hoover predicted that FDR's New Deal would not end the Depression, and it did not, though the unemployed waited and waited. Roosevelt nonetheless used the New Deal jobs to entrench himself in office, a tactic Hoover deplored. In the campaign of 1932 FDR had pilloried Hoover for deficit spending, yet the spending of his administration made a mockery of that criticism. During the 1932 campaign, much of Roosevelt's rhetoric proclaimed that Hoover was a spendthrift president who had gone too far in exploding federal power, although, simultaneously, he accused Hoover of being a do-nothing president. Sadly, much of this has been lost in the jumble of historical legends. The New Deal that began in 1933 and unfolded was not the New Deal promised in 1932, as Hoover clearly pointed out.[14]

Some of those who had earlier opposed Hoover now regretted losing him, as the New Deal produced layer upon layer of bureaucracy. The Democratic *Baltimore Sun* lamented that the New Deal was like Hoover with a second helping. Yet, to some degree, Hoover remained a loner in the Republican Party, in which many professional politicians had always considered him an interloper. They refused to renominate him not simply because his administration had been marred with failure but because they had never wanted him in the first place.[15]

Hoover himself was more unpopular than his ideas, which remain relevant. The election of 1932 marked a fork in the road of our political and economic history. The residue of opposition to the prolific spending of government, the growth of entitlements, and the addictive nature of welfare verify Hoover's critique, which provides a more comprehensive exposition of enlightened, sophisticated, humane conservatism than Ronald Reagan or Barry Goldwater enunciated. Hoover put flesh on the bones of theory. Yet, in subsequent elections, his name was seldom evoked by GOP presidential contenders except as a bogeyman. In foreign policy, only a few insulated scholars have used Hoover as a prophet of the dangers of overreach. Ironically, many of his ideas continue to gain credence, while Hoover himself is overlooked due to the stigma of the Great Depression. Few prophets in American history have been more scorned in their own country.[16]

Hoover was titular head of the GOP, but he wondered if he genuinely aspired to leadership of a party that seemed down and out. His friend Mark Sullivan wrote that he believed it would be a mistake to reveal the faintest interest in another term as president. For the moment, many in his party considered him neither a resource nor a leader but a millstone. Still, as an ex-president, Hoover immediately commanded an audience. As more and more Republicans came to see the New Deal as a threat to American institutions, some gravitated to Hoover. His life had been one of leadership. He needed to find new outlets for his energy without asserting himself too overtly in the beginning. He also nourished an ambition for exculpation, possibly in a political sense, but certainly in a historical manner. The ex-president helped organize a group of Republicans, many of whom had served in his administration, called the Republican Federal Associates. They constituted the embryo of opposition to the New Deal and possibly a stepping-stone for Hoover, yet in the short run the organization worked for the election of Republicans in the 1934 congressional elections. Among the most active were former Hoover cabinet members Ogden Mills and Walter F. Brown.[17]

When he left office Hoover seemed to have no aspirations for the 1936 GOP nomination, yet his friends urged him to remain in readiness should a call come. He maintained a prudent silence during the early months of the New Deal, though dismayed by the rush to legislate a hodgepodge of measures by a rubber-stamp Congress during the Hundred Days. Roosevelt's appetite for power might prove insatiable, he predicted. Hoover considered FDR's unsystematic inflation of the currency ill-advised and questioned his lack of consultation with congressional leaders, who nonetheless followed him. The ex-president did not oppose all aspects of the National Recovery Administration, yet he doubted that mandated scarcity could produce prosperity and warned that the new agency's monopolistic division of the markets would ruin small business. Hoover found many aspects of the early New Deal needlessly polarizing. Already, he had moral qualms about the New Deal, yet he considered it unseemly to enter the fray. He lamented the element of class war and the dicing of the population into interest groups, which reminded him of the march toward totalitarianism in Europe and the Soviet state. He was growing edgy, but he wanted to give the New Deal a chance and feared some would interpret criticism from him as spite. Hoover felt the flaws in the economy were flaws in individual men, not in the system. He worried not simply about the future of the country under the New Deal, but about the future of the GOP. There was no heir apparent, nor a spokesman grounded in experience. He cautioned prudence, not demagoguery, but he feared some in his party wanted to emulate the New Deal rather than redirect it. Hoover was tempted to speak out, but he resisted and instead tried to influence party policy behind the scenes.

Hoover disliked the prospect that Republicans would imitate the New Deal and he did not believe they could win on that basis. Privately, he conceded that elements of the New Deal were salutary, including some taken from his own administration. He had mixed feelings about the state of affairs in both parties but was not optimistic. He would reenter the public sphere, but timing was crucial.[18]

Hoover believed that if recovery occurred, it would take place in spite of, not because of, the New Deal, and also that the public would accept a more powerful, intrusive, leviathan state that crushed liberty. Hoover further worried that any recovery might not take place at all. He realized that if he criticized the New Deal and subsequently good times returned, he would be labeled a carping reactionary. So, for a variety of reasons, Hoover pondered his options. He did not race into battle, but he kept his powder dry. Hoover did, however, encourage surrogates to discharge volleys he considered inappropriate for himself. He also quietly began to cultivate Republican policies that might furnish an alternative to the New Deal, which appeared to him a runaway train. Further, he wanted to bind the GOP into a united fulcrum of opposition, because some congressmen were already tilting toward the forbidden apples of the New Deal. Even Republican National Chairman Everett Sanders was inclined to lean in that direction. Hoover's view, which was consistent throughout his life, was that responsible criticism was the mantra of the opposition party and that the two-party system was vital to American democracy. It was, in fact, the very purpose of freedom of speech. The ex-president pointed with alacrity to nations that lacked healthy opposition parties as they toppled down a rabbit hole into worlds of bizarre ideologies. However, criticism must be prudent and constrained, and it should focus on faulty policies, not indict the opposition as evil individuals. To cross these lines would be to lose credibility and to abuse freedom of speech. He did not believe in "fighting fire with fire." Moreover, he once admitted to fellow Republican Thomas E. Dewey that he might have signed much of the legislation Roosevelt had signed, though he hardly would have insisted on a rubber-stamp Congress.[19]

Hoover knew that he would be watched carefully, and he did not want to ignite prairie fires that would rage out of control. Neither did he believe in the aphorism "Divide and conquer," even to win elections. He never countenanced unscrupulous tactics to obtain political advantage, though certainly some of his surrogates indulged, and in later battles his wit could be biting. But negativity was never a major weapon in his arsenal, especially nitpicking of a personal nature. He persistently condemned policies, not people. Although he had more common sense than to deny the existence of evil in the world, or human imperfection, including his own, his chief villains were not persons but ideas, and his approach remained primarily leery of personal invective. Yet he persistently condemned policies that actually hurt people in the guise of helping them. Collectivism as a genre usually came to power by that route, he emphasized.

For all his caution, Hoover would have liked to make a political comeback in 1936. He wanted to prove his critics wrong. As the shadows of his life lengthened, he became more partisan as an ex-president than he had ever been as president, which led many to conclude that he had been more conservative as president than he actually was. The impression that Hoover was a hard-core conservative president probably owes a great deal to his crusades after his presidency. Primarily based on situational differences, he was more pragmatic as president. Further, he spent a long purgatory out of power, and if he never became a cynic, he doubtless grew dismayed and, beneath his stoicism, disappointed and impatient. He continued to avoid hyperbole, though he did indulge in wit, and he refused to join the American Liberty League, a group of conservative businessmen including Al Smith and John J. Raskob, Democrats and former opponents of Hoover. Neither did he campaign openly in the congressional elections of 1934.[20]

Upon retiring to Palo Alto, Hoover gingerly, and incrementally, reentered the political arena, remaining above partisan politics for about a year while he worked behind the scenes to mold policy and orchestrate criticism of the New Deal. He was disturbed by the lack of enthusiasm of GOP congressmen for defending his administration. As he tiptoed gingerly into the shark-infested waters of partisan politics, Hoover initially declined to criticize specific New Deal policies or to offer a tangible program of his own. Neither did he attack Roosevelt personally. Rather, he condemned the New Deal's overall philosophy of infringing on American liberties and leading to an aggrandizement of concentrated power designed to perpetuate the party of Jackson in power. Like Andrew Jackson, the contemporary Democrats practiced the spoils system with a vengeance.[21]

Some Republicans who believed Hoover was too tainted by the stigma of the Depression to make a viable candidate in 1936 identified the Republican Federal Associates as the seed of an organization to orchestrate his nomination and avoided connections with them. The association never became an important political tool and dissolved late in 1934. Hoover tacked to the winds and helped create a new organization designed to promote the return to sound money. With friends, he plotted a return to more active political involvement, beginning with lectures at universities and a series of articles for the daily press articulating traditional Republican principles.[22]

During the summer of 1934 Hoover returned to the bucolic outdoor beauty and male camaraderie of the Bohemian Grove summer encampment. Set amid a cathedral-like stand of redwoods in Northern California within a preserve of 2,800 acres, the site included some 250 camps of from two to twenty old friends and invited guests. Hoover's Caveman's Camp included his two sons, Dr. Ray Lyman Wilbur, two writers, and an oilman. In this idyllic setting, the stress and residual resentment of politics drained out of him. He continued the annual pilgrimage until 1962, when he was nearly ninety.[23]

Hoover played little role in the 1934 congressional elections, partly because his help was unwanted. Some candidates and party leaders were tilting toward a neutrality pact with the Democratic administration. Governor Alf Landon of Kansas was already planning a 1936 campaign for the nomination that to Hoover resembled a pale imitation of FDR.

Nonetheless, Hoover realized the inherent difficulties of campaigning against Roosevelt. While unemployment in the private sector remained virtually stagnant, employment in the public sector was exploding. The jobless were desperate, and much of the population seemed to accept the proposition that gift-wrapped patronage plums came free of cost to anyone, except perhaps the "money changers." Still, Hoover took no comfort in the election results. The Republicans lost yet more seats, defying the historical trend that the party that controls the White House usually suffers losses during off-year elections.[24]

In March 1935 Hoover escalated his criticism of the New Deal in a nationally broadcast speech at Sacramento, although he conceded that Roosevelt had created a Byzantine patronage machine that would make him difficult to dislodge. He continued to inveigh against inflationary policies, which, he explained, punished endowed universities and hospitals, savings accounts, pension plans, and insurance policies. Initially he attempted to phrase his criticism in terms of policies rather than personalities, but the ex-president could hardly conceal his disdain for the president's political opportunism. Still, he spoke in a calm voice and never shouted or resorted to demagoguery. He made it clear, however, that FDR's policies would not end the Depression and in time would shipwreck the country economically and strangle human liberty. Hoover now embarked upon the role of leader of the opposition with relish. He vowed to define Republicanism and explain how it differed from the philosophy of his nemesis in Washington.[25]

The ex-president attempted to explain that his administration had offered a blueprint for a more effective alternative. The Depression had been stopped by the summer of 1932, he argued, and reinvigorated by the November election, which spiked business fears by the uncertainty of Roosevelt's policies, while a bank panic during the interregnum nosedived the progress made to that point. The argument was plausible, and statistically arguable, yet Hoover had been demonized so consistently that the messenger poisoned the message. Journalist William Allen White, a Republican and a close friend of Hoover, feared the Republicans could not win merely by indicting the New Deal; they must be more constructive in describing their own program. There was no point in tearing down the house until the foundation of a new one was poured. Hoover wanted to indict and convict on the charges of unconstitutionality, incompetence, and government featherbedding. But that was insufficient. It exchanged the promise of a hot meal for a balanced budget. And times had been miserable when FDR took over, the Democrats retorted. Hoover wanted to raise the moral tone in politics and eliminate elements of class war and the spoils system that were creeping in. Roosevelt wanted a rubber-stamp Congress and a pliable Supreme Court, as well as an inert opposition party. The New Yorker seemed amoral, as if all that counted to him were material things. Hoover's core beliefs remained progressive, yet increasingly he represented the conservative wing of the Republican Party. Many in the GOP believed it was unlikely they could win on such principles, and even more unlikely with Hoover as the candidate.[26]

By mid-June Hoover believed he was making progress in saving the soul of a lost country and began seriously contemplating seeking the GOP nomination in 1936. However, the Republican Old Guard would have built a wall around the White House to keep Hoover out. The other obstacle was Hoover himself. He wanted his friends to wage the campaign for him without openly seeking the nomination himself, a method that had failed in 1920. There was no central organization, no fund-raising, only speeches, letters to editors, and the cultivation of friends. Efforts were made to compile a mailing list of men who had served Hoover in the CRB, the Food Administration, and the ARA, and to whet their appetites for a new crusade. However, the aspirant eventually dispatched a lieutenant to round up delegate support in the South.[27]

Meanwhile, other Republicans sought to spear the nomination, most prominently Alf Landon, a fresh face, less critical of the New Deal than Hoover. Landon was more popular than Hoover among farmers and seemed more inclined to commit early and run hard. Landon's chief advantages were the lack of a formidable GOP candidate and Hoover's residual unpopularity. The party's congressional delegation feared Hoover would drag them down with him. Neither did Hoover's game of hide-and-seek impress party professionals. William Allen White considered Hoover's unpopularity cruel and undeserved, yet cemented in place. "It still hangs on," White wrote. "And everything he says, as well as everything his friends say, is discounted. It is unbelievable."[28] Some Republican leaders warned that Hoover's nomination would result in another fusillade of Democratic mudslinging, circa 1932, and the result would be the same. By early 1936 Landon had emerged as the front-runner. In a poll of Nebraska farm voters, Hoover trailed Landon and Idaho senator William E. Borah. Adding momentum, William Randolph Hearst cast the support of his newspaper chain behind Landon. Ironically, the chief qualification of Landon was that he was not Hoover. The ex-president was much better known, had a wealth of experience in public service, and had won a tsunami victory in 1928. But the nomination over which they squabbled would not be worth much unless it was complemented by a strong anti-incumbent sentiment, and that was absent. Meanwhile, Hoover delivered about a speech a month, pounding home his theme of New Deal irresponsibility. He reminded voters of Roosevelt's 1932 promise to balance the budget, as well as other broken vows. He called for a balanced budget, a sound gold standard, and an end to pork-barrel public works. Unfortunately, there was nothing new in this. However sound these proposals might be in a theoretical sense, they resembled a rerun of the first Hoover administration. In November 1935 Hoover implied that he would not be a candidate in 1936, but he also implied that he would accept a draft. The *Review of Reviews* wrote that Hoover was the best-qualified candidate judged on any criterion but electability. Yet Hoover held back. He wanted the nomination to seek him, and while his excoriation of Roosevelt was strenuous, his assertion of his own availability was passive. The starter's gun for the nominating race had been fired, yet Hoover had failed to sprint out of the blocks.[29]

By February 1936, his campaign was as wobbly as a newborn calf. Sufficient funds to continue printing and distributing Hoover's speeches could not be raised. The GOP National Committee had refused to help, and Landon's strength was growing. A poll of sixteen hundred Ohio Republicans showed that only 4 percent supported Hoover's nomination. Hoover remained highly visible because of his attacks on the New Deal, yet he neglected the mundane task of gathering delegates, instead relying on speeches and friends. Some counseled Hoover to withdraw if prospects did not improve by May 1, but a few urged him to remain in through the convention and hope for a deadlock. Finally, on May 18, Hoover withdrew from the nominating campaign. The GOP, it appeared, loved Hoover, but it loved winning more.[30]

The taint of the Great Depression and the electoral debacle of 1932 still haunted Hoover. Governor Landon, the front-runner, was a popular personality yet a mediocre speaker who lacked experience in national and international affairs. Landon distanced himself from Hoover, wary that some of Hoover's stigma from the Depression might rub off on him. Landon planned on running slightly to the left of Hoover but somewhat to the right of FDR, gaining the moderate vote and making inroads into the usually monolithically Democratic South. Hoover disdained this tactic as "me too, but cheaper," implying that the governor was Roosevelt writ small. Hoover's influential friends arranged a prime-time speaking engagement at the Cleveland convention. Like an old-time evangelist, Hoover inspired the delegates with GOP orthodoxy and almost ignited a stampede to his standard. He still held a place in the hearts of the Republican faithful. "I think these people are trying to tell Mr. Hoover that they are ashamed of the way they doubted him and deserted him and that now they are trying to convince him that their hearts are with him," one spectator said.[31]

During the campaign, the Democrats dredged up Hoover and dragged him through the mud again, virtually ignoring Landon. Democratic orators, including President Roosevelt, reviled his predecessor, pounding him incessantly, making it a rerun of 1932. Landon was the real "forgotten man" of the election. He carried only two states, with nine electoral votes, Maine and Vermont. If Hoover was trounced in 1932,

Landon was virtually annihilated in 1936. Hoover himself would doubtless have lost overwhelmingly to the incumbent in 1936, but almost certainly he would have fared better than Landon and might have helped
generate more support for GOP congressional candidates. Landon was
no more a rousing speaker than Hoover and his attempts to straddle
made his speeches weaker in content. The Kansan wanted to reach out
and expand the Republican base while Hoover preferred to solidify the
base and reinforce it. Neither could have conceivably outflanked Roosevelt
in 1936, because the New York aristocrat had driven a silver stake through
the heart of Republican credibility.[32]

Following the 1936 slaughter at the polls, the Republican Party was
in disarray. Landon remained the titular head of the party, but as an
ex-president, Hoover retained as much, if not more, clout. During 1937
and 1938 a power struggle ensued between Hoover and Landon. They
had different visions for the GOP, and their followers believed the victor
in the clash would emerge as the front-runner for the 1940 nomination.
Both men considered a party reorganization vital, yet they veered in
opposite directions. Hoover wanted to purify the party of left-leaning
supporters of Landon and return to traditional Republican principles.
His vehicle for this reorientation was a large general conference to meet
in 1937, draft a set of Republican principles, and enunciate the party's
position prior to the 1938 congressional elections. Most Republicans in
Congress, however, preferred not to challenge the New Deal directly
and wanted to emphasize local issues. Landon's approach was more radical. He wanted to detach conservative Democrats from their party, woo
independents, and meld them with moderate Republicans to create a
third party as an alternative to the conservative GOP and the leftist
Democrats. Landon, like Hoover, wanted a conference, to serve as a
launching pad for the new party and, possibly, a second run at the White
House. Landon and Hoover were divided by personality, policy, and
organizational differences, and both wanted recognition as the Republican spokesman and, possibly, the 1940 nominee. Hoover considered
Landon's third-party idea impractical because third parties had been

relentlessly mowed down by major parties, despite Populist fervor for William Jennings Bryan in the 1890s and Progressive zeal for Theodore Roosevelt in 1912, both of whom were more engaging and charismatic than Landon. Further, Hoover considered the 1932 and 1936 elections aberrations. It might be more feasible, he believed, to resurrect the party that had dominated the 1920s than to quixotically spin off a new one.[33]

Despite media battles, speeches, and a great deal of political intrigue, neither man saw his vision materialize and neither conference ever met. Landon lost the backing of prominent Democrats who had initially expressed interest in his coalition, and Hoover's large general conference never moved beyond the planning stages. A face-saving compromise was arranged. Instead of a general meeting to formulate a united front on issues, the matter was handled by subcommittees of the Republican National Committee, which issued a watered-down, generic list of proposals. Hoover, though disappointed, professed to be satisfied, because his only purpose was to influence policy, not to reenter politics. The internal scrimmage ultimately produced little of lasting substance. Rather, the New Deal in 1937 and 1938 was weakened by its own excesses and a precipitous economic decline.[34]

Frustrated by a conservative, narrowly divided Supreme Court, which nullified legislation intended to implement New Deal objectives, in 1937 FDR proposed to pack the Court with additional judges appointed by him, thereby obtaining a liberal majority. Rebellion against the plan was nearly universal among both Democrats and Republicans. Even Democrats considered the bill a flagrant power grab and led the fight against it. Republican congressional leaders, content with the internecine strife, avoided comment to preserve the bipartisan nature of the opposition. Hoover, however, could not resist delivering a vehement speech denouncing the bill, which troubled GOP strategists, who feared his intervention might drive some Democrats to the president's defense. Hoover's rhetoric produced nothing more than an irritation, but it did estrange him from some congressional Republicans, at least temporarily. The Court-packing bill was soundly defeated, an embarrassment for the president.[35]

More choppy waters lay ahead for the incumbent, once considered invincible. In the summer of 1937 the economy plummeted, the worst sudden debacle in history, eclipsing the 1929 crash. It has been attributed to a backlog of overspending, a reduction in spending, overregulation, which paralyzed investment, or underregulation. Whatever the cause, the economy fell off a cliff. Between September of 1937 and the following June, industrial production plunged 33 percent, national income plummeted 13 percent, profits fell by an enormous 78 percent, payrolls eroded by 35 percent, and industrial stocks lost more than 50 percent in value. Manufacturing employment slid abruptly by 23 percent. Any hope that the Depression was ending was shattered. The Court-packing fiasco and the economic catastrophe, combined with simple battle fatigue among Democratic voters, opened a window of opportunity for the Republicans in the 1938 off-year elections. The economic and political furies also combined to bring the New Deal to a virtual standstill. In fact, except for the European war, the historical verdict on the New Deal's success in dealing with the Depression might remain a hung jury.[36]

In April 1938 Hoover claimed to have found another example of a Roosevelt power grab in New Deal legislation facilitating government reorganization, which the ex-president warned would permit the incumbent to perpetuate the spoils system. Forgetting that he had labored for reorganization during his own administration, Hoover descended into hyperbole by equating the reorganization bill with home-brewed Fascism. The ex-president was gratified when Congress handed his successor a thumping defeat on the bill, the House voting 204–196 against, including 108 Democrats who defected to the opposition. The Chief felt Roosevelt was on the ropes, dangling in a hangman's noose.[37]

Late in April Hoover resumed his attack, this time condemning the New Deal for encouraging immorality in government, which piggy-backed on inefficiency. The New Dealers had virtually invited every community into "a conspiracy to get its share from the federal grab bag." The New Deal had tested, and broken, Hoover's patience. He had never dipped into comparable invective during his entire public life, avoiding it even during the 1932 campaign when he was the target for Roosevelt's quiver of arrows. After Roosevelt's reign in the White House was terminated by the Grim Reaper in 1945, Hoover's voice never again reached a comparable decibel level. In Hoover's lifetime, no era matched the "creeping collectivism" of the New Deal and its mountain of bureaucracy that resembled Mount Everest. The Chief argued that unleashing free enterprise from regulatory entanglements and government favoritism would extract the nation from the grip of the Depression. Deliberately imposed scarcity would retard, not reward private initiative. There was more than an element of truth in Hoover's argument, and if he sometimes swerved into self-righteousness, self-righteous people are not inevitably wrong on the merits of their arguments.[38]

Hoover felt frustrated by being steamrollered consistently by the Roosevelt machine. He was unapologetic about his viewpoint. "One of the most discouraging things going on in the Republican Party is the constant apology being made for it," he reminded fellow Republicans. "The attitude on the part of many speakers implies that the party has no record of economic reform or humanitarian actions; that we must debase ourselves in sack cloth and apologies for the failure of our party; that we must acknowledge that the New Deal has the only righteousness in that field; that we must adopt New Deal methods; and that we will do it a little cheaper." He warned, "It [the GOP] can never win on that foundation." Hoover's angry words carried conviction and were clothed in articulate indignation.[39]

Hoover's purpose was not merely the triumph of abstract principle; he wanted to hit the bull's-eye in the 1938 elections. Silent in 1934, he planned three major speeches for 1938. He argued that Congress needed independent lawmakers instead of rubber stamps and felt driven by a sense of urgency. The stakes were high. Another defeat might be a knockout blow for the party of Lincoln. In addition to speaking, Hoover traveled through the Mountain and Western states, cultivating support. In his final speech at Philadelphia he rebutted FDR's claim to have restored stability and prosperity, pointing out that 11 million remained

unemployed. For the first time since Roosevelt had entered the White
House, in 1938 the Republicans handed him a thrashing reversal in the
congressional elections, gaining an additional eighty-one seats in the
House, seven in the Senate, and several governorships. Hoover could
reflect that he had contributed to the triumph, though events were in
the saddle, notably the 1937 recession and the failed Court-packing plan.
Further, the New Deal simply had not fulfilled its promise to end the
Depression and Roosevelt's star had dimmed. Hoover's three nationally
broadcast speeches were timely, and made an impact, nonetheless. He
believed they solidified the grudge that barred him from the White
House, though it hardly needed strengthening. Only Roosevelt knew his
reasons. But the feud intensified. FDR would no more let Hoover set foot
in the White House than he would free a caged tiger.[40]

THIRTEEN

Politics and Diplomacy Before the Second Great War

n December 1935 Hoover received an invitation to visit Belgium in order to be honored for his contributions to saving that nation from starvation during the Great War. The journey, his first return to Europe since 1919, was expanded to include fifteen European nations. On February 16, 1936, he arrived in Belgium to an enthusiastic reception. Awarding the American a special medal and giving him the title "Friend of the Belgian People," bestowed by King Albert, the grateful nation issued a stamp in his honor. Afterward, he was guest at a reunion dinner attended by 40 survivors of the 120 Belgians who had worked for him in the Commission for Relief in Belgium.[1]

A week later, Hoover was driven to France, where the people expressed their gratitude for his feeding of that nation. The University of Lille awarded him an honorary degree, the first of twelve he received in Europe. A street was named for him, and then he conferred with the French president in Paris. On March 3, after a brief stopover in Geneva, where he concluded the League of Nations stood in a state of collapse, he traveled to Vienna, where he received another degree. Sadly, he saw

European diplomacy disintegrating, demoralized. In all, Hoover spent seven weeks in Europe in 1938. Part of the trip was ceremonial and sentimental, but he also gathered intelligence about the state of European economic, military, and diplomatic conditions. He wanted to study the causes whereby some thirteen countries had abandoned free institutions established after the Great War and adopted some form of collectivist government. Hoover, two close friends, and a retinue visited Belgium, France, Switzerland, Austria, Czechoslovakia, Germany, Poland, Latvia, Estonia, Finland, Sweden, and England. They had personal discussions with twenty-two presidents, kings, and prime ministers, fifteen foreign ministers, a host of cabinet officers, editors, professors, and business and labor leaders—a total of more than 350 such interviews. The most significant part of his itinerary was his stopover in Germany. Hoover had many callers anxious to meet him in Germany. He was still more popular in Europe than in America, a figure of mythical proportions. Ordinary figures, such as professors, spoke in soft tones and were discreet, careful not to criticize. When several Germans were in the room together they talked in banalities. Only one or two offered any criticism of the Nazis. They seemed to believe they had mastered economics, though a few confided they were on the road to destruction. A few businessmen described how the Nazis had taken over their companies and reduced their standards of living. Wages and promotions were fixed by the government and men could not change jobs without government permission.[2]

Adolf Hitler issued an invitation to the ex-president. Reluctant to accept, Hoover was persuaded by the American ambassador that he might glean intelligence valuable to the U.S. government. The two men met alone, with only an interpreter. The scheduled courtesy call was extended to more than an hour by the führer, who did most of the talking. Hoover found him more intelligent than he had expected, lucid on many topics, with a firm grip on Germany's destiny. Yet the Reich chancellor's highly unstable personality included certain trigger points. Specific words or topics, such as Jews, democracy, and Communism, evoked explosions of manic, profane, uncontrollable rage. On some occasions Hoover had to calm the German by terminating conversations and moving on to more amenable topics. Hitler boasted of the economic progress Germany had made, and Hoover conceded the progress but added that it had come at the cost of a degree of regimentation that would prove unacceptable to Americans. Hoover did not feel that the führer wanted war with the West, at least not imminently, but the German dictator hinted indiscreetly that he might be compelled to seize the rich breadbasket of Ukraine. Hitler tried extremely hard to impress the American and seemed disappointed that he could not intimidate him, as the former president maintained his equanimity. Certainly there had been no meeting of minds. Hoover was struck by the fear that stalked the German streets. Average people seemed wary about speaking freely. Hoover could sense the presence of spies and believed his hotel phone might be tapped. Moreover, he was appalled by the darkest side of Hitler's Third Reich, the persecution of innocent, helpless Jews. Hoover did not know the full underside of the Reich, but he did have ominous forebodings.[3]

Hoover also met with the second-ranking Nazi, Hitler's Luftwaffe commander, Hermann Göring. Less bombastic than Hitler, but far more pretentious, Göring strove to impress the simple Quaker with his extravagant hunting lodge, where they dined on a luncheon catered by one of Berlin's finest restaurants. Carinhall was located northeast of Berlin, on a lake, surrounded by a forest. The lodge was constructed around a central court with low buildings on each side. Opposite the great hall stood offices for the staff officers and servants who served Göring. The great hall, where they were greeted by other guests, was about two hundred feet long by fifty feet wide. A huge fireplace sat at one end and a mammoth plate-glass window through which the lake could be viewed, at the other. The walls were lined with paintings, tapestries, and statues worth millions of dollars, making the room resemble a museum. After lunch, the group enjoyed coffee in another large room decorated with Göring's hunting trophies. As Hoover departed, Göring aligned some twelve to sixteen huntsmen garbed in green uniforms, carrying hunting horns, on which they played a Wagnerian melody. The conversation had focused largely on production. Göring mined Hoover's brain for ideas on standardization and waste reduction, which the American had introduced as commerce secretary and which Göring wanted to transplant to Germany. The German was evidently a great admirer of Hoover's industrial and engineering expertise. Both Göring and Hitler seemed to respect Hoover and were eager to obtain his respect in return. Hoover was not rude, but he remained noncommittal and focused on his fact-finding mission.[4]

Hoover planned to remain in Britain only overnight to catch the *Normandie* home but was delayed in port five days by fog, which gave him the chance to talk with British leaders and journalists. He told reporters he did not think war could happen for at least a year. In a meeting with Prime Minister Neville Chamberlain, he explained that he believed the Germans would be ready for war in eighteen months. Chamberlain agreed completely, adding that the weak spot in Europe was France, which feared Germany and tried to overcompensate by arming to the teeth. The French alliance with Russia made it certain that if war broke out, it would begin in the West, where Hitler would attack the weakest nation first, Chamberlain said. After speaking with the prime minister, Hoover had tea with King George VI, who was handicapped by his stuttering. Hoover sensed the strength had been sucked out of England by the last war, when their best had been drafted first and died first. They could not stand up to Germany, yet they were tenacious and would fight for their empire. He sensed the leaders he met were a notch below those he had known during the Great War. Notwithstanding the League of Nations, their foreign policy pivoted on balance-of-power politics on the continent.[5]

Hoover did not enter Russia on this trip, but from people he spoke with he pieced together a composite description of the country's situation. Russia's farmers worked on collective farms with two or three acres for private truck gardens. Members of the Communist Party were the new nobility. The upper echelon of the party was privileged. The number of churches had declined from 46,000 to less than 5,000. Liquidation of dissenters and classes was widespread. The czar had about 200,000 in camps for political convicts. Stalin raised this to 10 million. Hoover remarked to a statesman in a neighboring country, "Stalin seems to me equally a reincarnation of Ivan the Terrible and Lenin." The statesman replied, "Add to that something of Peter the Great and a large amount of Genghis Khan and you have him." The Russians were building a great army. They hated the Germans and feared the Western democracies. The Germans, unlike the Russians, did not try to conquer with their ideology but with force of arms. Communist threats played a large role in all the Fascist revolutions in Europe—Fascism seemed the lesser evil. It was also a different variation on the concept of the planned economy. Both Communism and Fascism proved that a collectivist economy was incompatible with personal liberty. Communism and Fascism were destined to clash, as the Anti-Comintern Pact showed.[6]

Upon arriving in America, Hoover seemed less optimistic after ruminating over world conditions during the voyage home. He described the continent as "a rumbling war machine, without the men in the trenches," a breeding ground for dictators, nations piling up debts and erecting an unstable balance of power, ruled by cynical politicians or totalitarian tyrants. The talk of quarantines and collective actions by the Roosevelt administration made him nervous. He did not believe America could save Europe from the hangman's noose from which it was dangling. It had tried and failed to do that in the Great War. The statesman said that to couple America's fate with that of Britain and France would perpetuate imperialism and possibly entangle the United States in an alliance with the Soviet Union, a nation focused on aggression. Hoover believed America could and should, if necessary, accept a world with dictatorships if they did not touch the United States' own shores. "We can never herd the world into the paths of righteousness with the dogs of war," he warned. Hoover continued to believe in the power of world opinion to save the world from destruction. America's job was to set a moral example. "Decency is still news," he explained. Prosperity might preserve that elusive peace.[7]

Upon his return to San Francisco, Hoover addressed a large crowd and was vividly descriptive about conditions in Europe. Unlike in his earlier speeches, he minced no words. Those who believed in totalitarian states were expected to sell their souls to the government, he said. Personal property was no longer respected. "If you carry over the old idea that perhaps it belongs to you, then you go to a concentration camp to rest your nerves," he said sarcastically. "You will also be taught to sing cheerful songs in the recreation hours and to march all about. You have social security if you conform. If you do not conform you get security in a concentration camp. . . . Altogether I am glad Europe is still 7,200 miles from California."[8]

All of the dictatorships tried to superimpose a collectivist managed economy on individual liberty and failed to make them synchronize. Some were triggered by intense internal or external threats or economic hardship. But the systems were incompatible, and they led to tyranny. Hoover warned that they would destroy American democracy if pushed too far here. In Europe, fourteen nations with 240 million people had mixed a planned economy with individual liberty and destroyed individual liberty. It had gone furthest in Germany and Russia. It was destined to fail everywhere. In a material sense, Germany was better than it had been five years earlier, yet individual liberty had been destroyed.[9]

By 1938 Hoover had shifted his focus from a critique of FDR's domestic policies to the overriding concern of diplomacy. He feared the president was incrementally leading the nation into a second world conflagration that would incubate more tragic consequences than the first failed crusade. Hoover had never been a hard-core isolationist. In the context of the 1920s and of his own presidency he was an internationalist. Despite his Quaker heritage, he was not a pacifist, though he was a reluctant warrior. Hoover wanted to pursue all avenues short of war before engaging in conflict, and then to fight only in self-defense. Yet he was troubled by the overconfident idea that America could liberate the world or extricate Europe from the cauldron of its chaos. His twenty years of life abroad made him unconvinced of Europe's ability to avoid war, and even more uncertain of America's ability to purge the continent of the demons of war. He believed the Wilsonian experience should have taught America these lessons the hard way. In 1938 he feared Roosevelt was moving in just the opposite direction. In addition to the heinous, baneful international repercussions, Hoover feared the domestic conse-quences of another war. The United States would incur an enormous expansion of the national debt, digging a fiscal hole that would require generations to pay. Moreover, the regimentation necessary to fight a war would leave a permanent imprint on American democracy, he believed. "Those who would have us again go to war to save democracy might give a little thought to the likelihood that we would come out of any such struggle a despotism ourselves," he warned.[10]

From 1938 to 1941 Hoover carried on a crusade against American entry into World War II. Hoover's prominent role in the debate over war versus armed neutrality kept him in the public spotlight. After his return from Europe, events soon erupted uncontrollably. On August 22, 1939, the Soviet Union and Germany, to the consternation of the world, signed a nonaggression pact, which gave Germany the green light to attack Western Europe. Shortly afterward, on September 1, German troops surged into Poland without a declaration of war. Two days later, Britain and France responded by declaring war on Germany. On September 17, Russia attacked Poland from the east and soon the nation of Poland disappeared from the map. Hitler's invasion after Britain and France had vowed to defend Polish sovereignty would not have occurred if the democracies had not been given private assurances by Roosevelt that he would aid them, according to Hoover and his informants. The secret, imprudent Polish guarantee had deflected Hitler from his real objectives in the East. The guarantee constituted a tragic blunder on Roosevelt's part. Hoover called for immediate permission to sell solely defensive weapons to the democracies on a cash-and-carry basis. The measure passed but did not bar offensive weapons. Hoover believed the sale of offensive weapons such as bombers, mobile cannons, submarines, tanks, and poison gas would kill civilians and escalate the conflict. To the end of his life Hoover believed that Roosevelt's implied secret support of Britain and France had inspired them to guarantee Polish neutrality. Otherwise, they might have been spared. Hitler, he believed, had long coveted the breadbasket of Ukraine and the vast hinterlands to the east as settlements for his Aryan race, not more densely populated, smaller nations west of Germany. Moreover, he respected the British, whom he considered an Aryan people.[11]

During 1940 the German air force began softening up England for an invasion planned for that summer. The air war—the Battle of Britain—stretched resources of the island while U-boats took a toll at sea. With Britain lacking funds, cash-and-carry no longer worked. On January 6, 1941, Roosevelt proposed to permit the British to borrow weapons and return them after the war and allow American ships to transport them. Many pointed out the incongruity in proposing to give weapons back when the shooting ended. More ominously, the next step would be American convoys to protect the precious cargoes, and American boys, along with their ships, would be sent to the bottom by Nazi submarines. It was a back door to war, not to mention a rerun of American entry into World War I. Hoover did not publicly oppose lend-lease, though he felt some facets delegated excessive power to a president who might abuse it. He wanted to forbid the president to authorize convoys on his own volition. The bill passed on March 11, 1941, including the ex-president's amendment. America's fate was now irrevocably linked to Britain's.[12]

In one sense, Hoover's criticism of New Deal foreign policy was ironic. During his first administration Roosevelt had been significantly less involved in global affairs than Hoover had been during his single term. The New York aristocrat showed little inclination to cooperate with other nations economically, and he interpreted the interests of the United States more narrowly than Hoover had done. Hoover, for example, had made the first initiative to reach out to Latin America, negotiated naval disarmament, and proposed a highly ambitious program for land disarmament at Geneva in 1932. There was nothing in Roosevelt's first term vaguely comparable to Hoover's bold intergovernmental debt moratorium of 1931, nor had the New Deal president held summits in America with foreign leaders, as Hoover had done. Further, Roosevelt's knowledge of world affairs was more limited than Hoover's. Hoover had lived abroad for twenty years, had been an international businessman, and knew scores of foreign heads of state, diplomats, and generals. He had on-the-ground experience during the Great War and had fed Belgium, Central and Eastern Europe, and the Soviet Union. The crucial difference lay in the two men's temperaments. The Great War had not numbed Hoover to human suffering; it had sensitized him to it. His experience at Versailles had persuaded him that America could not impose its will on Europe and might overreach in the process. While not xenophobic, he was skeptical of European motives and offended by aristocratic pretensions. He feared that Roosevelt, with aristocratic inclinations of his own and a friend of Churchill, might be duped into putting the interests of Europe before those of America.

Hoover believed America should remain neutral in any international conflict, joining the war only if the United States itself or the Western Hemisphere were attacked, which he considered unlikely. By June 1939 Hoover also became concerned that Roosevelt's militant opposition to Japan might lead the United States into a war in a region where the country had no vital interests. Prior to Pearl Harbor, Hoover delivered twelve addresses dealing with the looming conflict over nationwide radio and scores of talks to local and regional audiences opposing America's entry into the war. He published eight articles on the subject in national magazines. One of his major concerns was that World War II might end with the collapse of Fascism, only to leave the United States confronted with the spread of Soviet Communism, which proved prophetic. He predicted that individual freedom would be trampled by the powerful Soviet military and propaganda machine. Hoover found little to choose from between Communism and Fascism and hoped America would let these two tyrannies fight each other.[13]

As an activist and a leader of his party, Hoover could not remain silent on the threat from war as it came to overshadow debates over the New Deal. He repeatedly harkened back to what he considered the lessons of the Great War: that the United States could not save Europe from its follies, nor preserve permanent peace on the continent. The first crusade had failed to achieve its purpose. There should not be a second one. Somewhat surprisingly, in view of his antipathy to war, he opposed the constitutional amendment proposed by Congressman Louis Ludlow of Indiana, which would have required a national referendum before declaring war. The world moved too rapidly for that, he asserted, and such an approach would be a deterrent to war only if every nation were a democracy. Self-defense and an impregnable Western Hemisphere were the best deterrents. Hoover believed the best offense was a good defense. The United States should be so strong that no nation would dare attack it, but the country should not taunt or bait other nations into doing so. U.S. foreign policy should not be provocative. America should not tempt fate. Hoover saw no imminent danger to America from the Third Reich, and he did not oppose the return of some German-speaking areas to Germany at Munich in 1938. Hoover had balked at stripping Germany of these regions at Versailles. The former chief executive now reminded Americans of the disarmament and conciliatory policies of his own administration, including creation of the Good Neighbor Policy frequently attributed to FDR. As Europe moved toward war incrementally, Hoover warned repeatedly that war would entangle America in the inferno. From late 1938 onward he inveighed against the inevitabilities of war.[14]

Frustrated by exclusion from an elective or administrative position, the elder statesman remained an active insider in the politics of the GOP. Increasingly, he engaged in a power struggle with Wendell Willkie, a former Democrat who alienated the conservative wing of the GOP with the compatibility of his views with the outlook of the Roosevelt administration. Willkie was popular with the public but not within the hierarchy of his party. The Republicans did not come together internally even after America entered the war following Pearl Harbor.

Just six weeks before Hitler attacked Poland, beginning World War II in Europe, Hoover expressed his qualms to his friend John C. O'Laughlin in a letter of July 18, 1939. Hoover feared that Roosevelt was making war more likely by encouraging the British and the French and alienating the Germans and the Italians. He based his observations on the origins of the First World War.[15]

Roosevelt made a comparable mistake versus Japan, Hoover believed. The Japanese wanted half the Pacific to become a Japanese lake, but left alone with their newly minted empire, they had no substantial quarrel with the United States, nor any illusions that they could defeat America in a prolonged slugfest. Instead of papering over their differences, Roosevelt's policies toward the Japanese provoked a war in the Pacific that mirrored the unnecessary war in Europe set up by the Polish guarantee. Hoover argued, possibly correctly in the short run, though probably not in the long run, that America had no vital interests in the Far East worth dying for. But Hoover's immediate differences with the Democratic president's Far Eastern policies from mid-1940 to Pearl Harbor were more tactical than strategic. The president believed sanctions would intimidate the Japanese and deter war, while Hoover believed they would inflame the proud island nation and provoke war. On both tactical fronts, the ex-president perhaps had the better argument. Over the long term, it is somewhat naïve, however, to insist that America could live at peace indefinitely, with its interests undisturbed, confronted by totalitarian, expansionist regimes at both doorsteps. Moreover, an unshackled Hitler might have ultimately divided Europe with Stalin, leaving the United States isolated and in peril, especially as German science was developing new weapons rapidly. The United States would have found itself constantly on edge, in a war of nerves, with a dictator more irrational than the men who sat in the Kremlin during the Cold War era. Speculation provides grist for the mill of historians. We shall

never know for certain but the lives of everyone now living would probably be much different had Hoover's view prevailed.[16]

In June 1941, Hitler launched a massive attack on the Soviet Union
despite a nonaggression pact with the Communist power. The invasion
provided Hoover and other opponents of the war with a powerful new
argument about why America should remain out. The war could no longer be characterized as a crusade of democracy against totalitarianism,
he pointed out, because the Soviets were equal aggressors. After all, they
had invaded Poland, Latvia, Estonia, and Finland and had freed Hitler
to attack the West by signing the infamous neutrality pact. On practical
grounds, Hoover argued that the Soviets were as dangerous a world
predator as the Germans, possibly a greater threat. Thereafter, it was in
America's interest to let the power-mongering dictators bleed their countries white, weakening for the later showdown, while men such as Harry
Truman, Robert Taft, Joseph P. Kennedy, and numerous prominent Americans argued a similar perspective. The United States had no business
siding with either dictator, the man from Missouri advised. The more of
one another they killed, the better. Senator Taft joined the chorus in proclaiming the totalitarian regimes equally invidious, neither worthy of
American aid. Hoover also believed the titanic struggle being waged on
the eastern front relieved Britain of the imminent threat of invasion.
Aiding the Soviets could no longer be justified on the grounds of protecting Britain, he believed.[17]

Hoover appears wrong on the major issue that America could live
with Hitler, though, on the other hand, the United States coexisted in an
armed peace with the Soviet Union for about fifty years following the
war. He was correct on many specifics, such as the arbitrary, improvised
method with which FDR dealt with serious diplomatic problems, and the
erroneous decisions that sometimes resulted. On the rare occasions when
he intervened in military affairs, such as the North African and Italian
campaigns, and dividing authority in the Pacific theater, FDR might have
erred strategically as well. On the larger issue of escorted military aid to
Britain, Hoover was probably right that it would inevitably involve us in

war but probably wrong in his thesis that Britain could survive without American participation. On employing sanctions against Japan, Hoover proved prophetic that punitive steps were more likely to incite the Japanese than to intimidate them. Hoover relied largely on historical precedent, logic, and common sense, while Roosevelt trusted intuition. Neither was infallible, nor was any other national leader of that era. In retrospect, it is difficult to discern the end, regardless of the tactics employed, turning out much differently than it did. Hoover is unlikely to have proven an aggressive war president militarily, yet the home front doubtless would have been better organized.

Most of Hoover's prodigious energies during the war were channeled into writing. He felt humiliated by being excluded from the councils of government, yet he still wanted to remain relevant. It was during the war that he enhanced and launched a career in writing on a scale he had never anticipated previously. Though the work was laborious for such a perfectionist, Hoover foresaw usefulness beyond the present time. He had the opportunity to contribute to the historical record and to posterity.

The war in Europe opened another opportunity for Hoover to lead a major effort in food relief and perhaps to step back into the national scene and reconcile with Roosevelt. Through intermediaries, Roosevelt issued an invitation to the former president to visit the White House to advise on food relief and perhaps assume personal control. Hoover was puzzled by the invitation and suspected the president's motives. Hoover was involved in organizing another bid for the Republican nomination in 1940 and believed that FDR hoped to distract him from politics.[18]

Hoover probably misjudged the White House's motivation. The real impetus came from Eleanor Roosevelt, who viewed it as a common-sense attempt to make use of Hoover and at least diminish the hostility between the rivals. The offer was relayed by Myron Taylor, who found the former president unreceptive and unwilling to go to Washington. Hoover told him such relief should be handled by the Red Cross, now much stronger than in 1927, when it had carried the major burden of

Mississippi River flood relief in collaboration with Hoover. Erecting a new government bureaucracy when an infrastructure already existed would only delay relief, the former ARA chairman argued. Taylor was disappointed by the response, almost incredulous that Hoover would reject a long-coveted opportunity to emerge from exile, but he dutifully reported the conversation to FDR. A second emissary followed soon afterward: Norman Davis, a veteran diplomat, friend of both Roosevelt and Hoover, who now headed the American Red Cross. Davis bluntly told him that the task was beyond the resources of the Red Cross and invited Hoover to accept the offer. Instead, Hoover prepared an elaborate plan specifying how the Red Cross could consummate the project. Davis carried it back to the Red Cross board, which rejected the scheme as impractical. Of all those involved, Eleanor was the most disappointed. "Mr. Hoover turned us down," she said. "He refused to call on the President." It was an unfortunate misunderstanding. Hoover could have done extraordinary good for the famished, helped repair his own image, and feasibly opened the door to healing the animosity. Eleanor was more generous than some of the White House staff about Hoover's motives for rejecting the overture. She felt his chief concern was not his own political ambitions, but keeping America out of war, which he believed clashed with White House policies.[19]

With the failure of Roosevelt's initiative and the refusal of the Red Cross to act, the Polish government, to which Hoover remained a hero, appealed directly to the ex-president. This time he was more responsive, although the results were limited. Hoover turned to his old colleagues in the CRB, who, as usual, rallied to his cause. They agreed to create a skeleton organization, the Commission for Polish Relief. The committee established canteens to furnish two hundred thousand meals per day to hungry children. At rallies attended largely by Polish Americans, the group raised more than $1 million. Hoover's modest relief effort soon acquired another client when the Soviets invaded Finland in early December of 1939. Hoover was eager to aid the Finns, inspired by a combination of his contempt for Moscow and his admiration of the Finns for

retiring their World War I debt and for bravely resisting the overpower-
ing onslaught, inflicting heavy casualties on the invaders. Hoover con-
sulted with Davis and the Red Cross and offered to collaborate in the
relief of Finland, but his offer was rejected. The entangled thicket of
relief involved a tundra of turf wars and petty personal jealousies. To be
sure, there were daunting practical problems as well.[20]

Roosevelt also showed a petty side. He rebuked Davis for allowing
Hoover to preempt relief, which made the president look bad, he told the
Red Cross chairman. The administration, in an attempt to embarrass
Hoover, publicly released the account of Roosevelt's approaches to Hoover
to assume leadership of relief. Replying tit for tat, Hoover released his
side of those negotiations. Somewhat surprisingly, most of the press sided
with Hoover. The *New York Journal-American* termed the administration's
role "shoddy politics" and the *Baltimore Sun* called Roosevelt's tactics "A
Smear That Failed." *Newsweek* was blunter still. "Few administrations in
American history ever went to greater lengths to smear a predecessor
than this one," the magazine wrote.[21]

Hoover expanded rather than curtailed the scope of his relief activities after FDR's 1940 reelection. He wanted to be useful, but on his own
terms. FDR and Hoover both allowed pride and jealousy to cloud their
better judgment. As the war expanded, Europe became overrun with
refugees from the nations invaded and FDR obtained a congressional
appropriation of $50 million to assist the Red Cross, funneled through
the administration. Hoover was denied a role, which he resented but
expected. The Master of Emergencies attempted to create a private relief
organization to aid the democracies occupied by German and Russian
soldiers but made little headway. He had hoped to distribute food to the
German-occupied civilian populations of Poland, Norway, and the Netherlands through an organization modeled on the CRB. Hoover asked the
governments-in-exile of the occupied nations to furnish the funds and
encountered a solid wall of resistance from the British, especially from
Prime Minister Winston Churchill, who believed such assistance would

undermine the effectiveness of the British blockade. It was Germany's responsibility to feed these peoples, Churchill argued, and he had no intention of relieving them of that responsibility.[22]

In December 1939 *Time* speculated that the 1940 potential GOP presidential candidates were watching Hoover. He was the missing link, the enigma of the campaign. *Time* estimated that the Californian would control two hundred of the one thousand delegates on the opening ballot. He remained the most convincing critic of the New Deal's domestic and foreign policies. Yet, *Time* added, "the star performer was poison at the box office."[23] The magazine explained that most Republicans, even the party professionals, considered Hoover the ablest man in the party, yet preferred another candidate, and the polls bore out that conclusion. Throughout 1939 and into the fall of 1940 the ex-president was ranked high in ability but remained the first choice as a candidate for very few of his fellow Republicans.[24] The GOP wallowed in the position of a disgruntled, habitually losing baseball team that kept its star player on the bench. They would let him pinch-hit for other players occasionally, yet never promote him to the starting lineup. The reason: he had once struck out.

The 1940 nominating campaign and subsequent election occurred during the midst of a nationwide debate over foreign policy, though Hoover strove to point out the structural weaknesses of the New Deal, the dangers of collectivism, and Roosevelt's greed for personal power. In his Lincoln Day speech in New York the former president reprimanded the New Deal for producing the greatest divisions in the fabric of the nation since Lincoln's time. The rivalry between Hoover and Landon continued. Landon felt certain that Hoover coveted the nomination or wanted to name the standard-bearer. Both men strove to mend fences with Thomas E. Dewey of New York, a rising star in the party. The Hoovers were spending more time in New York, which provided opportunities for socializing with the Deweys.[25]

Hoover made his final attempt for the GOP presidential nomination in 1940. As he had in his past campaigns, he adopted a covert strategy that was overly passive, hoping for a coup at the convention, in which he would galvanize the delegates with a stirring speech that would have them stampeding to his banner. Hoover's approach was ineffectual and lacked vitality. Though he remained the most experienced and most respected individual in his party, and retained a core of loyal supporters, rank-and-file Republicans questioned his electability. In retrospect, the other GOP candidates nominated did not fare well either, and the humiliation of the Depression was not attached to Hoover alone—he was merely its most visible symbol. It was attached to the entire Republican Party, which faced an entrenched Democratic machine that mowed down the opposition by exchanging jobs for votes, serving spiced invective, and promoting a suave, politically adroit though economically illiterate leader.

Hoover desperately wanted the nomination, and he believed Roosevelt might be vulnerable, due to the third-term issue, the economic recession of 1937–38, the aborted Court-packing plan, and the fact that the nation remained mired knee-deep in the muck of the Depression. Therefore, the 1940 Republican nomination would be a greater prize than the 1936 selection. However, competition for the nomination was fervent and many Republicans remained doubtful that the warmed-over candidate slaughtered in 1932 could prevail. The field became more crowded when Senator Robert A. Taft of Ohio declared his candidacy in August 1939. Next to himself, Taft was Hoover's first choice, but he would not abandon his own ambitions to support Taft prior to the convention. Taft put out feelers to Hoover about nudging California's uncommitted delegation toward him, but the ex-president balked. As the convention approached and Hoover realized it would be his last chance to escape the purgatory of political rejection, he shed some of his inhibitions in campaigning. Though no glad-hander, he showed a glimmer of humor and an appealing human side. People saw a Hoover they could like as well as respect.[26]

Hoover's campaign for the 1940 nomination was temporarily deflected by his involvement in war relief. He seemed more energized to undertake relief activities than to cultivate delegates, organize, raise funds, or deliver political speeches. Hoover became lackadaisical about the nomination and conceded that he had become a long shot. During the critical month of January 1940 he made few decisions, delivered no speeches, and seemed to have lost interest in the campaign, completely preoccupied with relief for Finland. Attention in political circles focused on other candidates.[27]

Moreover, Hoover's friends warned him against taking undue risks. They advised that by announcing as a candidate early and openly, the ex-president might relinquish his credibility as a trustworthy critic of the New Deal, making his comments appear self-serving. Hoover reconsidered. Publicly, he remained available, but he backed away from plans to shift his campaign into high gear. Subtly, he was better organized at the grassroots level than in 1936. He had established a core of supporters in the Western states constituting a potentially substantial bloc of Hoover-leaning delegates. Yet it was a disadvantage, especially in raising money, to remain reticent while other candidates focused single-mindedly on the nomination. Further, he realistically recognized Roosevelt's continued popularity. People felt comfortable with him in the White House as threats loomed from abroad. Roosevelt, for his part, was running as a peace candidate. As the campaign progressed, foreign policy overshadowed domestic policy. Yet if there were risks in declaring his candidacy openly, there were even greater risks in waging a second stealth campaign, which had not worked in 1936. With the stakes higher in 1940, rival candidates had the opportunity to gather momentum and galvanize support. Hoover backed off. His earlier tendency to mingle and cultivate delegates, to seek the nomination more openly, had been but a dalliance. The spark of ambition did not ignite. He realized he was a long shot to win either the nomination or the election. Sadly, he also realized this would be his last chance. Hoover's head told him the quest was unlikely, and his heart was not entirely in it either. The ex-president still had many admirers, and he was self-taught at campaigning and raising money. Without the war there would have been no third term, and probably no desire for one on the part of the president or the population. Further, Hoover had learned by trial and error, and while he wanted to win, he at least wanted to influence the outcome. Beyond the election, he wanted to influence the principles on which the campaign was fought and won. This was a more modest, more realistic goal. Hoover took the obligations of the loyal opposition seriously.

Hoover's bid for the nomination in 1936 had not included any grass-roots organizational work, but in 1939 he created groups called the Republican Circles to build a base for his nomination in the Western states. Each adherent to the circles was a Hoover partisan. By late March of 1940 Hoover wrote his friend Arch Shaw that he had just completed a round of meetings with groups in the circles, one meeting per night. However, by this time, U.S. Senator Robert A. Taft, son of former president William Howard Taft of Ohio, had declared his candidacy. Now Hoover was not alone on the Republican right. He wanted to move the GOP back to core center-right principles and cease flirting with the New Deal. Although Hoover worried that Dewey might threaten his own aspirations, he also feared Landon lurking on the left. The old wounds in the party remained raw. It would be imprudent to squander this golden GOP opportunity to return to power and move the party's center of gravity to center-right at a time when the incumbent had been weakened. Moreover, Roosevelt sent mixed messages prior to the convention, and there was the possibility that FDR might retire. Hoover continued to monitor the spread of his Republican Circles as they expanded into Montana, Idaho, Washington, Oregon, and California. With his Western base secure, Hoover would command a strong position at the convention.[28]

Hoover had superior experience to any other pretender for the throne, yet his credentials were marred by his thrashing in 1932. In an aggressive speech to the delegates on June 25, 1940, the ex-president disparaged FDR as a power-craving autocrat who was leading America toward collectivism at home and into a preventable war abroad. He warned that FDR had exaggerated the danger from Germany in order to prolong his own tenure in the White House. Hoover's hope to sway the delegates to his standard was frustrated by a faulty microphone, probably tampered with by foes, that left his voice virtually inaudible. Instead, the delegates turned to an unlikely, inexperienced ex-Democrat, Wendell Willkie, who lacked Hoover's assets but also lacked his liabilities.[29]

Roosevelt's strategy in his third campaign followed the script of his first two. He largely ignored Willkie and again pulverized Hoover, hitting below the belt if necessary. Perhaps the worst aspect of the Democratic campaign was not its defamation of Hoover in a personal sense but its irrelevancy to the situation at hand. Poised on the brink of war, with unemployment still at high levels, Democratic orators carped about conditions back on March 4, 1933. The first volley was fired at the Democratic convention and the subsequent attacks never ceased. Keynote speaker Alben Barkley fired both barrels at Hoover: "We inherited chaos eight years ago," he maintained. "We inherited a lack of confidence. . . . The Americans had been led to the brink of precipice by the fallacies of a smug and blind regime."[30]

Hoover wanted to make a difference in the 1940 campaign. Willkie was weak among the conservative base, which the ex-president believed he could help energize. Yet Willkie was cautious and indecisive, and his entourage was riddled with dissent. Some of his advisers considered the ex-president a pariah who would be a liability to the campaign. Yet other Republicans would be critical if the ex-president were not invited to participate. Landon tried to tiptoe around the subject. Hoover had considered Landon's campaign disorganized, yet Landon had seemed like Solomon compared to Willkie. Further, Hoover feared that the nominee, to an even greater extent than Landon, did not offer voters a clear alternative to the New Deal. He found him personally likable, charming, even effusive, with undeniable magnetism, but it seemed no one was in control. For all his charm, Willkie was simply not a strong leader. Hoover feared he would be pulverized at the polls.[31]

Charles Halleck, who had placed Willkie's name in nomination at Philadelphia, arranged a meeting between the two men on August 12, hoping to cobble together a tacit alliance or at least dissipate the arctic atmosphere that prevailed. The meeting went poorly. Willkie invited Elliott Roosevelt, the president's son, to pose for photos with him in Hoover's presence. Willkie vaguely promised that Hoover would make several major talks—only two or three, the ex-president learned. On the other hand, Hoover found the businessman's personal charm refreshing, but he confided to a friend that the campaign was in disarray. He offered some organizational ideas, none of which was accepted. The former president's speeches were not delivered until late October, after most minds were decided. At Columbus, Ohio, Hoover attacked the third term and FDR's overreach for power. His speech was punctuated by humor, and Hoover's journalist friend Mark Sullivan commented that it was "an unanticipated and highly agreeable experience to hear an audience laugh at practically every second or third sentence of a speech by Herbert Hoover."[32] Several days later, a second speech, at Lincoln, Nebraska, was also well received. The energized campaigner focused his firepower on FDR's foreign policies, accusing the president of dangerous dabbling and lack of competence in dealing with global matters. At Salt Lake City on November 1, Hoover wrapped up his campaign, returning to domestic policies and the theme of usurpation of power. Roosevelt punched back, again ignoring Landon. "Back in 1932," he bristled, "these leaders were willing to let workers starve if they could not get a job. Back in 1932, they were not willing to guarantee collective bargaining." Then, in the cruelest cut, "Back in 1932, they met the demands of unemployed veterans with troops and tanks."[33]

In late 1940 Hoover wrote Chief Justice Charles Evans Hughes in an effort to encourage him to resign his office a few weeks before the election and campaign for Willkie, urging voters to repudiate FDR. Hughes felt this was unprecedented and would be neither prudent nor effective. When Hughes received Hoover's letter he responded that he had already been approached by Willkie himself and had declined. If nothing were done, Hoover's letter stated, Willkie was certain to lose. In retrospect, Hoover regretted sending the letter because he decided Willkie was intellectually a lightweight, little improvement on Roosevelt.[34]

Dismayed by Willkie's nomination, Hoover nonetheless had campaigned for him. He pilloried the incumbent for surreptitiously leading the nation into war while pretending to be a peace lover. Some of Roosevelt's purported peace measures were in fact war measures, he believed. On both domestic and international issues, the president reeked of intellectual dishonesty, the former president told friends. Roosevelt's shattering of the third-term precedent and thunderous victory drained Hoover. Yet he remained resolute. He continued relief efforts and rested his case before the bar of history.[35]

Roosevelt swamped Willkie by 5 million votes and consigned Hoover permanently to the status of an ex-president. Hoover's friend reporter Paul Smith echoed what many said of Willkie—that he had an attractive personality, yet lacked philosophical depth, sophistication, and philosophical grounding. He considered himself a liberal, but this was a losing proposition in a race against Roosevelt.[36]

On November 16, 1940, shortly after Willkie's defeat by FDR, Hoover invited the party's standard-bearer to his apartment at the Waldorf Astoria to discuss the recent election and to stiffen Willkie's resolution to fight against involvement in World War II. Hoover believed Willkie might be contemplating another run at the Republican nomination in 1944, something he wanted to avert. They concentrated on three topics: keeping the country out of war; measures short of war to help England; and the inevitable collapse of American democracy if the United States entered the war. They also discussed Willkie's defeat. Hoover told Willkie that many Republicans had voted against him. Ultimately, Willkie befriended Roosevelt, became an ardent internationalist, went on a Roosevelt-sponsored worldwide tour, and published a bestselling book, *One World*.[37]

Hoover learned of the attack on Pearl Harbor some hours later than many Americans. Arriving back at the Waldorf after a pleasant weekend with friends, he found two dozen reporters camped at the Waldorf Towers, clamoring for his opinion on the war. The next day, Congress, at the president's request, declared war. Hoover advised Robert Taft that he would be happy to travel to Washington and offer ideas on the food situation. He also expressed gratitude that Roosevelt had limited his initial request for a war to the Pacific and he hoped it could be contained to a one-front war.[38]

Immediately after Pearl Harbor, Hoover issued a statement lending his total support to President Roosevelt and calling upon the country to unite to win the war. "American soil has been treacherously attacked by Japan," he stated. "Our decision is clear. It is forced upon us. We must fight with everything we have. I have believed alternative policies would have been better," he explained. "But whatever our differences of view may be as to the causes that led to this situation, those are matters to be threshed out by history." He continued. "Today there is just one job before the American people. We must defeat this invasion by Japan and we must fight it in any place that will defeat it. Upon this job we must and will have unity in America." He threw full support behind the man he had recently castigated. "We must have and will have support for the President of the United States in this war to defend America. We will have victory." Hoover even advocated giving Roosevelt "dictatorial economic powers."[39]

FOURTEEN

The Maelstrom of War

W hen Japanese bombs rained on Pearl Harbor on December 7, 1941, it altered the direction of Herbert Hoover's career. Looking back, he had lost all three of his major objectives since 1938, including his quest for redemption at the polls in 1940; his struggle to play a role in war relief of Europe; and his attempts to avert war. Now he ceased his open opposition to Franklin Roosevelt's policies and loyally supported the war effort, although privately he continued to compile FDR's diplomatic blunders for a work that would not be published until long after Hoover's death. The day following the Japanese attack, the ex-president summoned the nation to duty. "The president took the only line of action available to any patriotic American," he proclaimed. "He will and must have the full support of the entire country. We have only one job to do now and that is to defeat Japan."[1]

Hoover's feelings were complex. After the attack, Hoover unreasonably resented the lack of a second opportunity to reorganize food resources on the home front in service of the war effort. After America entered the war he offered his services through two intermediaries, publisher John C. O'Laughlin and Bernard Baruch, a Democratic businessman and a mutual friend of the president and Hoover. The commander in chief was caustic in his rejection of Baruch's entreaty, replying acidly, "Well, I'm not Jesus Christ. I'm not going to raise him from the dead."[2]

Hoover found himself in an anomalous situation. He had warned that placing economic sanctions on Japan was dangerous; it would not deter the Japanese warlords and might lead to military conflict. Some, but not all, of Hoover's fears were borne out. He was as surprised by the timing of the attack on Pearl Harbor as most Americans were; he also initially believed Nazi Germany would defeat Communist Russia. Ultimately, he conceded that the Soviets would triumph and was reconciled to their absorption of Estonia, Latvia, Lithuania, Bessarabia, half of Poland, and large chunks of Sweden. He warned his countrymen not to trust Stalin, inveighing, "Five years after this war we'll be arming Germany and Japan to help protect us from Russia." He believed Roosevelt and some of his advisers were naïve about Stalin's ambitions and the nature of Communism.[3]

During the war, Hoover muted his criticism of the Roosevelt administration and threw himself wholeheartedly into striving for victory and a just peace. Though he considered it unlikely that the incumbent administration would solicit his advice, he kept himself available. Hoover avidly desired a role in reorganizing the home front. He continued and even accelerated his customary hectic regimen, testifying at congressional hearings, writing articles, delivering speeches, and dabbling in Republican politics, though he no longer aspired to the White House. He hoped the articles and his speeches would sway public opinion, and, more important, establish a record for history. Hoover retained the respect of many in both parties and maintained a high profile in GOP politics. Although Hoover endeavored to mend fences between the liberal Willkie wing and the conservative wing of the GOP, the estrangement widened as Willkie moved left and courted favor with FDR. For his part, the former president solidified his alliance with Alf Landon.

Willkie lent no help to Republican candidates in the 1942 congressional elections, yet the GOP gained ten seats in the Senate and forty-seven in the House. Meanwhile, Willkie embarked on a worldwide goodwill tour that implicitly endorsed Roosevelt's liberal internationalist policies. This was the prelude to another attempt by Willkie to win the Republican nomination in 1944. Although Hoover conceded that he would not be offered a job helping to mobilize the home front, he nonetheless continued to desire a role in food relief.[4]

Hoover believed the president had bungled both foreign policy and domestic policy during the war, although he muted his criticism after the war began. The ex-president was concerned that the home-front effort was disorganized, ill coordinated, and hydra-headed, and that FDR had overbureaucratized the stateside machinery and created various agencies and bureaus with overlapping activities, which led to inefficiency. He pointed to inefficient production and distribution of food resources for domestic consumption, the military, and the worldwide famine certain to follow the war. He called for draft exemptions for some farmworkers, whom he considered as essential as munitions workers, and furloughs for others at harvesttime. Hoover believed the free market should be permitted to function as normally as practicable during wartime. Some Republicans advocated Hoover himself as the man best qualified to untangle the red tape. Instead, he published numerous articles, delivered speeches, and testified on Capitol Hill about topics related to efficient production and distribution of food. He also realized that some idealists among the New Dealers wanted to exploit the opportunity presented by the war to redistribute wealth and create a leviathan welfare state. Hoover believed coupling war mobilization with social reform would detract from the priority of winning the war. Further, the GOP conservative believed that some New Dealers, including the president himself, underestimated the moral evils of Communism. Indeed, a few even sympathized with it. Hoover himself possibly underestimated the moral evils of Nazism until he learned of the full horrors of the Holocaust, which appalled him. Hoover was also dismayed by elements of the president's diplomacy, which he considered too compliant to Soviet expansionism and British imperialism during the summit conferences held during the war. He believed the New Dealer was moving away from his earlier commitment to internationalism and self-determination for nations and returning to the old balance-of-powers concept in which the Great Powers divided the world into spheres of influence. Nonetheless, near the end of the war the Chief was less critical of Roosevelt's concessions at Yalta than were some of his friends, who believed Hoover staked too much on an updated successor to the League of Nations. He emerged as the voice of reason among the divided Republican factions.[5]

From 1939 to 1947, Hoover crusaded for food and medical relief for the civilian populations in the German-occupied nations in Europe. After an appeal to him by the exiled governments of Belgium, Norway, the Netherlands, and Greece, Hoover proposed that the American and British governments create a public organization to feed these nations. Churchill, with the backing of Roosevelt, refused. Upon their refusal, Hoover created the National Committee on Food for the Small Democracies, which operated from 1940 through 1942, subsisting on donations. However, its shipments were terminated by the British blockade. The Great Humanitarian also played an unofficial role in organizing the home front during the Second World War. He cooperated with farm and business organizations in staging numerous conferences inspiring methods to increase production and to resolve economic problems during the conflict. At their request, Hoover appeared before numerous congressional committees to testify about economic strategy and relief issues.[6]

Hoover's efforts to feed the destitute masses of war-ravaged Europe during and after World War II included some of the continent's largest concentrations of Jews and helped save millions from starvation. He pleaded with FDR to open the gates of America and admit Jews who were being persecuted in Europe, especially in Poland. The president replied that the only practical way to help the Jews was to win the war. In 1943, Hoover broadcast a speech before the Emergency Conference to

Save the Jewish People in Europe. The ex-president remarked that there
was no language that would either portray their agonies or describe
their oppressors. "To find relief for them is one of the great human problems today."[7] He called upon the Allies to provide food relief as well as
clothing and medicine to Jews who had escaped Germany to neutral
nations. During the same period, Rabbi Stephen S. Wise presented definitive evidence that Jews from Poland and Russia were being gassed and
cremated at sites such as Treblinka and Auschwitz. FDR's Jewish treasury secretary, Henry Morgenthau, pressured the president to act and
warned him that if he did not he might lose Jewish votes. Within days
of his meeting with Morgenthau, Roosevelt issued an executive order
creating the War Refugee Board. Its mission was described as to take
"effective measures for the rescue, transportation, maintenance and
relief of the victims of enemy oppression." The board's efforts resulted
in saving about two hundred thousand Jews and twenty thousand non-
Jews and laid to rest the argument that the only way to help the Jews was
to win the war.[8]

By late 1943 there was a consensus among most Americans in both
parties that Jews needed and deserved a homeland, but there was no
consensus on where that homeland should be. Most Jews desired land
in Palestine, their ancient home, but many Arabs vehemently rejected
the proposal and vowed to fight to prevent its implementation. Hoover
proposed a plan to create a homeland for Arabs in a fertile but uninhab-
ited portion of Iraq in order to open Palestine for the Jews, but political
leaders considered this impractical. Near the end of the war several proposals were considered to end the friction between Arabs and Jews.
Hoover viewed the issue in nonideological terms but recognized that
both Arabs and Jews had a historic claim to Palestine. The new United
Nations proposed to partition Palestine, creating both Arab and Jewish
states, which failed to satisfy passionate nationalists on either side. Further, the Western nations would not agree to any proposal that would
inhibit their access to Arab oil. Nonetheless, by 1944, when the full
extent of the Holocaust was realized, both party platforms endorsed

unrestricted Jewish immigration to Palestine and the creation of an independent Jewish state there. Both common sense and the logic of politics dictated the long-delayed conversion.[9]

Once he realized that he would not be invited to help his country organize for war, Hoover decided to devote the bulk of his time during the conflict to serving his nation in another way. He would put his words into thoughts for articles and books. The articles might serve the short-term purpose of influencing public opinion. The books, more importantly, would preserve the historical record of his life and history and serve future historians and policy makers with raw materials that would still be read long beyond his own lifetime. Hoover had always read books for pleasure as well as for information, and he hoped his own books would contribute in that respect. In the process, the ex-president perfected his prose by dint of repetition, hard work, and meticulous attention to detail, and became a more polished writer. His mature books are sprinkled with quips and jovial self-insight. Hoover wrote not only about events he recollected, reinforced by research, but about those that were happening as he wrote. Some were written for contemporaries, but most targeted posterity. He left a greater legacy in writing than any other president save Theodore Roosevelt. The Hoover books are fundamentally reliable as history. They are straightforward, and he tried to make them as objective as possible, though he was fallible. During this period, writing was not the ex-president's sole occupation, but it was the dominant one, and he grew to enjoy what had once been an arduous task. Near the end of his life, the former president became obsessed with completing the books he had planned before he died. Involuntarily retired from politics, he attended congressional hearings and political rallies, held press conferences, and continued his activities in Republican Party circles. He never relinquished his old friendships; loyalty was the mainstay of his life.

Hoover's first wartime book, *America's First Crusade*, published only a few weeks after Pearl Harbor, was based on an earlier series of four articles that had recently appeared in *The Saturday Evening Post*. The ex-president had hoped the book would be published in time to show by historical analogy that it was folly for America to become involved in the quarrels of Europe. He demonstrated the high expectations and tragic culmination of Woodrow Wilson's dream for a fair peace and a League of Nations. Hoover considered America and Europe fundamentally different, having grown apart over the centuries. He blamed the failure of the Treaty of Versailles and the League largely on the cynicism of European statesmanship but also in part on Wilson's flawed idealism. The author's major purpose was to avoid a repeat of the mistake of involvement in a European war. Unfortunately, the book did not appear until after Pearl Harbor, when its core message was no longer relevant. Some reviewers blamed Hoover for taking an overly defensive military posture.[10]

After Pearl Harbor, Hoover was no longer interested in debating the wisdom of war and turned to writing a second book, coauthored with his friend diplomat Hugh Gibson, that intended to outline the framework of an enduring peace at the war's end. Again, he used the Versailles conference as an example of what to avoid. This book, *The Problems of Lasting Peace*, attempted to provide guidelines for a more successful treaty than Versailles. By early 1942, they had completed a draft. They were gratified by the decision of *The Reader's Digest* to publish it in advance as one of their condensed books, which gave the study immediate exposure to 5 million readers. The authors began by succinctly summarizing centuries of European wars and peacemaking attempts. They portrayed Wilson as a sincere reformer outmaneuvered by the cunning tactics and sleight of hand of the self-seeking European leaders. The conferees sliced and diced the American president's Fourteen Points, leaving them in shreds. The authors developed guidelines for tactics they hoped would ensure the fabric of a lasting peace at the war's end. Some of the ideas were not original, yet the authors took a more systematic approach to negotiating a settlement than had been done at Versailles. The historical case study was a mixture of theory and practice.[11]

The authors assiduously spelled out their terms. The peace following the Second World War should be reasonable to victors and vanquished rather than punitive. It should be formulated over time rather than at one enormous, pressure-packed conclave. A long armistice should provide an interlude between the end of the fighting and the signing of the final document, to permit passions to cool. America should commit to joining an international organization, but one without power to impose its decisions by force. There should be no international army, but the United States and Britain should collaborate in utilization of air and sea power to maintain stability. The peace should initially be negotiated at a set of regional conferences before a larger gathering convened, and rulings should be enforced at the regional level; the United States must be largely responsible for the Western Hemisphere. The international organization ought to resort to the leverage of world opinion before using force. Hoover also opposed the continuation of international imperialism. His model peace would be rational and not dictated by a handful of nations.[12] The victors must disarm shortly after the disarming of the vanquished. Those who plotted aggression should be punished as war criminals, but ordinary conscripts were to be given the opportunity to rebuild their lives. As in *America's First Crusade*, the authors used Versailles as a primer of mistakes to avoid. "When we got there we had high ideals, high aims, and great eloquence," the authors wrote. For the future peace, "we must have something far more specific and definite." The key to a successful treaty was meticulous planning over an extended period and a generous spirit. The writers wanted the book to reach average Americans as well as academicians. Hoover decided to invest time and money to ensure broad dissemination of the book, because he considered its message vital. It was published by Doubleday, Doran; the ex-president arranged for the Hoover Institution to subsidize it, which reduced the retail price to $2, and he purchased copies to donate to libraries. The Book-of-the-Month Club made the volume one of its selections, helping it to become a bestseller. The president-turned-historian raised money from friends to promote the volume.[13]

The study took a pragmatic and generous approach to peacemaking. Hoover wanted to avoid sowing the seeds of a future war. Free trade must be guaranteed and Germany should not be dismembered. The former enemy nations must be disarmed and their leaders tried as war criminals. The Allies should construct machinery to permanently ensure peace. The treaty would build in methods for the peaceful resolution of disputes, such as arbitration and mediation. The most vexing long-term problems ought to be settled after a cooling-off period once the participants at the original conference had been dispersed. Such problems might be delegated to separate international commissions. The book received critical praise for its ideas, logic, and common sense. Senator Arthur Capper of Kansas, who had opposed the League of Nations, endorsed Hoover's analysis, as did journalist William Allen White, who had differed with the former president over foreign policy prior to Pearl Harbor. The elder statesman was gratified to learn the book was being used in some college classrooms.[14]

Hoover also embarked upon his longest project, finally published in 2011 as *Freedom Betrayed*, still incomplete at the time of his death and withheld for decades by his sons and other heirs because they considered it too controversial. The lengthy manuscript was written as a criticism of FDR's foreign policies before and during World War II and expanded to include the early years of the Cold War. One prominent theme was the opening Roosevelt's leadership provided for Communist expansion and the shrinking of the free world. The former president remained convinced that entry into the war had been a mistake, blaming Roosevelt and Stimson. Hoover built a case indicting the policies of FDR's administration, listing some fifteen crucial blunders in statesmanship. He told a friend that the first chapter must include the fatal step taken in allying the United States with the Soviet Union. "When Roosevelt put America in to help Russia as Hitler invaded," he said, "we should have let these two bastards annihilate themselves."[15] During the war Hoover also began work on three volumes of memoirs. The last was ultimately entitled *The Great Depression, 1929–1941*. He expected the books to be published posthumously, but he outlived his own expectations, and the final volume was published in 1951.

In January 1943 Hoover attempted to silence any speculation that he might become a candidate for the GOP presidential nomination once more. Well in advance of the following year's convention, he publicly took himself out of the race. He wrote a reporter, Kent Cooper of the Associated Press, dispelling rumors that he would seek the nomination. This time he was firm. The ex-president said he would even decline a draft. "I wish to reiterate again my statement that I will not again accept political office," he wrote. "I hope such misstatements will cease. I believe I can be of more service to my country at my time of life with an occasional discussion or by providing advice upon public affairs. I should like to be able to do so free from political imputation." For the first time since he had departed from the White House, Hoover had disavowed beyond question any desire to hold the office of president again. In addition, Hoover took no public role in the nominating campaign. He had reservations about virtually all the candidates. Unfortunately, the man he favored privately, Ohio senator John W. Bricker, was probably the weakest of the top four contenders.[16]

Republicans looked hopefully toward the presidential contest of 1944. The chief candidates were Willkie, Dewey, California governor Earl Warren, and Bricker, perhaps the most conservative of the serious candidates. Willkie had coveted the nomination since his defeat in 1940, and the interim had been one long campaign for him, but he dropped out of the race after losing badly in the early primaries. Neither Warren nor Bricker waged vigorous primary campaigns, and Dewey was clearly the front-runner. Hoover was not enthusiastic about Dewey, and the New Yorker kept a distance from the ex-president. The Chief considered Dewey able and intelligent, but vain and coldly calculating in his bid for votes. Hoover's speech at the convention once again was better received than that of any other speaker. Dewey received the nomination as expected. He offered second place on the ticket to Warren, who declined, then to Bricker, who accepted.[17]

The ex-president played no active role in the campaign. Dewey did not invite him to take part and Hoover did not offer. The incumbent won a fourth term, although by a smaller margin than in his earlier campaigns. The Democratic standard-bearer appeared weak and barely able to light a cigarette or hold a coffee cup because of trembling hands, yet he concealed his declining health from the public. Dewey's defeat only confirmed Hoover's belief that the GOP had nothing to gain by straddling issues and running candidates who seemed pale images of the New Deal.[18]

The Democrats dusted off Charles Michelson to slay the dragon of Hoover once more during the campaign. Whomever the GOP nominated, the Democrats inevitably ran against Hoover. It seemed like an endless rerun of 1932 newsreels, with stock villains. Roosevelt adviser Tommy Corcoran snidely remarked to a group of fellow Democrats, "We ought to be eternally grateful to Herbert Hoover, who has been our meal ticket for twelve years." Because Dewey realized this, he studiously avoided Hoover. The proud former president received a curt order from Dewey's campaign advisers to avoid the candidate. Once again, Hoover seemed ostracized by both parties. During his speech at the convention, Hoover chose to cool speculation and dodged photographers who sought to photograph Dewey near him. This was pragmatism on Dewey's part; he did chat with Hoover occasionally in private after he was safely nominated. For his part, Hoover's sparse comments were directed against Roosevelt's policies.[19] He grew increasingly critical of what he considered FDR's bungling of food supplies during the war. It was riven by a "muddle of uncontrolled food prices, local famines, profiteering, black markets, and stifled farm production." Having ignored the model that had served the nation well during the Great War, Roosevelt would face a crisis of world famine at the end of the present war, Hoover warned. The administration would be unprepared to deal with it. Hoover continued to hope that he could find a way to provide food relief to the occupied nations of Europe. However, Churchill was adamantly opposed and Roosevelt conceded.[20]

For Herbert Hoover, 1944 saw the death of his most beloved. Lou cherished the bucolic surroundings and the memories within the walls of her dream house at Palo Alto, but when her husband decided to move permanently into a hotel suite in New York to be near the political action, she loyally followed, never complaining. She adjusted her life-style to enjoy the social and cultural amenities of the metropolis. Lou attended plays and concerts, visited museums, shopped and collected, and continued to work with the Girl Scouts and other charities. Her life was never marred by prolonged maladjustment to circumstances. She was content, even proud, to live in Bert's shadow. Physically attractive in youth, she was still a beautiful woman as First Lady, proudly declining to die her white hair. Her physical vigor declined sharply after leaving the White House, and she lacked the vitality of her youth, though she remained optimistic and vivacious.[21]

Lou became slightly more active politically after leaving the White House. Like her husband, she believed the New Deal was harming the country. She objected to FDR's ideology and considered him obsessed with perpetuating himself in office. She feared the possibility of a dicta-torship entrenching itself in America. Lou's political evolution to the right continued after the 1936 election. If anything, she became some-what more conservative than her husband, though less vocal, and her emphasis lay in moving forward. Lou helped energize Pro-America, an organization of conservative women that had been created in 1932. During the 1940s Lou became involved in promoting her husband's books, especially those that emphasized patriotism. Her emphasis was on pos-itive programs, wholesome values, and ethical politics. Like her husband, she retained a steadfast interest in the welfare of children, education, and helping others. Lou could be fun loving and gregarious, but she pos-sessed an inner reserve, a sense of calm and purposefulness. She resem-bled her husband in possessing a deep reservoir of duty. Like Bert, she never complained.[22]

On Friday, January 7, 1944, Lou attended a concert by an old friend, Mildred Dilling, a harpist who had performed at the White House for the Hoovers. Lou invited Bunny Miller, Hoover's secretary, to accom-pany her. She suggested that she walk home, but she tired quickly and

hailed a cab. Often Bunny dined with Lou after concerts, but this evening Lou did not invite her in. Rather, she went straight to her room to
rest. Hoover and his old friend Edgar Rickard were at the apartment,
preparing to depart for dinner. Hoover stepped into Lou's bedroom to
kiss her good night and found her slumped on the floor, stricken by a
heart attack. Hoover cut through her dress, tried to resuscitate her, and
summoned the house doctor. The physician pronounced her dead. She
was sixty-nine. Although Hoover would live for another twenty years, he
would never find another, and would not try. He did not show much
emotion—he never did—but he must have felt hollow inside. He rarely
mentioned Lou after her death. Franklin Roosevelt transmitted a gracious telegram and Eleanor sent a personal handwritten letter. Hoover
responded in kind, with a telegram to FDR and a written note to Eleanor.[23] The grieving husband told his family, "I have lived with the loyalty
and tender affection of an indomitable soul almost fifty years." For her
part, Lou wrote to her sons in her will: "You have been lucky boys to
have had such a father and I am a lucky woman to have had my life's trail
alongside the path of three such men and boys."[24]

The following Monday some fifteen hundred mourners packed into
St. Bartholomew's Episcopal Church near the Waldorf for the former
First Lady's funeral. There were numerous celebrities, political figures,
and old friends, and two hundred Girl Scouts. A Quaker minister read
from the Bible. The service was simple, and there was no eulogy. Hoover's
two sons flanked the widower in a pew. Lou's body then traveled by rail
to Palo Alto, where she was interred. At the grave-site services at Palo
Alto before her family and a few intimate friends, Ray Lyman Wilbur
delivered a brief eulogy in which he said, "She was just as interested in
the smallest Girl Scout as in the biggest economic or political person."
Journalistic eulogies also emphasized the many lives she had touched.[25]
When the West Branch Quaker who had risen to the presidency died in
1964, Lou's body was disinterred and moved to lie beside his in the small
park on the grounds that include the Herbert Hoover Presidential Library,

where they can be together in death as in life. On his deathbed, Hoover requested that his library close Lou's papers to researchers for at least twenty years. She had written some angry words about a few people who had maligned her husband during political campaigns, and he did not want to stir those memories. The delay in processing and opening her papers probably contributed to her becoming an underappreciated, sparsely studied First Lady.[26]

The grieving ex-president was deluged with sympathetic letters and telegrams. Lou's death left a void in his life that was never adequately filled. He wrote even more furiously and passionately, driving himself ferociously to the end of his life. He leaned even more heavily on his old male friends. Hoover, of course, made some new friends, but they could not displace those he had bonded with in his earlier work. Being in public service or politics together is like fighting a war jointly, or playing a team sport. It produces a bonding that is lifelong. Holed up in his suite in the Waldorf, Hoover was haunted by the memory of his mother and his wife. He was alone with his heaps of book projects, his reading material, artifacts of his travels, honorary degrees, awards, and valuable collectibles. His permanent companion was a Siamese cat he named "Mr. Cat." Yet he was never bored by idleness, remained in contact with friends, and was visibly stoic.[27]

The ex-president continued to monitor developments in the war and diplomacy. He received unofficial briefings from the War Department and remained on cordial terms with War Secretary Henry L. Stimson. He learned as early as December 1944 of the race to develop a nuclear bomb. Late in January 1945, when FDR left for a parley at Yalta with Stalin and Churchill, Hoover expressed his skepticism of the outcome of Great Power diplomacy to Ray Lyman Wilbur. He predicted that Roosevelt would return with a bundle of Stalin's promises, which would flee like frightened antelope. Hoover was distrustful of the agreements reached at Yalta, but he confided to Landon that, publicly, at least, it would be unwise to oppose them because it would only divide the American people—and it would be futile as well. Hoover said that if the agreements had elements of success, he would be gratified, though he was skeptical of that outcome. However, he wanted them to succeed because he wanted world peace. Increasingly, however, Roosevelt's diplomacy near the end of the European war emphasized realpolitik at the expense of his earlier ideals expressed in the Atlantic Charter. With some resignation, Hoover conceded that the only viable option was to use the new international organization to rectify the shortcomings of the Great Power agreements. Such an arrangement reminded him of Wilson's strategy at Versailles, which had resulted in a war. Hoover had the disturbing sense of history repeating itself.[28]

On April 12, 1945, President Roosevelt died at Warm Springs, Georgia, his private aquatic resort for people with disabilities. Although he had long been ill, his death shocked the nation. Hoover was gracious in his response to the passing of the man who had tried to destroy him politically and had denied him even the minimum courtesies customarily extended to a former chief executive. "The nation sorrows at the passing of its president," the Chief said in a statement to the press. "Whatever differences there may have been, they end in the regrets of death," he added. "The new president will have the backing of the country. While we mourn Mr. Roosevelt's death, we shall march forward." Although eight years older than Roosevelt, Hoover had outlived his archenemy. In the final days, Eleanor had sought to reconcile the men, but her husband had obstinately refused.[29] Hoover hoped to stimulate a revival of conservatism in the post-Roosevelt era. Already he was collaborating in the liftoff of a new conservative journal, *Human Events*, to compete with liberal and radical journals such as *The New Republic*, *The Nation*, and *New Masses*, which had achieved near dominance in universities and among the intellectual elite.[30]

On May 8, 1945, Germany surrendered, and Hoover immediately turned his attention to the feeding of postwar Europe, especially the saving of children from imminent famine. Meanwhile, war continued to rage in the Pacific. American marines crept incrementally closer to the home islands, the battles growing increasingly bloody. President Truman sought a negotiated peace but also pondered use of a powerful new weapon, the atomic bomb, which could destroy an entire city. Hoover knew of the attempt to build a superbomb, but its sudden use on Japanese cities revolted him. It lifted war to a new level of destruction and killed noncombatants, including children, indiscriminately. He had consistently opposed the bombing of civilian populations, and he considered the atomic bombs literal overkill. Hoover now faced an uncertain future. Many Americans considered prewar noninterventionists such as Hoover unpatriotic, no different from extreme isolationists or Nazi sympathizers, forgetting the polls that showed a majority of Americans opposed going to war before Pearl Harbor. The new president was a wild card in the deck.[31]

Hoover opposed the Dumbarton Oaks draft of the United Nations Charter and proposed several amendments, some of which were subsequently incorporated into the charter written at San Francisco in June 1945. Between March 25 and March 28 the ex-president had published four articles outlining his ideas for a successor to the League of Nations. He attempted to apply lessons learned from its failure to the new document. In his unofficial capacity, the GOP spokesman exerted his influence on world politics and, theoretically, as a political philosopher, in trying to shape the framework of the new organization. His desire for an enduring peace had not been dimmed by the maelstrom of war; in fact, it had been enhanced. His articles and public statements mirrored ideas he had previously discussed in *The Problems of Lasting Peace*. The new organization should be decentralized, with regional peacekeeping bodies. Sufficient time should be devoted to drafting the document in order to get it right. Once done, it could not be easily undone. The defeated powers should be disarmed totally and immediately; the victors should be disarmed partially and incrementally. Hoover stated that the UN must ban military alliances and specifically define aggression. It should wrap the skeleton of its framework in spiritual garments and study the causes of war. Ex–New Dealer Raymond Moley praised Hoover's recommendations. Hoover's former adversary told the elder statesman that his suggestions for the charter were "exactly what is needed at this time of confusion and drift." He added that "the country never needed you more than it needs you now" and urged him to speak up. In their elder years, the men had become close friends.[32]

Although the UN Charter rejected most of Hoover's recommendations while adopting a few, the GOP spokesman spoke out in favor of the completed document, as he had for ratification of the imperfect Treaty of Versailles. In postwar America, many Republican leaders opposed the successor to the League of Nations. The role that Hoover played in advocating a largely, if not completely, bipartisan foreign policy after Pearl Harbor was significant, though he was not alone in closing ranks. However, the wartime allies had not even waited until the war ended, much less observed a cooling-off period, to draft a tentative plan for peace. Neither had they defined aggression, created regional subgroups, or made immediate plans for disarmament. The Republican statesman disliked the Security Council's veto power, which he believed might paralyze action, which it often did. The draft did contain a "bill of rights" pertaining to nations, one of Hoover's suggestions. Despite its shortcomings, he backed the organization on July 18, in an address in San Francisco devoted to the UN, stating that it probably was as good as was reasonable to expect. The Great Humanitarian of the Great War added the caveat that Americans should not expect the updated version of the League to ensure a lasting peace. Enforcement would lie in the hands of the Great Powers, who had already begun to quarrel before the war ended. Hoover followed up with a speech at Long Beach on August 11, where he warned that a growing number of nations were succumbing to the clutches of Communism. A short time later, the ex-president's longtime nemesis Hiram Johnson, with whom he had reconciled, died. One by one, Hoover was outliving his friends and foes alike. Some of the statesman's friends suggested him as a temporary appointment to fill the Senate seat, but

Governor Earl Warren appointed wealthy publisher William Knowland. Hoover's appointment was probably unrealistic because he had lived chiefly in New York since 1940.[33]

Although he was never invited to join the Roosevelt administration's efforts to win the war, Hoover served his country in a variety of ways during the conflict. Following his presidency he had become a leader of the Boys Clubs of America (BCA) and by 1936 was already chairman of the board. The BCA appealed to Hoover's sense of voluntarism, self-help, patriotism, and community service. Clubs operated in urban areas, offering wholesome recreation, vocational training, and the opportunity to bond with adult mentors and other boys. Hoover also viewed clubs as an alternative to street gangs bred by city slums, which generated juvenile delinquency. During World War II, the BCA was a leader in mobilizing the home front to win the war. It emphasized patriotism and physical fitness and showed the advantage that democracy gave boys for choosing their occupation and obtaining an education. It also trained teenage boys in skills needed by the armed services and by war industries. Most clubs had an indoor swimming pool, offered a variety of team and individual sports, and provided free, regular physical and dental examinations. They offered classes in carpentry, woodcraft, electrical skills, writing, painting, typing, radio operations, photography, and model airplane building. They also instructed boys in music, drama, and comedy, staged shows, and sponsored marching bands. They maintained libraries including fiction, nonfiction, newspapers, and magazines. Stories were read aloud to younger children. Their chief objective was to prepare boys from low-income families for the responsibilities they must face. During the war a large number of members left the BCA to enter the military, and many returned afterward. Hoover quickly became the BCA's most visible promoter and most prolific fund-raiser, tapping his network of wealthy friends, corporations, and foundations, delivering speeches nationwide, and sending out thousands of personal letters. Despite a shortage of resources during the war, the Andrew W. Mellon Foundation donated $10,000 in 1943, and that year the W. K. Kellogg

Foundation gave $25,000. Hoover also assisted the organization with generous bequests from friends. He frequently spoke at the annual banquet. Hoover operated primarily at the national level, but he also delivered speeches to help clubs in major cities raise money for large capital expenditures, such as buildings and equipment. He later became an important fund-raiser for a building in New York City, named after him, to house the national headquarters.[34]

FIFTEEN

The Truman Years

H erbert Hoover's relationship with Harry S. Truman was more complicated than his association with Roosevelt. Truman was a professional politician, a product of the notoriously corrupt Pendergast machine
of Kansas City who believed, as do most politicians, that survival came
first, which meant winning. A political realist, he was not above hyperbole to win votes, and, as Hoover discovered, party loyalty sometimes
came ahead of personal loyalty. He was politically expedient and willing
to cut expeditious deals.[1]

Yet by the standards of politics, Truman was an honest man. For
Hoover, the new president's temperament was a refreshing change after
Roosevelt. He lacked FDR's conceit, vindictiveness, and unquenchable
thirst for power. Competent and decisive, though not brilliant, the former Missouri senator was an average speaker who did not dominate
Congress as FDR did. He was kind, yet hardheaded and practical, less
idealistic than Hoover, and more liberal. Basically fair, usually modest,
he had never ambitiously sought the presidency. Like Hoover, he could
be blunt, had simple tastes and a happy marriage, and was religious, yet

occasionally profane. The product of small-town, rural America, Truman, like Hoover, had experienced poverty and had worked with his hands. Both men were individualists, sometimes pugnaciously so.

Self-educated, Truman was the last president without a college education. He was reasonably well-read, though he lacked Hoover's erudition and philosophical depth. Still, Truman and Hoover enjoyed a mutual respect that deepened to affinity. As the only two living ex-presidents for a time, they developed a relationship that blossomed into empathy and friendship. Though they belonged to opposing political parties, their political ideologies were anchored primarily in common sense. Each man was suspicious of the liberal intellectuals who had gravitated to the New Deal and influenced FDR. Both men could identify each other's inconsistencies perhaps more easily than they could see their own foibles. "One day I find in him a devoted public servant," Hoover said of Truman, and "the next time I find him to be a Pendergast-machine politician who will do anything for a vote." Truman could praise a Hoover speech as spellbinding in 1948 and a few weeks later accuse him of leading the nation into the Okefenokee Swamp of the Great Depression.[2]

Hoover's intuition told him Truman would be a change for the better. FDR had trampled his reputation after the 1932 campaign, but he now hoped that the new president would dam the stream of vitriol. Truman soon began to invite Hoover back into the fold of public service with incremental steps, overtures of respect that in time blossomed into a cordial friendship, though never a political alliance, comparable to the twilight correspondence of Thomas Jefferson and John Adams. Unlike Jefferson and Adams, Hoover and Truman went beyond expressions of mutual admiration to active, nonpolitical collaboration.

Henry Stimson helped arrange the initial contact by inviting Hoover to meet with him, explaining Truman was amenable to befriending Hoover. The former president was wary at first, questioning the man's motives. He wanted the invitation to originate with the president, he informed Stimson, partly because that was the only way to shield himself from the leftists in the Democratic entourage. They could hardly belittle the actions of their own leader. Several friends of Hoover talked with Truman, striving to set up a meeting. Truman was quite interested; he said the former chief executive would have his total attention and the visit would be substantive, not merely a formality.[3]

After turning down several invitations to meet with Stimson, who had now served in the cabinet of two Republican and two Democratic presidents, Hoover finally met with his former secretary of state on May 13, 1945. Although Stimson had never been Hoover's favorite cabinet member, he was always deferential and had great respect for his former boss. Despite his initial misgivings, Hoover was encouraged by what Stimson told him about Truman. He departed with the impression that Truman could prove to be a better president than Dewey might have been. He seemed to have more steel in his backbone.[4]

In May, Hoover began to flesh out some ideas for a compromise peace with Japan that would save American lives, preserve Japanese sustainability as an economic power, restore Chinese sovereignty, and stifle Soviet expansion. He believed the Japanese had given Korea a better government than it had before they occupied the peninsula. He did not know the timetable of the plan to use the atomic bomb, but if he had, he would have opposed it. He later complained that the A-bombs that scorched Japan needlessly killed women and children and opened opportunities for expansion to the Soviets. Hoover discussed his plan with his friend Joseph P. Kennedy, who agreed on the main points, including Hoover's idea of making it appear that the overture for peace originated with Chiang Kai-shek and permitting the Japanese to retain Emperor Hirohito.[5]

Hoover was concerned with Soviet expansionism in Asia, pointing out that Stalin had a ravenous appetite for swallowing smaller nations. To prolong the war against Japan, he observed, "we are likely to have won the war for Russia's benefit just as we have done in Europe." Hoover drew up a memorandum summarizing his plan for Stimson. He stated that Japan should be compelled to withdraw from China, including Manchuria, but retain Korea and Formosa. Japan would be required to fully disarm, but no reparations would be exacted. Hoover's plan would preserve capitalism and free trade throughout the region and Japan would be spared an American military government. In many respects it might have produced a better outcome than the one that actually occurred. Because the terms were relatively generous and Japan would save face by keeping Korea and Formosa, as well as by surrendering directly to Chiang, it is reasonable to expect they might have accepted.[6]

At the time FDR died, Hoover had written the new president, "All Americans will wish you strength for your gigantic task. You have the right to call for any service in aid of the country." Thus Hoover had already made himself available when Truman became interested in seeking the ex-president's advice about food relief. Truman also believed it had been rude of Roosevelt to exclude Hoover from any service or recognition. When the opportunity occurred, however, Hoover wanted a personal invitation from the new president. After his long absence, he did not want to seem presumptuous, and he also considered it beneath the dignity of a former president to call upon a sitting president uninvited. Hoover also knew that some of the New Deal holdovers in the new administration opposed inviting him. His pride was another factor, and he wanted to be certain he was welcome. Finally, on May 24, 1945, Truman wrote, "If you should be in Washington, I would be most happy to talk over the European food situation with you. Also it would be a pleasure for me to become acquainted with you."[7]

When Hoover finally met Truman on May 28, he explained his plan for relief to the president, a plan he had already discussed with Stimson and with several of Truman's emissaries. They had opposed some specific details, such as Hoover's belief that the army was the institution best equipped to handle the logistics of relief. Hoover emphasized that the next ninety days were critical in averting famine. The two men discussed domestic food conditions, which Hoover said were entangled in red tape. Abroad, he urged Truman not to trust Stalin and to protect American interests. War would be folly, however. It might decimate the remnants of Western civilization. Truman listened carefully to a plan Hoover had earlier discussed with Stimson to make peace overtures to Japan through Chiang Kai-shek. Hoover's plan would end the war quickly, before the Soviets could grab portions of the Japanese Empire. Truman asked his new friend to provide a detailed memorandum explaining the peace plan. Hoover hurried home to compose his memorandum and to summarize his thoughts on food relief. Though he liked Truman, Hoover did not seriously expect to be called to service. He speculated that his meeting was nothing more than a courtesy and assumed Truman might have political motives. In reality, Truman liked Hoover's ideas, although he did not implement all of them. Further, he was impressed by the former president's cogent presentation and the quality of his mind. Already, he respected Hoover at a distance.[8]

Early in 1946, after the president had abruptly ended the war by the atomic bombing of Hiroshima on August 6, 1945, and Nagasaki on August 9, Truman invited Hoover to visit the White House again. In a productive meeting, the men laid explicit plans to maximize Hoover's availability to the new administration and tap his residual reservoir of humanitarian instincts. It launched Hoover on a second career in relief, provided him a sense of purpose, and, he later commented, added ten years to his life. The common purpose marked the genesis of a bond between the president and the ex-president. It also furnished the opportunity Hoover had long sought: the opportunity to resurrect his reputation. On March 16, 1946, the Master of Emergencies delivered a nationwide radio appeal for food conservation in order to save 500 million people from famine, then departed on a special C-54 christened *The Faithful Cow*. Hoover traveled throughout Europe, gathering statistical data, unplugging bottlenecks, and interviewing presidents, prime ministers, and food experts, as well as collecting documents for his War Library. He was received by Pope Pius XII, whom he asked to intercede with Latin American leaders, especially Juan Perón of Argentina, who controlled a large surplus of beef. The former president, constantly on the move, took no time away from work. The Chief seemed to thrive on activity. His most important assignment was to collect data on the precise food needs of the malnourished countries and to identify others that had surplus food to export. Everywhere, he preached the gospel of conservation. At the beginning of his tour, the Great Humanitarian had estimated an 11-million-ton gap in cereal necessities, yet he trimmed that by 4 million tons by implementing stringent conservation pledges. He also proposed to expand a feeding program for 40 million undernourished European children. At the conclusion of his travels he spoke to an international radio audience from London about "hundreds of millions" of people waging a personal war against hunger. Badly undernourished children were prey to diseases such as tuberculosis, rickets, and anemia in their weakened condition. Part of Hoover's itinerary included the Indian subcontinent, where he talked with the country's leader, Jawaharlal Nehru, and Mahatma Gandhi.[9]

In April President Truman feared the American voluntary food conservation program was faltering and asked Hoover to return to deliver a series of speeches inspiring his countrymen. Hoover dissented; he wanted to continue his mission through Asia. They compromised when Hoover halted in Cairo to deliver a radio broadcast distributed worldwide, calling for greater sacrifice to avert famine before the next harvest. The appeal seemed effective, and he continued his trek eastward. From Japan, Hoover distributed a press dispatch. The Japanese faced starvation. "Japan must have food imports," he stressed. "Without them, all Japan will be on a ration little better than that which the Germans gave to the Buchenwald and Belsen concentration camps," he pleaded. "Moreover, unless there are food imports the people will not have the stamina to work upon reconstruction or in the fields for the next crop."[10]

Hoover returned to America to find imminent rail and shipping strikes and a crippling coal stoppage frustrating food deliveries to the hungry nations. He warned that the coal strike might cause hundreds of thousands of deaths abroad. "If the railroad strike takes place it will mean death to millions," he continued. "If the shipping strike takes place it will be a holocaust. . . . There is only 30 to 60 days' supply of food in the famine area of 27 nations. They have five months to go until the next harvest."[11]

On May 13 Hoover summarized his eight-week inspection in the form of a yardstick of hunger. Two days later, President Truman responded that "the collection of basic facts had been an arduous and difficult task" and that the former president had "provided a great service to your country and to humanity in making possible for each of us to know better the extent of world distress and to measure the magnitude of our responsibilities." Truman then asked Hoover to undertake yet another journey, to Latin America, to ascertain the prospect of obtaining food exports to the famished nations. Hoover quickly consented, urging the grain-producing nations to undertake conservation to furnish grain to the bread-starved nations. One day later Hoover and Truman discussed his trip personally and issued a request to Stalin to join the food-conservation effort, though Hoover considered the prospect dim. The ex-president explained to the sitting chief executive that only a truculent attitude toward the Russians made the slightest impression on Stalin. On May 25 Hoover complained about the selfishness of labor unions that incited strikes, which caused suffering to millions. Long a supporter of labor, he now felt that leaders of big unions had grown arrogant and threatened not only American transportation but also international trade. They should not take prosperity for granted, he cautioned. America had suffered severely from the war, and self-seeking attitudes could devastate the economy.[12]

In late May, Hoover embarked on a trip of Latin America with a twenty-five-day itinerary. "Mr. Hoover's willingness to undertake these arduous assignments underscores his deep patriotism and his high qualifications," the *Columbus (OH) Evening Dispatch* wrote. Hoover elicited promises for the export of 2 million tons of food in the Southern Hemisphere. Argentina had been especially cooperative after President Truman's emissary strove to patch up shaky relations with the southern nation. Hoover helped arrange the sale of the Latin American surplus, dispatching Liberty ships to transport the grain to European and Asian ports. The trip involved physical pain for the aging statesman. A fall in the bathtub caused a contusion in his back. Upon his return, Hoover's friend the publisher John C. O'Laughlin informed him that the Truman administration was extremely gratified by his efforts. Truman was attempting to override resistance from holdovers from the Roosevelt administration to restore the original name, Hoover Dam, to the massive structure near Las Vegas that Harold Ickes had spitefully renamed Boulder Dam. O'Laughlin also wrote that Truman planned to continue to consult Hoover about national policies.[13]

On June 28, 1946, Hoover delivered his last major internationally broadcast speech about food relief at Ottawa via the Canadian Broadcasting Corporation. He thanked the Canadians for their contributions and explained that along with the United States, Australia, and Argentina, they had shouldered 90 percent of the burden of world relief. At Truman's request, he had covered fifty thousand miles, including all nations experiencing food deficits and the major providers of surpluses, except for Australia and South Africa. He had "discussed crops, animals, calories, rations, stocks, ships, railroads, supplies and hunger with the Presidents, the Prime Ministers, the good officials of each of these nations." The honorary chairman of the Famine Emergency Committee concluded that hunger had been arrested in every nation except China. He was still concerned about feeding the children and made recommendations that ultimately resulted in the creation of the United Nations International Children's Fund.[14]

After years of neglect, Hoover now found himself influential in Truman's circle. "I am delighted that you have come into your own again," Ray Lyman Wilbur wrote to him. Chester Davis, the operational leader of the Famine Emergency Committee, had adopted Hoover's recommendations and organized the committee as chiefly a conservation vehicle, creating local famine-emergency committees and retail organizations, and utilizing housewife pledges and a youth organization, all designed to continue at least until the harvest in August. A week later Secretary of Agriculture Clinton Anderson invited him to return to Washington for another round of discussions concerning food problems. Anderson wrote to thank the unretired humanitarian for his efforts in resolving worldwide food problems and averting a famine.[15]

On January 18, 1947, President Truman asked the elder statesman to again take wing, this time to inspect and report on conditions in Germany and Austria. Hoover insisted that his mission should go beyond food and include a survey of the entire economy in those nations, and that he would summarize his conclusions in a report. At that time, the so-called Morgenthau Plan was partially in effect for the defeated powers, providing for Germany's deindustrialization and reduction to a pastoral state subsisting primarily on farming. Hoover viewed his expedition as a tool to gain leverage to pry Germany back into the European and world economies. Despite the atrocities committed by German leaders, Hoover believed a scorched-earth policy would drag down all of Europe, and America as well, into a pit of economic torment. There could be no European recovery without German recovery, he concluded. Germany must be permitted all heavy manufacturing except weaponry in order to obtain exports to exchange for badly needed raw materials. Nor should Germany be stripped of its industrial areas. Denying Germany its industrial prowess would be an exercise in self-flagellation for the rest of the world. Further, a pro-Western Germany would be a barrier to Communist expansion in the heartland of Europe. Hoover argued to Truman and his assistants on grounds of self-interest. Moreover, keeping Germany in poverty would require American taxpayers to support the German citizens. An unspoken argument was that Hoover's views commanded influence among the new GOP majority in Congress and that any policy he opposed might be rejected. His impact on the foreign policies of the Truman administration, both because of policies he supported and because of those he opposed, was substantial. He had logic and his congressional clout working in his favor. Moreover, the British, who ultimately merged their zone with the Americans, agreed with much of Hoover's philosophy.[16]

Although Hoover's impact on Truman's policies toward Germany was sometimes underestimated in America, partly because much of it occurred behind the scenes, it was appreciated in Germany. When the former president visited Germany in 1954, he was praised by Chancellor Konrad Adenauer. "We . . . owe it to your political farsightedness, to your comprehensive knowledge of economic life that we could again build up our country and our economy after the ravages of the Second World War," Adenauer explained. "The limitations upon our economy were relaxed and, thanks to the magnanimous aid of the American people, we could begin the reconstruction of our native land." Hoover's magnanimity also benefited Germany in other ways. In February 1947 Hoover testified before the House Committee on Foreign Affairs in favor of Truman's request for $350 million for relief of Germany and Austria, and he collaborated with Secretary of State George C. Marshall in shepherding the legislation through. Hoover lined up Republican votes for the measure in a Congress now dominated by the GOP. After the measure passed, Major General William H. Draper, economic adviser to the headquarters of the European command, wrote Hoover, "There is no question in my mind that your report on food saved the day for our deficiency appropriation and I hope will prove equally effective with respect to the 1948 appropriation." Draper added, "Both Germany and all of those interested in the attainment of American objectives in Europe owe you a deep debt of gratitude."[17]

As with Germany, Hoover was a voice of humane self-interest about policy toward Japan. Despite U.S. citizens' understandable ill feeling, "we must confine punishment to the war leaders and we must live with his 80,000,000 people," Hoover advised. Japan, like Germany, must be restored to its full potential of peaceful industry and take its place in the family of nations. As Germany was the cornerstone of prosperity and a barrier to Communist expansion in the West, Japan played a similar role in the East. Japan must export enough to pay for its imports; otherwise, it would be dependent on American taxpayers indefinitely. There was no point in the United States punishing itself simply to wreak revenge on the Japanese. "Chains on any productive area are chains on the whole world," the ex-president warned. "We need a larger vision." Japan posed a strong ideological dam against the spread of Communist subversion as well as against Russian military threats. Historian Gary Dean Best concludes, "Again, it is difficult to avoid the conclusion that Hoover had a decisive influence on the change of policy toward Japan for largely the same reasons as in the case of Germany."[18]

Hoover was skeptical of the expansive degree of Truman's defense commitments and insisted that financial assistance should be in the form of loans rather than grants, lest the demand for aid become open-ended. He had to be persuaded to support the degree of commitment implied in the defense of Europe in the Truman Doctrine, announced in early March of 1947. The president promised to thwart Communist threats posed against Greece and Turkey by Soviet expansionism with a $400 million appropriation for military aid, coupled with a broad statement that America would aid any nation threatened by Communist aggression. Hoover's Republican friends in Congress frequently asked his opinion of this extension of America's role as a defender of virtually any nation. Many Republicans feared this was biting off more than American resources could digest. Hoover remained discreetly silent in public because he wanted to retain clout both with GOP solons and with administration shapers of foreign policy and play the role of an honest broker. Privately, he was unconvinced about an unrestricted commitment. Similarly, Hoover publicly supported the Marshall Plan of economic aid to reconstruct the European economy and foster trade with America, yet he had doubts about its scope and some of its details. Further, he felt hurt about not being consulted before it was announced. The former president proved much more amenable to supporting a bipartisan foreign policy when he was taken into the confidence of policy makers. He believed Secretary of State George C. Marshall was out of his element in the intricate details of European diplomatic intrigue.

He was inviting the Europeans to gang up on America for handouts. Some greedy nations might pit America versus Russia as rival Santa Clauses.[19]

The Republican statesman had a more conservative and more cautious view of spending commitments than Truman and the Democrats. He believed that America should not pursue a unilateral foreign aid policy as a matter of prudence and economy. It should ask other nations who could afford to lend help, such as Canada, Argentina, and South Africa, which had not been damaged by the war, to chip in. The loans would become a political issue when the time arose to repay them, as they had following World War I, and it would be more appropriate to offer them on a multilateral basis. The United States and other contributors could utilize a vehicle such as the World Bank that would minimize nationalistic considerations. The contributing nations might purchase debentures in the bank, spreading the risk and the credit. As a moral matter, Hoover did not believe friends bought outright were any more reliable friends than ladies of the night. Moreover, if the European nations sincerely wanted to restore prosperity, they should tighten their belts and return to the six-day workweek until they surmounted the crisis. Further, the Europeans should create a "customs and transportation union" as "a practical first step towards a United Nations of Europe," a prophetic idea.[20]

Hoover was a fiscal conservative, but he was no Scrooge. In a memorandum to Massachusetts representative Christian Herter, an old friend, Hoover explained that Americans should not really expect the foreign loans to be repaid. They would actually be gifts, but to call them that would encourage a demand that would outstrip the supply. Some basic needs would be considered outright humanitarian relief. Other "loans" could be repaid in kind with raw materials and products America needed. Hoover also saw the reconstruction of Europe interconnected with that of Germany and Japan. "It is simply crazy for us to build up productivity in foreign countries out of American resources, and at the same time, to tear down productivity in these two areas."[21] Alf Landon worked in concert with Hoover on the Marshall Plan. He proposed to Congressman Joseph Martin that Congress should establish a board to administer the foreign aid appropriation and that Hoover should be a member. On the left, some feared Hoover was exerting entirely too much influence in the administration. Former vice president Henry A. Wallace, dumped in favor of Truman in 1944, now editor of the liberal *New Republic*, complained that Roosevelt's successor had reversed many of FDR's plans for the postwar world. Worse yet, "it is Hoover's thinking which guides our foreign policy." It was an exaggeration and a backhanded compliment, but a tribute to the distance Hoover had come.[22]

Late in 1947 the Republican Congress passed and Truman signed an act that established a committee to study and provide recommendations for reorganization of the executive branch in the interest of economy and efficiency, and the committee members chose Hoover to chair it. This proved to be the Chief's most sweeping contribution to domestic policy during Truman's administration. The committee's report was to be delivered after the 1948 election, and Hoover and congressional Republicans expected to be dealing with a Republican president sympathetic to paring down the bureaucracy and scaling back federal power, with a shift of responsibility to the states. Hoover labored strenuously to inject his vision of government into the committee's report. After the reelection of Truman in 1948 he realized that his intention to reduce the New Deal bureaucracy would fall short of realization, yet the report nonetheless was stamped with his crafting. A steady stream of reports flowed from the commission to Congress recommending specific changes in the administrative structure of the executive branch. Hoover's model provided for a clear chain of command, a reduction of the numerous agencies reporting directly to the president—grouping agencies by purpose and function—and the use of standardized language to describe specific tasks. His principle was to simplify, streamline, and trim fat. The commission proposed what became the General Services Administration to centralize purchasing and save money by bulk purchasing and the prevention of overlap. The commission proposed abolishing numerous government agencies, consolidating others, and returning yet others to the private sector. It called for centralization of all public works in the Department of the Interior. Another recommendation was creation of a new department to deal with welfare and education. Overall, the report reflected Hoover's belief in the reduction of waste and duplication and his preference for decentralization and states' rights.[23]

Drafting a fine-tuned model government was one thing. Enactment encountered opposition from special interests and bureaucrats with turf to protect. Truman vowed to collaborate and congratulated Hoover on his gargantuan effort, but Hoover was not fully satisfied with the president's follow-through. Fully aware of the political consequences of every change, Truman told Hoover he would have to take into account the viewpoints of the responsible bureaucrats, especially when changes entailed the shifting of tasks from one department or agency to another. Tucked into every nook and cranny of the government were enclaves of jealously guarded jobs, power, and prestige. Hoover's friends helped organize and finance a private "Citizens Committee" to lobby Congress to enact the reforms. Hoover did not directly affiliate with the organization, but he complemented its efforts by delivering speeches and radio addresses and appearing before congressional committees.[24]

Hoover was tied up pushing through Congress the recommendations of the Hoover Commission during the 1949 debate over American membership in the North Atlantic Treaty Organization (NATO), but he considered the alliance a questionable proposition for Americans. It added nothing to U.S. defense and stretched thin America's commitments, and the NATO members, except Britain, made paltry efforts to contribute to their own protection. During the Korean War, Hoover lamented that our NATO allies made minuscule contributions. He opposed MacArthur's offensive north to the Yalu River and encouraged the general to use air power rather than ground troops as his primary weapon. Hoover considered limited wars against Communists worldwide diversions that might weaken America; he favored a powerful nuclear deterrent as an alternative. He supported Truman's initial response, as he loyally backed every war, but he believed MacArthur, his close friend, had sapped American resources by taking the offensive. Although a warrior with words, Hoover was a reluctant combatant who was extremely wary about overseas commitments. A vehement ideological foe of socialism, Communism, and any form of collectivism, he also resisted militarism, which he considered a waste of lives and resources, except for self-defense. He would not strike first but when attacked would fight with every ounce of strength.[25]

The GOP statesman was heartened by the thunderous Republican victory in the 1946 congressional elections. His party gained control of Congress for the first time since 1928. He considered it more than a turnover in personnel; it symbolized an ideological triumph. The New Deal had lost its luster, and the appeal of collectivism was fading. Hoover set an agenda for the new Congress. Foremost must come labor reform. Big labor had gripped America by the throat and now threatened to strangle productivity. Hoover took comfort in the ascendancy of Senator Robert A. Taft to the chairmanship of the Senate Labor Committee and worked closely with Taft to thrash out provisions for a new labor law restricting the power of big labor and ending abusive practices. He also helped assemble a GOP consensus for its passage. Hoover was disillusioned by the evolution of labor, which he had always championed, into a new form of monopoly that imposed its will on an unprotected public. He felt that big labor sometimes staged strikes for ideological purposes. Such strikes affected the lives of millions of innocent bystanders. Hoover believed the president and the courts should have the power to end strikes that threatened the public welfare. He also advocated compulsory arbitration. One of the principal accomplishments of the 80th Congress, in Hoover's mind, was enactment of the Taft-Hartley Act, a GOP bill designed to restore balance to labor relations, which had shifted in favor of unions since the New Deal's Wagner Act of 1935. Due to several crippling strikes in 1946 that caused national hardship, and the internecine labor wars of the 1930s, punctuated by violence, the public mood had turned against big labor. Hoover felt that the unions had grown enormously in size and influence and possessed more power in some respects than the federal government. Taft, one of the chief architects of the measure, became one of the front-runners for the 1948 GOP presidential nomination due to his pivotal role in enacting the legislation. The bill defined specific unfair practices by labor, limited the role of Communists in union leadership, and required a cooling-off period before strikes jeopardizing the national welfare could materialize. Fought bitterly by the Democrats, it was enacted over Truman's veto.[26]

Dewey and Taft were the chief contenders for the GOP nomination. Hoover believed either could defeat Truman in a year when the Democrats were splintered. Although he strongly preferred Taft, he designed a compromise to help avoid a deadlock resulting in the nomination of a weaker candidate. Should either Taft or Dewey stumble in the early ballots, the weaker would transfer his delegates to the leader, ensuring his nomination. Both agreed, and when Taft's bid faltered, the Ohioan facilitated Dewey's nomination. The New Yorker would run with a united party behind him. For many of the delegates, the pinnacle of the convention was Hoover's speech. In his fourth consecutive address to a GOP conclave since departing from the White House, the ex-president delivered his most moving discourse. He attacked the New Deal's foreign and domestic policies and peppered his speech with references to moral and spiritual ideals and bedrock Republican principles. He said the next president would serve during perilous times due to the Communist threat. Hoover insisted that America must conserve, set priorities, and curtail waste. Further, the United States should not foster an interminable dependency on America by the European nations, which must become self-sustaining. Hoover's speech was an invocation to follow the Boy Scout motto: "Be prepared." A journalist who heard the speech wrote, "Never in his 74 years has he had a higher moment. It was astounding," he marveled. "They drew the man to their hearts as they had forgotten to do through his long period of public service. They seemed to be trying to make up for their lapse of affection and understanding."

Hoover told a friend that he had received a handwritten note from President Truman terming the speech the greatest "since Lincoln's Gettysburg Address."[27]

Hoover's energy was devoted to his work chairing the Committee on Government Reorganization, and he made no plans to campaign. Yet when both Truman and Democratic representative Sam Rayburn of Texas resorted to Hoover bashing, reviving the epitaphs of Roosevelt's ghostwriters, Hoover felt inclined to leap into the fray. Dewey, however, made no overture to the ex-president. Hoover felt that the bitterness of the campaign caused him to lose some of the gains he had made in restoring his reputation and he made no secret of his lack of respect for politicians who resorted to hypocrisy in the name of political expediency. Putting aside the goodwill he demonstrated earlier, Truman returned to his status as a machine politician. The Democrat and his surrogates blamed Hoover for single-handedly provoking the Great Depression, then sitting on it, without remorse. Truman veered left and tried to compete with the radical third-party candidate, Henry A. Wallace, in the North. Still a fourth candidate, Governor J. Strom Thurmond of South Carolina, appealed to conservatives, especially the Southern bloc. Dewey tried to straddle issues, mimicking Landon and Willkie. Instead, he alienated regular Republicans such as Hoover. Truman marshaled a razor-thin comeback victory.[28]

Much of the battering he was taking from Democrats in the campaign was soothed by the glow of human affection when Hoover returned to his birthplace to celebrate his seventy-fourth birthday at West Branch, Iowa, on August 10, 1948. Columnist Anne O'Hare McCormick wrote that "the former President's homecoming was the counterpart in personal terms to the address he delivered at the Republican convention a few weeks ago. In Philadelphia he was the elder statesman calling upon the party he once led," she explained. "In West Branch he was the country boy grown old and mellow and renowned. The burden of his speech was not that he is self-made but that he is America-made, the product of this society and this system." It was a poetic tribute to the nation that had helped make and mold him. "He has seen far more of this tortuous and tortured world than most political leaders, and the sum of his experience, distilled into this testament, is that there is nothing like America." *Newsweek* explained that the outpouring of affection, at least in West Branch, brought a measure of redemption, an indication of how far he had come. "It also meant vindication for his ideas—ideas which had been jeered at during the depression but had since regained respect." *U.S. News and World Report* heaped on another accolade when it wrote that "Mr. Hoover, a former President, may have more influence on the country now than he ever did while he was in the White House."[29]

A year later, Hoover celebrated his seventy-fifth birthday by delivering a speech at Stanford's Institution on War, Revolution, and Peace, which he had founded thirty-four years earlier. During these years, Hoover had helped raise more than $3.45 million in private contributions for the library, which had grown exponentially. Hundreds of individuals and some thirty-six governments had contributed to its holdings, he revealed. The institution preserved records of wars and revolutions, archiving the errors of troubled times in order to avert the mistakes of the past. Its documents in its area of specialization were unduplicated anywhere. It was not dead storage; it continued to grow as history evolved. The institution was funded entirely by grants and private donations. It never received one cent of government funds. Scholars from throughout the world utilized its resources. The library was not for his generation alone, Hoover explained. It taught stern lessons to coming generations in the hope that it could prevent future war, revolution, and genocide. Respect for Hoover attracted invaluable documents to the collections, and he also proved the library's most effective fund-raiser. Along with the Boys Clubs and Stanford University, the Hoover Institution on War, Revolution, and Peace constituted his chief charitable commitment. Hoover shifted his focus beyond the library to the world and to the next generation of Americans, and he sought to engage his audience in the quest for tempering the growth of collectivism—a dangerous fallacy, he believed.

At best, it wasted money, and at worst it enslaved peoples. Americans must remain a progressive people, he said, and collectivism was the antithesis of progress. Hoover went on to describe the tangle of bureaucracy that had grown and the cost to taxpayers compelled to feed the weeds sown by gratuitous and misdirected spending. A major enemy of individual liberty had become the massive burden of red tape that entangled lowly individuals in its quest for infinite bureaucracy. Further damaging was the polarization of the country into rapacious private pressure groups.[30]

Hoover now considered his abstention from the 1948 campaign a mistake. Thus, the seventy-six-year-old former president decided to deliver several speeches prior to the 1950 congressional elections because he understood the high stakes. However, he believed he could be most effective if he presented his addresses in a nonpartisan format. Most of his speeches were related to the great debate over military strategy that had recently commenced. Hoover argued that the policies of the Truman administration had overextended America and compromised the country's ability for self-defense. Further, the Truman Doctrine, the Marshall Plan, and NATO burdened American taxpayers. The great debate over military strategy began with Truman's decision to enter NATO, extended through the Korean War, and culminated during the Eisenhower administration, when Hoover essentially won his point. His chief ally in reliance on use of air and sea power rather than on ground troops was Senator Robert A. Taft. Hoover, Taft, and Eisenhower himself considered air power a cheaper, more efficient weapon. Hoover went further than Eisenhower; he opposed stationing American divisions in Europe to flesh out NATO, arguing that they would pose little realistic resistance to a massive Soviet ground assault, which would overwhelm and slaughter the outnumbered NATO troops. Fighting a ground war against Communism in Europe or Asia would be brutally suicidal and accomplish nothing, Hoover argued bluntly. The elder statesman reiterated his complaints about the stubborn negligence of America's NATO allies, save for Britain, to contribute meaningfully to their own protection, while simultaneously spending on extravagant social programs. Moreover, it was unhealthy for the Europeans to be completely dependent on the Americans. The GOP spokesman presciently pointed out that the United States could never fight everyone else's wars for them; it was a task worthy of Sisyphus. In the long run, even after Communism imploded, this proved all too true. Where the local will is lacking, America cannot impose a stable, just world order. The United States must depart sooner or later, and its well-intentioned nation building only delays the inevitable. On December 20, 1950, as American forces were driven back by the Chinese in Korea, Hoover delivered a speech that called for assessing the strength of the ground forces arrayed against the United States before the country became engaged in another conflict such as Korea.[31]

Hoover calibrated the odds of winning a worldwide ground war against the United States' Communist adversaries. Opposed to some 800 million people and more than three hundred combat divisions available to the Communist world, the United States and its only reliable major ally, Great Britain, could muster only sixty combat divisions on the ground, yet the United States possessed an overwhelming advantage in air and sea weaponry. Moreover, trying to match the Soviet land forces would bankrupt America. Before agreeing to dispatch ground divisions to Europe, America must ascertain the degree to which the Europeans were willing to contribute. Yet air and naval resources provided a potent deterrent and, if necessary, a far more powerful offensive weapon. While these forces deterred attack, the United States and Britain could buy time for the Communist system to collapse from within. To act otherwise would engage additional Koreas, at great expense and loss of life, with negligible gain. This stood in stark contrast to Truman's policy of dispatching Eisenhower to Europe to command American ground forces there. Press reaction could be calibrated by the political affiliation of the newspaper or journal. The Democratic press distorted Hoover's message by labeling it "isolationist" or "appeasement," a withdrawal to the Western Hemisphere. As Hoover explained his defense theories, it became clear that he intended to place limits on assistance only to countries who contributed nothing to their own defense. Moreover, he extended America's defense perimeters to Britain, Japan, Taiwan, and the Philippines, with Taft adding Australia and New Zealand, not to mention all of North and South America. The nuclear umbrella protected nations in Western Europe and Southern Asia. This defense would be more cost-efficient than attempting to match the Soviets and the Chinese and their allies man for man. Also, U.S. air power could strike anywhere, almost instantly, like a lightning bolt. Taft emphasized air power's great mobility and offensive potential. The massive Soviet land army, its vast territory, and the Russian winter provided no defense against air power. Naval power could complement air superiority. The Soviets, with few warm-weather ports, were unlikely to develop a formidable navy. In the air, the United States had only to maintain the technological advantage the country already possessed. Further, the advocates of air power did not rule out ground support for nations that devoted sufficient resources to their own land armies. Because Hoover's defense program promised more defense for less money, it appealed to fiscal conservatives. Later, it was described as "More Bang for the Buck." Hoover's plan was viewed as GOP doctrine. Some considered it dangerous because it left no option for fighting limited wars and potentially made every war a nuclear war.[32]

After Truman excoriated Hoover for failing to end the Great Depression, Hoover refused to attend the ex-president's seventieth birthday party in 1954. Hoping to repair Hoover's hurt feelings, Truman paid a courtesy call on him in New York in October 1955 and the men chatted amiably. Later that month the GOP ex-president attended a meeting with sponsors of the Truman Presidential Library who were seeking to raise $200,000 in the Southwest as part of the $2 million they needed to erect the building in Truman's hometown, Independence, Missouri. In July 1957 Hoover traveled to Independence, where he helped dedicate the Truman Presidential Library along with Chief Justice Earl Warren, Eleanor Roosevelt, Senator William Knowland, House Speaker Sam Rayburn, Congressman Charles Halleck, and other dignitaries. In a brief speech,

Hoover stated that it was important that Americans disperse the history of the nation throughout the land rather than limiting it to Washington, DC. Libraries should go to the people as well as people go to libraries. Their status as the only living ex-presidents brought Hoover and Truman back together, the scars of the political wars healed, and the two men resumed their friendship. The ex-presidents genuinely liked each other and developed a relationship that almost approached intimacy. In 1958, Truman, who had had his gall bladder removed, consoled Hoover, who was recovering from a similar operation. A year later, Hoover sent an ailing Bess Truman a bouquet of white mums and yellow roses. He invited Truman to the Bohemian Grove and recalled that his friend's visit to the Waldorf was "my intellectual stimulant of the month" after Truman visited in March 1960. Later, after Truman gave his friend a copy of his most recent book, Hoover wrote that "it goes into the file of most treasured documents." Truman responded with equal kindness: "I didn't receive a single birthday telegram that I appreciated more than I did yours." He wrote in July 1963 that they understood each other. Indeed they did. Historians have compared their postpresidential correspondence to the twilight missives of John Adams and Thomas Jefferson, old adversaries who consummated a profound friendship in their declining years.[33]

Many gave Hoover credit for eloquently and tirelessly campaigning, election after election and in between, to educate the public and keep the flame of conservatism flickering. Journalist Mark Sullivan wrote, "It was during these years that Mr. Hoover, in private life, strove passionately with word and pen, in addresses, magazine articles, and books, to make America see the virtues of individualism, [and] the perils of the collectivism which threatened to supplant it."

Sullivan believed, "That patient and laborious work of public education . . . will be Mr. Hoover's real distinction in history."[34]

SIXTEEN

The Republicans Return to Power

n 1951 Hoover began to closely follow the GOP presidential nominating campaign. He considered the election crucial, the Republicans' best opportunity since Roosevelt to elect a president, and perhaps the last opportunity they would have during his lifetime. Hoover strongly backed his old friend Senator Robert A. Taft. During the early months Hoover maintained a pose of neutrality, though behind the scenes he orchestrated Taft's campaign, persuading Joseph P. Kennedy, his old friend and a Democrat, to contribute $5,000 to the candidate's coffers. The chief obstacle to Taft's nomination was the popularity of General Dwight D. Eisenhower, a war hero yet an amateur in politics. Hoover feared that the famous general, the favorite of the liberal, internationalist wing of the GOP, would become another "me too" candidate like Landon and Willkie. Ike's supporters, however, argued that the Kansan was more likely than Taft to sweep a Republican Congress in on his coattails.[1]

The nomination at the Republican National Convention, held in June 1952 in Chicago, hinged on contested delegations from a few Southern states. Hoover offered to mediate the controversy through a compromise in which he and two other senior Republicans would examine the delegate claims and seat them on a case-by-case basis. Ike's campaign manager, Henry Cabot Lodge Jr., rejected Hoover's scheme, and the Eisenhower delegations were seated.[2] Hoover, conceding that his candidate could no longer win, attempted to persuade Taft to withdraw in favor of Douglas MacArthur. Taft said he would withdraw after the first ballot if his cause appeared hopeless. Unfortunately for the Taft supporters, Eisenhower won on the first ballot. Many Republicans considered Taft more qualified and a purer Republican, yet considered Eisenhower more electable.[3]

On the second night of the convention, Hoover delivered his address. Using a teleprompter for the first time, he needed glasses, which Chairman Joe Martin accidentally crushed when he pounded his gavel. Nonetheless, Hoover's speech was applauded thunderously by the delegates, less because of its ideological content than because of its tone of moral uplift and nostalgia for the old party warrior, who had kept the torch of Republican philosophy burning through five consecutive Democratic administrations. Hoover condemned the minor scandals of the Truman administration but focused more on the incumbent's failures in foreign policy. The Democrats had been extremely gullible in trusting the Soviets to keep their promises, and nation after nation had fallen under the domination of the hammer and sickle. "The ghosts of the Four Freedoms now wander amid the clanking chains of a thousand slave camps," said the once awkward speechwriter who had made himself a phrasemaker.[4] When Hoover delivered his speech, the 1952 nomination had already been settled. Eisenhower had won virtually all the contested delegates and was certain to win. Nonetheless, Hoover endorsed Taft as a matter of principle because he believed in his heart the Ohio senator would have made a superior president. He gained respect in some quarters for his action. One daily wrote, "He could have remained silent, packed his grips and gone home, the ovations of his party music in his ears. But Mr. Hoover was never a man to bid for popularity by doing or failing to do something." Instead, he went ahead and spoke his mind. "So feeling as he did that Senator Taft best fulfilled his ideas of the type of leadership he thought America needed, he endorsed the Senator, full knowing that his only reward would be a sharing in another political defeat." The editorial concluded, "Even Eisenhower partisans, of whom we count ourselves among the first, will honor Mr. Hoover's final act of courage. He is a man who ploughs the row to the end."[5] The *Washington Daily News* led with the headline "Herbert Hoover Is Our Real Mr. Republican." Robert C. Ruark concluded, "I just wish we could return Herbert Hoover for President, because I am certain we could win with him and fetch a little sanity back home."[6] The *Wall Street Journal* concluded that Hoover had received the longest and most enthusiastic reception of anyone who had spoken at the convention.[7]

Hoover expressed regret to Taft that his old friend would lose his last, best chance to capture the presidency. Truman, mired in scandals at home and bogged down abroad, had grown unpopular, and the Democratic candidate, Adlai Stevenson, while polished, and popular among liberals, appeared to be an elitist intellectual who failed to connect with ordinary Americans. He seemed too leftist ideologically and projected a cold, haughty demeanor. "I am sorry beyond expression," Hoover wrote to Taft. "We did our best." He remained cool toward Eisenhower, issuing an abrupt statement: "Being a Republican, I shall vote the Republican ticket." As to a possible role in the campaign, Hoover remarked, "I am going fishing." He was still annoyed by Eisenhower's support for stationing U.S. troops in Europe, nor could he forgive Lodge and others in the Eisenhower camp for what he considered the stealing of disputed delegates at the nominating convention. Nonetheless, Eisenhower treated Hoover respectfully and courted his favor. Like the press, Ike had been impressed by the loyalty to Hoover among bedrock Republicans and the reception he had received at the GOP convention. After waiting three weeks for nerves to cool after the convention, the candidate wrote a generous letter to the elder statesman expressing regret for not being able to visit him personally at the Chicago conclave. The general also expressed his interest in meeting with the venerable Republican to consult with him about the Hoover Commission reports and other matters, signing the missive, "With my sincere and respectful regards." In response, the ex-president sent the newcomer to politics a gift of his memoirs, and further correspondence followed. Ike wrote that only Hoover could understand the way he was besieged on all sides by people telling him different things, and he knew he could rely on his experience.[8]

Eisenhower employed his strongest asset, acquired as a general leading a coalition of armies: the combination of a calm, genial, yet firm personality and an ability to deal with people and to conciliate conflicting opinions. Ironically, the general, like Hoover, was born into a pacifist sect, the Mennonites. Hoover came to the defense of his friend and fellow Quaker Richard Nixon when the vice presidential candidate was accused of maintaining a secret fund, rumored to be for lavish living. Hoover argued that Nixon should remain on the ticket, stating publicly, "If everyone in the city of Washington possessed the high level of courage, probity and patriotism of Senator Nixon, this would be a far better nation." Nixon wrote Hoover that none of the thousands of endorsements he received gratified him more than Hoover's.[9]

The issue of whether Hoover should deliver a televised appeal for the GOP ticket was delicate. Hoover was reluctant to assert a role, fearing that Ike, like Dewey, might consider him a liability. Finally persuaded to call, the elder statesman was pleasantly surprised to learn that the Eisenhower campaign had been hoping he would volunteer. However, there was some difficulty raising the $50,000 necessary to pay for the broadcast. When Senator Everett McKinley Dirksen of Illinois learned of the problem, he personally provided the funds. On October 18, the aging ex-president delivered a stirring defense of Republican principles and policies to a national audience over CBS. He targeted younger voters who had never lived under a GOP administration. Within forty-eight hours, some thirty-five thousand viewers wrote to request copies of the speech.[10]

Nonetheless, in 1952 the Democrats once again used Hoover as a scapegoat for the Depression. One circular, entitled "Change Back to

What?," featured photos of breadlines, Hoovervilles, men begging for jobs, and tramps trudging the highways in search of work. The propaganda piece read, "The Republicans said it was wrong for the Government to give relief to the hungry and the homeless."[11] In addition, the Democrats published a tabloid, distributed to 5 million potential voters, featuring a photograph showing then Major Eisenhower directing the ejection of the 1932 Bonus marchers from Washington under the byline "General Ike Helps Rout the Vets." An accompanying article stated that he was using force against the ex-soldiers at the orders of President Herbert Hoover. The tabloid focused on the theme that the Republican Party had caused the Depression, then proceeded to make it worse by neglect, and that later the Democrats had restored prosperity.[12] Meanwhile, large numbers of Republicans doubted Eisenhower's fealty to the GOP. He had never before expressed interest in public office and had not taken clear positions on partisan issues. Initially, Hoover intended to vote for Eisenhower but otherwise remain uninvolved. Not until mid-October did he publicly endorse the Republican nominee. Whatever his doubts, Hoover did not want to see the Democrats' grip on the White House continue. For his part, Ike adroitly courted the elderly ex-president and felt his support would be helpful in the West and in solidifying the GOP base.[13] On November 6, 1952, Hoover enthusiastically watched via television as an avalanche of Republican votes buried the Democrats beneath an Eisenhower landslide. Hoover had waited for this moment since he had left the White House almost twenty years earlier. At the suggestion of Clare Boothe Luce, Eisenhower telephoned Hoover and told him he would try to bring as much integrity to the presidency as Hoover had brought to it. Hoover considered the election a referendum not only on politics, but on his core values. It had been a long, lonely road back. He realized it would not be possible to roll back the tide of big government completely, but at least in Eisenhower he had a fiscal conservative in the Executive Mansion. Although the two men did not agree on all issues, they established a relationship of mutual respect that endured. Also, Hoover was beginning to come to terms with the past and to renew his hope for the future. Eisenhower honored his aged predecessor by placing him at the front of his inaugural parade.[14]

In the years since his presidency, Hoover had grown more conservative. It was difficult to recall, even for Hoover himself, that the conservative wing of the Republican Party had once evinced the same doubts about President Hoover's GOP credentials that Hoover now felt about Eisenhower's. Still, there were substantial similarities. Both had earned their reputations largely as administrators. Neither was a professional politician, and Eisenhower, like Hoover, had been cultivated by Democrats before formally declaring himself a Republican. Each had a reputation for a placid temperament but could be explosive, and each possessed more drive and ambition than was superficially evident. Ike, like Hoover, would be more conservative as ex-president than as president. If one word could sum up Hoover's feelings, it would be "vindication," even though he would have been happier with Taft or MacArthur in the White House. Nonetheless, Hoover's lifelong ability to improvise did not fail him. The relationship was not warm initially, but it grew, as both men recognized in each other qualities they admired. The bond began with mutual respect and built on that foundation. More than a month after the election, on December 23, 1952, Eisenhower invited Hoover to lunch, at which they were joined by the incoming secretary of state, John Foster Dulles, and in January Hoover attended the new president's inauguration. Hoover did not always agree with Eisenhower's policies, but he made himself an ally, not an adversary. By December 1953 Hoover described his relations with the president to Hugh Gibson, writing that at first "there was coldness—and even some hostility. Gradually that has evaporated but I am not in any inner circle of influence."[15]

Eisenhower trusted Hoover's political judgment and agreed with it more than Truman had. He respectfully listened to Hoover's advice and sometimes solicited it, though he did not inevitably follow it. The chief executive kept his door open to the former president and also made social overtures to him. In May 1953, he invited his new friend to a stag dinner that included such Hoover friends as Lewis Strauss, Douglas MacArthur, and the conservative treasury secretary, George Humphrey. A few weeks later the president extended congratulations to Hoover on his seventy-ninth birthday, expressing gratitude that recent events had united them. Ike said he anticipated even closer relations in the future. One journalist wrote to Hoover that Eisenhower's ascendancy to the White House represented "the splendid vindication by millions of American voters of those political principles which you consistently espoused and defend against attack, and worse, indifference."[16]

Hoover was disappointed with Eisenhower's first defense budget, which called for a smaller air force than he had recommended, yet he did not publicly criticize the president. "I am still regarded by many of the public as a Republican leader," he wrote a friend, explaining that if he opposed the administration it would "at once be heralded as a split in the Party." Hoover was a consummate realist. He elaborated that Ike's was "the only Republican administration we have or hope to reelect in our time." Eisenhower continued to cultivate Hoover's friendship, extending an invitation in August 1954 to join him on a fishing trip to Colorado. Hoover, who rarely declined an opportunity to fish, readily agreed. Ike said the only people at the camp would be Hoover, himself, and possibly the owner of the lodge—and the president would do all the cooking. The elder statesman found Ike a genial companion but not sufficiently serious about fishing and overpunctilious about cooking.[17]

In 1953 the Republican Congress approved a bill sponsored by two GOP congressmen providing for a second government reorganization commission with broader powers than the previous commission Hoover had chaired under Truman. Hoover was appointed by Eisenhower to serve, and at the first meeting the commission elected him chair. It has become known as the Second Hoover Commission. Unlike the first commission, it contained a majority of Republicans and had no vice chairman. Hoover personally appointed every member of the numerous task forces that researched and reported on specific bottlenecks in the federal bureaucracy. Although the first commission had focused primarily on reorganization within individual agencies, its successor also explored, and attempted to eliminate, overlap among agencies. It was specifically authorized to probe and sever from the bureaucracy the government functions that competed with private enterprise. This provoked the wrath of Democrats, who feared Hoover might use the commission to dismantle functions of the New Deal, which was precisely his objective. He was eager to push such changes through Congress expeditiously, lest the Democrats regain control of that body in the 1954 off-year elections.

As Hoover had feared, the 1954 congressional elections returned the Democrats to control of Congress. This proved a hurdle to implementation of the recommendations of the Second Hoover Commission. The senior public servant professed himself pleased with Eisenhower, Dulles, Defense Secretary Charles Wilson, Treasury Secretary George Humphrey, and Agriculture Secretary Ezra Taft Benson. The trouble, he believed, came from other quarters outside the White House and the cabinet. After a brief goodwill trip to Germany, Hoover redoubled his efforts to crank out reams of recommendations from the Second Hoover Commission. The commission submitted 145 administrative recommendations that could be implemented by executive orders and an additional 167 that required legislation. The Democratic Congress proved a redoubtable obstacle to many of the proposed reforms, and, overall, the Second Hoover Commission ostensibly accomplished less than the first. However, Hoover reflected that even those not implemented might have educational value. Hoover always came in under budget. Democratic Senator John McClellan, chairman of the Committee on Government Operations, later reminisced that "at the expiration of both the Commissions [Hoover] headed, he returned to the Treasury of the United States a 'surplus.' That is, he got the job done without spending all the appropriations Congress gave him—a rarity, I regret to say, in Washington today." McClellan added that this served to verify that Hoover lived "up to the principles of good government for which he so squarely stands."[18]

Hoover was pleased that "the administration, without admitting it, has adopted my proposals in the Great Debate—of course without any acknowledgement as to where they got it. Anyway, it is all to the good." By mid-January 1954, Hoover believed that, as a whole, the "New Look" defense policy of the administration was close to what he had advocated. The New Look relied primarily on a large, nuclear-armed Strategic Air Command, expanding to bases around the globe. Gradually, the United States encircled the Soviet Union with air and naval bases, placing every major target within striking distance. Ground forces were now considered the auxiliary rather than the first line of defense. Moreover, America accelerated its submarine, aircraft carrier, and missile programs. Further, late in 1953 the still feisty ex-president signed a mammoth petition urging the United States to veto the admission of Communist China to the United Nations. In early 1954 a proposed constitutional amendment by Hoover's friend Ohio senator John W. Bricker to outlaw executive agreements such as those negotiated by FDR from becoming effective without congressional ratification became a heated issue. Hoover favored the amendment but took no public stand on the measure, which was defeated. In May and June of 1954 the French found it difficult to repel attacks by Communist guerrillas in Vietnam. Hoover advised against sending American troops to aid the French, warning that it would prove a greater sinkhole of manpower than Korea. Moreover, in Vietnam the United States would be upholding imperialism, and the chances for success in the long term there were minuscule, given the determination of the Vietnamese nationalists to win independence. It would be a serious error to aid in the perpetuation of vestiges of the British and French empires, a practice that was already giving America "the stigma of colonial exploitation which we little deserve in view of our long history of sympathy with people striving to be free."[19]

Hoover certainly detested Communism, but his foreign policy strategy was forged more on practical than on ideological grounds. He pointed out that America must adopt a resurgence of nationalism in an aggressive postwar world, in which Americans were almost uniquely self-critical. Patriotism should become fashionable; the United States had little to be ashamed of. Idealism coupled with realistic self-interest must undergird U.S. policies in the Cold War. So far as the UN proved useful, the United States should utilize it, but the country should not overestimate its efficacy. It was primarily a debating society that furnished a forum for anti-American diatribes. It would not and could not protect America or small democracies confronted with Communist aggression. The United States should recognize and accept the fact that some nations had resorted to neutrality to protect themselves. America should be parsimonious with military and economic aid. It had already been proven that the United States could not buy reliable friends. Economic aid rarely improved living standards among the poor in the recipient nations, because it was skimmed off by the rich.[20]

In November 1954 Hoover traveled to Germany at the invitation of Chancellor Konrad Adenauer to be honored for his contributions to Germany's restoration as an industrial power with democratic institutions. Adenauer met Hoover at the airport in Bonn and lauded him "as one of the great men of the world who has placed himself in the service of humanity." At dinner, the chancellor heaped more praise on the American for helping revive the German economy from postwar restrictions. Hoover replied by commending a healthy degree of German nationalism and said Germany must become the economic fulcrum of Western Europe. West German president Theodor Heuss told the aging humanitarian, "Your name is blessed by millions of nameless people." Hoover departed with an optimistic farewell. "Today, under your wise statesmanship," he informed Adenauer, "West Germany is about to attain her independence and to become a partner in the defense of freedom from the common danger." Hoover briefed the president on his trip and Eisenhower said Hoover was the most qualified man he could have dispatched to undertake the healing of the vital nation in the heart of Europe.[21]

The 1956 convention marked the centennial of the birth of the GOP. Hoover had planned a fishing trip, but Eisenhower asked the ex-president to deliver a brief speech. The thirty-first president used the commemoration to celebrate the party's principles rather than deal in programmatic details. Safeguarding the vitality of free men and nations was the primary objective. He praised "the genius of our people, their devotion to personal liberty and their sustaining devotion to personal liberty and religious beliefs." Although he rarely mentioned it, Hoover's elder son, Herbert Jr., was making a contribution to statecraft by serving as the undersecretary of state under John Foster Dulles. Herbert Jr. helped untangle a diplomatic thicket that threatened to halt the flow of oil from Iran to the West. Meanwhile, early in 1953, Hoover's longtime devoted friend Senator Taft, now the majority floor leader, was diagnosed with cancer. Despite his own advanced age, Hoover visited his stricken comrade at every opportunity. Loyalty to friends was a consistent, lifelong trait. When Taft died on the last day of July, Hoover issued a press release describing his remorse for the passing of the man he had known since their mutual work in food relief during the Great War. In February 1955, Hoover's older brother, Tad, died. In old age the West Branch native, now a New Yorker, thrived on work and memories. Shortly after Tad's death, Hoover's boyhood home in Newberg, Oregon, was opened to the public.[22]

When Hoover indicated that he did not plan to attend the 1956 GOP convention, Ike personally asked him to go and to deliver an address. "You exemplify in more ways than I am sure you realize the dignity and the spirit of the Republican Party," the president wrote, "and I know that every delegate to the Convention would be keenly disappointed, as would I, if you were not there to lend your counsel and advice." Hoover decided to make the trip and was gratified by the thunderous applause with which his speech was received. It was his sixth speech before the quadrennial gathering. He used the occasion to warn of the dangers of Communism. Afterward, the former president wrote Eisenhower to give thanks "for a President who has, amid stupendous difficulties, kept the world at peace and lifted American public life again to the levels of integrity." In late October, Hoover was heartened by the Hungarian Revolution, then helped raise money for refugees after the anti-Communist uprising was suppressed by the Soviet Union. He mobilized some of his aging World War I assistants, who helped provide medicine and clothing for refugees and aided some to immigrate to America. Unlike the crises for which the earlier ARA had mobilized, in this one food was not a major need. By February 1957, most of the early immigrants had been settled and the government took over the program. Hoover devoted the remainder of the year to writing. Although Hoover and Ike were superficially congenial friends, Hoover did express reservations about Eisenhower's aptitude for the presidency. He said the ex-general was decent and sincere in his desire to do the right thing, yet he had little knowledge about economics, politics, or the art of governing.[23]

Hoover did not slow down, and he never lost his zest for an active life. During his eighty-fifth year he traveled some fourteen thousand miles and delivered twenty speeches. He had long since outgrown his tendency as president to mumble in a nearly inaudible voice and had blossomed into a poignant, sometimes witty speaker. His speeches were sprinkled with original humor, epigrams, and aphorisms, and his writing now displayed this style as well. Moreover, Hoover had grown to enjoy public speaking and was in great demand, with far more invitations than he could accept. He still painstakingly wrote every speech himself and picked out of his rhetorical garden every gratuitous weed. Hoover was either on the road, fishing at his favorite haunts, or immersed in writing, wherever he went, but chiefly at the Waldorf Towers, surrounded by secretaries and interrupted by friends and dignitaries, whom he greeted cheerfully; then he returned to writing, which had become his passion in old age. As some men turned to drink, gambling, or women, Hoover turned to writing. It was his avocation and his vocation. He had once struggled; now he excelled. Hoover also continued to speak, to testify before congressional committees, and to perform ceremonial tasks at the government's request. He was now fully acclimated to continent hopping by plane. In April 1958, shortly after Hoover's gall bladder removal, Eisenhower called to ask if he would represent the United States for the celebration of July Fourth at the Brussels World's Fair. By the end of April, the elderly statesman's doctor gave his permission for the trip and Eisenhower provided a government plane. Belgium was the place where Hoover had leaped up on the world stage, and memories flooded back. The man who had fed Belgium twice within a generation was given a hero's welcome. Hoover's July Fourth speech was a rousing defense of American values and his country's role in the world. He noted that his nation's ideals included compassion and the sharing of its technological innovations. His was a generous nation, Hoover reminded his audience at the fair. "Never after victory did we ask for an acre of territory, except a few military bases to protect the free nations. We have never asked for reparations or economic privileges," he continued. "On the contrary, we made gigantic gifts and loans to aid nations in war and reconstruction, including Communist Russia." On July 5, which was declared "Hoover Day," he spoke about the achievements of the CRB during the First World War. The *New York Times* wrote that it had been an excellent idea to send Hoover to represent America and that "once more Mr. Hoover has been an honor to his country."[24]

Back at home, Hoover assessed the condition of his nation. In the late 1950s he grew concerned that Americans were becoming too materialistic. He cited crime statistics as an index of moral decay. The boy who had attended rural schools worried that fashionable progressive education discouraged study of fundamental subjects such as math. He shared the fear of many of his countrymen in the aftermath of Sputnik that America was falling behind in science. The Iowa orphan believed many young people were preoccupied with entertainment and neglected religious grounding. However, Hoover had positive suggestions. He wanted to implement tougher educational standards. He pointed out that wholesome recreational opportunities such as those provided in his beloved Boys Clubs could provide alternatives to crime and idleness, pointing out that his clubs had reduced youth crime by 75 percent in one St. Louis suburb. In 1959, his eighty-fifth year, Hoover accepted twenty-three awards from groups such as the Jewish Theological Seminary and the U.S. Lawn Tennis Association. He laid three cornerstones for public buildings, dedicated four Boys Clubs, and devoted as much time as possible to his "pavement boys," the

newest incarnation of his love of children. He argued that with $10 mil-
lion invested in a Boys Club in Harlem he could do more to deter juvenile
delinquency than any police program.[25]

The Eisenhower administration virtually cribbed its defense strategy
from Hoover. However, he continued to warn about America becoming
overextended, particularly in preserving the colonial empires of its allies,
which, he believed, would be lost ultimately to changing times. With the
French colonial empire in Indochina staggering, Hoover expressed the
strong opinion that the United States should never dispatch troops to
reinforce French imperialism. He was almost in equal parts an opponent
of Communist aggression and an opponent of war. Always an opponent
of colonialism, Hoover said that the United States "should cease to support colonial exploitation even by our friends." The present world, destabilized by interminable Communist expansion, had only confirmed his
belief that it had been wrong for the United States to enter the European
war. Yet in his public statements, he was careful to be less critical of
Republican foreign policies than he had been when a Democrat sat in the
White House. He did not want to weaken the president or hurt GOP
congressional candidates. In January 1957 several congressmen asked for
Hoover's opinion on a request by the president to authorize the chief
executive to use American armed forces in the Middle East to preserve
peace, and also for $400 million in economic assistance to the region.
The aging statesman replied to the first request, "On the understanding
that these proposals extend only to Russian Communist military aggression and to economic aid I am in full agreement with the President." He
elaborated when asked to do so by a senator, responding "that the United
States should use its military forces to aid Middle East states to repel any
military aggression in the region," and that he backed "continued economic aid in the region." Hoover had to some degree shifted his reluctance to intervene abroad because of the strategic importance of the
Middle East, including its petroleum resources, to American interests,
because the matter did not involve a lack of commitment on the part of

America's allies, such as he perceived the case to be in Western Europe, and because he wanted to back a Republican president.[26]

Hoover remained dubious of some of Eisenhower's domestic policies. He felt the president had not compelled the New Dealers to turn tail and run. He was less critical of the president's foreign policy, which he felt, overall, was sound, yet he lamented the lackadaisical attitude of the United States' Western European allies toward their own defense. He questioned whether the Europeans possessed the intestinal fortitude to defend themselves. The only option was to let them stew in their own juices, deterring a major war with nuclear intimidation until infatuation with the Communist utopia ended. Nonetheless, Eisenhower had avoided war while also avoiding concessions to Communism, such as Roosevelt had made. Hoover was gratified that Ike had largely, if not entirely, adopted the reliance on air power he had advocated during the great debate.

Hoover realized that Eisenhower's two terms had not restored the GOP to the place it had held before FDR as the nation's majority party. The party needed to be rebuilt, and while Eisenhower had to his credit fiscal austerity and a period of peace and prosperity, he had failed to get down in the trenches to fight the hard battles necessary to rejuvenate and rebuild the GOP. Thus, his two terms, built on personal popularity rather than on ideology, represented an interlude rather than a trend. Three consecutive defeats of the GOP in congressional elections confirmed the ex-president's appraisals. Some of Hoover's close friends never ceased wishing that the Quaker, rather than the general, had occupied the White House during the 1950s.

Still a public presence, the aged ex-president remained active in politics, charities, and writing. He seemed to have shifted the gears of the evolution of age into reverse. He received more speaking invitations than he could fulfill. In December 1959, he became a member of the board of trustees of the conservative Americans for Constitutional Action, which worked to elect conservative candidates to public office. Hoover did not intend to play a role in the 1960 Republican campaign. When party leaders asked him to deliver a speech at the quadrennial convention, he tried to beg off, but he consented to deliver a short address at Chicago. This was destined to be his fourth "farewell" appearance, and his last. Hoover considered Vice President Nixon to be Ike's logical successor. He favored Barry Goldwater for the vice presidency yet considered it unlikely the delegates would pair two Westerners. Of the Eastern candidates, Hoover preferred Henry Cabot Lodge Jr., whom Nixon selected. Hoover liked Nixon personally but considered the fellow Quaker, like Eisenhower and Lodge, to the left of Goldwater and himself. Hoover opened his speech with a touch of nostalgia and irony. "In each of the last three Conventions I bade you an affectionate goodbye," he said. "Apparently my goodbyes did not take," he explained. "Unless some miracle comes to me from the Good Lord, this is finally it." Hoover focused on moral, spiritual, and philosophical themes. He said that America was experiencing "a frightening moral slump" with an infection of Marxism undermining religious institutions. Churches and organizations devoted to character building and moral uplift needed additional aid. Hoover summoned the GOP to "stop this moral retreat, to lead the attack and recapture the meaning of the word—America."[27]

Hoover went on to say that the federal government should abstain from the use of the military to enforce the law by use of federal troops within any state except in the case of rebellion. Agricultural policy should be based on the premise of paying farmers to reduce the surplus by leasing marginal acreage and returning such land to pasture or forests. He also suggested that the government vow to avoid competition with private enterprise in a way that would appeal to both business and unions. He pointed out that workers on government projects had no bargaining leverage over wages or working conditions and could be terminated at will by the government—which was true at that time. Perhaps Hoover's most penetrating observations pertained to his critique of the GOP candidate's performance in his first debate with Kennedy. He found Nixon's presentation weak and pointed out numerous errors the nominee had committed. He advised Nixon to address Kennedy directly, to challenge him more forcefully. Nixon had agreed with Kennedy's premises five times rather than attacking them aggressively and defining their differences. JFK did not, by contrast, concur with Nixon a single time. Hoover urged Nixon to clearly delineate the lines of demarcation, suggesting that Nixon paint Kennedy as a big-government exemplar of the New Deal. The ex-president pointed out that Nixon should focus on identifying flaws in Kennedy's program. Finally, and most obviously, Nixon's appearance was unkempt. He did not appear presidential. He looked like a frightened rabbit. "Either he was ill or he was not shaven, or not properly made up. Or if he were made up, it was a terrible job and he should get a better make-up technician." Hoover remained an astute critic of his own party in his final campaign, and he did not mince words. In an additional memorandum to Kentucky senator Thruston Morton pertaining to campaign strategy, Hoover viewed Nixon as losing ground to Kennedy as the campaign progressed. He advised the party's candidate to emphasize that Kennedy's promises would require greater spending and tax increases. Nixon should advocate scaling down government and slashing taxes. Some $10 billion annually could be saved by taking the government out of work that could be done more efficiently by private enterprise. This would permit tax reductions. Minimizing government bureaucracy and reducing taxes would reap millions of votes.[28]

Hoover liked Nixon personally but was pessimistic about his chances. Like Ike, he considered the Californian too willing to compromise. Eisenhower, however, had an advantage Nixon did not; he was a war hero. On November 8, 1960, Hoover cast his vote for the Republican ticket. He refused to predict an outcome, stating that he was no prophet. However, James A. Farley, who had directed FDR's 1932 campaign and was now Hoover's neighbor in the Waldorf Towers, predicted Kennedy would win all but fifteen states. The two men, now warm friends, met at the polls, shook hands, and posed for photos together. Asked if he had voted a straight party ticket, Hoover responded, "Any man who has been

President of the United States at the hands of his party always sticks with his party." Farley proved correct about the victor but far too optimistic about Kennedy's margin of victory. Kennedy edged Nixon by one of the narrowest margins in the century. When the returns were in, Joseph Kennedy called the Waldorf to share his enthusiasm with his old friend. The Kennedy family always treated Hoover with respect. Hoover suggested that Nixon and Kennedy meet and shake hands before photographers as a display of reconciliation and national unity. Nixon was reluctant, but Joseph Kennedy helped arrange the meeting.[29]

Notwithstanding his eighty-six years, Hoover planned to fly to Washington for JFK's inauguration, only to find the airports closed because of a rare snowstorm. Kennedy wanted the older man's presence to the extent that he sent a plane to fly him to Washington. Hoover and Kennedy enjoyed mutual respect, even fondness. At a reception in Palm Beach the young president sought out the elder statesman for advice. Hoover offered none, but told him not to worry because as president, Kennedy would be bombarded with advice. On April 17, 1961, American-trained Cuban exiles invaded Cuba at the Bay of Pigs and were quickly routed after Kennedy failed to provide promised air support. Hoover supported the attempt to overthrow Castro but said that he would have destroyed Castro's entire army with American ground troops if necessary. Overcoming his Quaker inhibitions, the ex-president fulminated that America could not tolerate a Soviet-backed enclave nestled ninety miles due south of Key West. On April 28 the president sought the counsel of Hoover and General MacArthur, successively, at the Waldorf Towers. Kennedy eventually appointed Hoover as honorary chairman of his pioneering Peace Corps initiative. Kennedy's thoughtfulness continued. He sent John McCone of the CIA to brief the ex-president on security issues.[30]

Hoover remained relatively close to the Kennedys. In May 1963 the president dropped by the Waldorf for a visit while attending a birthday party in New York City. Later that year Hoover wrote the president's mother, Rose Kennedy, stating that now he, like her husband, required a wheelchair, but "I am in a better way than he for I have begun to walk with the help of two good nurses." In November, Hoover grieved for the young president struck down in his prime by an assassin's bullet. He issued a press release stating that Kennedy "loved America and has given his life for his country. I join our bereaved nation in heartfelt sympathy for Mrs. Kennedy and their two children."[31]

The assassination of John F. Kennedy depressed the old man more than any event in years. Allan decided to spend the night with his father in his Waldorf suite to help calm his nerves. Truman and Eisenhower rushed to Washington to consult with the newly sworn-in president Lyndon Johnson, and in turn Johnson telephoned Hoover to complete the circle of unity among the living presidents. The next morning Hoover cabled the new president, "I am ready to serve our government in any capacity, from office boy up." He also dispatched a note to the widow, Jacqueline Kennedy, conveying his heartfelt remorse. "You were always wonderful to my husband and he admired you so much," she wrote back. The grieving widow paid a call on Hoover at the Waldorf, where he played with her youngest child, John-John.

Lyndon Johnson's initial address to Congress was delivered in somber tones. Afterward, Hoover wrote him "that all Americans who heard your stirring words will evidence appreciation by their cooperation and response." On December 9, LBJ, while in New York for a funeral, impulsively decided to call on Hoover at the Waldorf, bringing with him Earl Warren and Mayor Robert Wagner. Two weeks later, Johnson telephoned to express Christmas greetings to the revered ex-president.[32]

The 1964 campaign was the last one of Hoover's life. Richard Nixon visited his apartment to discuss politics, but Hoover said he was unlikely to endorse any candidate in the primaries, although he liked Barry Goldwater. The Arizona senator was probably the closest to his ideological soul mate of any GOP nominee. Hoover was gratified by Goldwater's telephone call from the convention to personally inform him that he had selected Representative William Miller of New York as his running mate. The conclave was the first Republican gathering he had missed since leaving office. The octogenarian told Goldwater that he could not be there in person, but he offered to write a letter of endorsement that could be read to the convention. The six-hundred-word epistle was read to the delegates by Illinois senator Everett Dirksen. On August 9, Goldwater paid a courtesy call on Hoover at the Waldorf and found the old man brimming with enthusiasm for the cause. Hoover fervently backed Goldwater yet doubted he could defeat LBJ, swept up in an outpouring of sympathy for the slain Kennedy.[33]

On October 3, 1964, Goldwater penned a gracious note to Hoover thanking him for his sage advice and subtle support during the campaign. "This campaign will chart the course of conservatism in America for years to come, and I am counting on your efforts to make it a continued success," the Arizona senator wrote. But Hoover had only two weeks to live. He died on October 20, 1964, before voters defeated the man who came closest to embodying his philosophy of any candidate nominated by the GOP since Hoover had departed the White House in 1933.[34]

SEVENTEEN

Tempest and Triumph

On October 22, 1964, the presidential campaign was temporarily
halted to permit both candidates to fly to New York City, where
Herbert Hoover's body lay in state at St. Bartholomew's Episcopal Church.
Some 17,500 mournful citizens filed by his coffin the first day. The setting was ornate, yet the ceremony itself was in keeping with the simplicity of Hoover's youth.[1]

From New York, the casket traveled by train to the nation's capital.
It was carried from Union Station on a caisson drawn by seven horses,
and a crowd stood seven deep along sidewalks while soldiers fired a
twenty-one-gun salute as Hoover made his final trip to the Capitol. Afterward, the casket was flown to Cedar Rapids, where 5,000 mourners met
the plane, and then driven to its final resting place at West Branch,
where 75,000 gathered for the burial on the grounds of the Hoover
Library. Later, Lou, who had been buried at Stanford, was moved to a
grave adjoining her husband's.[2]

The peripatetic life that had begun in a tiny whitewashed cottage at
the corner of Main and Downey streets in the idyllic hamlet of West

Branch had ended ninety years and two months later in a $32,000-per-year suite in the Waldorf Astoria, high above Manhattan's Park Avenue. Born to a father who shod horses, Bertie had risen to the pinnacle of American power and had lived to witness the space race, yet he never relinquished the values inculcated by his Quaker parents and relatives.[3]

Hoover circled the world as a trailblazing engineer. Between 1914 and 1923, he had earned himself titles such as the "Great Humanitarian," the "Napoleon of Mercy," and "Samaritan to a Continent." He had managed, orchestrated, and assisted an array of relief operations unparalleled in world history, all without a cent of remuneration, declining even expenses. During and after World War I he was responsible for the delivery of nearly 34 million metric tons of food, clothing, and medicine to those endangered by famine and pestilence in Europe and Asia. These supplies were worth some $5,234,000,000 in the currency of his time, an estimated $50 billion today. Most of these undertakings were initiated by Hoover; none of them could have been accomplished without him. Hoover fed an estimated 83 million people and was doubtless responsible for saving more lives than any individual in history. This does not even include the role he played when beckoned by President Truman to survey relief needs and supplies in the wake of World War II, the distribution of which he did not personally supervise.[4]

Returning to his homeland after the war, under presidents Harding and Coolidge he made an obscure cabinet post the most important force behind 1920s prosperity and became the greatest commerce secretary in history and one of the three or four most influential men in America. Hoover's presidency was a disappointment, but he redeemed himself by sheer persistence, character, and steadfast unselfishness. Often swimming against the tide during the 1930s and 1940s, he wrote industriously, spoke widely, raised money for charities, and created one of the world's great research facilities, the Hoover Institution on War, Revolution, and Peace at Stanford. Returned to public service by Harry Truman, he played leading roles in relief and in government reorganization and became the glue of the GOP during its own political exile, which lasted until 1953. If suffering brings redemption, Hoover knew both the agony and the ecstasy, regaining respect and deference, if never the adulation he had commanded prior to his presidency. He outlived most of his enemies and persuaded much of the public that he was a useful citizen of sterling character. When he was asked how he had survived the ostracism of the Roosevelt era, his eyes twinkled and he cackled, "I outlived the bastards."[5] Yet he never quite achieved historical vindication. If democracy is a cruel and fickle employer, historians abet the process of adulation and demonization to a degree often undeserved at both extremities. Herbert Hoover is the only U.S. president who never made the cover of *Time* as a sitting president—although he was on the cover four times while out of office.[6]

During the thirty-one years from the end of his presidency to his death, Hoover served as the purest spokesman of American conservatism. While the country veered increasingly leftward during the New Deal, his views remained remarkably consistent. He never strayed from his conviction that free-market capitalism, reasonably regulated, produced the world's highest standard of living. Inextricably linked were the fundamental American values of political, religious, and intellectual freedom, which contributed to the quality of life and complemented the cornucopia of productivity.[7]

Nonetheless, Hoover questioned the efficacy of selfish big business, an octopus second only to the government bureaucracy that could strangle individual initiative and siphon off the nation's wealth. Considering many businessmen narrow-minded and self-serving, he never believed money was an end in itself. He was as inveterate a foe of business monopoly as he was of government bureaucracy, and he remained proud of his party's early role in containing both. Having sprung from the grass roots, Hoover believed the core of sagacity lay in the lower realms of government, bottom-up, not top-down. Too much government inspired a demand for more government to solve the dilemmas it had created itself.[8]

Because Hoover was frequently on the losing side of the ideological debates of the 1930s and 1940s, historians have been too quick to leap to the conclusion that he was wrong on the merits of his causes, or even misguided to raise the arguments. Yet today, his ideas remain at the heart of American politics. In the 1980s, a groundswell of conservatism swept Ronald Reagan into power, reigniting the debate about big government, fiscal policy, welfare, overregulation of business, special interests, and endemic public spending. Hoover's concern that prodigious public debt would eventually paralyze the government in time of real need still resonates with voters. Today, polarization and paralysis increasingly characterize American politics, yet at the core we remain a centrist nation, whether right-center or left-center. Although political prophets, like biblical prophets, are often scorned in their own lands, they are as necessary today as they were in Jeremiah's times. It is possible that the "weaning of America" for which Hoover yearned might yet take place.

Hoover remained proudly patriotic throughout his life, yet he worried about the future of his nation during his declining years. He questioned whether America had become a country of sheep, splintered into selfish interest groups. In their seeking economic security as their chief priority, he worried that they might shut the door to other values. "Freedom is the open window," Hoover said, "through which pours the sunlight of the human spirit, of human dignity."[9]

Hoover's life was one of undeniable accomplishment and indefatigable industriousness, even in lost causes. But most important about his life are his ideas, his ideals, and his character, which stand undiminished generations after his death. For him, there was no substitute for hard work and perseverance. In almost any pursuit, drive was more important than intelligence. Herbert Hoover did not gain the whole world, but neither did he lose his soul.

ACKNOWLEDGMENTS

My gratitude begins with my devoted wife, Lauren Priegel, who has lived not only with me, but also with Hoover for the duration of our marriage and has exercised loving patience; and my daughters, Leah and Hannah, who are sources of love, inspiration, and pride. My two closest friends, David Luhrssen and Phil Deeken, undertook so many requests for aid, large and small, that they deserve a great share of the credit. David took time away from his own hectic schedule as a writer to edit and reorganize much of the material in the manuscript and to rescue me from my own follies. He is, quite simply, the best writer I know. David unselfishly devoted many hours to editing, streamlining, trimming, and consolidating the book and smoothing my prose with no more tangible reward than my thanks. Phil's contributions were varied and so numerous they are impossible to enumerate, and he was my chief computer guru. He transported me to places far and near when I was hopelessly lost. My other computer expert, Stephen Baldwin, also contributed hugely, as did Cliff Rogers. Phil, a jack-of-all-trades, spent months at my home untangling computer snafus with the patience of Job, tutoring me about online mastery, and sometimes taking dictation, as did two former students, Chris Harley Rupp and Rosie Millman. Computer mavens themselves, they were long-suffering with a writer less understanding of technology than themselves. Another friend and neighbor, Carla Otterson, was my nearby computer expert who coaxed out of my computer and printer their best efforts. None of my other helpers enjoyed the advantage of such proximity.

My graduate student Peter Lund tracked down scores of obscure references. My guardian angel at the University of Wisconsin–Milwaukee for decades has been Anita Cathey, joined more recently by Kathy Kreugel and Barisha Letterman, and Kathy's predecessor, Cynthia Barnes. My students and colleagues at the University of Wisconsin–Milwaukee, my academic home for thirty-five years, were a source of stimulation and encouragement. My ex-student, the former Meredith Vnuk, located, ordered, and purchased every book written on Hoover, in or out of print, and mailed them to me at West Branch, which necessitated combing, usually by computer, hundreds of rare-book stores at no charge for her prodigious, time-consuming work. As you may surmise, this was a team effort by a group that bonded in a common cause. My agent, Bridget Matzie of Zachary Shuster Harmsworth, the finest literary agent I have encountered, worked ceaselessly to place the manuscript. She was untiring, patient, painstaking, good-natured, and persistent, and Todd Shuster, my other agent, intervened several times to rescue a project that resembled roadkill. I also want to acknowledge the role of Jacob Moore, my early agent at ZSH. My editor, Brent Howard at NAL/Penguin Random House, was all that a writer can ask for, and more. Discovering Brent was like being dealt a deuce and drawing to an inside straight.

It would take a book of its own to name individually the treasure trove of lifetime friends I developed during my years at the Herbert Hoover Presidential Library. I took from them the lesson that not only can writing a presidential biography be arduous; it can be uplifting, given appropriate camaraderie. Thank you all for laughing at my jokes, even the puns. It starts at the top, with the library director during my residency, Timothy Walch, his successor, Thomas Schwartz, the director of the Hoover

Presidential Library Association (now the Hoover Foundation) Rebecca Allgood, and her successor, Jerry Fleagle. Competence actually does sprout on trees in West Branch, though it is a bit less common than corn, including my style of humor. The Reading Room was presided over by a maestro, Matt Schaefer, assisted by the able reference expert Spencer Howard, also an accomplished musician. Lynn Smith and Craig Wright were crucial and untiring in obtaining photographs for no reward but gratitude. Jim Detlefsen fine-tuned the computers. Everyone from the manager of the bookstore and gift shop to the library security guards treated me not as an intruder but as family.

I wish to pay tribute to the other Hoover scholars I befriended, especially George H. Nash, Kendrick A. Clements, Hal Wert, and, through reputation, the late Gary Dean Best. I appreciate the support and encouragement of Margaret Hoover in my attempt to capture her great-great-grandfather as he actually was. Like birds of a feather, we instinctively flocked together. I want to thank Leo P. Ribuffo of George Washington University for sharing his knowledge of conservatism and for writing letters of recommendation for grants and awards and for his friendship since graduate school. Chris Chappell of Palgrave Macmillan helped launch my career as a Hoover scholar. And then there were my dedicated photocopiers at West Branch, graduate student Heather Martens, college student Laura Fraise, and West Branch high schoolers Seth Honemann, Molly Whiteside, and Megan O'Neil. At the Hoover Institution at Stanford University, my wife, Lauren, was my sole photocopier, research aide, and inseparable companion.

Without the funding of grants awarded by the Earhart Foundation (four), the National Endowment for the Humanities, the American Historical Association, the American Philosophical Society, the Bradley Foundation, the American Council of Learned Societies, and the University of Wisconsin–Milwaukee, this project would never have achieved liftoff, much less reached its destination.

My spiritual gurus David Bobrowich, Gregory Hoag, Anna Maria Casper, Joan Hoss, and the late Nancy Retzlaff and Victoria Leigh kept me sane and energized.

ESSAY ON SOURCES

Most of my primary research was undertaken in the enormous collections about Hoover at the Herbert Hoover Presidential Library at West Branch, Iowa, where I spent fifteen consecutive months during my sabbatical of 2006–7 as well as shorter periods during the summers of other years. In addition, I spent about six weeks photocopying material, with the help of my wife, Lauren Priegel, from the Herbert Hoover Papers at the Hoover Institution at Stanford University, a smaller collection chiefly devoted to the Chief's early career. There is some overlap between the collections at Stanford and West Branch.

At West Branch I found the Reprint File of articles and the Clipping File of newspapers to be among the most valuable resources. Although I thoroughly combed the correspondence of each period of Hoover's life and found some nuggets, most of Hoover's personal and professional letters were cursory, usually dictated. The exceptions were the long, intimate letters Hoover wrote to his brother, Tad, while the Chief worked as an engineer in Australia and China. I also photocopied every oral history transcript, about three hundred, but they proved of marginal value because the oral history project began after Hoover's death and the recollections dated primarily to the postpresidential period, which was thoroughly covered in clippings, Hoover's books, and correspondence. One notable exception was a lengthy transcript of an oral history interview with Allan Hoover and his wife, Margaret, after Bert's death, which contained a plethora of information about family life. I also obtained information about the family from the small collection of the papers of Lou Henry Hoover, an unusually gifted writer.

The presidential library housed every book, dissertation, and master's thesis written on Hoover. I read all of the books and most of the dissertations, as well as many theses. My research assistants photocopied hundreds of magazine and newspaper articles, too numerous to list individually, set aside by me. A collection of unpublished diaries at the presidential library proved vital. The most important were the Joel T. Boone Diary, the Theodore G. Joslin Diary, the James H. MacLafferty Diary (copyright Stanford University), the Henry L. Stimson Diary (microfilm edition), and the Edgar Rickard Diary.

I methodically combed the Hoover papers at the presidential library, organized chronologically by period. These included the Pre-Commerce Period, the Commerce Period, the Campaign and Transition Period, the Presidential Period, and the Post-Presidential File. I studied "The Bible," a set of books containing typed copies of Hoover's articles, addresses, and public statements, 1892–1964. I examined collections of papers of George Edward Akerson, the American Child Health Association, the American Relief Administration Bulletin, the Lawrence Richey Papers, and the Allan Hoover Papers.

At the Hoover Institution Archives at Stanford I examined the George Barr Baker Papers, the Herbert Hoover Subject Collection, the Edward Eyre Hunt Papers, the Mark Sullivan Papers, and the Ray Lyman Wilbur Papers. All of these men were intimate friends of Hoover, and their papers revealed numerous insights into Hoover's work and his personality.

My days at the Hoover Library and the Hoover Institution were devoted to note taking and setting aside longer material for photocopying. Away from the libraries I read and took notes on the photocopied documents as well as on books, articles, dissertations and theses, and my massive mound of photocopied data. On weekends in West Branch I also enjoyed the camaraderie at Herb and Lou's tavern, directly below the apartment I rented, and at Palo Alto, Lauren and I enjoyed the local restaurants and markets and spent weekends as tourists in San Francisco.

The best overviews of Hoover's life to date are David Burner's *Herbert Hoover: A Public Life* (New York: Alfred A. Knopf, 1979), and Richard Norton Smith, *An Uncommon Man: The Triumph of Herbert Hoover* (New York: Simon and Schuster, 1984). Both are dated, and Burner stops in 1933, although Hoover lived until 1964. David M. Kennedy provides a fair overview of Hoover's presidency in the early chapters of *Freedom from Fear: The American People in Depression and War, 1929–1945* (New York: Oxford University Press, 1999). Joan Hoff, *Herbert Hoover: Forgotten Progressive* (Boston: Little, Brown and Company, 1975), is compact and fair. Wilton Eckley, *Herbert Hoover* (Boston: Twayne, 1980), is another succinct biography. David Hinshaw, *Herbert Hoover: American Quaker* (New York: Farrar, Straus and Company, 1950), includes thoughtful personality analysis. The best popular biography, although unfootnoted, is Alfred Steinberg, *Herbert Hoover* (New York: G. P. Putnam's Sons, 1967). Another view of Hoover's personality is included in a study by his press secretary, Theodore G. Joslin, *Hoover Off the Record* (Garden City, NY: Doubleday, Doran and Company, Inc., 1934; repr., New York: Books for Libraries Press, 1971). Craig Lloyd's *Aggressive Introvert: Herbert Hoover and Public Relations Management, 1912–1932* (Columbus: Ohio State University Press, 1972), brims with keen observations. William E. Leuchtenburg has written two broad studies chiefly about the Quaker, *Herbert Hoover* (New York: Henry Holt, 2009), and *The Perils of Prosperity, 1914–1932* (Chicago: University of Chicago Press, 1958). Frank T. Nye, *Doors of Opportunity: The Life and Legacy of Herbert Hoover* (West Branch, IA: Herbert Hoover Presidential Library Association, Inc., 1988), complements the other Hoover biographies. Catherine Owens Peare, *The Herbert Hoover Story* (New York: Thomas Y.

Crowell Company, 1965), adds to the long list of Hoover biographies. Hal Wert has written the best monograph about Hoover's hobby and includes rich biographical data: *Hoover: The Fishing President: Portrait of the Private Man and His Life Outdoors* (Mechanicsburg, PA: Stackpole Books, 2005). Harold Wolfe wrote a fond portrait, *Herbert Hoover: Public Servant and Leader of the Loyal Opposition* (New York: Exposition Press, 1956). Eugene Lyons has written a penetrating general biography, *Herbert Hoover: A Biography* (Garden City, NY: Doubleday, 1964). Another portrait is Dorothy Horton McGee, *Herbert Hoover: Engineer, Humanitarian, Statesman* (New York: Dodd, Mead and Company, Inc., 1967). Among the complete biographies, another capable one is Carol Green Wilson, *Herbert Hoover: A Challenge for Today* (New York: Exposition Press, 1968).

Any reader interested in the early life of Herbert Hoover should begin with George H. Nash's three monumental tomes, which carry the story of Hoover's life to 1918: *The Life of Herbert Hoover: The Engineer, 1874–1914* (New York: Norton, 1983); *The Life of Herbert Hoover: The Humanitarian, 1914–1917* (New York: Norton, 1988); and *The Life of Herbert Hoover: Master of Emergencies, 1917–1918* (New York: Norton, 1986). Nash has also written an account of Hoover's collegiate years as well as his lifelong connection with his alma mater in *Herbert Hoover and Stanford University* (Stanford, CA: Hoover Institution Press, 1988). Hoover himself provides great detail in volume 1 of his memoirs, *Years of Adventure, 1874–1920* (New York: Macmillan Company, 1951), and recounts his childhood with brevity in *A Boyhood in Iowa* (New York: Aventine Press, 1931). Hoover reminisces about fishing in *Fishing for Fun—and to Wash Your Soul*, edited by William Nichols (West Branch, IA: Hoover Presidential Library Association, 1963). Also see Mitchell V. Charnley, *The Boy's Life of Herbert Hoover* (New York: Harper and Brothers, 1931); William Hard, *Who's Hoover?* (New York, 1928); Will Irwin (a journalist friend of Hoover's), *Herbert Hoover: A Reminiscent Biography* (New York: Grosset & Dunlap, 1928); Vernon Kellogg (another Hoover friend), *Herbert Hoover: The Man and His Work* (New York: Appleton and Company, 1920); Rose Wilder Lane, *The Making of Herbert Hoover* (New York: Century,

1920), a superficial sketch; Walter Liggett, *The Rise of Herbert Hoover* (New York: H. K. Fly Company, 1932); and Earl Reeves, *This Man Hoover* (New York: A. L. Burt Company, 1928). The bulk of these are superficial, written primarily before Hoover went into politics, but some, written by persons who knew Hoover quite well personally, include original insights into his personality.

Hoover wrote highly detailed accounts of his relief efforts during and after the Great War, including *America's First Crusade* (New York: Charles Scribner's Sons, 1938) and in volumes, cumulatively entitled *An American Epic*, all published by Henry Regnery (Chicago) over the span from 1959 to 1964. Frank M. Surface ably describes Hoover's organization of the agricultural sector during and after World War I in *American Food in the World War and Reconstruction Period: Operations of the Organization Under the Direction of Herbert Hoover, 1914 to 1924* (Stanford, CA: Stanford University Press, 1931). The Quaker describes Woodrow Wilson and his own experience at the Versailles Peace Conference in *The Ordeal of Woodrow Wilson* (New York: McGraw-Hill, 1958), the only biography of a president written by another president. Perhaps Hoover's most important relief effort came in the Soviet Union while he was secretary of commerce. This gargantuan rescue is described in an 817-page book, Bertrand M. Patenaude's *The Big Show in Bololand: The American Relief Expedition to Soviet Russia in the Famine of 1921* (Stanford, CA: Stanford University Press, 2002). One of the more interesting chapters in Hoover's life, his direction of massive flood relief, is described in John M. Barry, *Rising Tide: The Great Mississippi Flood of 1927 and How It Changed America* (New York: Simon and Schuster, 1997). See also Pete Daniel, *Deep'n as It Come: The 1927 Mississippi River Flood* (New York: Oxford University Press, 1977).

In his memoirs, Hoover chose to encapsulate his entire political career in volume 2, *The Cabinet and the Presidency, 1920–1933* (New York: Macmillan Company, 1952). The most useful studies of Hoover's economic policies, aside from those that deal with his presidency, are Kendrick A. Clements, *Hoover, Conservation, and Consumerism: Engineering the Good*

Life (Lawrence: University Press of Kansas, 2000), and Clements, *The Life of Herbert Hoover: Imperfect Visionary, 1918–1928* (New York: Palgrave Macmillan, 2010), which dissects Hoover's tenure as secretary of commerce. Clements views Hoover as an economic seer who occasionally erred. Also useful is Joseph Brandes, *Herbert Hoover and Economic Diplomacy: Department of Commerce Policy, 1921–1928* (Pittsburgh, PA: University of Pittsburgh Press, 1962). Hoover's tenure at Commerce is also the subject of Ellis W. Hawley, ed., *Herbert Hoover as Secretary of Commerce: Studies in New Era Thought and Practice* (Iowa City: University of Iowa Press, 1981). While commerce secretary, Hoover wrote *American Individualism* (New York: Doubleday, Doran & Company, 1922), in which he defines his personal philosophy and the factors that make America unique.

The literature on the presidency of the Quaker is not exhaustive but is varied. Among the most comprehensive are Glen Jeansonne, *The Life of Herbert Hoover: Fighting Quaker, 1928–1933* (New York: Palgrave Macmillan, 2012), and Martin L. Fausold, *The Presidency of Herbert C. Hoover* (Lawrence: University Press of Kansas, 1985). See also Fausold and George T. Mazuzan, eds., *The Hoover Presidency: A Reappraisal* (Albany: State University of New York Press, 1974). Arthur Train wrote an early defense of the Hoover administration, *The Strange Attacks on Herbert Hoover: A Current Example of What We Do to Our Presidents* (New York: John Day Company, 1932). Hoover's fishing retreat from the stresses of the presidency is colorfully described in Darwin Lambert's depiction of Camp Rapidan, his fishing camp, in *Herbert Hoover's Hideaway* (Luray, VA: Shenandoah History Association, Inc., 1971).

The best place to begin an account of the Hoover administration policies lies in volume 3 of his memoirs, *The Great Depression, 1929–1941*, which includes Franklin D. Roosevelt's first two terms (New York: Macmillan Company, 1952). For an excellent general account of Hoover's Depression policies see Harris Gaylord Warren, *Herbert Hoover and the Great Depression* (New York: W. W. Norton & Company, 1967). A good overall description of the Depression can be found in T. H. Watkins, *The Hungry Years: A Narrative History of the Great Depression in America* (New York: Henry Holt

and Company, 1999). Two of Hoover's lieutenants, Ray Lyman Wilbur and
Arthur Mastick Hyde, edited *The Hoover Policies* (New York: Charles
Scribner's Sons, 1937). Two other Hoover confederates produced *The Hoover
Administration: A Documented Narrative* (New York: Charles Scribner's
Sons, 1936). Lee Nash, ed., *Understanding Herbert Hoover: Ten Perspec-
tives* (Stanford: Hoover Institution Press, 1987) includes a variety of essays
by ten Hoover experts. Edgar Eugene Robinson and Vaughn Davis Bornet,
Herbert Hoover: President of the United States (Stanford, CA: Hoover Institution Press, 1975), is a character portrait with substantial insight. Timothy Walch has edited documentary collections that yielded significant
letters and personal data, including *Uncommon Americans: The Lives and
Legacies of Herbert and Lou Henry Hoover* (Westport, CT: Greenwood Press,
2003); and with Dwight M. Miller, *Herbert Hoover and Franklin D. Roosevelt:
A Documentary History* (Westport, CT: Greenwood Press, 1998); and also
with Miller, *Herbert Hoover and Harry S. Truman: A Documentary History*
(Worland, WY: High Plains Publishing Company, 1992), which traces the
blossoming of a warm friendship.

Most books about Hoover focus on his economic policies, especially
his role in the Great Depression. Among them are William J. Barber,
*From New Era to New Deal: Herbert Hoover, the Economists, and American
Economic Policy, 1921–1933* (New York: Cambridge University Press, 1985).
Edward Robb Ellis provides an overview in *A Nation in Torment: The
Great American Depression, 1929–1939* (New York: Capricorn Books, 1970),
as does John A. Garraty in *The Great Depression* (San Diego, CA: Har-
court Brace Jovanovich, 1986), and Albert U. Romasco, *The Poverty of
Abundance: Hoover, the Nation, the Depression* (New York: Oxford University
Press, 1968). Murray N. Rothbard provides a libertarian interpretation
of the Depression in *America's Great Depression* (Los Angeles: Nash Publishing, 1972), as does Amity Shlaes in *The Forgotten Man: A New History
of the Great Depression* (New York: Harper, 2008). On the opposite side
of the political spectrum is Arthur Schlesinger Jr.'s account in *The Age of
Roosevelt: The Crisis of the Old Order, 1919–1933* (Boston: Houghton Miff-
lin Company, 1957). Jordan A. Schwarz also views Hoover negatively in

The Interregnum of Despair: Hoover, Congress, and the Depression (Urbana: University of Illinois Press), as does Gene Smith, *The Shattered Dream: Herbert Hoover and the Great Depression* (New York: William Morrow, 1970). A detailed account of the economic catastrophe is available in Charles P. Kindleberger, *The World in Depression, 1929–1939*, revised and enlarged edition (Berkeley: University of California Press, 1986). For positive revisionist essays, see Carl E. Krog and William Tanner, eds., *Herbert Hoover and the Republican Era: A Reconsideration* (Lanham, MD: University Press of America, 1984).

Maury Klein, *Rainbow's End: The Crash of 1929* (New York: Oxford University Press, 2001), concentrates primarily on the stock market crash and the period preceding it. Donald J. Lisio focuses on a dramatic event during the Depression in *The President and Protest: Hoover, MacArthur, and the Bonus Riot* (Columbia: University of Missouri Press, 1974). Lisio has also written an account of racial politics in the South during the 1928 nominating campaign, *Hoover, Blacks, and Lily-Whites: A Study of Southern Strategies* (Chapel Hill: University of North Carolina Press, 1985). One of Hoover's chief tools designed to combat the Depression is the topic of James Stuart Olson, *Herbert Hoover and the Reconstruction Finance Corporation, 1931–1933* (Ames: Iowa State University Press, 1977). Perhaps the best account of Hoover's agricultural policies is David E. Hamilton, *From New Day to New Deal: American Farm Policy from Hoover to Roosevelt, 1928–1933* (Chapel Hill: University of North Carolina Press, 1991).

Several books have been written about the Chief's foreign policies. These include Louis P. Lochner, *Herbert Hoover and Germany* (New York: Macmillan Company, 1960); George J. Lerski, *Herbert Hoover and Poland: A Documentary History of a Friendship* (Stanford, CA: Hoover Institution, 1977); William Starr Myers, *The Foreign Policies of Herbert Hoover, 1929–1933* (New York: Charles Scribner's Sons, 1940); and Raymond G. O'Connor, *Perilous Equilibrium: The United States and the London Naval Conference of 1930* (Westport, CT: Greenwood Press, 1969), the study of a successful naval disarmament conclave orchestrated by Hoover. Norman E. Saul,

Friends or Foes: The United States and Soviet Russia, 1921–1941 (Lawrence: University Press of Kansas, 2006), has exceptional insight into the mercurial relationship. L. Ethan Ellis discusses foreign policy under Harding, Coolidge, and Hoover in *Republican Foreign Policy, 1921–1933* (New Brunswick, NJ: Rutgers University Press, 1968). Among the most useful surveys is Robert H. Ferrell, *American Diplomacy in the Great Depression: Hoover-Stimson Foreign Policy, 1929–1933* (New Haven, CT: Yale University Press, 1974).

Lou Henry Hoover is an underrated First Lady, but a handful of sympathetic biographies exist. The best is Dale Mayer, *Lou Henry Hoover: A Prototype for First Ladies* (Hauppauge, NY: Nova History Company, 2004). See also Mayer's edited work, *Lou Henry Hoover: Essays on a Busy Life* (Worland, WY: High Plains Publishing Company, 1994). Somewhat more recent is Nancy Beck Young, *Lou Henry Hoover: Activist First Lady* (Lawrence: University Press of Kansas, 2004). Lou's definitive biography remains to be written, although her personal papers are sparse. For insights on the Hoover family see Hulda Hoover McLean, *Genealogy of the Herbert Hoover Family* (Stanford, CA: Hoover Institution, 1967), as well as her *Uncle Bert: A Biographical Portrait of Herbert Hoover* (published by the author, 1974), and her account as compiler of the president's mother *Hulda's World: A Chronicle of Hulda Minthorn Hoover, 1848–1884* (West Branch, IA: Hoover Presidential Library Association, 1989).

The outstanding survey of Hoover's postpresidential life was written by the late Gary Dean Best, *The Life of Herbert Hoover: Keeper of the Torch, 1933–1964* (New York: Palgrave Macmillan, 2013). The preeminent expert on Hoover's postpresidential activities, Best wrote an earlier, more detailed two-volume account, *Herbert Hoover: The Postpresidential Years, 1933–1964*, vol. 1, *1933–1945*, and vol. 2, *1946–1964*, both published by Hoover Institution Press (Stanford, CA, 1983).

A great deal can be gleaned from Hoover's own books, thirty-three in all, too numerous to cite individually. His speeches have been published in a series cumulatively entitled *Addresses upon the American Road*, 8 vols. (New York: Charles Scribner's Sons, 1938–61). The Chief's study of the Great War, *America's First Crusade* (New York: Charles Scribner's Sons, 1942), was published during a writing-intensive period. *The Challenge to Liberty*, in which he condemned all forms of collectivism, originally written during the 1930s, was republished in Rockford, Illinois, by the Herbert Hoover Presidential Library Association, in 1971. During the Second World War Hoover wrote two books warning about the methods needed to prevent another conflagration, *The Problems of Lasting Peace* (Garden City, NY: Doubleday, Doran & Company, Inc., 1942), and with Hugh Gibson, *The Basis of Lasting Peace* (New York: D. Van Nostrand Company, Inc., 1945). Hoover's Presidential Papers were published in four volumes between 1974 and 1977. Perhaps Hoover's most important postwar books, dealing with attacks on the foreign and domestic policies, were not published until decades after his death: *Freedom Betrayed: Herbert Hoover's Secret History of the Second World War and Its Aftermath*, edited by George H. Nash (Stanford, CA: Hoover Institution Press, 2011), and *The Crusade Years, 1933–1935: Herbert Hoover's Lost Memoir of the New Deal Era and Its Aftermath*, also edited by Nash (Stanford, CA: Hoover Institution Press, 2013). In these lengthy posthumous tomes the Quaker speaks more frankly than he had dared do during his public life. Hoover's later writing was designed primarily to set the record straight. He became a historian of the events he had witnessed and in which he had played a role. His writing actually crested during his eighties. Both the quantity and the quality are remarkable.

ENDNOTES

Prologue

1. David Hinshaw, *Herbert Hoover: American Quaker* (New York, 1950), 63.
2. *Iowa City Press-Citizen*, August 12, 1989, Reprint File, Herbert Hoover Presidential Library (hereafter cited as HHPL); George H. Nash, afterword to *The Life of Herbert Hoover: Keeper of the Torch, 1933–1964*, by Gary Dean Best (New York, 2013), 470.
3. "Herbert Hoover," 1874–1964, White Book 2, HHPL.
4. *Iowa Press-Citizen*, August 12, 1989, Reprint File, HHPL.
5. Ibid.
6. Glen Jeansonne, *The Life of Herbert Hoover, 1928–1933: Fighting Quaker* (New York, 2012), chaps. 1, 5–6, 9–11.
7. Ibid., chaps. 1, 11, 13, 18.
8. See Gary Dean Best, *The Life of Herbert Hoover, 1933–1964: Keeper of the Torch* (New York, 2013), passim.

Chapter 1. A Quaker Orphan on the Frontier

1. Eugene Lyons, *Herbert Hoover: A Biography* (Garden City, NY, 1964), 1; David Burner, *Herbert Hoover: A Public Life* (New York, 1979), 6; Theodore J. Hoover, "Memoranda, Being a Statement of an Engineer," 1939, Acct. 585, Box 1, Herbert Hoover Presidential Library (hereafter cited as HHPL), 16.
2. T. Hoover, "Memoranda," 1–6; Burner, *Hoover: A Public Life*, 4; George H. Nash, *The Life of Herbert Hoover: The Engineer, 1874–1914* (New York, 1983), 1–3; James R. Bowers, "Herbert Hoover: Ambivalent Quaker" (master's thesis, University of Illinois Legal Center, 1981), 52–60.
3. Vernon Kellogg, *Herbert Hoover: The Man and His Work* (New York, 1920), 14; Richard Norton Smith, *An Uncommon Man: The Triumph of Herbert Hoover* (New York, 1984), 63; Will Irwin, *Herbert Hoover: A Reminiscent Biography* (New York, 1928), 6.

4. T. Hoover, "Memoranda," 26; Alfred Steinberg, *Herbert Hoover* (New York, 1967), 14; Kellogg, *Hoover: The Man and His Work*, 14–15.

5. T. Hoover, "Memoranda," 13–16; Montessori quote from Herbert Hoover, *The Memoirs of Herbert Hoover*, vol. 1, *Years of Adventure, 1874–1920* (New York, 1951), 5.

6. T. Hoover, "Memoranda," 13–14, 16; Lyons, *Hoover: A Biography*, 16; William Eckley, *Herbert Hoover* (Boston, 1980), 16.

7. Steinberg, *Herbert Hoover*, 16–17.

8. Herbert Hoover, *Hoover After Dinner: Addresses Delivered by Herbert Hoover* (New York, 1933), 125–26.

9. Ibid., 129.

10. Lyons, *Hoover: A Biography*, 12.

11. David Hinshaw, *Herbert Hoover: American Quaker* (New York, 1950), 62.

12. Theodore Joslin, ed., *Hoover Off the Record* (New York, 1917), 310; Mitchell V. Charnley, *The Boy's Life of Herbert Hoover* (New York, 1931), 37, 43–45; Hinshaw, *Hoover: American Quaker*, 4.

13. Steinberg, *Herbert Hoover*, 21–24.

14. Martin Fausold, *The Presidency of Herbert Hoover* (Lawrence, KS, 1985), 3–4.

15. Herbert Hoover to Lewis L. Strauss, Christmas 1953, Subject File, HHPL.

16. Ibid.

17. James Quinton Cahill, "Herbert Hoover's Early Schooling and Its Place in Presidential Politics," *Annals of Iowa* 61, no. 2 (Spring 2002): 156–59, 176; *Iowa Press-Citizen*, July 10, 1928, White Book 1, HHPL.

18. Charnley, *Boy's Life of Herbert Hoover*, 37; T. Hoover, "Memoranda," 35; Lyons, *Hoover: A Biography*, 12.

19. T. Hoover, "Memoranda," 18–19, 20–25.

20. Ibid., 24–25; Steinberg, *Herbert Hoover*, 19.

21. Cahill, "Herbert Hoover's Early Schooling," 185; Irwin, *Hoover: A Reminiscent Biography*, 12.

22. Irwin, *Hoover: A Reminiscent Biography*, 15–17.

23. T. Hoover, "Memoranda," 26–27.

24. Steinberg, *Herbert Hoover*, 19–20; Irwin, *Hoover: A Reminiscent Biography*, 11; Hoover, *Memoirs*, 1:31.

25. T. Hoover, "Memoranda," 36.

26. Smith, *An Uncommon Man*, 66.

27. Steinberg, *Herbert Hoover*, 26–27; T. Hoover, "Memoranda," 22–23, 37–40; Nash, *Hoover: The Engineer*, 11.

28. Steinberg, *Herbert Hoover*, 26–28; Hoover, *Memoirs*, 1:6; Stratton, *Herbert Hoover's Home Town*, 53 (source of Wally quote).

29. Steinberg, *Herbert Hoover*, 29; Nash, *Hoover: The Engineer*, 12; Charnley, *Boy's Life of Herbert Hoover*, 55; Irwin, *Hoover: A Reminiscent Biography*, 27; Hoover, *Memoirs*, 1:10–11.

30. Irwin, *Hoover: A Reminiscent Biography*, 28; Herbert Hoover, *On Growing Up*, ed. William Nichols (New York, 1962), 147, 157.

31. Nash, *Hoover: The Engineer*, 17.

32. Burner, *Hoover: A Public Life*, 14.

33. Steinberg, *Herbert Hoover*, 31–32; Quote from Kendrick A. Clements, *Hoover, Conservation, and Consumerism: Engineering the Good Life* (Lawrence, KS, 2000), 17.

34. Steinberg, *Herbert Hoover*, 33.

35. Nash, *Hoover: The Engineer*, 17.

36. Hoover, *Memoirs*, 1:11–12.

37. Smith, *An Uncommon Man*, 67.

38. T. Hoover, "Memoranda," 67–68; Charnley, *Boy's Life of Herbert Hoover*, 62–65; Nash, *Hoover: The Engineer*, 19–20; Joan Hoff, *Herbert Hoover: Forgotten Progressive* (Boston, 1975), 10–11.

39. Burner, *Hoover: A Public Life*, 14–15; Charnley, *Boy's Life of Herbert Hoover*, 65–66; Hal Elliott Wert, *Hoover: The Fishing President: Portrait of the Private Man and His Life Outdoors* (Mechanicsburg, PA, 2005); T. Hoover, "Memoranda," 67–68.

40. Burner, *Hoover: A Public Life*, 15; Smith, *An Uncommon Man*, 68; Clements, *Hoover, Conservation, and Consumerism*, 14; Nash, *Hoover: The Engineer*, 23.

41. Wert, *Hoover: The Fishing President*, 33, 42–47.

42. Hoover, *Memoirs*, 1:13–14.

43. Smith, *An Uncommon Man*, 417; Nash, *Hoover: The Engineer*, 25.

44. Burner, *Hoover: A Public Life*, 14–15; Steinberg, *Herbert Hoover*, 35; Hoover, *Memoirs*, 1:114.

45. Steinberg, *Herbert Hoover*, 32–36; Kellogg, *Hoover: The Man and His Work*, 27–30; Harold Wolfe, *Herbert Hoover: Public Servant and Leader of the Loyal Opposition* (New York, 1956), 17; Irwin, *Hoover: A Reminiscent Biography*, 31–33; Hoover, *Memoirs*, 1:14.

46. Irwin, *Hoover: A Reminiscent Biography*, 32–33; Steinberg, *Herbert Hoover*, 36–38; Hoover, *Memoirs*, 1:15.

47. Steinberg, *Herbert Hoover*, 37.

48. Ibid., 38–39; George H. Nash, *Herbert Hoover and Stanford University* (Stanford, CA, 1988), 3–5.

49. Nash, *Hoover and Stanford University*, 5; Steinberg, *Herbert Hoover*, 39.

Chapter 2. Cardinal Red

1. George H. Nash, *Herbert Hoover and Stanford University* (Stanford, CA, 1988), 3–5; Hal Elliott Wert, *Hoover: The Fishing President: Portrait of the Private Man and His Life Outdoors* (Mechanicsburg, PA, 2005), 49; Will Irwin, *Herbert Hoover: A Reminiscent Biography* (New York, 1928), 34–37; *The Story of Hoover*, White Book 1, n.p., unpaginated, HHPL.

2. Herbert Hoover, *The Memoirs of Herbert Hoover*, vol. 1, *Years of Adventure, 1874–1920* (New York, 1951), 16–17; Irwin, *Hoover: A Reminiscent Biography*, 39–41; Vernon Kellogg, *Herbert Hoover: The Man and His Work* (New York, 1920), 34–37; Mitchell V. Charnley, *The Boy's Life of Herbert Hoover* (New York, 1931), 80–81.

3. Kellogg, *Hoover: The Man and His Work*, 37, 40–42, 56–57; Nash, *Hoover and Stanford University*, 6.

4. Nash, *Hoover and Stanford University*, 6; Harold Wolfe, *Herbert Hoover: Public Servant and Leader of the Loyal Opposition* (New York, 1956), 17–18.

5. Alfred Steinberg, *Herbert Hoover* (New York, 1967), 43–44; Nash, *Hoover and Stanford University*, 6–7; George H. Nash, *The Life of Herbert Hoover: The Engineer, 1874–1914* (New York, 1983), 28.

6. Steinberg, *Herbert Hoover*, 43–44.

7. Irwin, *Hoover: A Reminiscent Biography*, 45–47; Nash, *Hoover and Stanford University*, 20; quote from Wilton Eckley, *Herbert Hoover* (Boston, 1980), 20.

8. Irwin, *Hoover: A Reminiscent Biography*, 45–46.

9. Richard Norton Smith, *An Uncommon Man: The Triumph of Herbert Hoover* (New York, 1984), 69; Nash, *Hoover and Stanford University*, 6–7; *Herbert Hoover's Days at Stanford*, Pre-Commerce Papers, Box 63, Stanford, 1895, n.p., HHPL.

10. Nash, *Hoover and Stanford University*, 8; Charnley, *Boy's Life of Herbert Hoover*, 90–91.

11. Charnley, *Boy's Life of Herbert Hoover*, 93–95; Irwin, *Hoover: A Reminiscent Biography*, 49–50; Craig M. Lloyd, *Aggressive Introvert: Herbert Hoover and Public Relations Management, 1912–1932* (Columbus, OH, 1972), 7.

12. Irwin, *Hoover: A Reminiscent Biography*, 50–52; Charnley, *Boy's Life of Herbert Hoover*, 95–98.

13. Steinberg, *Herbert Hoover*, 45–46.

14. Ibid., 46–47; Hoover, *Memoirs*, 1:21; Charnley, *Boy's Life of Herbert Hoover*, 88.

15. Steinberg, *Herbert Hoover*, 50–51; Nash, *Hoover and Stanford University*, 7–8; *Stanford Daily*, February 14, 1940, Post-Presidential Papers (hereafter cited as PPP), Box 159, Football, 1940–63, HHPL; Hoover Speech to the National Football Foundation Hall of Fame, New York City, December 6, 1960, PPP, Box 159, Football, HHPL.

16. Irwin, *Hoover: A Reminiscent Biography*, 58–61; *Stanford Illustrated Review*, December 1931, PPP, Box 159, Football, 1940–63, HHPL; Stanford Football Varsity, 1894 Team, PPP, Box 159, Football, 1940–63, HHPL.
17. Charnley, *Boy's Life of Herbert Hoover*, 112–13.
18. Stanford, *Hoover's Days at Stanford*, 1895, Pre-Commerce Papers, Box 63, unpaginated; Wolfe, *Hoover: Public Servant*, 18.
19. *The Story of Hoover*, excerpt from White Book 1; Steinberg, *Herbert Hoover*, 59–60.
20. Nash, *Hoover: The Engineer*, 35; *The Story of Hoover*, excerpt from White Book 1.
21. *The Story of Hoover*, excerpt from White Book 1; Charnley, *Boy's Life of Herbert Hoover*, 103–5; Irwin, *Hoover: A Reminiscent Biography*, 53–54.
22. Irwin, *Hoover: A Reminiscent Biography*, 53–57; Charnley, *Boy's Life of Herbert Hoover*, 103–5; Nash, *Hoover and Stanford University*, 10–12; Ray Lyman Wilbur, "Herbert Hoover: A Personal Sketch," 7–9; Articles about or by Herbert Hoover, Pre-Commerce Papers, Box 26, HHPL.
23. Charnley, *Boy's Life of Herbert Hoover*, 109–10.
24. *New York Evening Post*, September 26, 1928, White Book 2, HHPL; Smith, *An Uncommon Man*, 69–70; "Sons of the Stanford Red: Hoover—Pioneer," *Stanford Illustrated Review* 21, no. 1, 110–12, HHPL.
25. Irwin, *Hoover: A Reminiscent Biography*, 66.
26. Steinberg, *Herbert Hoover*, 60–61; Hal Elliott Wert, *Hoover: The Fishing President: Portrait of the Private Man and His Life Outdoors* (Mechanicsburg, PA, 2005), 53–54; Helen B. Pryor, *Lou Henry Hoover: Gallant First Lady* (New York, 1969), 18–25.
27. Wert, *Hoover: The Fishing President*, 53–59; Pryor, *Lou Henry Hoover*, 27.
28. Smith, *An Uncommon Man*, 71–72.
29. Nash, *Hoover: The Engineer*, 38; Wert, *Hoover: The Fishing President*, 55–57; Nancy Beck Young, *Lou Henry Hoover: Activist First Lady* (Lawrence, KS, 2004), 9–10.
30. Smith, *An Uncommon Man*, 71–72; Steinberg, *Herbert Hoover*, 60–61, 69; Irwin, *Hoover: A Reminiscent Biography*, 63–64, 67; Pryor, *Lou Henry Hoover*, 26–28.
31. David Burner, *Herbert Hoover: A Public Life* (New York, 1979), 17–18; Nash, *Hoover: The Engineer*, 36–37; Nash, *Hoover and Stanford University*, 13–15; "Herbert Hoover's Days at Stanford," 1895, unpaginated, Pre-Commerce Papers, Box 63, HHPL.
32. Nash, *Hoover: The Engineer*, 38–39; Steinberg, *Herbert Hoover*, 59; Irwin, *Hoover: A Reminiscent Biography*, 62.
33. Nash, *Hoover and Stanford University*, 17–18; Nash, *Hoover: The Engineer*, 39; Wert, *Hoover: The Fishing President*, 59; Charnley, *Boy's Life of Herbert Hoover*, 120–21; Hoover, *Memoirs*, 1:23–24.
34. Irwin, *Hoover: A Reminiscent Biography*, 66–67.

Chapter 3. The Great Engineer

1. Alfred Steinberg, *Herbert Hoover* (New York, 1967), 65–66; Will Irwin, *Herbert Hoover: A Reminiscent Biography* (New York, 1928), 68.
2. George H. Nash, *The Life of Herbert Hoover: The Engineer, 1874–1914* (New York, 1981), 48–49.
3. Irwin, *Hoover: A Reminiscent Biography*, 69–70; Herbert Hoover, *The Memoirs of Herbert Hoover*, vol. 1, *Years of Adventure, 1874–1920* (New York, 1951), 25–26; Nash, *Hoover: The Engineer*, 45–46; Steinberg, *Herbert Hoover*, 67.
4. David Burner, *Herbert Hoover: A Public Life* (New York, 1979), 21–24; Mitchell V. Charnley, *The Boy's Life of Herbert Hoover* (New York, 1931), 127–35; Vernon Kellogg, *Herbert Hoover: The Man and His Work* (New York, 1920), 60–63; Hoover, *Memoirs*, 1:25–27; Information for Biographers of Herbert Hoover, Articles about or by Herbert Hoover, Pre-Commerce Papers, Box 25 (probably 1916), 5, Herbert Hoover Presidential Library (hereafter cited as HHPL).
5. Hugh Gibson, "Herbert C. Hoover," *Century Magazine*, August 1917, 510; Irwin, *Hoover: A Reminiscent Biography*, 74; Steinberg, *Herbert Hoover*, 71; Hoover, *Memoirs*, 1:28.

6. Steinberg, *Herbert Hoover*, 71–74; Kellogg, *Hoover: The Man and His Work*, 67–68; Unmarked clipping, March 28, 1897, Album 51, Box 69, Pre-Commerce Papers, Clippings, 1900, HHPL.

7. Hoover to friends, April 16, 1897, Pre-Commerce Papers, Box 1, Australia, 1897–98, HHPL.

8. Kellogg, *Hoover: The Man and His Work*, 68–70.

9. Hoover to Tad and May, undated, 1897, Pre-Commerce Papers, Box 1, Australia, 1897–98, HHPL.

10. George H. Nash, *Herbert Hoover and Stanford University* (Stanford, CA, 1988), 21.

11. Hoover to Tad, September 27, 1897, Pre-Commerce Papers, Box 1, Australia, 1897–98, HHPL.

12. Hoover to Tad, February 15, 1898, Pre-Commerce Papers, Box 1, Australia, 1897–98, HHPL.

13. Hoover to Tad, undated [1897], Pre-Commerce Papers, Box 1, Australia, 1897–98, HHPL.

14. Hoover to Tad, June 6, 1897, June 1898 (undated), July 9, 1897, Pre-Commerce Papers, Box 1, Australia, 1897–98, HHPL; Steinberg, *Herbert Hoover*, 77–80; Kellogg, *Hoover: The Man and His Work*, 74.

15. Nash, *Hoover: The Engineer*, 64–65, 74–79, 84; Hoover, *Memoirs*, 1:33; Irwin, *Hoover: A Reminiscent Biography*, 80–81; Kellogg, *Hoover: The Man and His Work*, 74–75; Steinberg, *Herbert Hoover*, 80–82.

16. Hoover to Tad, undated, April 1898, July 1898, Pre-Commerce Papers, Box 1, Australia, 1897–98, HHPL.

17. Hoover to Tad, undated, April 1898, July 1898, Pre-Commerce Papers, Box 1, Australia, HHPL.

18. Hoover to Tad, undated, 1898, Pre-Commerce Papers, Box 1, Australia, HHPL.

19. Hoover to Tad, November 1, 1898, Pre-Commerce Papers, Box 1, Australia, 1897–98, HHPL.

20. Hoover to Tad, November 2, 1898, Pre-Commerce Papers, Box 1, Australia, 1897–98, HHPL.

21. Hal Elliott Wert, "Hoover's Brush with the Boxers," *History Today* 61, no. 9 (September 2011): 36–37; Richard Norton Smith: *An Uncommon Man: The Triumph of Herbert Hoover* (New York, 1984), 75; Hoover, *Memoirs*, 1:36; Dale Mayer, *Lou Henry Hoover: A Prototype for First Ladies* (New York, 2004), 46; Nash, *Hoover and Stanford University*, 22.

22. Helen B. Pryor, *Lou Henry Hoover: Gallant First Lady* (New York, 1969), 36–37, 45–47; Mayer, *Lou Henry Hoover*, 52–54; *Chicago Daily News*, June 12, 1929.

23. Mayer, *Lou Henry Hoover*, 57–58, 125–28; Wert, "Hoover's Brush with the Boxers," 39.

24. Wert, "Hoover's Brush with the Boxers," 36–38, 41–43.

25. Hal Elliott Wert, *Hoover: The Fishing President, Portrait of the Private Man and His Life Outdoors* (Mechanicsburg, PA, 2005), 73; Mayer, *Lou Henry Hoover*, 57.

26. Nash, *Hoover: The Engineer*, 112–13; Mayer, *Lou Henry Hoover*, 55; Wert, "Hoover's Brush with the Boxers," 38; Steinberg, *Herbert Hoover*, 87; Hoover to Tad, undated, 1899, Pre-Commerce Papers, Box 1, HHPL.

27. Wert, *Hoover: The Fishing President*, 71–73; Hoover, *Memoirs*, 1:61–64; Steinberg, *Herbert Hoover*, 88–92.

28. Nash, *Hoover: The Engineer*, 105–7; Burner, *Hoover: A Public Life*, 34–36.

29. Steinberg, *Herbert Hoover*, 87–89; Wert, *Hoover: The Fishing President*, 73.

30. Steinberg, *Herbert Hoover*, 86–93; Kellogg, *Hoover: The Man and His Work*, 87–90; Hoover, *Memoirs*, 1:40–44; Irwin, *Hoover: A Reminiscent History*, 85; Mayer, *Lou Henry Hoover*, 56–57.

31. Wert, "Hoover's Brush with the Boxers," 40–41; Nash, *Hoover: The Engineer*, 117, 118; Pryor, *Lou Henry Hoover*, 48; Mayer, *Lou Henry Hoover*, 73.

32. Mayer, *Lou Henry Hoover*, 71; Nash, *Hoover: The Engineer*, 120–23.

33. Wert, "Hoover's Brush with the Boxers," 40–41; Charnley, *Boy's Life of Herbert Hoover*, 164–69; Steinberg, *Herbert Hoover*, 98–101.

34. Irwin, *Hoover: A Reminiscent Biography*, 90–91, 95–96; Hoover, *Memoirs*, 1:51; Charnley, *Boy's Life of Herbert Hoover*, 165–67; Wert, "Hoover's Brush with the Boxers," 41; Steinberg, *Herbert Hoover*, 104.

35. Wert, "Brush with the Boxers," 41; Hoover, *Memoirs*, 1:40; Steinberg, *Herbert Hoover*, 97–99.

36. Wert, "Brush with the Boxers," 41–43; Hoover, *Memoirs*, 1:52–53; Steinberg, *Herbert Hoover*, 102; Kellogg, *Hoover: The Man and His Work*, 95; Nash, *Hoover: The Engineer*, 121–23.

37. George H. Nash has the most detailed account of the intricately tangled negotiations. See Nash, *Hoover: The Engineer*, 124–47; Lou Henry Hoover to Theodore Hoover, 1920 [?], "Chinese Story," 8–10, Pre-Commerce Papers, Box 10, HHPL; Hoover to Tad, July 15, 1901, Pre-Commerce Papers, Box 1, HHPL; Charnley, *Boy's Life of Herbert Hoover*, 172–74.

38. Hoover, *Memoirs*, 1:99–103; Steinberg, *Herbert Hoover*, 106.

39. Hoover, *Memoirs*, 1:103–4; Nash, *Hoover: The Engineer*, 184–90; Hoover to Tad, April 15, 1901, Pre-Commerce Papers, Box 1, HHPL.

40. Hugh Gibson, "Herbert C. Hoover," *Century Magazine*, August 1917, 513–14; Theodore J. Hoover, "Memoranda, Being a Statement of an Engineer," 1939, Acct. 585, Box 1, HHPL, 276; Hoover, *Memoirs*, 1:90.

41. Nash, *Hoover: The Engineer*, 224–25; Hoover, *Memoirs*, 1:74–75; Burner, *Hoover: A Public Life*, 44; Kellogg, *Hoover: The Man and His Work*, 102–3; Mildred Houghton Comfort, *Herbert Hoover, Humanitarian* (Minneapolis, MN, 1960), 75.

42. Steinberg, *Herbert Hoover*, 116–17.

43. Eugene Lyons, *The Herbert Hoover Story*, excerpted in White Book 2, HHPL.

44. Comfort, *Hoover, Humanitarian*, 74–75.

45. Irwin, *Hoover: A Reminiscent Biography*, 109–11; Comfort, *Hoover, Humanitarian*, 74; Steinberg, *Herbert Hoover*, 112; Hoover, *Memoirs*, 1:75–77.

46. "Keeping the Wolf from the World's Door: The Story of Herbert Hoover," Reprint File, unmarked clipping, September 1918, White Book 2, HHPL; Hoover, *Memoirs*, 1:83–85; Nash, *Hoover: The Engineer*, 246–75; Harold Wolfe, *Herbert Hoover: Public Servant and Leader of the Loyal Opposition* (New York, 1956), 27–28.

47. Nash, *Hoover: The Engineer*, 345–49; Wert, *Hoover: The Fishing President*, 76–78, 82–83; Mayer, *Lou Henry Hoover*, 119.

48. Nash, *Hoover: The Engineer*, 353–71; Charnley, *Boy's Life of Herbert Hoover*, 183; Steinberg, *Herbert Hoover*, 115.

49. Hoover, *Memoirs*, 1:91–95; Kellogg, *Hoover: The Man and His Work*, 109–10; Irwin, *Hoover: A Reminiscent Biography*, 116.

50. Burner, *Hoover: A Public Life*, 521; Nash, *Hoover: The Engineer*, 411–25; "Hoover's Seven American Business Pilgrimages," *Magazine of Business* 52, no. 4 (April 1928): 1–6, Commerce Box 268, Hoover, Herbert, Biography, 1928, HHPL; "Mining—Burma Mines," Report of May 5, 1914, 1–4, Pre-Commerce Papers, Box 50, HHPL.

51. Nash, *Hoover: The Engineer*, 380, 384–85; Steinberg, *Herbert Hoover*, 116.

52. T. Hoover, "Memoranda," 176–77.

53. Ibid., 176.

54. Kellogg, *Hoover: The Man and His Work*, 107; Irwin, *Hoover: A Reminiscent Biography*, 106–8; Ray Lyman Wilbur, "Herbert Hoover: A Personal Sketch," 12, Pre-Commerce Papers, Box 26, Articles about or by Herbert Hoover, HHPL; Herbert Hoover (handwritten), ca. 1916, 11, Information for Biographers, Pre-Commerce Papers, HHPL.

55. Hoover, *Memoirs*, 1:102–6; Nash, *Hoover: The Engineer*, 426–37; Steinberg, *Herbert Hoover*, 116–19; Irwin, *Hoover: A Reminiscent Biography*, 112–13; Charnley, *Boy's Life of Herbert Hoover*, 194–96.

56. Steinberg, *Herbert Hoover*, 119; Kellogg, *Hoover: The Man and His Work*, 108–9; Nash, *Hoover: The Engineer*, 441–44.

57. Kellogg, *Herbert Hoover: The Man and His Work*, 108–10; Charnley, *Boy's Life of Herbert Hoover*, 195–96; Nash, *Hoover: The Engineer*, 444–46.

58. Bradley S. Tice, *Herbert Hoover's Intellectual Development* (Bloomington, IN, 2004); Burner, *Hoover: A Public Life*, 68; Nash, *Hoover and Stanford University*, 24–25; Nash, *Hoover: The Engineer*, 489, 510–13; Craig M. Lloyd, *Aggressive Introvert: Herbert Hoover and Public Relations Management, 1912–1932* (Columbus, OH, 1972), 12–13; David S. Jordan to Charles D. Norton, secretary to President Taft, October 7, 1910; Norton to Jordan, October 14, 1910, Recommendations, Letter of, Pre-Commerce Papers, Box 60, 1910, HHPL.

59. Tice, *Hoover's Intellectual Development*, 11–13; Hoover, *Memoirs*, 1:117–18; Burner, *Hoover: A Public Life*, 69–70; Nash, *Hoover: The Engineer*, 494–95; Pryor, *Lou Henry Hoover*, 69–70; Wert, *Hoover: The Fishing President*, 86–87.

60. Nash, *Hoover: The Engineer*, 491–95; Hoover, *Memoirs*, 1:119; Irwin, *Hoover: A Reminiscent Biography*, 118–19; Mayer, *Lou Henry Hoover*, 129–33.

61. Lloyd, *Aggressive Introvert*, 14.

62. "Herbert Hoover, Biographical Sketch," *The World's Work*, unpaginated clipping, April 1915, Pre-Commerce Papers, Box 25, Articles about Herbert Hoover, HHPL; Eugene Lyons, *Herbert Hoover: A Biography* (Garden City, NY, 1964), 56.

Chapter 4. The Great Humanitarian

1. Alfred Steinberg, *Herbert Hoover* (New York, 1967), 126–27; David Burner, *Herbert Hoover: A Public Life* (New York, 1979), 62; Craig M. Lloyd, *Aggressive Introvert: Herbert Hoover and Public Relations Management, 1912–1932* (Columbus, OH, 1972), 20–22, 32.

2. Hugh Gibson, "Herbert C. Hoover," *Century Magazine*, August 1917, 514; Steinberg, *Herbert Hoover*, 126; Grey quote from Dale Mayer, *Lou Henry Hoover: A Prototype for First Ladies* (New York, 2004), 157; Hoover quote from Herbert Hoover, *The Memoirs of Herbert Hoover*, vol. 1, *Years of Adventure, 1874–1920* (New York, 1951), 137.

3. Will Irwin, *Herbert Hoover: A Reminiscent Biography* (New York, 1928), 127–31; Hoover, *Memoirs*, 1:142–45; Gary Dean Best, *The Politics of American Individualism: Herbert Hoover in Transition, 1918–1921* (Westport, CT, 1975), 4–5; Joan Hoff, *Herbert Hoover: Forgotten Progressive* (Boston, 1975), 44.

4. Hoff, *Hoover: Forgotten Progressive*, 44; Hal Elliott Wert, *Hoover: The Fishing President: Portrait of the Private Man and His Life Outdoors* (Mechanicsburg, PA, 2005), 89–91; Steinberg, *Herbert Hoover*, 217–29; Hoover, *Memoirs*, 1:141–46.

5. Steinberg, *Herbert Hoover*, 130–31; Kellogg, *Hoover: The Man and His Work*, 137–52; Gibson, "Herbert C. Hoover," 515; Irwin, *Hoover: A Reminiscent Biography*, 133–35.

6. Irwin, *Hoover: A Reminiscent Biography*, 133; Hoover, *Memoirs*, 1:155; Richard Norton Smith, *An Uncommon Man: The Triumph of Herbert Hoover* (New York, 1984), 81.

7. Irwin, *Hoover: A Reminiscent Biography*, 133–34; Herbert Hoover, *An American Epic*, vol. 1, *The Relief of Belgium and Northern France, 1914–1930* (New York, 1969), 2–3; Harold Wolfe, *Herbert Hoover: Public Servant and Leader of the Loyal Opposition* (New York, 1956), 37.

8. *New York Times*, October 21, 1928.

9. Irwin, *Hoover: A Reminiscent Biography*, 135.

10. George H. Nash, "'An American Epic': Herbert Hoover and Belgian Relief in World War I," *Prologue* 7 (Spring 1989): 86.

11. George H. Nash, *The Life of Herbert Hoover: The Humanitarian, 1914–1917* (New York, 1988), 94.

12. Irwin, *Hoover: A Reminiscent Biography*, 141–43, 172–75.

13. "The Story of Belgium," *Hearst's Magazine*, November 1917, 384, CRB (Commission for Relief in Belgium) Printed Misc., 1914–20, Pre-Commerce Papers, Box 32, HHPL.

14. Hoover, *American Epic*, 1:29; CRB Pamphlets, pamphlet on "Babies' Milk Funds," Pre-Commerce Papers, Box 11, HHPL.

15. Pamphlet on War Orphans, CRB Pamphlets and Printed Material, Pre-Commerce Papers, Box 31, HHPL.

16. CRB Speech, Lou Henry Hoover, October 1915, 11, Pre-Commerce Papers, HHPL; Edward Eyre Hunt, "Hoover of the C.R.B.," *World's Work* (June 1917), 166, Reprint File, HHPL; Hoover, *Memoirs*, 1:176.

17. *New York Times*, October 21, 1921, White Book 4, HHPL.

18. Bertrand Patenaude, *The Big Show in Bololand: The American Relief Expedition to Soviet Russia in the Famine of 1921* (Stanford, CA, 2002), 29; Burner, *Hoover: A Public Life*, 79–83.

19. Hunt, "Hoover of the C.R.B.," 168.

20. Steinberg, *Herbert Hoover*, 132–33.
21. Lewis R. Freeman, "Hoover and the Belgians," *Outlook*, September 1915, 81–83.
22. Ibid., 82.
23. Steinberg, *Herbert Hoover*, 134–35.
24. Gary Dean Best, *The Politics of American Individualism: Herbert Hoover in Transition, 1918–21* (Westport, CT, 1975), 6.
25. David Hinshaw, *Herbert Hoover: American Quaker* (New York, 1950), 10. See also Nash, *Hoover: The Humanitarian*, 121.
26. Vernon Kellogg, "Herbert Hoover, as Individual and Type," *Atlantic Monthly* (March 1918), 80, White Book 1, HHPL.
27. Ray Lyman Wilbur, 1928 Campaign Speech, Campaign and Transition Papers, Box 34, Biographical Sketches of Hoover, 1931–39, HHPL.
28. Hoover, *Memoirs*, 1:165–67.
29. Steinberg, *Herbert Hoover*, 137–38.
30. Smith, *An Uncommon Man*, 86.
31. Irwin, *Hoover: A Reminiscent Biography*, 147–48.
32. Hoover, *American Epic* 1:86, 437; "The Story of Belgium," 383–85, CRB Printed Misc., 1914–20, Pre-Commerce Papers, Box 32, HHPL.
33. Nash, *Hoover: The Humanitarian*, 143–51; Burner, *Hoover: A Public Life*, 89–90; Hoover, *Memoirs*, 1:199–202.
34. Steinberg, *Herbert Hoover*, 141–42.
35. Woodrow Wilson to Herbert Hoover, September 20, 1915, Public Relations of the CRB—Documents, vol. 2, 198, Pre-Commerce Papers, Box 31, HHPL.
36. Nash, *Hoover: The Humanitarian*, 194.
37. Steinberg, *Herbert Hoover*, 136–37.
38. Best, *The Politics of American Individualism*, 6.
39. Kellogg, *Hoover: The Man and His Work*, 150–76; Pamphlet on Belgian Relief, CRB, Pamphlets and Printed Materials, Pre-Commerce Papers, Box 31, HHPL; Lloyd, *Aggressive Introvert*, 39; Minutes Compiled by the New York Office, 1914–19, Pre-Commerce Papers, Box 37, HHPL.
40. Hoover, *Memoirs*, 1:167–71; CRB, Minutes compiled by New York Office, 1914–19, Pre-Commerce Papers, Box 37, HHPL.
41. Steinberg, *Herbert Hoover*, 142–44.
42. Irwin, *Hoover: A Reminiscent Biography*, 152–53, 168; CRB Balance Sheets and Accounts, October 1914–September 30, 1920, 8, Pre-Commerce Papers, Box 31, HHPL; Reprint File.
43. Nash, "An American Epic," 84; Wolfe, *Hoover: Public Servant*, 47; Hinshaw, *Hoover: American Quaker*, 325–26.
44. Quotation from Sonja Schoepf Wentling and Rafael Medoff, *Herbert Hoover and the Jews* (Washington, DC, 2012), 4.
45. Ray Lyman Wilbur, Biographical Sketches of Hoover, 1931–39, 3, Campaign and Transition Papers, 1928, Box 34, HHPL.
46. Kellogg, *Hoover: The Man and His Work*, 197–98, 208; George H. Nash, *The Life of Herbert Hoover: Master of Emergencies, 1917–1918* (New York, 1986), 16–17, 23–25; Burner, *Hoover: A Public Life*, 113.
47. Burner, *Hoover: A Public Life*, 98–99; Nash, *Hoover: Master of Emergencies*, 39–40, 50–54, 66, 71–73.
48. Quote from Wilbur, Biographical Sketches, 4, Campaign and Transition Papers, Box 34, 1931–39, HHPL; Kellogg, *Hoover: The Man and His Work*, 199–200; Ray Lyman Wilbur, "Herbert Hoover: A Personal Sketch," [1919], 18–19, Articles about or by Herbert Hoover, Pre-Commerce Papers, Box 26, HHPL.
49. Rhondda quote from Kellogg, *Hoover: The Man and His Work*, 217. See also Steinberg, *Herbert Hoover*, 144–45; Irwin, *Hoover: A Reminiscent Biography*, 195.
50. Eugene Lyons, *Herbert Hoover: A Biography* (Garden City, NY, 1964), 102.

51. Vernon Kellogg, "Herbert Hoover, as Individual and Type," *Atlantic Monthly*, March 1918, White Book 1, HHPL; Irwin, *Hoover: A Reminiscent Biography*, 193.

52. Nash, *Hoover: Master of Emergencies*, 41.

53. Quote from Nash, *Hoover: Master of Emergencies*, 136. Also see Witold S. Sworakowski, "Herbert Hoover, Launching the Food Administration, 1917–18"; in Lawrence E. Gelfand, ed., *Herbert Hoover: The Great War and Its Aftermath, 1914–1923* (Iowa City, IA, 1979); "Food Control—A War Measure," Address by Herbert Hoover Before the Pittsburgh Press Club, April 18, 1918, 3–7, Public Statements, 1917–20, Pre-Commerce Papers, Box 60, HHPL.

54. Hoover, *Memoirs*, 1:240–41; Ray Lyman Wilbur, *The Memoirs of Ray Lyman Wilbur*, ed. Edgar Eugene Robinson and Paul Carroll Edwards (Stanford, CA, 1960), 258–59.

55. Lloyd, *Aggressive Introvert*, 46–51; Nash, *Hoover: Master of Emergencies*, 41–43, 156–59; Sworakowski, "Hoover, Launching the Food Administration," 57.

56. *Minneapolis Journal*, February 4, July 29, 1918; *Washington Star*, February 3, 1918; other unmarked clippings, Clipping File (hereafter cited as CF), White Book 2, HHPL.

57. Nash, *Hoover: Master of Emergencies*, 166–67; Kellogg, *Hoover: The Man and His Work*, 242–46; Irwin, *Hoover: A Reminiscent Biography*, 197–98.

58. Kellogg, *Hoover: The Man and His Work*, 199–201, 223–31, 235–36; Hoover, *Memoirs*, 1:245–47; Articles about or by Herbert Hoover, "Hoover Biography," [1919 or 1920], anon., Pre-Commerce Papers, Box 26, HHPL; Burner, *Hoover: A Public Life*, 107–10; Nash, *Hoover: Master of Emergencies*, 343–45.

59. Nash, *Hoover: Master of Emergencies*, 419–24; Steinberg, *Herbert Hoover*, 149–52; Hoover, *Memoirs*, 1:263, 286; Best, *The Politics of American Individualism*, 11–12.

60. Irwin, *Hoover: A Reminiscent Biography*, 204–7.

61. Nash, *Hoover: Master of Emergencies*, 431, 365–67, 377–78; Irwin, *Hoover: A Reminiscent Biography*, 206–9; Helen B. Pryor, *Lou Henry Hoover: Gallant First Lady* (New York, 1969), 113.

62. Hinshaw, *Hoover: American Quaker*, 95–96; Kendrick A. Clements, *Hoover, Conservation, and Consumerism: Engineering the Good Life* (Lawrence, KS, 2000), 32; Lyons, *Hoover: A Biography*, 100; Kellogg, *Hoover: The Man and His Work*, 216–17.

Chapter 5. Samaritan to a Continent

1. Herbert Hoover, *The Memoirs of Herbert Hoover*, vol. 1, *Years of Adventure, 1874–1920* (New York, 1951), 283–85.

2. Kendrick A. Clements, *The Life of Herbert Hoover: Imperfect Visionary, 1918–1928* (New York, 2010), 10–12; Royal J. Schmidt, "Hoover's Reflections on the Versailles Treaty," in Lawrence E. Gelfand, ed., *Herbert Hoover: The Great War and Its Aftermath, 1914–1923* (Iowa City, IA, 1979), 66–83.

3. David Burner, *Herbert Hoover: A Public Life* (New York, 1979), 114–16; Gary Dean Best, *The Politics of American Individualism: Herbert Hoover in Transition, 1918–1921* (Westport, CT, 1975), 12–13; Hoover, *Memoirs*, 1:296–99.

4. Alfred Steinberg, *Herbert Hoover* (New York, 1967), 161–62.

5. Best, *The Politics of American Individualism*, 12–13; Hoover, *Memoirs*, 1:329–33.

6. Clements, *Imperfect Visionary*, 6; Chronology of the American Relief Administration, White Book 2, 27–29, HHPL; Hoover, *Memoirs*, 1:302–4.

7. Clements, *Imperfect Visionary*, 6–10; Hoover, *Memoirs*, 1:395.

8. *New York Times*, March 10, 1919; Hoover, *Memoirs*, 1:333; Steinberg, *Herbert Hoover*, 162–63.

9. Hoover, *Memoirs*, 1:397–414; Steinberg, *Herbert Hoover*, 170–71; Will Irwin, *Herbert Hoover: A Reminiscent Biography* (New York, 1928), 242.

10. Hoover, *Memoirs*, 1:363–64; Steinberg, *Herbert Hoover*, 10, 171–72.

11. Wentling and Medoff, *Herbert Hoover and the Jews*, 5.

12. Ibid., 33, 14, 7.

13. Best, *The Politics of American Individualism*, 13–14; Clements, *Imperfect Visionary*, 16–17; Irwin, *Hoover: A Reminiscent Biography*, 240.

14. Clements, *Imperfect Visionary*, 18; Hoover, *Memoirs*, 1:318–19.

15. Steinberg, *Herbert Hoover*, 168; Irwin, *Hoover: A Reminiscent Biography*, 234; Clements, *Imperfect Visionary*, 17.

16. Hoover, *Memoirs*, 1:325–26; Steinberg, *Herbert Hoover*, 169; Clements, *Imperfect Visionary*, 23; Irwin, *Hoover: A Reminiscent Biography*, 235; *Congressional Record—House* 69, 202, excerpted in White Book 2, HHPL.

17. *National Cyclopedia of American Biography*, 18–20, Pre-Commerce Papers, Box 26, Articles about or by Herbert Hoover, HHPL; "Chronology of the American Food Administration," 27–29, White Book 2, HHPL; Sketch of Hoover, Post-Presidential Papers, Box 39, 1945, Sketches of Hoover, 1940–49, HHPL, 10; Hoover, *Memoirs*, 1:321–23.

18. Steinberg, *Herbert Hoover*, 180; Hoover, *Memoirs*, 1:422–26; Best, *The Politics of American Individualism*, 13–14; *Congressional Record—House* 69 (1928), 202, excerpted in White Book 2, HHPL.

19. George H. Nash in Lee Nash, ed., *Understanding Herbert Hoover: Ten Perspectives* (Stanford, CA, 1987), 35; Hoover, *Memoirs*, 1:472.

20. "Hoover Biography," Articles about or by Herbert Hoover, anonymous, 1919 or 1920, 35, Pre-Commerce Papers, Box 26, HHPL.

21. Clements, *Imperfect Visionary*, 29–31, 49; Steinberg, *Herbert Hoover*, 180–81; Craig Lloyd, *Aggressive Introvert: Herbert Hoover and Public Relations Management, 1912–1932* (Columbus, OH), 312–13.

22. Richard Norton Smith, *An Uncommon Man: The Triumph of Herbert Hoover* (New York, 1984), 93–94.

23. Clements, *Imperfect Visionary*, 39; Steinberg, *Herbert Hoover*, 181–82.

24. Clements, *Imperfect Visionary*, 30, 37–40, 42–47; Best, *The Politics of American Individualism*, 38–39, 41–51.

25. Best, *The Politics of American Individualism*, 24–25.

26. Ibid., 26.

27. Steinberg, *Herbert Hoover*, 181.

28. Best, *The Politics of American Individualism*, 28–32.

29. The best summary of Hoover's role in the 1920 campaign is Clements, *Imperfect Visionary*, chap. 20, 49–69. See also Gary Dean Best, "The Hoover-for-President Boom of 1920," *Mid-America* 25, no. 4 (October 1971): 227–44.

30. The quotation is from Lloyd, *Aggressive Introvert*, 80–81. See also Louis W. Liebovich, *Bylines in Despair: Herbert Hoover, the Great Depression, and the U.S. News Media* (Westport, CT, 1994), 18; Ray Lyman Wilbur, *The Memoirs of Ray Lyman Wilbur*, ed. Edgar Eugene Robinson and Paul Carroll Edwards (Stanford, CA, 1960), 371–74; Best, *The Politics of American Individualism*, 19, 35.

31. Timothy Walch and Dwight M. Miller, eds., *Herbert Hoover and Franklin D. Roosevelt* (Westport, CT, 1998), 5–6, 8.

32. Best, *The Politics of American Individualism*, 54–57; Best, "The Hoover-for-President Boom of 1920," 227–30.

33. Best, *The Politics of American Individualism*, 82–87; Campaign of 1920, Hoover Republican Club of California, Press Releases—Campaign Issues, League of Nations, April 1920, 1–2, Pre-Commerce Papers, Box 29, HHPL.

34. Best, *The Politics of American Individualism*, 112–15; "The 1920 Lightning That Did Not Strike Herbert Hoover," unsigned, 3–4, Pre-Commerce Papers, Box 27, HHPL; Harold Wolfe, *Herbert Hoover: Public Servant and Leader of the Loyal Opposition* (New York, 1956), 88; Herbert Hoover, *The Memoirs of Herbert Hoover*, vol. 2, *The Cabinet and the Presidency, 1920–1933* (New York, 1952), 35.

35. Patrick Renshaw, *Franklin D. Roosevelt* (New York, 2004), 36.

36. Hoover, *Memoirs*, 2:419–20; Frank M. Surface and Raymond L. Bland, *American Food in the World War and Reconstruction Period* (Stanford, 1931), 244; Statement by M. Pichon, French Foreign Minister, Translation, April 6, 1919, 1–3, Relief-Russia, 1919–20, Pre-Commerce Papers, Box 60, HHPL.

37. Benjamin N. Weisman, *Herbert Hoover and Famine Relief to Soviet Russia, 1921–1923* (Stanford, 1974), 1–7; Clements, *Imperfect Visionary*, 149, 157, 159.

38. Steinberg, *Herbert Hoover*, 188. See also memo from Thomas McCormick, "Famine Relief Work in Russia, 1917–1921," 1–2, American Relief Administration, Russia, Misc., 1922–27, Box 30, Commerce Papers, HHPL.

39. Clements, *Imperfect Visionary*, 39; Bertrand Patenaude, *The Big Show in Bololand: The American Relief Expedition to Soviet Russia in the Famine of 1921* (Stanford, CA, 2002), 39; Burner, *Hoover: A Public Life*, 130–32.

40. Patenaude, *Big Show in Bololand*, 6; Clements, *Imperfect Visionary*, 149.

41. Clements, *Imperfect Visionary*, 155.

42. Patenaude, *Big Show in Bololand*, 59, 67.

43. Ibid., 1, 67, 75.

44. Ibid., 264–68.

45. Clements, *Imperfect Visionary*, 153–55; Patenaude, *Big Show in Bololand*, 60–61.

46. Patenaude, *Big Show in Bololand*, title page to part 1.

47. Ibid., 77, 81; Clements, *Imperfect Visionary*, 156. Haskell quote from Patenaude, *Big Show in Bololand*, 125.

48. Patenaude, *Big Show in Bololand*, 102, 108–9. Quote on 102.

49. Ibid., 104.

50. Ibid., 107.

51. Ibid., 72.

52. Ibid., 127, 135.

53. Clements, *Imperfect Visionary*, 157, 160; Sketch of Hoover, 1945, 10, Sketches of Hoover, 1940–49, Box 39, HHPL.

54. Steinberg, *Herbert Hoover*, 189.

55. Smith, *An Uncommon Man*, 95.

56. Transcript, White Book 2, June 29, 1948, HHPL.

57. *Washington Post* and *Times Herald*, February 25, 1959, White Book 2, HHPL.

Chapter 6. Secretary of Commerce, Locomotive of the Economy

1. See Kendrick A. Clements, *The Life of Herbert Hoover: Imperfect Visionary, 1918–1928* (New York, 2010), 103, for quotation. See also Harris Gaylord Warren, *Herbert Hoover and the Great Depression* (New York, 1967), 26; Robert K. Murray, "Herbert Hoover and the Harding Cabinet," in Ellis W. Hawley, ed., *Herbert Hoover as Secretary of Commerce: Studies in New Era Thought and Practice* (Iowa City, IA, 1981), 20–21.

2. Murray, "Herbert Hoover and the Harding Cabinet," 33–34; Hoover to Harding, November 29, 1921, Commerce Papers (hereafter cited as CP), Box 480, President Harding, 1921, October–November, Herbert Hoover Presidential Library (hereafter cited as HHPL); Hoover Memoranda to Harding, March–May, 1923, CP, Box 481, HHPL; George B. Christian to Hoover, March 17, 1921, CP, Box 480, President Harding, HHPL; Christian to Hoover, April 14, April 29, 1921, CP, Box 480, President Harding, HHPL; Harding to Hoover, March 11, 1929, CP, Box 480, President Harding, HHPL; Harding to Hoover, May 14, 1921, CP, Box 480, President Harding, HHPL.

3. Clements, *Imperfect Visionary*, xi. For the best synopsis of Hoover's philosophy see Herbert Hoover, *American Individualism* (New York, 1922), published while he was secretary of commerce.

4. Clements, *Imperfect Visionary*, x–xii, 232–33; Ellis W. Hawley, "Herbert Hoover, the Commerce Secretariat, and the Vision of an Associative State, 1921–1928," *Journal of American History* 61, no. 1 (June 1974): 117; David Hinshaw, *Herbert Hoover: American Quaker* (New York, 1950), 121–22; David Burner, *Herbert Hoover: A Public Life* (New York, 1979), 157.

5. Murray, "Herbert Hoover and the Harding Cabinet," 30–33. On tax policy see Hoover to Harding, November 28, 1921 (memo enclosed), CP, Box 480, President Harding, 1921,

October–November, HHPL; Harding to Hoover, December 6, 1921, CP, Box 480, President Harding, 1921, December, HHPL.

6. Clements, *Imperfect Visionary*, 105–6, 286–87, 314, 343; Hawley, "Herbert Hoover, the Commerce Secretariat," 137; Harold Wolfe, *Herbert Hoover: Public Servant and Leader of the Loyal Opposition* (New York, 1956), 103–5.

7. Clements, *Imperfect Visionary*, 143.

8. Ellis W. Hawley, "Herbert Hoover and Economic Stabilization, 1921–1922," in Hawley, *Herbert Hoover as Secretary of Commerce*, 44; Alfred Steinberg, *Herbert Hoover* (New York, 1967), 186–87.

9. Craig Lloyd, *Aggressive Introvert: Herbert Hoover and Public Relations Management, 1912–1932* (Columbus, OH, 1972), 134–38; Burner, *Hoover: A Public Life*, 164–66; George T. Odell, "Producing Half a Billion Dollars in Business," *Trade Winds* (May 1925), 8–11, CP, Box 121, Commerce Department Achievements, HHPL; David M. Kennedy, *Freedom from Fear: The American People in Depression and War, 1929–1945* (New York, 1999), 48.

10. Burner, *Hoover: A Public Life*, 177; Hawley, "Herbert Hoover and Economic Stabilization, 1921–1922," 55–56, 62–64; Clements, *Imperfect Visionary*, 117–18, 119–22, 251; Hoover to Thomas O'Neill, October 20, 1921, CP, Box 507, Railroads, Strikes, 1921, October 17–20, HHPL; Hoover to Robert A. Taft, September 25, 1922, CP, Box 593, Taft, Robert A, 1923–28, HHPL.

11. Lloyd, *Aggressive Introvert*, 139–41; Wolfe, *Hoover: Public Servant*, 101–2. See the exchange of letters engineered by Hoover including Harding to Judge Gary, June 13, 1923 [ghosted by Hoover], CP, Box 481, President Harding, 1923, June–December, HHPL, and Hoover to Harding, April 8, 1922, CP, Box 234, Gary, Elbert H., 1920–26, HHPL.

12. Richard Norton Smith, *An Uncommon Man: The Triumph of Herbert Hoover* (New York, 1984), 99; Wolfe, *Hoover: Public Servant*, 92; Hawley, "Herbert Hoover, the Commerce Secretariat," 120–22.

13. Hawley, "Herbert Hoover, the Commerce Secretariat," 123–29; Clements, *Imperfect Visionary*, 110–11, 254–55; *Congressional Record—House* 69 (1928), 203, White Book 2, HHPL; CP, Box 120, Department Achievements, 1921–23, HHPL; CP, Box 191, Elimination of Waste in Industry, 1925, March–December, and 1927–28 and undated, HHPL.

14. Clements, *Imperfect Visionary*, 221–24, 288, 322–23; Statement by Secretary Hoover to *Christian Science Monitor* on Housing, March 25, 1922, 1–6, CP, Box 89, *Christian Science Monitor*, 1922–25, HHPL; Analysis of Housing, #1, CP, Box 63, Building and Housing, 1921, HHPL.

15. Clements, *Imperfect Visionary*, 240–46, 362–63; Herbert Hoover, *The Memoirs of Herbert Hoover*, vol. 2, *The Cabinet and the Presidency, 1920–1933* (New York, 1952), 177–79; Lewis L. Strauss Memo on War Debts, 1–2, CP, Box 78, Strauss, Lewis L., HHPL.

16. Burner, *Hoover: A Public Life*, 184–85; Clements, *Imperfect Visionary*, 242, 307–8; Hoover to Mr. R. W. Farr, August 31, 1921, CP, Box 208, Foreign Bond Speculation, 1921, HHPL; Hoover Memo to Harding Warning of Foreign Loans, November 30, 1921, CP, Box 480, President Harding, 1921, October–November.

17. Hoover, *Memoirs*, 2:49; Clements, *Imperfect Visionary*, 265–68; Smith, *An Uncommon Man*, 102.

18. *San Francisco Examiner*, August 1, 1923, CP, Box 481, President Harding, Illness, Tributes, Letters of Sympathy, 1923, July–August, HHPL; Hoover, *Memoirs*, 2:49–51; Steinberg, *Herbert Hoover*, 192–93.

19. Statement of President Coolidge, CP, Box 476, President Coolidge, 1924, January; Steinberg, *Herbert Hoover*, 193–94; Hoover, *Memoirs*, 2:54.

20. Hoover, *Memoirs*, 2:54–55.

21. Eugene Lyons, *Herbert Hoover: A Biography* (Garden City, NY), 170; Wolfe, *Hoover: Public Servant*, 95; Hoover to Coolidge, November 3, 1924; Bascomp Slemp [Coolidge's secretary] to Hoover, November 3, 1924; Hoover to Coolidge, November 11, 1924, all in CP, Box 477, President Coolidge, October–November, HHPL. For an example of a speech Hoover wrote for Coolidge see paragraphs of the president's message on Muscle Shoals, November 19, 1923, CP, Box 476, President Coolidge, 1923–November, HHPL.

22. Martin L. Fausold, *The Presidency of Herbert Hoover* (Lawrence, KS, 1985), 21.

23. For Coolidge's brief snubbing of Hoover, for which he apologized, see *Los Angeles Times*, April 16, 1920; *Washington Star*, April 20, 1920; *New York World*, April 20, 1920; *New York Times*, April 20, 1920, all in President Coolidge, Statements to the Press, News Accounts, April 16–20, 1920, CP, Box 479, Coolidge, Statements to the Press, HHPL.

24. Radio Division, Department of Commerce, CP, Box 1, Accomplishments of the Department of Commerce, 1921–28, 1–2, HHPL; "Radio Talk by Secretary Hoover, Washington, DC, March 24, 1924, 1–9, CP, Box 489, Radio, Correspondence, Press Releases, Misc., 1924, January–March, HHPL; Hoover to Secretary of State, January 5, 1923, CP, Box 501, Radio-International Problems, 1923–27 and undated, HHPL; Ray Lyman Wilbur and Arthur Mastick Hyde, *The Hoover Policies* (New York, 1937), 207–14.

25. Interview given by former president Hoover in 1952—reminisces about radio, Hoover and Radio, 3, "Radio Gets a Policeman," Post-Presidential Papers (PPP), Box 103, Campaign, 1952, HHPL.

26. "Hoover Helps Transmit TV," CP, Box 598, Television, 1926–27; Smith, *An Uncommon Man*, 100; Clements, *Imperfect Visionary*, 354.

27. Wilbur and Hyde, *The Hoover Policies*, 216–19; Hoover, *Memoirs*, 2:133–34; Interview with Hoover published in *Boston American*, October 13, 1924, CP, Box 39, Aviation, 1922–24, 1–3; Summary on Civil Aeronautics, 1927, CP, Box 479, 1–2, President Coolidge, November–December, HHPL; Secretary of Commerce, Aviation 1926–28, CP, Box 40, 1–3, Aviation, 1926–28 and undated, HHPL; Summary, 1921–28, Activities in the Aeronautical Line, CP, Box 1, Accomplishments of the Department of Commerce, 1921–28 (summarized).

28. Hoover, *Memoirs*, 2:72; CP, Box 120, Achievements, 1924, May–June, press release, June 26, 1924, 1–2, HHPL; Clements, *Imperfect Visionary*, 295.

29. Kendrick A. Clements, *Hoover, Conservation, and Consumerism: Engineering the Good Life* (Lawrence, KS, 2000), 79.

30. Clements, *Imperfect Visionary*, 371.

31. Will Irwin, *Herbert Hoover: A Reminiscent Biography* (New York, 1928), 305; Clements, *Hoover, Conservation, and Consumerism*, 79.

32. Wilbur and Hyde, *The Hoover Policies*, 255–59; Hoover, *Memoirs*, 2:112–16; Burner, *Hoover: A Public Life*, 178–82; Wolfe, *Hoover: Public Servant*, 105; Coolidge Appoints Hoover to St. Lawrence Commission, Coolidge to Hoover, March 10, 1924, CP, Box 477, President Coolidge, 1924–March, HHPL.

33. Wolfe, *Hoover: Public Servant*, 105–6; Clements, *Hoover, Conservation, and Consumerism*, 132–33; Wilbur and Hyde, *The Hoover Policies*, 279–82.

34. Clements, *Imperfect Visionary*, 125, 300–301; Hoover to Coolidge, March 14, 1925; Everett Sanders to Hoover, March 16, 1925, CP, Box 477, President Coolidge, 1925–March, HHPL.

35. Clements, *Hoover, Conservation, and Consumerism*, 61–64.

36. Clements, *Imperfect Visionary*, 274–75.

37. Clements, *Hoover, Conservation, and Consumerism*, 66–71; Wilbur and Hyde, *The Hoover Policies*, 241–45; press release, June 30, 1924, Accomplishments in Fishing, CP, Box 120, 1924, May–June, HHPL; Summary of Accomplishments, Bureau of Fisheries, CP, Box 1, 1921–28, 1–3, HHPL.

38. Joseph Brandes, "Product Diplomacy: Herbert Hoover's Anti-Monopoly Campaign at Home and Abroad," 191–203, in Hawley, *Herbert Hoover as Secretary of Commerce*; "Herbert Hoover's Fight Against Raw Material Monopoly," 1921–28, 1–11, CP, Box 1, Accomplishments of the Administration, HHPL; Hoover Statement to the House Committee on Interstate and Foreign Commerce on Monopolies of Raw Materials Imports to the U.S., January 6, 1925, 1–2, CP, Box 135, HHPL.

39. Investigation of Raw Materials Controlled by Cartels, CP, Box 121, Commerce Department Achievements, 1924, August–December and undated, 11–14, HHPL; Hoover to Senator Arthur Capper, December 10, 1925, CP, Box 77, Arthur Capper, 1914–28, HHPL; Hoover, *Memoirs*, 2:79–84; *Congressional Record—House* 69 (1928), 203, White Book 2, HHPL.

40. Lloyd, *Aggressive Introvert*, 139.
41. Press release, December 31, 1925, Hoover, "Economic Prospects for 1926," CP, Box 188, Economic Situation in the U.S., 1925–28, 5–6, HHPL.
42. *New York Evening Post*, January 3, 1927.
43. See the exchange of letters including I. L. Lenroot to D. R. Crissinger, November 23, 1925; Crissinger to Lenroot, December 10, 1925; Lenroot to Crissinger, December 23, 1925, all in CP, Box 199, 1925–33, HHPL. For a synopsis of the 1925 and 1927 negotiations, respectively, see Clements, *Imperfect Visionary*, 104, 305, and 368–69.
44. Frederick Simpich, "The Great Mississippi Flood of 1927," *National Geographic Magazine* 52, no. 3 (September 1927), 243–89. Quotes on 245.
45. *New York Times*, April 26, 1927.
46. Estimate of Damage, Mississippi Valley Flood Relief Work, Misc., January–April, 1928, CP, Box 397, 1–5, HHPL; Bruce Alan Lohof, "Hebert Hoover and the Mississippi Valley Flood of 1927: A Case Study of the Political Thought of Herbert Hoover" (PhD diss., Syracuse University, 1968), 131–32; Pete Daniel, *The 1927 Mississippi River Flood* (New York, 1977), 62.
47. Lohof, "Herbert Hoover and the Mississippi Valley Flood of 1927," 138–43; Daniel, *The 1927 Mississippi River Flood*, 93–98; Simpich, "The Great Mississippi Flood of 1927," 269.
48. John M. Barry, *Rising Tide: The Great Mississippi Flood of 1927 and How It Changed America* (New York, 1997), 321–23; *New York Age: The National Negro Weekly*, June 25, 1927; Hoover to Moton, December 23, 1927; Hoover to R. E. Malone, July 5, 1927, both in CP, Box 404, Mississippi Valley Flood Relief Work, Negroes, HHPL. In the letter to Malone, Hoover expresses gratitude for the loving cup.
49. Simpich, "The Great Mississippi Flood of 1927," 270, 287; Lohof, "Herbert Hoover and the Mississippi Valley Flood of 1927," 81–82, 88–91; Barry, *Rising Tide*, 253–58.
50. Smith, *An Uncommon Man*, 101.
51. Lohof, "Herbert Hoover and the Mississippi Valley Flood of 1927," 269, 272.
52. Barry, *Rising Tide*, 288.
53. For a summary of Hoover's plans for a resettlement corporation see Burner, *Hoover: A Public Life*, 195–96. For correspondence relating to the conference with philanthropists see William Schieffen to Hoover, February 6, 1928, Robert Moton to Hoover, February 27, 1928, Hoover to Mr. Embry [first name missing], March 6, 1928, all in CP, Box 435, Negroes, Plan to Make Good Farm Land in South Available, 1927–28, HHPL.

Chapter 7. Into the White House

1. Donald R. McCoy, "To the White House: Herbert Hoover, August 1927–March 1929," in Martin Fausold, ed., *The Hoover Presidency: A Reappraisal* (Albany, NY, 1974), 29–30.
2. David Hinshaw, *Herbert Hoover: American Quaker* (New York, 1950), 138.
3. McCoy, "To the White House," 30.
4. Ibid., 30–31; Hinshaw, *Hoover: American Quaker*, 137–39.
5. *New York Times*, February 6, 1928, CF, HHPL; James J. Davis, *Presidential Primaries: Road to the White House* (Westport, CT, 1980), 295.
6. Martin Fausold, *The Presidency of Herbert Hoover* (Lawrence, KS, 1985), 22–23; Maury Klein, *Rainbow's End: The Crash of 1929* (New York, 2001), 139.
7. *Grand Rapids Herald*, October 9, 1927, CF, HHPL.
8. *Jackson (MI) Citizen Patriot*, September 7, 1927, CF, HHPL.
9. *St. Louis Post-Dispatch*, December 21, 1927, CF, HHPL.
10. *Springfield (MA) Republican*, January 27, 1928, CF, HHPL.
11. Harris Gaylord Warren, *Herbert Hoover and the Great Depression* (New York, 1967), 32.
12. *Orange (NJ) Daily Courier*, January 6, 1928, CF, HHPL; telegram, Louis B. Mayer to Mark L. Requa, April 20, 1928, telegram, Cecil B. De Mille to Mark L. Requa, April 20, 1928, CP, Box 78, HHPL.

13. Dale Carnegie to Hoover, December 15, 1927, CP, Box 78, Carnegie, Dale, 1927, HHPL; Ray Lyman Wilbur, *The Memoirs of Ray Lyman Wilbur*, ed. Edgar Eugene Robinson and Paul Carroll Edwards (Stanford, CA, 1960), 387–89; Joan Hoff, *Herbert Hoover: Forgotten Progressive* (Boston, 1975), 123–25.

14. *Chicago Tribune*, February 23, 1928, CF, HHPL.

15. Kendrick A. Clements, *The Life of Herbert Hoover: Imperfect Visionary, 1918–1928* (New York, 2010), 404.

16. David Burner, *Herbert Hoover: A Public Life* (New York, 1979), 197–98.

17. Donald Lisio, *Hoover, Blacks, and Lily-Whites: A Study of Southern Strategies* (Chapel Hill, NC, 1985), 38, 48–49, 51–55.

18. Clements, *Imperfect Visionary*, 401; Burner, *Hoover: A Public Life*, 198–200.

19. Harold Wolfe, *Herbert Hoover: Public Servant and Leader of the Loyal Opposition* (New York, 1956), 117; McCoy, "To the White House," 34–35.

20. Burner, *Hoover: A Public Life*, 200; *Chicago Tribune*, June 7, 1928, June 8, 1928, CF, HHPL; *Chicago Daily News*, June 11, 1928, CF, HHPL; Helen P. Pryor, *Lou Henry Hoover: Gallant First Lady* (New York, 1969), 151.

21. E. S. Rochester, *Coolidge-Hoover-Work: An Intimate Review of an Epochal Campaign for the Presidency of the United States* (Washington, DC, 1929), 48; *Chicago Tribune*, June 15, 1928, CF, HHPL; *Chicago Daily News*, June 15, 1928, CF, HHPL; McCoy, "To the White House," 35–36.

22. Fausold, *The Presidency of Herbert Hoover*, 25.

23. Burner, *Hoover: A Public Life*, 200–201; Clements, *Imperfect Visionary*, 400.

24. Alfred Steinberg, *Herbert Hoover* (New York, 1967), 200–201.

25. Hubert Work Scrapbook, clippings from *Toledo Times*, June 29, 1928; *Washington Post*, July 1, 1928; *New York Times*, July 8, 1928; *Chicago Tribune*, July 3, 1928, July 5, 1928; *Philadelphia Inquirer*, August 26, 1928, Box 1, Hoover Institution Archives, Stanford University.

26. Hal Elliott Wert, *Hoover: The Fishing President, Portrait of the Private Man and His Life Outdoors* (Mechanicsburg, PA, 2005), 160.

27. *Buffalo Evening News*, July 20, 1928, Campaign and Transition Papers (hereafter cited as C&TP), Box 75, HHPL; *Chicago Daily News*, July 20, 1928, CF, HHPL.

28. Fausold, *The Presidency of Herbert Hoover*, 26–27; Wilbur, *Memoirs*, 398–99; *Buffalo Evening News*, August 13, 1928, C&TP, Box 75, Subject: Anecdotes, HHPL.

29. William Starr Myers and Walter H. Newton, *The Hoover Administration: A Documented Narrative* (New York, 1936), vi.

30. Hoover, *The New Day* (Stanford: Stanford University Press, 1928), 36.

31. Ibid., 41.

32. Ibid., 17–33; *Chicago Daily News*, August 13, 1928, CF, HHPL; *Buffalo Evening News*, August 12, 1928, C&TP, Box 75, Anecdotes, HHPL.

33. Hoover, *The New Day*, 11.

34. Ibid., 37.

35. *Chicago Daily News*, August 13, 1928, CF, HHPL.

36. Herbert Hoover, *The Memoirs of Herbert Hoover*, vol. 3, *The Great Depression, 1919–1941* (New York, 1952), 343.

37. Compilation of clippings, August 13, 1928, CF, HHPL.

38. Fausold, *The Presidency of Herbert Hoover*, 29; McCoy, "To the White House," 42–43.

39. *New York World*, June 24, 1928; *Chicago Daily News*, October 18, 1928; *Chicago Tribune*, September 28, October 19, 1928, all in CF, HHPL.

40. *Chicago Tribune*, September 30, October 1, 1928, CF, HHPL.

41. Editorial, *Washington Post*, September 28, 1928, CF, HHPL.

42. Timothy Walch and Dwight M. Miller, eds., *Herbert Hoover and Franklin D. Roosevelt* (Westport, CT, 1998), 24–26.

43. Ibid., 27.
44. Editorial, *Chicago Daily News*, November 6, 1928, November 7, 1928, CF, HHPL; George H. Nash, *Herbert Hoover and Stanford University* (Stanford, CA, 1988), 91–92. Final quote from *Chicago Daily News*, November 8, 1928, CF, HHPL.
45. Editorial, *Washington Post*, November 8, 1928, CF, HHPL.
46. *Chicago Daily News*, November 7, 1928, CF, HHPL.
47. Hoff, *Hoover: Forgotten Progressive*, 128.
48. Burner, *Hoover: A Public Life*, 285–86; *Chicago Daily News*, July 19, 1929, Reprint File, HHPL; DeConde, *Hoover's Latin-American Policy*, 15–17; Wolfe, *Hoover: Public Servant*, 126–27; Robert H. Ferrell, *American Diplomacy in the Great Depression: Hoover-Stimson Foreign Policy, 1929–1933* (New Haven, 1957), 217; French Strother, "Four Years of Hoover: An Interpretation," *New York Times*, February 26, 1933, transcript, Reprint File, HHPL; McCoy, "To the White House," 46–47; Wert, *Hoover: The Fishing President*, 173–76.
49. Louis W. Liebovich, *Bylines in Despair: Herbert Hoover, the Great Depression, and the U.S. News Media* (Westport, CT, 1994), 85; Hoff, *Hoover: Forgotten Progressive*, 133–34; Burner, *Hoover: A Public Life*, 208–9; Theodore G. Joslin Diaries, Box 10, F 7, August 27, 1931, HHPL; Fausold, *The Presidency of Herbert Hoover*, 34–37; unmarked clipping, Associated Press, July 7, 1929, CF, HHPL.

Chapter 8. Getting a Grip on the Presidency

1. *New York Times*, May 12, 1929, Clipping File (hereafter cited as CF), Herbert Hoover Presidential Library (hereafter cited as HHPL).
2. Davis W. Houck, "Rhetoric as Currency: Herbert Hoover and the 1929 Stock Market Crash," *Rhetoric and Public Affairs* 3, no. 2 (2000): 161.
3. Quoted in David M. Kennedy, *Freedom from Fear: The American People in Depression and War, 1929–1945* (New York, 1999), 11.
4. Editorial, "The Trend of Events," *Outlook and Independent*, March 20, 1929, 450.
5. *Chicago Daily News*, March 2, 1929, Reprint File, HHPL.
6. Martin L. Fausold, *The Presidency of Herbert Hoover* (Lawrence, KS, 1985), 39–40; Nancy Beck Young, *Lou Henry Hoover: Activist First Lady* (Lawrence, KS, 2004), 5; *Chicago Daily News*, March 4, 1929, CF, HHPL; Helen B. Pryor, *Lou Henry Hoover: Gallant First Lady* (New York, 1969), 163–65; Donald R. McCoy, "To the White House, Herbert Hoover, August 1927–March 1929," in Martin L. Fausold, ed., *The Hoover Presidency: A Reappraisal* (Albany, NY, 1974), 48–49; Louis W. Liebovich, *Bylines in Despair: Herbert Hoover, the Great Depression and the U.S. News Media* (Westport, CT, 1994), 89.
7. Fausold, *The Presidency of Herbert Hoover*, 41; *Chicago Daily News*, April 14, 1929, CF, HHPL; Theodore Joslin, "Hoover's First Year," *World's Work*, March 1930, 6–65, 118–20, Reprint File, HHPL; Liebovich, *Bylines in Despair*, 84–85; Lawrence Richey to Arthur Brisbane, January 2, 1932, White Book 2, HHPL.
8. David Burner, "Before the Crash: Hoover's First 8 Months in the Presidency," in Fausold, *The Hoover Presidency*, 50–58.
9. Richard Norton Smith, *An Uncommon Man: The Triumph of Herbert Hoover* (New York, 1984), 108; Fausold, *The Presidency of Herbert Hoover*, 56; Richard Norton Smith, "Herbert Hoover and the Third Way," in Timothy Walch, ed., *Uncommon Americans: The Lives and Legacies of Herbert and Lou Henry Hoover* (Westport, CT, 2003), 256–57.
10. David Burner, *Herbert Hoover: A Public Life* (New York, 1979), 234; French Strother, "Four Years of Hoover: An Interpretation," *New York Times*, February 26, 1933, transcript, Reprint File, HHPL.
11. Burner, *Hoover: A Public Life*, 219; Joan Hoff, *Herbert Hoover: Forgotten Progressive* (Boston, 1975), 8, 159–60; *Christian Science Monitor*, March 11, 1925, CF, HHPL.

12. Theodore Joslin, *Hoover Off the Record* (New York, 1934), 73, 207–12.
13. Burner, *Hoover: A Public Life*, 212; James D. Calder, "Herbert Hoover's Contributions to the Administrative History of Crime Control Policy," transcript prepared for delivery at Southwest Political Science Association Convention, 1981, 1–4, Reprint File, HHPL.
14. *Chicago Daily News*, April 22, 1929, CF, HHPL; Robert P. Lamont to Charles L. McNary, April 18, 1929, Presidential Papers (hereafter cited as PP), Subject File (hereafter cited as SF), Box 127, Farm Matters, Export Debenture Plan, 1929, January–April; Jordan A. Schwarz, "Hoover and Congress: Politics, Personality and the Presidency," in Fausold, *The Hoover Presidency: A Reappraisal*, 96; David E. Hamilton, *From New Day to New Deal: American Farm Policies from Hoover to Roosevelt, 1928–1933* (Chapel Hill, NC, 1991), 27–37, 48–50.
15. Harris Gaylord Warren, *Herbert Hoover and the Great Depression* (New York, 1967), 169–71; Fausold, *The Presidency of Herbert Hoover*, 66; Hamilton, *From New Day to New Deal*, 13–15.
16. Victor L. Albeg, "Hoover, the Presidency in Transition," *Current History* (October 1960): 213–19, Reprint File, HHPL; *New York Times*, April 16, 1929, CF, HHPL.
17. Fausold, *The Presidency of Herbert Hoover*, 37, 53, 93–95; Edward Eyre Hunt, "The Fight on the Depression, First Phase," transcript, Box 335, HH Presidential Files, Stanford University (hereafter cited as HHPF), undated, 95–96.
18. Kennedy, *Freedom from Fear*, 49; Alfred Steinberg, *Herbert Hoover* (New York, 1967), 206–8.
19. Hoover, *Memoirs*, 2:315; Vaughn Davis Bornet, "Herbert Hoover's Planning for Unemployment and Old Age Coverage, 1921 to 1933," in Lawrence E. Gelfand, ed., *The Quest for Social Security: Papers on the Origins of the American Social Security System* (Washington, DC, 1982), 35–71, Reprint File, HHPL; Kennedy, *Freedom from Fear*, 90; Harold Wolfe, *Herbert Hoover: Public Servant and Leader of the Loyal Opposition* (New York, 1956), 159–61; Ray Lyman Wilbur and Arthur Mastick Hyde, *The Hoover Policies* (New York, 1937), 91–92; Burner, *Hoover: A Public Life*, 261.
20. Hoover, *Memoirs*, 2:316; Bornet, "Herbert Hoover's Planning for Unemployment," 38–47.
21. Fausold, *The Presidency of Herbert Hoover*, 63–65; Maury Klein, *Rainbow's End: The Crash of 1929* (New York, 2001), 28–30, 115.
22. Klein, *Rainbow's End*, 48–49, 175–93.
23. Ibid., 194; Wolfe, *Hoover: Public Servant*, 217; Hal Elliott Wert, *Hoover: The Fishing President: Portrait of the Private Man and His Life Outdoors* (Mechanicsburg, PA, 2005), 194; *New York Times*, October 26, 1929, CF, HHPL; *New York Evening Post*, October 29, 1929, CF, HHPL.
24. Kennedy, *Freedom from Fear*, 38–40; Louis W. Liebovich, *Bylines in Despair: Herbert Hoover, the Great Depression, and the U.S. News Media* (Westport, CT, 1994), 192; David Hinshaw, *Herbert Hoover: American Quaker* (New York, 1950), 154–55; Burner, *Hoover: A Public Life*, 249; James T. Shotwell, Carnegie Endowment for International Peace, Division of Economics and History, Annual Report for the Year 1932, 6, in Edward Eyre Hunt, "The Fight on the Depression, Second Phase," Box 336, HHPF.
25. Kennedy, *Freedom from Fear*, 40–41; *New York Times*, January 3, 1933, CF, HHPL; R. Gordon Hoxie, "Hoover and the Banking Crisis," Commentary on the Hoover Presidential Seminar, August 7, 1974, unpaginated, Reprint File, HHPL.
26. Kennedy, *Freedom from Fear*, 53–55; Fausold, *The Presidency of Herbert Hoover*, 75–76; Burner, *Hoover: A Public Life*, 252; *New York Times*, November 17, 1929, CF, HHPL; *New York Herald Tribune*, November 19, 1929, CF, HHPL; *New York Evening Post*, November 19, 1929, CF, HHPL; *New York World*, November 21, 1929, CF, HHPL; William Starr Myers and Walter H. Newton, *The Hoover Administration: A Documented Narrative* (New York, 1936), 28.
27. *New York Herald Tribune*, November 19, 1929, November 27, 1929, CF, HHPL; *New York Evening Post*, November 25, 1929, CF, HHPL; Craig Lloyd, *Aggressive Introvert: Herbert Hoover and Public Relations Management, 1912–1932* (Columbus, OH, 1972), 157.
28. John Spargo, *The Legend of Hoover Who "Did Nothing,"* 18–19, Box 226, March 21, 1936, HHPF; Houck, "Rhetoric as Currency," 151–81, 170.
29. Robert Sobel, *Herbert Hoover at the Onset of the Great Depression, 1929–1930* (Philadelphia, 1975), 62–63.

30. The *New York Times* and the *New York Herald Tribune* are quoted in Smith, *An Uncommon Man*, 117.

31. See Amity Schlaes, *The Forgotten Man: A New History of the Great Depression* (New York, 2007) and *Coolidge* (New York, 2013); and Murray N. Rothbard, *America's Great Depression* (Los Angeles, 1972).

32. Wolfe, *Hoover: Public Servant*, 148; *New York Herald-Tribune*, February 4, 1930, CF, HHPL; *New York Times*, April 27, 1930, CF, HHPL; unmarked clipping, "Chief Justice Hughes," SF, PP, Box 193, Judiciary—Supreme Court of the U.S., Appointment of Hughes as Chief Justice, HHPL; *Los Angeles Times*, February 15, 1930, SF, PP, Box 193, Judiciary—Supreme Court of the U.S., Appointment of Hughes as Chief Justice, HHPL.

33. Burner, *Hoover: A Public Life*, 235: Donald Lisio, *Hoover, Blacks, and Lily-Whites: A Study of Southern Strategies* (Chapel Hill, NC, 1985), 205–8; Fausold, *The Presidency of Herbert Hoover*, 88–90; Hinshaw, *Hoover: American Quaker*, 176–77; *New York Herald Tribune*, March 29, 1930, CF, HHPL.

34. Lisio, *Hoover, Blacks, and Lily-Whites*, 228–37; Wolfe, *Hoover: Public Servant*, 148.

35. *New York Times*, May 8, 1930, CF, HHPL.

36. *Minneapolis Journal*, May 8, 1930, CF, HHPL.

37. Editorial, *New York Herald Tribune*, May 5, 1930, CF, HHPL.

38. *New York Herald Tribune*, May 21, 1930, CF, HHPL; *New York Evening Post*, May 10, 1930, CF, HHPL; Fausold, *The Presidency of Herbert Hoover*, 93.

39. Theodore G. Joslin Diaries, Box 10, F 7, February 15, 1932, HHPL; James H. MacLafferty Diary, Box 1, February 16, 1932, 6, HHPL, copyright Stanford University; *New York Herald Tribune*, February 16, 1932, CF, HHPL; *New York Evening Post*, February 16, 1932, CF, HHPL; Lisio, *Hoover, Blacks, and Lily-Whites*, 246.

Chapter 9. Holding a Finger in the Dike

1. Edward Eyre Hunt, "The Fight on the Depression, First Phase," Box 335, 98–102, Herbert Hoover Presidential Files, Hoover Archives, Stanford University; Martin L. Fausold, *The Presidency of Herbert Hoover* (Lawrence, KS, 1985), 63–73; *New York World*, May 3, 1930, Clipping File (hereafter cited as CF), Herbert Hoover Presidential Library (hereafter cited as HHPL), West Branch, Iowa; *New York Herald Tribune*, May 4, 1930, CF, HHPL; Nancy Beck Young, *Lou Henry Hoover: Activist First Lady* (Lawrence, KS, 2004), 93–108.

2. Edward Eyre Hunt, "The Fight on the Depression, Second Phase," 1935, 57, Herbert Hoover Presidential Files, Hoover Archives, Stanford University; *New York Times*, April 2, 1930, October 12, 1930, CF, HHPL; *U.S. Daily News*, September 21, 1931, CF, HHPL; *New York World*, October 11, 1930, October 21, 1930, CF, HHPL; David Hinshaw, *Herbert Hoover: American Quaker* (New York, 1950), 65.

3. David M. Kennedy, *Freedom from Fear: The American People in Depression and War, 1929–1945* (New York, 1999), 88.

4. David Burner, *Herbert Hoover: A Public Life* (New York, 1979), 265–66; Ray Lyman Wilbur and Arthur Mastick Hyde, *The Hoover Policies* (New York, 1937), 371–75; William Starr Myers and Walter H. Newton, *The Hoover Administration: A Documented Narrative* (New York, 1936), 52–53; Hunt, "The Fight on the Depression, First Phase," Box 335, 103–4, Herbert Hoover Presidential Files, Hoover Archives, Stanford University; *New York Times*, January 28, 1931, CF, HHPL; *U.S. Daily News*, April 28, 1931, CF, HHPL; *New York Herald Tribune*, April 28, 1931, CF, HHPL; *New York Evening Post*, October 22, 1930, October 23, 1930, CF, HHPL.

5. *Chicago Daily News*, February 5, 1930, CF, HHPL.

6. E. Francis Brown, "Mr. Hoover Faces Nation's Problem," *Current History* (January 1932), 32: 575–83; Herbert Hoover, *Memoirs*, vol. 3, *The Great Depression, 1919–1941* (New York, 1952), 175.

7. Hoover, *Memoirs*, 3:175.

8. Ibid., 55.

9. Kennedy, *Freedom from Fear*, 47.

10. Burner, *Hoover: A Public Life*, 260.

11. Hoover, *Memoirs*, 3:56.

12. Presidential Papers (hereafter cited as PP), Subject Files (hereafter cited as SF), Box 55, Accomplishments of the Administration, 1930, January–June; *New York Herald Tribune*, December 17, 1929, CF, HHPL.

13. Theodore Joslin, *Hoover Off the Record* (Garden City, NY, 1934), 33.

14. Richard Norton Smith, "Herbert Hoover and the Third Way," in Timothy Walch, ed., *Uncommon Americans: The Lives and Legacies of Herbert and Lou Henry Hoover* (Westport, CT, 2003), 257–58; Albert U. Romasco, *The Poverty of Abundance: Hoover, the Nation, the Depression* (New York, 1963), 34, 55; Louis W. Liebovich, *Bylines in Despair: Herbert Hoover, the Great Depression and the U.S. News Media* (Westport, CT, 1994), 148–49; Kendrick A. Clements, *Hoover, Conservation, and Consumerism: Engineering the Good Life* (Lawrence, KS, 2000), 173–74; *U.S. Daily News*, October 9, 1931, CF, HHPL; *New York Times*, November 30, 1929, October 19, 1930, July 3, 1931, CF, HHPL; *Chicago Daily News*, February 22, 1929, CF, HHPL.

15. Richard Norton Smith, *An Uncommon Man: The Triumph of Herbert Hoover* (New York, 1984), 111; Myers and Newton, *The Hoover Administration*, 33; Maury Klein, *Rainbow's End: The Crash of 1929* (New York, 2001), 246.

16. Myers and Newton, *The Hoover Administration*, 32–33; *New York Times*, July 3, 1930, CF, HHPL; "The Tyrannies of Minorities in American Life," *Current History* (July 1931): 543–46.

17. Burner, *Hoover: A Public Life*, 262, 267; *New York Times*, June 19, 1930; *New York Herald Tribune*, April 3, 1930, CF, HHPL; Joslin, *Hoover Off the Record*, 75.

18. Wilbur and Hyde, *The Hoover Policies*, 197–200; James H. MacLafferty Diary, June 5, 1930, June 26, 1930, Box 1, HHPL, copyright Stanford University; *New York Times*, June 28, 1931, CF, HHPL; *New York Evening Post*, June 26, 1930, CF, HHPL; Editorial, *New York Herald Tribune*, June 26, 1930, June 29, 1930, CF, HHPL.

19. Clements, *Hoover, Conservation, and Consumerism*, 89; Kennedy, *Freedom from Fear*, 63; *New York Herald Tribune*, April 17, 1930, CF, HHPL.

20. Clements, *Hoover, Conservation, and Consumerism*, 180; David E. Hamilton, "Herbert Hoover and the Great Drought of 1930," *Journal of American History* 68, no. 4 (March 1982): 850–54; Robert Sobel, *Herbert Hoover at the Onset of the Great Depression, 1929–1930* (Philadelphia, 1975), 99–100.

21. Wilbur and Hyde, *The Hoover Policies*, 399–401; Hinshaw, *Hoover: American Quaker*, 249; John Spargo, *The Legend of Hoover Who "Did Nothing,"* transcript, Box 226, March 21, 1936, 20–25, Herbert Hoover Presidential Files, Hoover Archives, Stanford University; Hunt, "The Fight on the Depression, First Phase," Box 335, 98–99, Herbert Hoover Presidential Files, Hoover Archives, Stanford University.

22. Myers and Newton, *The Hoover Administration*, 55–56; MacLafferty Diary, September 16, 1930, September 19, 1930, Box 1, HHPL, copyright Stanford University; *New York Times*, September 22, 1929, August 17, 1930, CF, HHPL; *New York Herald Tribune*, September 3, 1930, October 14, 1930, November 7, 1930, CF, HHPL; *New York Evening Post*, October 10, 1930, CF, HHPL; *New York World*, July 14, 1930, CF, HHPL.

23. Kennedy, *Freedom from Fear*, 59–61; Louis W. Liebovich, *Bylines in Despair: Herbert Hoover, the Great Depression, and the U.S. News Media* (Westport, CT, 1994), 124–25; *New York Evening Post*, November 6, 1930, CF, HHPL; *New York Times*, December 5, 1930, Editorial, November 5, 1930, CF, HHPL.

24. Fausold, *The Presidency of Herbert Hoover*, 132–35; Spargo, *The Legend of Hoover Who "Did Nothing"*; *New York Evening Post*, November 8, 1930, November 14, 1930, CF, HHPL; *New York Times*, November 8, 1930, CF, HHPL.

25. Message to Congress, December 2, 1930, in *New York Times*, December 3, 1930, in Sobel, *Herbert Hoover at the Onset of the Great Depression*, 95–98.

26. Editorial, *Boston Transcript*, March 7, 1931, CF, HHPL.

27. Herbert Hoover, *The Memoirs of Herbert Hoover*, vol. 2, *The Cabinet and the Presidency, 1920–1933* (New York, 1952), 340–44; Burner, *Hoover: A Public Life*, 290–91; Fausold, *The Presidency of Herbert Hoover*, 172–73; Robert H. Ferrell, *American Diplomacy in the Great Depression: Hoover-Stimson Foreign Policy, 1929–1933* (New Haven, CT, 1957), 68–86; *New York Times*, October 6, 1929, CF, HHPL; Darwin Lambert, "Herbert Hoover's Hideaway," bulletin no. 4, Shenandoah National Historical Society, 1971, 77–81.

28. Eugene Lyons, *Herbert Hoover: A Biography* (Garden City, NY, 1964), 256–57, 269–73; Myers and Newton, *The Hoover Administration*, 71–73; Kennedy, *Freedom from Fear*, 70–72; Ferrell, *American Diplomacy in the Great Depression*, 107–12.

29. Henry L. Stimson and McGeorge Bundy, *On Active Service in Peace and War* (New York, 1948), 201–11; *U.S. Daily News*, June 23, 1931, CF, HHPL; *New York Evening Post*, December 15, 1931, December 23, 1931, CF, HHPL; *New York Herald Tribune*, December 20, 1931, CF, HHPL.

30. *New York Times*, July 24, 1931, March 24, 1932, CF, HHPL; Wilbur and Hyde, *The Hoover Policies*, 411–13; Ferrell, *American Diplomacy in the Great Depression*, 116–19.

31. *New York Evening Post*, November 7, 1931, November 19, 1931, Editorial, July 21, 1932, CF, HHPL; *New York Times*, November 18, 1931, CF, HHPL; *New York Herald Tribune*, November 18, 1931, CF, HHPL.

32. Ferrell, *American Diplomacy in the Great Depression*, 198–204; Fausold, *The Presidency of Herbert Hoover*, 189; *New York Times*, October 24, 1931, October 25, 1931, October 26, 1931, October 27, 1931, CF, HHPL; *New York Evening Post*, October 26, 1931, October 27, 1931, CF, HHPL; *New York Herald Tribune*, October 26, 1931, Editorial, October 27, 1931, CF, HHPL.

33. Richard Nelson Current, *Secretary Stimson: A Study in Statecraft* (Rutgers, NJ, 1954), 67–70; Ferrell, *American Diplomacy in the Great Depression*, 123–26; Burner, *Hoover: A Public Life*, 293–94.

34. Current, *Secretary Stimson*, 74–90; Wilbur and Hyde, *The Hoover Policies*, 599–603; William Starr Myers, *The Foreign Policies of Herbert Hoover* (New York, 1940), 154–57.

35. Harold Wolfe, *Herbert Hoover: Public Servant and Leader of the Loyal Opposition* (New York, 1956), 197–202; Hoover, *Memoirs*, 2:367–73; Stimson and Bundy, *On Active Service in Peace and War*, 239–44; Joslin, *Hoover Off the Record*, 176–77; Burner, *Hoover: A Public Life*, 295–97.

Chapter 10. Fighting the Depression

1. E. Francis Bacon, "Mr. Hoover Faces Nation's Problems," *Current History* (January 1932): 575–83; William Starr Myers and Walter H. Newton, *The Hoover Administration: A Documented Narrative* (New York, 1936), 145–46; Mark Sullivan, "Congress Strife Rouses Third Party Initiatives," *Washington Sunday Times*, January 18, 1931, CF, HHPL.

2. *New York Times*, December 9, 1931, CF, HHPL.

3. Martin L. Fausold, *The Presidency of Herbert Hoover* (Lawrence, KS, 1985), 155–56.

4. *U.S. Daily News*, December 9, 1931, CF, HHPL.

5. Harris Gaylord Warren, *Herbert Hoover and the Great Depression* (New York, 1967), 148–57; *New York Herald Tribune*, December 17, 1931, CF, HHPL.

6. James Stuart Olson, *Herbert Hoover and the Reconstruction Finance Corporation, 1931–1933* (Ames, IA, 1977), 34–38; Fausold, *The Presidency of Herbert Hoover*, 154–55: David Burner, *Herbert Hoover: A Public Life* (New York, 1979), 272–73; Theodore Joslin Diaries, Box 10, F 4, January 22, 1932, HHPL; Theodore Joslin, *Hoover Off the Record* (New York, 1971), 165–66; *New York Times*, January 22, 1932, CF, HHPL; Editorial, *New York Times*, January 22, 1932, CF, HHPL; *New York Evening Post*, January 22, 1932, CF, HHPL.

7. Albert U. Romasco, *The Poverty of Abundance: Hoover, the Nation, the Depression* (New York, 1964), 190–91; Ray Lyman Wilbur and Arthur Mastick Hyde, *The Hoover Policies* (New York, 1937), 423–24.

8. David M. Kennedy, *Freedom from Fear: The American People in Depression and War, 1929–1945* (New York, 1999), 75–77; Burner, *Hoover: A Public Life,* 270.

9. James H. MacLafferty Diary, Box 1, February 19, 1932, 1–2, HHPL, copyright Stanford University; Theodore G. Joslin Diaries, Box 10, F 7, February 15, 1932, HHPL; *New York Times,* January 29, 1932, February 12, 1932, CF, HHPL; *New York Herald Tribune,* February 11, 1932, Editorial, February 17, 1932, February 25, 1932, CF, HHPL.

10. *New York Times,* February 17, 1932, CF, HHPL.

11. The Garner quotes are from Herbert Hoover, *The Memoirs of Herbert Hoover,* vol. 3, *The Great Depression, 1929–1941* (New York, 1952), 101; Kennedy, *Freedom from Fear,* 61–64; *New York Times,* December 10, 1931, CF, HHPL.

12. Myers and Newton, *The Hoover Administration,* 186–87, 197, 223; Wilbur and Hyde, *The Hoover Policies,* 450–56; Murray K. Rothbard in Joseph Huthmacher and Warren I. Susman, eds., *Herbert Hoover and the Crisis of American Capitalism* (Cambridge, MA, 1973), 47; Joslin Diaries, Box 10, F 7, March 26, 1932, HHPL; Romasco, *The Poverty of Abundance,* 222; *Chicago Daily News,* March 25, 1932, June 30, 1932, CF, HHPL; *New York Times,* June 9, 1932, June 30, 1932, CF, HHPL; Taylor-Gates Collection, B-2, A-IV-2, Budget, 1–2, PP, HHPL.

13. Fausold, *The Presidency of Herbert Hoover,* 164–65; *New York Herald Tribune,* January 30, 1932, CF, HHPL; *New York Times,* February 17, 1932, CF, HHPL.

14. *New York Herald Tribune,* June 25, 1932, CF, HHPL.

15. Hoover, *Memoirs,* 3:109–10; *New York Times,* May 29, 1932, CF, HHPL.

16. Message to House of Representatives, PP, SF, Box 82, 1–4, Bills-Relief, Garner-Wagner-Rainey bills, H.R. 12353, 12445; 1932, Statements and Press Releases, HHPL; Myers and Newton, *The Hoover Administration,* 225–29; James H. MacLafferty Diary, Box 1, HHPL, copyright Stanford University, July 11, 1932, July 12, 1932.

17. Olson, *Herbert Hoover and the Reconstruction Finance Corporation,* 67–73, 89; Hoover, *Memoirs,* 3:153–54; Jordan A. Schwarz, *The Interregnum of Despair: Hoover, Congress, and the Depression* (Urbana, IL, 1979), 164.

18. Myers and Newton, *The Hoover Administration,* 235; Hoover, *Memoirs,* 3:160–63; *New York Times,* July 17, 1932, CF, HHPL; *New York Herald Tribune,* August 2, 1932, CF, HHPL; James H. MacLafferty Diary, Box 1, July 11, 1932, July 12, 1932, HHPL, copyright Stanford University.

19. Romasco, *The Poverty of Abundance,* 102–3.

20. Ibid., 97–102; Robert Sobel, *Herbert Hoover at the Onset of the Great Depression, 1929–1930* (Philadelphia, 1975), 63–64; Burner, *Hoover: A Public Life,* 238–39; Harold Wolfe, *Herbert Hoover: Public Servant and Leader of the Loyal Opposition* (New York, 1956), 231–33.

21. Joslin, *Hoover Off the Record,* 64–67, 262–66; Wolfe, *Hoover: Public Servant,* 250–51.

22. Edward Eyre Hunt, "The Fight on the Depression, Second Phase," Box 336, Herbert Hoover Presidential Files, Stanford University, 66–71; Wilbur and Hyde, *The Hoover Policies,* 203–5; Liebovich, *Bylines in Despair,* 155–56; *Washington Evening Star,* August 4, 1932, CF, HHPL; Interview with General Douglas MacArthur by the Press at 11 p.m., July 28, 1932, PPP, SF 214, MacArthur, General Douglas, Corres., 1942–46, HHPL.

23. Alfred Steinberg, *Herbert Hoover* (New York, 1967), 232–33.

Chapter 11. Democracy Is a Harsh Employer

1. *Chicago Tribune,* February 23, 1932, Clipping File (hereafter cited as CF), Herbert Hoover Presidential Library (hereafter cited as HHPL).

2. *New York Herald Tribune,* August 12, 1932, CF, HHPL.

3. *Chicago Daily News,* August 13, 1932, CF, HHPL.

4. *New York Herald Tribune,* August 13, 1932, CF, HHPL.

5. Roy V. Peel and Thomas C. Donnally, *The 1932 Campaign: An Analysis* (New York, 1935), 164–65.

6. Theodore Joslin, List of Comments, Observations, January 1931–33, 2, HHPL.

7. George R. Nutter to Hoover, October 4, 1932, Presidential Papers (hereafter cited as PP), Subject File (hereafter cited as SF), Box 352, Republican National Committee, Correspondence—Speech Suggestions, 1932, October, HHPL.

8. *New York Herald Tribune*, August 31, 1932, CF, HHPL; Theodore G. Joslin Diaries, Box 10, F7, October 18, 1932, HHPL; *Chicago Tribune*, August 12, 1932, CF, HHPL; David Burner, *Herbert Hoover: A Public Life* (New York, 1979), 307–9; Louis W. Liebovich, *Bylines in Despair: Herbert Hoover, the Great Depression, and the U.S. News Media* (Westport, CT, 1994), 193–94.

9. *New York Herald Tribune*, September 14, 1932, CF, HHPL; Theodore Joslin Diaries, Box 10, F7, September 7, 1932, September 11, 1932, HHPL.

10. Joslin Diaries, Box 10, F 7, October 3, 1932, October 5, 1932, HHPL.

11. Joslin Diaries, Box 10, F 7, October 5, 1932, October 7, 1932, HHPL; Theodore Joslin, *Hoover Off the Record* (Garden City, NY, 1934), 299–313; Harold Wolfe, *Herbert Hoover: Public Servant and Leader of the Loyal Opposition* (New York, 1956), 289–93; Roger Daniels, *Franklin D. Roosevelt: Road to the New Deal, 1882–1939* (Urbana, IL, 2015), 108.

12. Alfred Steinberg, *Herbert Hoover* (New York, 1967), 229.

13. John Spargo, *The Legend of Hoover Who "Did Nothing,"* March 21, 1936, Herbert Hoover Presidential Files, Hoover Archives, Stanford University.

14. Wolfe, *Hoover: Public Servant*, 293–94.

15. Steinberg, *Herbert Hoover*, 234; Richard Norton Smith, *An Uncommon Man: The Triumph of Herbert Hoover* (New York, 1984), 28.

16. Joslin, *Hoover Off the Record*, 295–96.

17. *New York Herald Tribune*, October 1, 1932, CF, HHPL.

18. *New York Times*, September 30, 1932, CF, HHPL.

19. Ibid.; *New York Herald Tribune*, October 1, 1932, October 12, 1932, October 14, 1932, October 19, 1932, CF, HHPL.

20. Theodore Joslin Diaries, Box 10, F 7, October 15, 1932, HHPL; *New York Times*, October 12, 1932, October 15, 1932, CF, HHPL; *New York Herald Tribune*, October 16, 1932, October 17, 1932; Wilton Eckley, *Herbert Hoover* (Boston, 1980), 72.

21. Joslin, *Hoover Off the Record*, 322.

22. Timothy Walch and Dwight M. Miller, eds., *Herbert Hoover and Franklin D. Roosevelt* (Westport, CT, 1998), 56–61.

23. *New York Herald Tribune*, October 27, 1932, CF, HHPL; Editorial, *Los Angeles Times*, October 31, 1932, CF, HHPL.

24. *New York Times*, November 1, 1932, CF, HHPL; *New York Herald Tribune*, November 1, 1932, CF, HHPL.

25. Wolfe, *Hoover: Public Servant*, 394–97; Joslin Diaries, Box 10, F 7, October 31, 1932, November 1, 1932, HHPL; *New York Herald Tribune*, November 1, 1932, Editorial, November 1, 1932, CF, HHPL.

26. Joslin, *Hoover Off the Record*, 324–25.

27. Joslin Diaries, Box 10, F 7, November 5, 1932, HHPL.

28. Walch and Miller, *Hoover and Roosevelt*, 64.

29. Eckley, *Herbert Hoover*, 73.

30. Burner, *Hoover: A Public Life*, 316–17.

31. Gary Dean Best, *The Life of Herbert Hoover: Keeper of the Torch, 1933–1964* (New York, 2013), 4–5.

32. Kennedy, *Freedom from Fear*, 104–8; Wolfe, *Hoover: Public Servant*, 316–18; Walch and Miller, *Hoover and Roosevelt*, xxi–xvii.

33. Best, *Hoover: Keeper of the Torch*, 2; Olson, *Herbert Hoover and the Reconstruction Finance Corporation, 1931–1933*, 99–100; Lawrence Sullivan, *Prelude to Panic: The Story of the Bank Holiday of 1932–1933* (Washington, DC, 1936), 47–54; Mark Sullivan, "Recent Runs on Banks Traced to Publicity of R.F.C. Loans," *New York Herald Tribune*, February 7, 1933, CF, HHPL; Daniels, *Roosevelt: Road to the New Deal*, 125.

34. Sullivan, *Prelude to Panic*, 23.

35. Joslin, *Hoover Off the Record*, 327; Theodore Joslin to Hoover, February 25, 1933, February 26, 1933, Banking Crisis, Presidential Log and Documents, Box 36, 2, HHPL.

36. Norman Beasley, *Politics Has No Morals* (New York, 1949), 100–101, excerpted in White Book 2, HHPL.

Chapter 12. Challenging the New Deal

1. Theodore J. Hoover, "Memoranda, Being a Statement of an Engineer," 1939, Acct. 585, Box 1, 277–80, Herbert Hoover Presidential Library (hereafter cited as HHPL).

2. Gary Dean Best, *The Life of Herbert Hoover: Keeper of the Torch, 1933–1964* (New York, 2013), 3.

3. Richard Norton Smith, *An Uncommon Man: The Triumph of Herbert Hoover* (New York, 1984), 169–71; Herbert Hoover, *The Crusade Years, 1933–1955: Herbert Hoover's Lost Memoir of the New Deal Era and Its Aftermath*, ed., with an introduction by George H. Nash (Stanford, CA, 2013), 467–68.

4. Quote from Herbert Hoover, *The Memoirs of Herbert Hoover*, vol. 3, *The Great Depression, 1919–1941* (New York, 1952), 345–46. Also see David Burner, *Herbert Hoover: A Public Life* (New York, 1979), 327; Harold Wolfe, *Herbert Hoover: Public Servant and Leader of the Loyal Opposition* (New York, 1956), 359.

5. Hoover, *The Crusade Years*, 9, 468–69; Alfred Steinberg, *Herbert Hoover* (New York, 1967), 235–37; Hoover to Stimson, July 9, 1934, quoted in Timothy Walch and Dwight M. Miller, eds., *Herbert Hoover and Franklin D. Roosevelt* (Westport, CT, 1998), 158.

6. Smith, *An Uncommon Man*, 172–74; Wolfe, *Hoover: Public Servant*, 360–61; David Hinshaw, *Herbert Hoover: American Quaker* (New York, 1950), 301–4; Hal Elliott Wert, *Hoover: The Fishing President: Portrait of the Private Man and His Life Outdoors* (Mechanicsburg, PA, 2005), 230–35, 240–41, 286–87.

7. Hoover, *The Crusade Years*, xvii–xix; Wilton Eckley, *Herbert Hoover* (Boston, 1980), 79–83; Eugene Lyons, *Herbert Hoover: A Biography* (Garden City, NY, 1964), 342.

8. Hoover, *Memoirs*, 3:447.

9. Hoover, *The Crusade Years*, xx–xxii. Quote on xx. Also see Eckley, *Herbert Hoover*, 88–89; Wert, *Hoover: The Fishing President*, 233; and Joan Hoff, *Herbert Hoover: Forgotten Progressive* (Boston, 1975), 213.

10. Hoover to William R. Castle, September 14, 1939, Neutrality and Embargo Bill, 1–2, Post-Presidential Papers (cited hereafter as PPP), Neutrality Legislation, Herbert Hoover Presidential Library; Hoover to John O'Laughlin, September 24, 1939, in Walch and Miller, *Hoover and Roosevelt*, 175–76.

11. *New York Times*, March 24, 1940, White Book 1, HHPL.

12. The best source for the overview of Hoover's interpretation of the Depression and his own and Roosevelt's policies is Hoover, *Memoirs*, vol. 3.

13. See the discussion in Hoff, *Hoover: Forgotten Progressive*, 214. The bulk of the paragraph constitutes ruminations of the author and of Hoover based on postwar developments.

14. Gary Dean Best, *Herbert Hoover: The Postpresidential Years, 1933–1964*, vol. 1, *1933–1945* (Stanford, CA, 1983), xiii–xiv.

15. Ibid., 1:xiv–xv.

16. Ibid., 1:xvi.

17. Ibid., 1:1–4.

18. Ibid., 1:5–9; Best, *Hoover: Keeper of the Torch*, 8–11; Eckley, *Herbert Hoover*, 87; Walch and Miller, *Hoover and Roosevelt*, 157–58.

19. Best, *Hoover: The Postpresidential Years*, 1:9–11; Burner, *Hoover: A Public Life*, 329.

20. Hoover, *Memoirs*, 3:455; Best, *Hoover: Keeper of the Torch*, 28; Burner, *Hoover: A Public Life*, 330.

21. Best, *Hoover: The Postpresidential Years*, 1:9–15; Ray Lyman Wilbur and Arthur Mastick Hyde, *The Hoover Policies* (New York, 1937), 28–31.

22. Best, *Hoover: The Postpresidential Years*, 1:1, 10–17; Burner, *Hoover: A Public Life*, 328–29.

23. Best, *Hoover: The Postpresidential Years*, 1:27.

24. Best, *Hoover: Keeper of the Torch*, 28–31; Best, *Hoover: The Postpresidential Years*, 1:29–31; Hinshaw, *Hoover: American Quaker*, 299–301.

25. Lyons, *Hoover: A Biography*, 348; Best, *Hoover: The Postpresidential Years*, 1:33–37, 51.

26. Wilbur and Hyde, *The Hoover Policies*, 628–32; Hoover, *Memoirs*, 3:388–89; Hoff, *Hoover: Forgotten Progressive*, 211–14.

27. Best, *Hoover: The Postpresidential Years*, 1:42–43, 53.

28. Ibid., 1:41.

29. Best, *Hoover: Keeper of the Torch*, 25, 36–43; Best, *Hoover: The Postpresidential Years*, 1:44–46, 52–55. The *Review of Reviews* is quoted in Clair Everett Nelsen, "The Image of Herbert Hoover as Reflected in the American Press" (PhD diss., Stanford University, 1956).

30. Best, *Hoover: The Postpresidential Years*, 1:48–50, 54; Best, *Hoover: Keeper of the Torch*, 44–47; Wolfe, *Hoover: Public Servant*, 366–67.

31. Steinberg, *Herbert Hoover*, 237.

32. Ibid., 236–37; Best, *Hoover: Keeper of the Torch*, 54–55; Smith, *An Uncommon Man*, 229–30, 235–38; Hoover, *The Crusade Years*, 94–99, 102–9; Best, *Hoover: The Postpresidential Years*, 1:74, 75, 76.

33. Hoover, *The Crusade Years*, 161–66; Best, *Hoover: Keeper of the Torch*, 58–60, 61–74; Smith, *An Uncommon Man*, 245–49; press release, n.d., [1938] Post-Presidential Papers, Box 95, Campaign 1938, Clippings and Printed Matter; Hoover to John Hamilton, April 23, 1937, PPP, Box 270, Republican Mid-Term Conference, Correspondence, 1937–39.

34. Hoover Meetings with Republicans, 1937, PPP, Box 270, Republican Mid-Term Conference, HHPL; Hoover Calendar, 1937; Meetings and Interviews, Hoover Calendar on Mid-Term Conference, PPP, Box 270, HHPL; Smith, *An Uncommon Man*, 245, 249.

35. Hoover, *Memoirs*, 3:370–74; Lyons, *Hoover: A Biography*, 355; Smith, *An Uncommon Man*, 241–43.

36. Best, *Hoover: The Postpresidential Years*, 1:99; Best, *Hoover: Keeper of the Torch*, 75–76, 88.

37. Best, *Hoover: The Postpresidential Years*, 1:104–5.

38. Ibid., 1:107–8.

39. Ibid., 1:109.

40. Hoover, *The Crusade Years*, 197; Best, *Hoover: The Postpresidential Years*, 1:111–15.

Chapter 13. Politics and Diplomacy Before the Second Great War

1. Richard Norton Smith, *An Uncommon Man: The Triumph of Herbert Hoover* (New York, 1984), 251–57; David Burner, *Herbert Hoover: A Public Life* (New York, 1979), 332.

2. Smith, *An Uncommon Man*, 252–53; Herbert Hoover, *The Crusade Years, 1933–1955*, ed. George H. Nash (Stanford, CA, 2013), 112, 113, 127.

3. Smith, *An Uncommon Man*, 253–54; Gary Dean Best, *The Life of Herbert Hoover: Keeper of the Torch, 1933–1964* (New York, 2013), 80; Eugene Lyons, *Herbert Hoover: A Biography* (Garden City, NY, 1964), 357; Louis P. Lochner, *Herbert Hoover and Germany* (New York, 1960), 134–36.

4. Best, *Hoover: Keeper of the Torch*, 80–81; Hoover, *The Crusade Years*, 125–26; Gary Dean Best, *Herbert Hoover: The Postpresidential Years, 1933–1964*, vol. 2, *1946–1964* (Stanford, CA, 1983), 103; Lochner, *Herbert Hoover and Germany*, 138.

5. Hoover, *The Crusade Years*, 141–45.

6. Ibid., 136–39.

7. Smith, *An Uncommon Man*, 258–59.

8. Ibid., 259; Hoover, *The Crusade Years*, 152; Lochner, *Herbert Hoover and Germany*, 145.

9. Hoover, *The Crusade Years*, 149, 152.

10. Herbert Hoover, *Freedom Betrayed: Herbert Hoover's Secret History of the Second World War and Its Aftermath*, ed. George H. Nash (Stanford, CA, 2011), xviii–xx.

11. Hoover, *Freedom Betrayed*, xxxii–xxxiii; Best, *Hoover: Keeper of the Torch*, 112–13.

12. Best, *Hoover: Keeper of the Torch*, 159–66; Hoover to William R. Castle, March 1, 1941, quoted in Timothy Walch and Dwight M. Miller, eds., *Herbert Hoover and Franklin D. Roosevelt* (Westport, CT, 1998), 184–85; Smith, *An Uncommon Man*, 295–98.

13. Sketch of Herbert Hoover composed for the Associated Press, 1945, Biographical Sketches of Hoover, Post-Presidential Papers (hereafter cited as PPP), Box 39, 1940–49, 7, Herbert Hoover Presidential Library (hereafter cited as HHPL).

14. Herbert Hoover, "America and the World Crisis," New York City, October 26, 1938, in Hoover, *America's Way Forward* (New York, 1938), PPP, Box 95, Campaign of 1938, Clippings and Printed Matter, 2; Best, *Hoover: Keeper of the Torch*, 100.

15. Timothy Walch and Dwight M. Miller, eds., *Herbert Hoover and Franklin D. Roosevelt* (Westport, CT, 1998), 166–67.

16. Best, *Hoover: Keeper of the Torch*, 150. A good collection of Hoover's noninterventionist addresses and articles prior to Pearl Harbor can be found in Sketch of Herbert Hoover composed for the Associated Press, Biographical Sketches of Hoover, PPP, Box 39, 1940–49, esp. 6–7, HHPL. The best example of Hoover's interpretation of why the United States went to war in Europe and in Asia can be found in Hoover, *Freedom Betrayed*, sec. 10, "The Road to War," 247–310. See also "A Step-by-Step History of Poland," 585–607, in Hoover, *Freedom Betrayed*. The section on Poland includes some redundancy.

17. Gary Dean Best, "Herbert Hoover and the Great Debates in Foreign Policy, 1940–1941 and 1950–1951," in *Understanding Herbert Hoover: Ten Perspectives*, ed. Lee Nash (Stanford, CA, 1987), 113.

18. Smith, *An Uncommon Man*, 274.

19. Ibid., 274–75; Walch and Miller, *Hoover and Roosevelt*, 171–79; Hal Elliott Wert, *Hoover: The Fishing President: Portrait of the Private Man and His Life Outdoors* (Mechanicsburg, PA, 2005), 268–69.

20. Smith, *An Uncommon Man*, 277–78; Burner, *Hoover: A Public Life*, 333; Lyons, *Hoover: A Biography*, 359–60; Mayer, *Lou Henry Hoover*, 319–20; Walch and Miller, *Hoover and Roosevelt*, 181–83.

21. Smith, *An Uncommon Man*, 279.

22. Hoover, *Freedom Betrayed*, xlvii.

23. Best, *Hoover: Keeper of the Torch*, 125.

24. Ibid., 126.

25. Ibid., 103–4; Harold Wolfe, *Herbert Hoover: Public Servant and Leader of the Loyal Opposition* (New York, 1956), 381–83; Walch and Miller, *Hoover and Roosevelt*, 181.

26. Ibid., 114–15; Wert, *Hoover: The Fishing President*, 267.

27. Ibid., 126.

28. Ibid., 104–6.

29. Hoover, *Freedom Betrayed*, xliii–xliv; Wolfe, *Hoover: Public Servant*, 385–86.

30. Smith, *An Uncommon Man*, 288.

31. Best, *Hoover: The Postpresidential Years*, 2:167–70, 172–73; Best, *Hoover: Keeper of the Torch*, 150.

32. Smith, *An Uncommon Man*, 289.

33. Ibid., 290.

34. Hoover, *The Crusade Years*, 489–91.

35. Hoover, *Freedom Betrayed*, xliv–xlvi.

36. Smith, *An Uncommon Man*, 290.

37. Hoover, *The Crusade Years*, 445–47, 454.

38. Smith, *An Uncommon Man*, 306.

39. Sketch of Herbert Hoover composed for the Associated Press, 1945, 7, Biographical Sketches of Hoover, PPP, Box 39, 1940–49, HHPL.

Chapter 14. The Maelstrom of War

1. Herbert Hoover, *Freedom Betrayed: Herbert Hoover's Secret History of the Second World War and Its Aftermath*, ed. George H. Nash (Stanford, CA, 2011), lvi.
2. Ibid., lvii.
3. Richard Norton Smith, *An Uncommon Man: The Triumph of Herbert Hoover* (New York, 1984), 318.
4. Ibid., 317–19; Hoover, *Freedom Betrayed*, lvii, lix. Hoover had also been considered an internationalist during his own presidency, viewed by his own party as excessively liberal because of his support for the League of Nations and his backing of the regulation of American business. Many former Progressives, in fact, became opponents of the New Deal.
5. Gary Dean Best, *Herbert Hoover: The Postpresidential Years*, vol. 1, *1933–1945* (Stanford, CA, 1983), 207, 210, 221; Gary Dean Best, *The Life of Herbert Hoover, 1933–1964: Keeper of the Torch* (New York, 2013), 236–38.
6. Activities in World War II, Biographical Sketches of Hoover, Box 34, 1931–39, 2, Herbert Hoover Presidential Library (cited hereafter as HHPL).
7. Best, *Hoover: Keeper of the Torch*, 234–35.
8. Sonja Schoeph Wentling and Rafael Medoff, *Herbert Hoover and the Jews* (Washington, DC, 2005), 115–18.
9. Ibid., 135, 137, 144–45.
10. Best, *Herbert Hoover: The Postpresidential Years*, vol. 1; Smith, *An Uncommon Man*, 310–11.
11. Best, *Hoover: The Postpresidential Years*, 1:207.
12. Best, *Hoover: Keeper of the Torch*, 193–209.
13. Best, *Hoover: The Postpresidential Years*, 1:213.
14. Smith, *An Uncommon Man*, 316; Best, *Hoover: The Postpresidential Years*, 1:213–16.
15. Smith, *An Uncommon Man*, 212.
16. Best, *Hoover: Keeper of the Torch*, 213, 246.
17. Ibid., 244–48; Smith, *An Uncommon Man*, 332–33; PPP, Box 39, 1940–49, Biographical Sketches of Hoover, 7–8, HHPL.
18. Smith, *An Uncommon Man*, 338; Best, *Hoover: The Postpresidential Years*, 1:260; Best, *Hoover: Keeper of the Torch*, 249–50.
19. Smith, *An Uncommon Man*, 332–33.
20. Best, *Hoover: The Postpresidential Years*, 1:247–50.
21. Nancy Beck Young, *Lou Henry Hoover: Activist First Lady* (Lawrence, KS, 2004), 293.
22. Ibid., 110, 170–83; David Burner, *Herbert Hoover: A Public Life* (New York, 1979), 334.
23. Best, *Hoover: Keeper of the Torch*, 241–42; Sketch of Hoover, PPP, Box 39, Biographical Sketches of Hoover, 1940–49, 8, HHPL; Dale Mayer, *Lou Henry Hoover: A Prototype for First Ladies* (New York, 2004), 330–31.
24. Alfred Steinberg, *Herbert Hoover* (New York, 1967), 243.
25. Young, *Lou Henry Hoover*, 186; Smith, *An Uncommon Man*, 329.
26. Smith, *An Uncommon Man*, 329–30; Helen B. Pryor, *Lou Henry Hoover: Gallant First Lady* (New York, 1969), 251.
27. Smith, *An Uncommon Man*, 20.
28. Best, *Hoover: The Postpresidential Years*, 1:262–63.
29. Best, *Hoover: Keeper of the Torch*, 252–53.
30. Ibid., 256.
31. Smith, *An Uncommon Man*, 349–50; Best, *Hoover: Keeper of the Torch*, 269–70; Clair Everett Nelsen, "The Image of Herbert Hoover as Reflected in the American Press" (PhD diss., Stanford University, 1956), 185–87.
32. Biographical Sketches of Hoover, 1931–39, Box 34, 2, HHPL; Best, *Hoover: Keeper of the Torch*, 256–58.
33. Best, *Hoover: Keeper of the Torch*, 269–70.

34. Boys Clubs of America Annual Report, 1945, Post-Presidential Papers (hereafter cited as PPP), Box 75, Boys Clubs of America (BCA) Correspondence, Armstrong, David, 1945, June–July, n.d., June; Elmer R. Murphy to Hoover, November 29, 1937, PPP, Box 71, BCA, Corres.; Hoover to Edwin S. Webster, February 8, 1943, PPP, Box 72, BCA, Corres., General, 1943; Hoover to Paul Mellon, May 4, 1943; D. D. Shepard to Hoover, May 18, 1943, PPP, Box 77, BCA, Corres., Hall, William E., May 1943–December 1944; A Brief Report of the Executive Director to the Board of Directors, Corres., Armstrong, David, n.d. May 1942–December 1942.

Chapter 15. The Truman Years

1. Richard Norton Smith, *An Uncommon Man: The Triumph of Herbert Hoover* (New York, 1984), 341.
2. Ibid.
3. Gary Dean Best, *Herbert Hoover: The Postpresidential Years*, vol. 1, *1933–1945* (Stanford, CA, 1983), 269–71; Herbert Hoover, *Freedom Betrayed: Herbert Hoover's Secret History of the Second World War and Its Aftermath*, ed. George H. Nash (Stanford, CA, 2011), 535–38; Gary Dean Best, *The Life of Herbert Hoover: Keeper of the Torch, 1933–1964* (Stanford, CA, 2013), 262–65.
4. Best, *Hoover: The Postpresidential Years*, 1:269–70.
5. Best, *Hoover: Keeper of the Torch*, 270; Joan Hoff, *Herbert Hoover: Forgotten Progressive* (Boston, 1975), 255; David Burner, *Herbert Hoover: A Public Life* (New York, 1979), 335.
6. Best, *Hoover: Keeper of the Torch*, 267–68.
7. Smith, *An Uncommon Man*, 341; Timothy Walch and Dwight M. Miller, eds., *Herbert Hoover and Harry S. Truman: A Documentary History* (Worland, WY, 1992), 4–5; Steinberg, *Herbert Hoover*, 240; Sketch of Hoover, Post-Presidential Papers (hereafter cited as PPP), Box 39, Biographical Sketches of Hoover, 1940–49, Herbert Hoover Presidential Library (cited hereafter as HHPL).
8. Burner, *Hoover: A Public Life*, 335; Walch and Miller, *Hoover and Truman*, 44–47.
9. Best, *Hoover: Keeper of the Torch*, 281–85; Smith, *An Uncommon Man*, 351; Steinberg, *Herbert Hoover*, 240–41; Walch and Miller, *Hoover and Truman*, 10–13; Clair Everett Nelsen, "The Image of Herbert Hoover as Reflected in the American Press" (PhD diss., Stanford University, 1956), 190–91; David Hinshaw, *Herbert Hoover: American Quaker* (New York, 1950), 330–33.
10. Best, *Hoover: Keeper of the Torch*, 285.
11. Ibid., 285–86.
12. Ibid., 286–87.
13. Ibid., 290; Gary Dean Best, *Herbert Hoover: The Postpresidential Years, 1933–1964*, vol. 2 (Stanford, CA, 1983), 291–93; Eugene Lyons, *Herbert Hoover: A Biography* (New York, 1964), 388–90.
14. Best, *Hoover: Keeper of the Torch*, 290–91; Wolfe, *Hoover: Public Servant and Leader of the Loyal Opposition* (New York, 1956), 421–22, 426.
15. Best, *Hoover: Keeper of the Torch*, 291–92.
16. Steinberg, *Herbert Hoover*, 242; Best, *Hoover: Keeper of the Torch*, 298–301; Best, *Hoover: The Postpresidential Years*, 2:298–301; Hoover, *The Crusade Years*, 263–64.
17. Best, *Hoover: Keeper of the Torch*, 298–301; Walch and Miller, *Hoover and Truman*, 14–15, 188–226, 247–50; Joan Hoff, *Hoover: Forgotten Progressive*, 258–64. For a detailed account see Louis P. Lochner, *Herbert Hoover and Germany* (New York, 1960).
18. Best, *Hoover: Keeper of the Torch*, 302–3; Smith, *An Uncommon Man*, 344–47.
19. Best, *Hoover: Keeper of the Torch*, 312; Hoff, *Hoover: Forgotten Progressive*, 258–60; Smith, *An Uncommon Man*, 366–70; Walch and Miller, *Hoover and Truman*, 118–26, 247–50.
20. Best, *Hoover: Keeper of the Torch*, 311–14; Hoff, 258–59; Wolfe, *Hoover: Public Servant*, 427.
21. Best, *Hoover: Keeper of the Torch*, 314–15.
22. Ibid., 315–16. See also Smith, *An Uncommon Man*, 366–70.

23. Hinshaw, *Hoover: American Quaker*, 336–44; Smith, *An Uncommon Man*, 372–75; Lyons, *Hoover: A Biography*, 397–99.

24. Kendrick A. Clements, *Hoover, Conservation, and Consumerism: Engineering the Good Life* (Lawrence, KS, 2000), 200–201; Lyons, *Hoover: A Biography*, 400–402.

25. Hoff, *Hoover: Forgotten Progressive*, 264–65; Smith, *An Uncommon Man*, 388–91.

26. Best, *Hoover: Keeper of the Torch*, 294–97, 317, 326, 327; Wolfe, *Hoover: Public Servant*, 423; Hoover, *The Crusade Years*, 262–63.

27. Best, *Hoover: Keeper of the Torch*, 327–29; Hoover, *The Crusade Years*, 272–73.

28. Hoover, *The Crusade Years*, 275–76; Smith, *An Uncommon Man*, 377; Wolfe, *Hoover: Public Servant*, 428–30.

29. Best, *Hoover: Keeper of the Torch*, 330–32; Hoover, *The Crusade Years*, 276–77; Wolfe, *Hoover: Public Servant*, 429–30.

30. Hoover, *The Crusade Years*, 286–89.

31. Ibid., 295, 309–13; Wolfe, *Hoover: Public Servant*, 440–42.

32. Best, *Hoover: Keeper of the Torch*, 359–64.

33. Ibid., 428; Smith, *An Uncommon Man*, 421; Walch and Miller, *Hoover and Truman*, includes numerous fond letters between the ex-presidents, 211–40, and a kind eulogy to Hoover by Truman in June 1965.

34. Mark Sullivan, quoted in Hoover, *The Crusade Years*, 260–61.

Chapter 16. The Republicans Return to Power

1. Richard Norton Smith, *An Uncommon Man: The Triumph of Herbert Hoover* (New York, 1984), 397; Gary Dean Best, *Herbert Hoover: The Postpresidential Years*, vol. 2, *1946–1964* (Stanford, CA, 1983), 358.

2. Smith, *An Uncommon Man*, 397.

3. For the negotiations between Hoover and Lodge over the seating of delegates see Telegram, Henry Cabot Lodge Jr., to Press, June 24, 1952, Post-Presidential Papers (hereafter cited as PPP), Box 102, Campaign, 1951–52; Hoover to Lodge, June 26, 1952, PPP, Box 102, Campaign, 1951–52; Lodge to Hoover, July 1, 1952, PPP, Box 102, Campaign, 1951–52, Herbert Hoover Presidential Library (cited hereafter as HHPL); Smith, *An Uncommon Man*, 397–99.

4. Smith, *An Uncommon Man*, 399.

5. Unmarked clipping, PPP, Box 34, Biographical Material, 1933–64, HHPL.

6. Robert C. Ruark, "Herbert Hoover Is Our Real Mr. Republican," *Washington News*, July 9, 1952, PPP, Box 102, Campaign, 1951–52, Printed Material and Clippings, HHPL.

7. *Wall Street Journal*, July 15, 1952, PPP, Box 102, Campaign, 1951–52, Printed Material and Clippings, HHPL.

8. Smith, *An Uncommon Man*, 399–400.

9. Ibid., 400.

10. Ibid., 401.

11. Tract, "Change Back to What?" [1952], Democratic Party, PPP, Box 102, Printed Material, HHPL.

12. *New York Times*, October 24, 1952, PPP, Box 102, Campaign of 1951–52, Printed Material and Clippings, HHPL.

13. Smith, *An Uncommon Man*, 399–401; W. D. C. McPeeley to Hoover, October 11, 1952, PPP, Box 102, Campaign 1951–52, Corres.; J. H. Redhead, Managing Director, National Association of Manufacturers, to Hoover, August 23, 1951, HHPL.

14. Best, *Hoover: The Postpresidential Years*, 2:364; Smith, *An Uncommon Man*, 401–3.

15. Best, *Hoover: The Postpresidential Years*, 2:365, 366, 371, 375.

16. Smith, *An Uncommon Man*, 407; Gary Dean Best, *The Life of Herbert Hoover: Keeper of the Torch, 1933–1964* (New York, 2013), 387, 388. The quote is from Best.

17. Best, *Hoover: Keeper of the Torch*, 392, 398.

18. Ibid., 417.
19. Ibid., 398, 399, 400, 401. Quote on 404.
20. Ibid., 405.
21. Smith, *An Uncommon Man*, 408; Best, *Hoover: Keeper of the Torch*, 407–8.
22. Best, *Hoover: The Postpresidential Years*, 2:372, 398, 399, 400, 401.
23. Ibid., 2:402; Smith, *An Uncommon Man*, 408–9; Hal Elliott Wert, *Hoover: The Fishing President: Portrait of the Private Man and His Life Outdoors* (Mechanicsburg, PA, 2005), 325.
24. *New York Times* quoted in Best, *Hoover: The Postpresidential Years*, 2:407. See also Smith, *An Uncommon Man*, 421, 422; Wert, *Hoover: The Fishing President*, 332–33.
25. Smith, *An Uncommon Man*, 19, 423.
26. Best, *Hoover: The Postpresidential Years*, 2:376, 378, 380, 383, 403.
27. Smith, *An Uncommon Man*, 19; for quotes see Best, *Hoover: Keeper of the Torch*, 440, 442–43.
28. "The Great Debate," observations by Hoover on the first Kennedy-Nixon debate, 1960, to Thruston Morton, Chairman, RNC, September 15, 1960, PPP, Box 105, HHPL.
29. Wert, *Hoover: The Fishing President*, 340–42; *New York Times*; *New York Herald Tribune*; *New York Journal American*; *Stanford Daily*; November 9, 1960, PPP, Indiv. File 1391, 23, HHPL; Smith, *An Uncommon Man*, 423.
30. John Sparkman to Kennedy, December 16, 1960, PPP, Box 296, Kennedy, John F., Inaugural, 1960–61; Bunny Miller to Admiral Lewis Strauss, January 19, 1961; Best, *Hoover: Keeper of the Torch*, 420, 448, 449; Best, *Hoover: The Postpresidential Years*, 2:420; Smith, *An Uncommon Man*, 424.
31. Best, *Hoover: The Postpresidential Years*, 2:427, 428.
32. Smith, *An Uncommon Man*, 426–27.
33. Ibid., 427; Best, *Hoover: Keeper of the Torch*, 459–60.
34. Ibid., 460, 461, 462.

Chapter 17. Tempest and Triumph

1. Gary Dean Best, *Herbert Hoover: The Postpresidential Years, 1933–1964*, vol. 2, *1946–1964* (Stanford, CA, 1983), 432.
2. Ibid., 2:433.
3. Ibid., 2:432; Richard Norton Smith, *An Uncommon Man: The Triumph of Herbert Hoover* (New York, 1984), 15.
4. George H. Nash, afterword to *The Life of Herbert Hoover: Keeper of the Torch, 1933–1964*, by Gary Dean Best (New York, 2013), 271.
5. Smith, *An Uncommon Man*, 15.
6. "Editor's Desk," *Time*, March 11, 2013, n.p.
7. Best, *Hoover: The Postpresidential Years*, 2:434–35.
8. Ibid., 2:437; Smith, *An Uncommon Man*, 21.
9. Smith, *An Uncommon Man*, 24.

INDEX